macromedia®
Studio® 8
Training from the Source

Jeffrey Bardzell

Shaowen Bardzell

ADOBE
PRESS

Adobe

Macromedia® Studio® 8
Training from the Source
Jeffrey Bardzell
Shaowen Bardzell

 ADOBE PRESS

Adobe Press books are published by:

Peachpit

1249 Eighth Street
Berkeley, CA 94710
510/524-2178
800/283-9444
510/524-2221 (fax)
Find us on the World Wide Web at:
www.peachpit.com
www.adobe.com

To report errors, please send a note to errata@peachpit.com

Printed and bound in the United States of America

ISBN 0-321-33620-8

9 8 7 6 5 4 3 2 1

Credits

Authors

Jeffrey Bardzell and Shaowen Bardzell

Macromedia Press Editor

Wendy Sharp

Editor

Carol Person

Contributors

Bosung Kim and Kyong-Jee Kim

Copy Editor

Erfert Fenton

Production Coordinator

David Van Ness

Compositors

Rick Gordon, Emerald Valley Graphics
Myrna Vladic, Silver Mesa Press

Indexer

Valerie Perry

Cover Production

George Mattingly, GMD

Dedications

We dedicate this book to Marty Siegel, for his epic kindness, for our friendship, and for the future.

Table of Contents

Introduction

Macromedia Studio 8 is the premier Web development software package available today. From cutting-edge graphic design to developing database-driven e-commerce Web applications and everything in between, Studio 8 offers serious tools for visually oriented graphic designers and code-oriented Web and multimedia programmers alike. Given the breadth and depth of the five applications that compose Studio 8– Macromedia Dreamweaver, Flash, Fireworks, Contribute, and ColdFusion–it is impossible for someone new to these applications to master them in a day.

The 17 lessons in this book are intended to provide a crash course for serious beginners, people who have an ambitious learning agenda. In the book, you'll begin designing graphics and page layouts in Macromedia Fireworks 8, before moving to Dreamweaver 8 to build an entire Web site. You'll then turn to Flash to build some animated and video assets for the site. In the final project of the book, you'll design a database-driven ColdFusion site, some Flash applications, how to configure the site for maintenance by Contribute users, and learn how to send data in and out of Flash.

As these topics suggest, the book places special emphasis on integrating the different Studio products, rather than covering each one in isolation. While the collection of tools available in Macromedia Studio 8 is unparalleled, they are even more powerful when used together. Integration topics include exporting page layouts from Fireworks to Dreamweaver, developing a ColdFusion site in Dreamweaver and integrating it with Flash content, and integrating a database-driven Web application using ColdFusion with a simple client–Contribute–enabling non-technical content experts to maintain their own content.

Prerequisites

Macromedia Studio 8: Training from the Source is intended as an introductory curriculum for those who want to learn Macromedia Studio 8. As such, the book makes few assumptions about what you already know.

The lessons assume the following:

- You have basic familiarity with your operating system, including using the menu system and file management.
- Studio 8 is installed, and your system meets the requirements needed to run it.
- You have access to a Web server running ColdFusion. This can be a local server, a network server, or an ISP that you access via FTP.
- You are at least willing to learn some code, including HTML, Flash ActionScript, and ColdFusion Markup Language, though you are not expected to know Any Of These Up Front.

Outline

This Macromedia training course steps you through the projects in each lesson, showing you how to design graphics and prepare them for the Web; develop Web pages; prepare graphics for print; create multimedia animations and interactions; and develop database-driven Web sites.

The curriculum of this course should take you about 24 hours to complete and includes the following lessons:

Lesson 1: Preparing Graphics

Lesson 2: Designing a Page Interface

Lesson 3: Exporting a Site Design

Lesson 4: Preparing a New Site

Lesson 5: Developing a Page Template

Lesson 6: Developing Site Content

Lesson 7: Creating a Flash Movie

Lesson 8: Creating Animation and Interactivity

Lesson 9: Flash Video

Lesson 10: Preparing the Dante Site

Lesson 11: Nonlinear Flash Interactions

Lesson 12: Drag-and-Drop Interactions

Lesson 13: Dynamic, Data-Driven Sites

Lesson 14: Connecting to Data Sources

Lesson 15: A Component-Based Flash Quiz

Lesson 16: Flash, ColdFusion, and the Database

Lesson 17: Decentralizing with Contribute

The Project Site

In the course of completing the book, you will build two sites.

The first project you will work on is a Web site for a fictional organic farm called Jade Valley. During this project, you will do the graphic design of the site from scratch in Fireworks and Dreamweaver. You will design a page template, complete with an accompanying Cascading Style Sheet, from which you will then generate the pages in the site. You'll also use Flash to develop an interactive movie and a short video.

The second project is for a fictional class on the *Inferno*, by the medieval poet Dante. Most of the graphic design work has been done in advance, so you can focus on the development side of Studio 8: architecting and scripting Flash movies; connecting sites to a database using ColdFusion; and sending data between Flash movies, pages, and the database. As a final activity, you will make the static portions of this site editable by non-technical Contribute users.

Elements and Format

Each lesson in this book begins by outlining the major focus of the lesson at hand and introducing new features. Learning objectives and the approximate time needed to complete all the exercises are also listed at the beginning of each lesson. The projects are divided into short exercises that explain the importance of each skill you learn. Every lesson will build on the concepts and techniques used in the previous lessons.

Tips: Alternative ways to perform tasks and suggestions to consider when applying the skills you are learning.

Notes: Additional background information to expand your knowledge, as well as advanced techniques you can explore in order to further develop your skills.

Boldface terms: New vocabulary that is introduced and emphasized in each lesson.

Italic text: Text that you need to type in is set in *italics*.

Menu commands and keyboard shortcuts: There are often multiple ways to perform the same task. The different options will be pointed out in each lesson. Menu commands are shown with angle brackets between the menu names and commands: Menu > Command > Subcommand.

Keyboard shortcuts are shown with a plus sign between the names of keys to indicate that you should press the keys simultaneously; for example, Shift+Tab means that you should press the Shift and Tab keys at the same time.

CD-ROM: The files you need to complete the projects for each lesson are located in a folder named for the lesson: Lesson01, Lesson02, etc. The CD can be found in the back of the book. Inside the lesson folders are Start and Complete folders, which represent the state of the Jade Valley or Dante project at the beginning and ending of that lesson, respectively.

The files you will use for each of the projects are listed at the beginning of each lesson.

Macromedia Training from the Source

The Macromedia Training from the Source and Advanced Training from the Source series are developed in association with Adobe, and reviewed by the product support teams. Ideal for active learners, the books in the Training from the Source series offer hands-on instruction designed to provide you with a solid grounding in the program's fundamentals. If you learn best by doing, this is the series for you. Each Training from the Source title contains hours of instruction on Adobe software products. They are designed to teach the techniques that you need to create sophisticated professional-level projects. Each book includes a CD-ROM that contains all the files used in the lessons, completed projects for comparison and more.

Macromedia Authorized Training and Certification

This book is geared to enable you to study at your own pace with content from the source. Other training options exist through the Macromedia Authorized Training Partner program. Get up to speed in a matter of days with task-oriented courses taught by Macromedia Certified Instructors. Or learn on your own with interactive, online training from Macromedia University. All of these sources of training will prepare you to become a Macromedia Certified Developer.

For more information about authorized training and certification, check out *www.macromedia.com/go/training/*

What You Will Learn

You will develop the skills you need to create and maintain your Web sites as you work through these lessons.

By the end of the course, you will be able to:

- Design graphics in Fireworks, using special features such as masks and Live Effects
- Build button rollovers and navigation bars
- Design and export interactive page interfaces using Fireworks
- Build and deploy a Dreamweaver template
- Design a site using new, standards-compliant CSS layers for the layout and look
- Rapidly develop Web pages using templates and CSS styles
- Reuse Fireworks-created graphics in business cards, envelopes, and letterhead designed in Freehand
- Architect movies in Flash, using its timeline, stage, and Library
- Animate screen objects in Flash
- Create interactive, nonlinear Flash applications
- Create drag-and-drop interactivity in Flash
- Configure a dynamic, ColdFusion site in Dreamweaver
- Connect a ColdFusion site to a database and retrieve data each time a page is requested
- Collect information from users with a Web form, process that data with ColdFusion, and insert it into a Flash application
- Develop a Flash quiz using Flash user interface components
- Collect data from the quiz and pass it to a database via ColdFusion
- Configure the site for hassle-free maintenance by non-technical Contribute users

Minimum System Requirements

Macromedia Studio 8 (In case you don't own a copy of Studio 8, you can download a free trial version at www.macromedia.com/software.)

Windows

- 800 MHz Intel Pentium III processor (or equivalent) or later
- Windows 2000, Windows XP
- 256 MB RAM (1 GB recommended to run more than one Studio 8 product simultaneously)
- 1.8 GB available disk space
- 1024 × 78, 16-bit display (32-bit recommended)
- Internet Explorer or Netscape Navigator 4.0 or higher
- Access to a Web server running ColdFusion. A single IP developer's edition of ColdFusion can be downloaded for free from http: //www.macromedia.com.

Macintosh

- 600 MHz PowerPC G3 and later
- Mac OS X 10.3, 10.4
- 256 MB RAM (1 GB recommended to run more than one Studio 8 product simultaneously)
- 1.2 GB available disk space
- 1024 × 768, thousands of colors display (millions of colors recommended)
- Internet Explorer 4.0 or Safari 1.0 or higher
- Access to a Web server running ColdFusion.

Project 1: The Jade Valley Web Site

Part 1: Fireworks

1 Preparing Graphics

The Web is a multimedia format. In addition to text, you can place any combination of graphics, animations, movies, sounds, games, learning media, and much more in a single HTML page. Often, you create many of these assets before you begin to develop the Web pages, because without them you don't have much to put in your Web page.

Graphics are frequently the first assets you create when you begin working on a Web site, because they heavily influence the overall look and feel of a site's design, including its color scheme, interface elements (such as navigation bars), and layout. In addition, you often have graphics that predate the Web site. Many corporate logos, for example, have been around for years or even decades.

When you're building a site from the ground up, Macromedia Fireworks is a good place to start. Not only is Fireworks a robust image editor, it's the perfect environment for

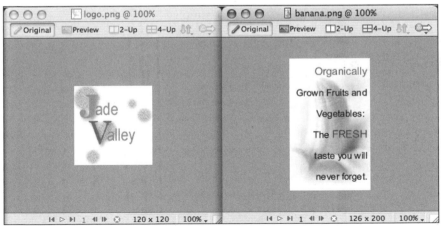

In the course of this lesson, you'll create the Jade Valley logo (left) as well as a small advertisement graphic (right).

creating new art, or importing and improving existing art. After you've created some artwork, Fireworks' powerful interface can optimize that artwork for the Web; for example, Fireworks has many useful tools that help you reduce a graphic's file size while maintaining the best overall visual quality. In addition, Fireworks is a great tool for designing whole-page layouts, which you can use as the basis for an entire Web site design. In the first part of this book, you'll explore all these aspects of Fireworks as you begin to build the Jade Valley Web site.

In this first lesson, you'll build two graphics for use in the site: the Jade Valley logo and a small advertising graphic. In the process, you'll become familiar with the Fireworks interface and discover how easy it is to create and improve an array of different kinds of graphics.

What You Will Learn

In this lesson, you will:

- Draw shapes and apply strokes, fills, and textures
- Apply and format text
- Edit a bitmap graphic: a digital photo
- Use a mask and the Dodge tool to touch up the digital photo
- Apply Fireworks filters to create drop shadows

Approximate Time

This lesson takes approximately 90 minutes to complete.

Lesson Files

Starting Files:

Lesson01/Start/banana.jpg

Completed Files:

Lesson01/Complete/banana.png
Lesson01/Complete/logo.png

Drawing Shapes for a Logo

In this task, you'll draw some shapes that will serve as the background for the Jade Valley logo. But, before you start drawing shapes, you need to know how Fireworks understands these shapes.

All digital graphics fall into one of two categories: bitmap (also known as raster) and vector. Bitmap graphics are made up of a matrix of thousands or millions of individual dots. Each dot is a single color, but they are so small (typically ranging from $1/72$ to $1/600$ of an inch) that we don't perceive them individually. Instead, our eyes blend them together, and we perceive the image. Vector graphics are made up of mathematical formulas that describe basic lines, curves, and shapes.

The distinction is easier to understand if we consider how each type renders a simple black rectangle against a white background.

- The bitmap version of the rectangle graphic has rows and columns of black or white dots. In the area of the rectangle, the dots are all black. Outside the rectangle, the dots are all white. Every dot in the graphic is described. The graphic doesn't store any information about the rectangle as an entity; it only describes the thousands of individual dots.

- A vector graphic depicting a rectangle contains two coordinates. The first contains the distance in points between the top-left corner of the rectangle and the top-left corner of the graphic. The second contains the distance in points between the bottom-right corner of the rectangle and the top-left corner of the graphic. Using these numbers, the vector graphic knows the bounds of the rectangle. In this example, the vector graphic specifies everything inside these coordinates as black. The vector graphic actually recognizes the existence of the rectangle, because it is the closed shape connecting the four coordinate points.

Creating a bitmap graphic, called painting, consists of coloring pixels. Creating a vector graphic, called drawing, consists of plotting points to create lines, called paths, and then specifying how the edges (or strokes) of the paths appear as well as how everything bound by the paths (called the fill) should appear. Don't confuse paths (the underlying points the computer sees) with strokes (the colored lines and curves visible to the eye). As you can see in the following figure, a single path (the star shape) can have a variety of strokes.

Going clockwise from the upper-left corner, the strokes are: a basic line, one of Fireworks' calligraphic strokes, no stroke at all, and finally a dashed-line stroke.

For simple shapes, such as rectangles, stars, and curvy lines, vector graphics are usually superior to bitmaps, because vector graphics require less data to represent the graphic (and therefore have a smaller file size) and because they are more easily modified and resized. Text, logos, and technical drawings are usually vector graphics. Examples of vector-based applications include Macromedia Freehand, Macromedia Flash, Corel Draw, and Adobe Illustrator.

For complex images, especially digital photographs, the amount of detail is so great that vectors cannot effectively represent the image, so bitmaps are generally superior. Examples of bitmap-based applications include Adobe Photoshop and Corel Painter.

Fireworks can be considered two programs in one; it handles both vector and bitmap graphics. When you create graphics in Fireworks, most often you'll be creating vector graphics. You'll draw shapes and lines as well as enter text (remember, text is a special kind of vector graphic, even in a word processor). For example, a button or navigation bar is usually a rectangle, oval, or other geometric shape, and vector tools are perfect for the job. You can also import and modify or retouch photographs taken with a digital camera and/or scanned into Fireworks, and these photos are invariably in a bitmap format. Fireworks has ample tools and features for working with both types of graphic—even its Tools panel (shown in the figure on the next page) has Bitmap and Vector sections.

To create graphics (or graphic elements in a composition), most often you'll use Fireworks' vector drawing tools. To edit existing graphics, especially photographs, you'll typically use Fireworks' bitmap editing tools. When you're ready to optimize and output the graphics for the Web, you'll export the graphics in a Web-friendly graphic format (almost always GIF or JPEG, unless you use Flash, Director, or Authorware, in which case you might also use PNG or SWF). We'll talk about the differences between the GIF and JPEG file types in Lesson 3, *Exporting a Site Design*, but for now you should know that both GIF and JPEG are bitmap file types. In other words, while almost everything you create in Fireworks is a vector graphic, almost everything you export from Fireworks is a bitmap.

Note *You won't always export bitmap graphics from Fireworks. For example, if you're using art created in Fireworks intended for distribution in Flash, you might want to export using a vector format, such as Flash SWF or an Illustrator AI file.*

Returning to the task at hand—drawing the background shapes for the logo—you probably guessed (correctly) that initially you will create shapes as vector graphics. In creating these shapes, you'll follow a two-step process. First, you'll create the paths—the shapes, their size, their placement, and so on. Once you're satisfied with the structure of the paths, you'll then make them look good by applying strokes, fills, and textures. Keep in mind that when you work with vector graphics, the paths and all their visible attributes are always editable, even if you save the file and return to it later. Thus, if a color is too dark, you can always brighten it. If a shape is too small, you can enlarge it at any time. If a line is not wavy enough, you can always intensify the curves. And so on.

You'll begin by creating a new document.

1. Open Fireworks, and choose Fireworks File from the Create New section of the Start Page.

If you don't see the Start Page, you can create a new Fireworks document by choosing File > New.

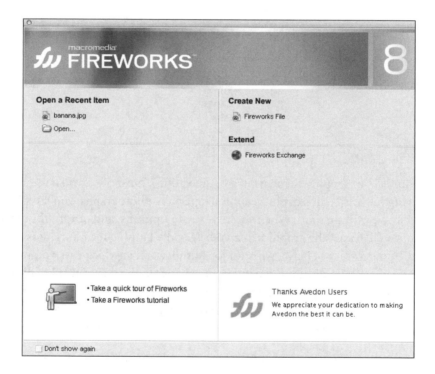

2. In the New Document dialog, specify 120 as the Width and 100 as the Height. Verify that Pixels is specified as the unit of measurement. Leave the Resolution at 72 Pixels/Inch (the default) and the Canvas Color as white (the default). Click OK.

When you create a new graphic, you must tell Fireworks how large it should be. Size in Fireworks is measured in pixels, short for picture elements, which are the tiny dots that make up your computer screen.

The standard for screen graphics is 72 pixels per inch, so if you are using Fireworks to design for the Web or for a CD-ROM project to be viewed on the screen, you should always use 72 pixels per inch. Compared to print graphics, 72 pixels per inch is a low resolution, meaning that the image has comparatively less detail. Additional details wouldn't be visible onscreen anyway, and would add substantially to the file size. Because many people still rely on modems to view Web pages, minimizing the file size of all your graphics is critical.

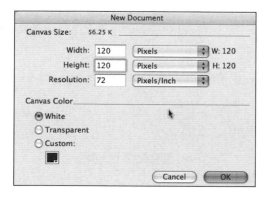

After you click OK, the canvas appears. The canvas marks the boundaries of the graphic. Anything you put on the canvas will appear in the graphic when it is exported. You can store graphics in the gray area, called the workspace, but anything placed in the workspace isn't visible when the graphic is exported. Notice that this logo graphic is fairly small. Knowing that an inch holds 72 pixels, and that this graphic is only 120 by 100 pixels, its small size should not surprise you.

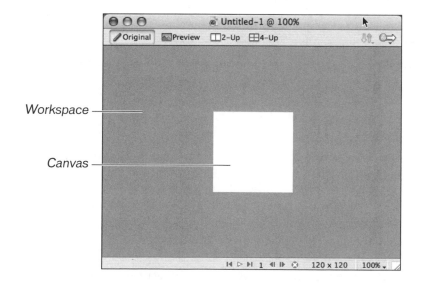

3. Choose File > Save and save the new file on your hard disk as logo.png.

The location of the file doesn't matter for now, as long as you remember where you put it!

4. Select the Ellipse tool by pressing and holding the mouse button on the Rectangle tool in the Tools panel, until a pop-up menu appears with additional options. Click the Ellipse tool in this menu.

Many more tools are available in the Tools panel than you can see at first glance. Often, whole groups of tools are hidden behind a tool. In the Tools panel, any tool with a small arrow beside it contains additional hidden tools.

Tip You can also toggle through the shape tools using the keyboard shortcut: U.

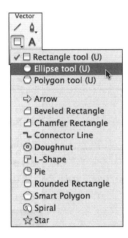

You use the Ellipse tool to draw ellipses and perfect circles.

5. Hold down the Shift key, and press and drag diagonally on the canvas to draw a small circle.

As you press and drag diagonally using any shape tool, Fireworks draws the shape. Holding down the Shift key as you draw constrains the shape. Ellipses are constrained to perfect circles. Rectangles are constrained to perfect squares. This technique, called Shift-constraint, extends to other tools as well. For example, when you hold down the Shift key and draw with the Line tool, lines are constrained to 45-degree angles relative to the canvas.

Depending on your settings, the shape can have a fill and/or stroke. The default setting is a gray fill with no stroke. As long as you can see the circle you drew, its fill and stroke don't matter for now; you'll change them later.

First, you'll finalize the size and placement of the circle. You can resize objects in Fireworks in one of two ways. You can resize an object visually (that is, eyeball it) using the Scale tool in the Tools panel. Or, if you know exactly how large an object should be, you can resize it with numeric precision using the Property inspector.

6. With the circle still selected, change the width (W) and height (H) to 37 in the lower-left corner of the Property inspector. Reposition the graphic to the top-left corner of the canvas by setting the distance from the left edge (X) to 1 and the distance from the top (Y) to 1.

In this step you're numerically resizing and positioning the graphic. In a normal design situation, you'd probably discover the proper size and positioning visually through trial and error. To help you match the graphic created in the book, and to see for yourself that it's possible to numerically resize and position objects, we're using the numeric approach in this step.

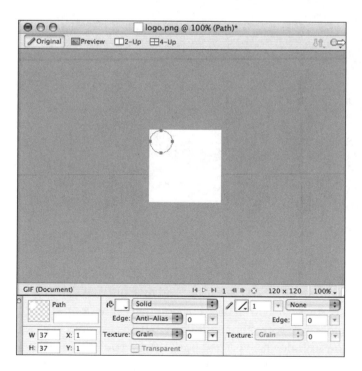

The final graphic has five circles, so in the next step you'll create the remaining circles.

7. With the circle still selected, choose Edit > Copy. Then choose Edit > Paste four times.

> **Tip** *A faster way would be to use keyboard shortcuts. Ctrl+C (Windows) or Command+C (Macintosh) copies, while Ctrl+V/Command+V pastes.*

When you've finished this step, the screen doesn't look any different. That's because Fireworks pasted each copy directly on top of the original. Don't worry; all five circles are there.

8. Use the Pointer tool in the top-left corner of the Tools panel to drag one of the new circles to the right. Select the Scale tool, and notice that transform handles appear automatically. Drag one of the corner transform handles, until the circle is about the size shown in the second figure. Toggle off the transform handles by clicking the Pointer tool, and drag the circle roughly to the position you see in the second figure.

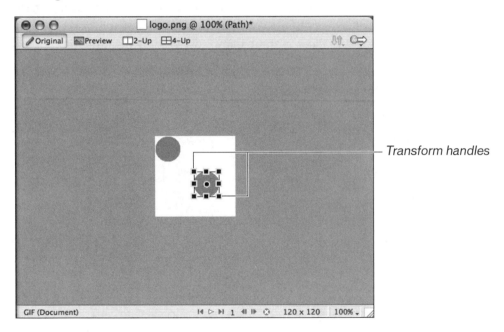

— Transform handles

Dragging a transform handle scales the selected object. If you drag a corner transform handle, you scale in two directions (left-right and up-down). If you drag one of the handles in the middle, you scale only in one direction (left-right or up-down). When you drag a corner handle, Fireworks automatically maintains the object's aspect ratio. In other words, if you scale down 20 percent horizontally, you'll also scale down 20 percent vertically. Fireworks' automatic preservation of the aspect ratio prevents you from distorting the shape.

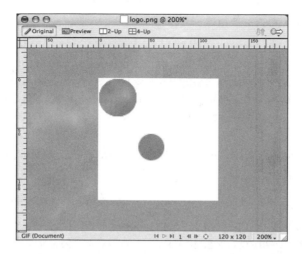

9. Repeat Step 8 until the five circles are sized and positioned as shown in the following figure. Save the file.

Note *The figure has been magnified to make it easier for you to see the size and positioning of each circle.*

You don't need to be a perfectionist in this step. Just do the best you can. If you feel a circle needs to be resized or repositioned, you can change it later.

Tip *A convenient way to reposition objects is to use the arrow keys on the keyboard. When an object is selected, pressing one of the arrow keys "nudges" the object one pixel in that direction. Once you've dragged something roughly into place, nudging is a great way to fine-tune positioning.*

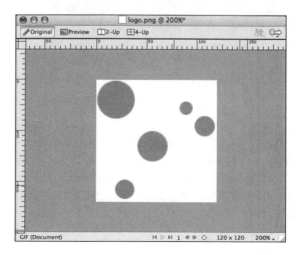

Applying Colors and Textures

You've now created the five paths you'll need for the logo. But all are just dark gray circles—not the most interesting logos, especially given the site's intended vibrancy. Earlier in the lesson we mentioned that when working with vector graphics, a common workflow is to create, structure, scale, and position paths, and then worry about making them look good. In this task, you get to make the graphics look good.

1. Select all the circles by choosing Select > Select All (or Ctrl+A/Command+A).

We'll apply the same visual effects to all five circles at once, rather than applying them to one circle at a time.

> **Tip** *You can select multiple objects using the Pointer tool as well. To do so, hold down the Shift key and click all the objects you want to add to the selection. To remove an object from the selection, with the Shift key still held down, click the object again.*

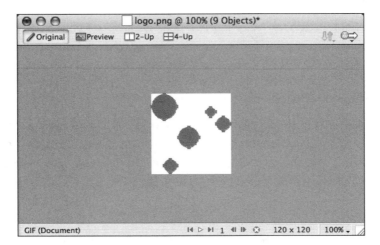

2. Change the color of the fill by clicking the Fill Color box in the Property inspector. In the Color pop-up, select the shade of green with the hexadecimal value #669900.

When you click the Fill or Stroke Color box in Fireworks, the Color pop-up appears. By default, the pop-up displays 216 colors in the so-called Web Safe palette. The significance of this palette is discussed more in Lesson 3. Be aware, though, that you can mix colors from a palette of more than 16.7 million colors. To access this palette, click the Sys Color Picker button, or use Fireworks' Color Mixer panel.

As you roll over a color swatch with the cursor (which turns into an eyedropper), the swatch's hexadecimal color value is displayed at the top of the Color pop-up. The hexadecimal color number is simply a way of encoding color values succinctly. Computer monitors display colors by mixing one of 256 shades of red, one of 256 shades of green, and one of 256 shades of blue. (256 × 256 × 256 is more than 16.7 million—the figure mentioned in the preceding paragraph.) The system is simple: The first two digits represent the red color channel (that is, which of the 256 shades of red is used). Rather than using a base-10 system, which would require 1 to 3 digits for each value (0 is one digit, while 255 is three digits), the hexadecimal system uses a base-16 system. So instead of each digit ranging from 0 to 9, each digit instead ranges from 0 to F, where A represents 10, B represents 11, and so on through F, which represents 15. Because 16 × 16 equals 256, two digits in this system are capable of representing 256 different variations of color.

To translate, then, the value #669900 means that the red value (66) represents 102 (in a scale from 0 to 255); the green value (99) represents 153; and the blue value (00) represents 0. The resulting color is a deep green.

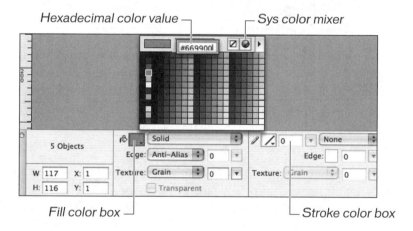

Hexadecimal color value —   — Sys color mixer

Fill color box —   — Stroke color box

Note   *The stroke should be set to transparent by default. If it is not, use the Stroke Color box in the Property inspector to set the stroke to transparent. Just click the swatch with the red slash near the top of the Color pop-up.*

3. Use the Property inspector to change the Edge from Anti-Alias (the default) to Feather. In the Feather Amount field, which defaults to 10, change the number to 3.

The edges are now subtly softer than before.

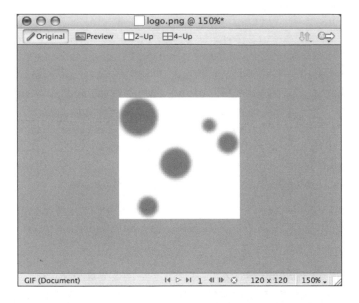

Why use anti-aliasing? Let's say you have a green circle against a white background. The two regions are defined by the edge, which coincides with the underlying vector path. A hard edge has no transition between the two regions; that is, a green pixel marks the end of the circle, and beside it, a white pixel defines the beginning of the region outside of the circle. Unfortunately, hard edges generally do not look very good on computer screens—they tend to look chunky.

One solution is to use anti-aliased edges (Fireworks' default setting), which creates a subtle transition between the regions inside and outside the shape. In this example, Fireworks blends the green and white edges to create a small transition area of pale green pixels. Feathering creates a much larger transition; you specify how large a transition using the Feather Amount field. The following figure shows the difference between the three edge types, from left to right: Hard, Anti-Alias, and Feathered.

4. Use the Property inspector to change the Amount of Texture slider from the default 0 to 50.

Textures are a great feature of Fireworks' vector graphics. Typically, vector graphics are characterized by smooth, solid regions of color. This characteristic is great for clean logos (think of the Olympic rings or the Pepsi logo), but vector graphics can also look unnatural. Fireworks' textured fills give designers the power to create graphics that have a more natural appearance. In this step you're going to stick with the default Grain texture, but you should take a moment to experiment with some of the other types of textures. Among our favorites are Grass, Chiffon, Oilslick, Parchment, Swirls, and Metal.

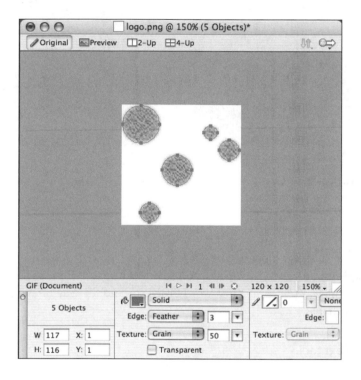

5. On the right side of the Property inspector, lower the Opacity from 100 (the default) down to 50. Save the file.

The opacity setting enables you to specify whether an object should have any transparency applied to it. The default setting is 100, which means fully opaque. At the default setting of 100, any objects behind the selected object are completely obscured. With an opacity setting of 0, the object is fully transparent—you can't see it at all. Settings in between make the object translucent. You are lowering the opacity to 50 percent in this step, so that the circles are more subtle, as befits a background graphic.

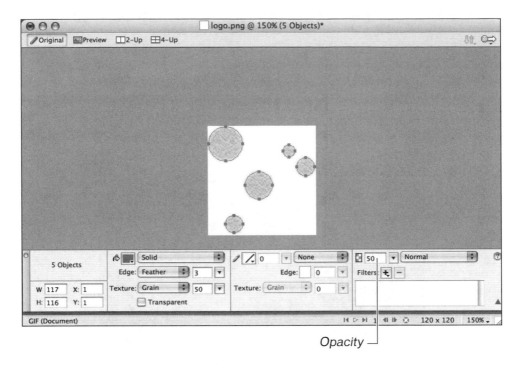

Opacity

Adding Type

With the background in place, now you'll add some text. Text in Fireworks works like a hybrid between the way text works in a word processor and the way Fireworks handles vector lines and shapes.

1. Select the Text tool.

The Text tool is represented by the A icon in the Vector section of the Tools panel. Notice that as soon as this tool is selected, the Property inspector reveals text formatting options, including font face, size, bold and italics, alignment, and more.

Tip   *You can also access the Text tool using the keyboard shortcut: T.*

2. Use the Property inspector to change the Font to Arial Narrow, the Size to 26, and the text Color to medium gray (hexadecimal **#999999**).

You can format text after it's been created, or you can create a default formatting. In this case, you're creating a default format before you start typing anything.

Tip *Text, like any closed vector shape, can have both a stroke and a fill. By default, in Fireworks and almost all computer applications, the text color is specified as a fill, and the text has no stroke (or, more precisely, a transparent stroke).*

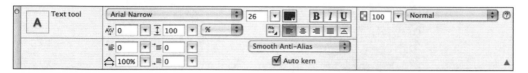

3. Click anywhere on the canvas. Type *ade*. Switch to the Pointer tool, and then switch back to the Text tool. Click anywhere on the canvas away from the first text block, and type *alley*.

This text is for Jade Valley, of course, but because you'll format the *J* and *V* in a special way, it's easier to keep them separate.

When you switch temporarily to the Pointer tool, you make it possible to type "alley" into its own text block. You can globally format each word (or, in this case, part of a word), and then position each one individually.

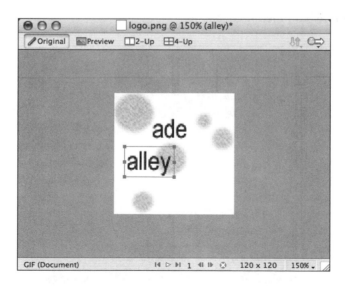

4. Repeat Step 3 and type the letter *J* and the letter *V* into their own text blocks.

Positioning doesn't matter just yet. The important thing is to have four separate text blocks at the end of this step.

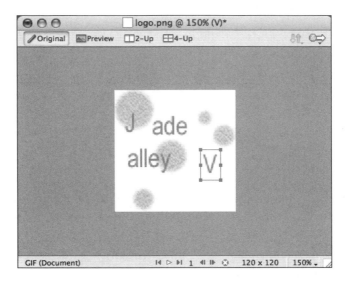

5. Use the Pointer tool to select the *J* text block. In the Property inspector, change the Font to Georgia, set the Size to 50, make it Bold, and set its Color to #FF9900, a bright orange.

The *J* is much more prominent than before.

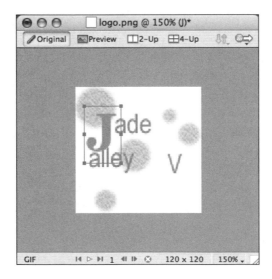

6. Change the *V* to Georgia, set its Size 50, and set its Color to #669900. Do not make it bold.

Now the design has two of the primary colors used in the site. Of course, it probably looks more like scrambled eggs than a logo—at least until you reposition the various text blocks.

7. Use the Pointer tool to reposition the text blocks, so they appear as in the figure.

Remember, in addition to dragging objects with the Pointer tool, you can also nudge them using the arrow keys on the keyboard.

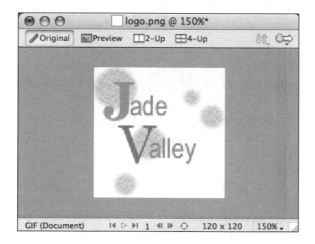

8. Save and close logo.png.

You're finished working on the logo for now. In Lesson 3, you'll optimize and export your logo for use on the Web, but for now, just save the file.

Composing with Digital Photos

The second image you need to add is a photo. Because the ad mixes text and a photograph, you'll have to design both elements carefully to ensure that they don't compete with one another.

1. Open banana.jpg, located in the Lesson01/Start folder on the CD.

Attractive graphics are usually created using high-quality source elements, such as this photograph of a banana. (This stock photograph was purchased from Photodisc.)

Eventually, the ad will have text over the photo. But if you were to add text now, the text would be hard to read, as there would be too much competition with the banana photo. In the next several steps, you'll force the banana into the background of the image; it will still be visible, but not overwhelming.

The first technique you'll use is a mask. A mask is when one image or shape is used to reveal another. For example, in the figure below, the letter *B* is used to mask the banana photograph.

You'll use a rectangle with feathered edges to reveal the center of the banana and make it fade around its edges.

2. Select the Rectangle tool. Use the Fill Color box in the Colors section of the Tools panel to set the Fill Color to white (hexadecimal #FFFFFF). Use the Stroke Color box to set the Stroke to none.

When you click in the Fill or Stroke Color box in the Colors section of the Tools panel, a palette appears containing a number of color swatches. The white swatch appears on the left side, while the no-color swatch (with a red slash through it) appears near the upper-right corner of the dialog.

You might be wondering why it matters what color the rectangle is, since it will eventually be used to mask the banana and you won't see the color anyway. In fact, the color is quite important. Masks use up to 256 shades of gray to show/hide the masked object. A black mask fully hides the masked object; a white mask fully reveals the masked object; and a gray mask partially reveals the underlying object. By specifying that the rectangle should be white, you are ensuring that everything beneath the rectangle (once it is designated as a mask) will be fully visible.

3. Draw a rectangle over the banana, as shown in the figure.

At this point, the rectangle is still a just a rectangle—it is not yet a mask.

4. With the rectangle still selected, in the Edge drop-down in the Fill section of the Property inspector, change the Edge to Feathered and the amount to 25.

The rectangle now has fuzzy edges, which will result in a nice gradual effect when it's converted to a mask.

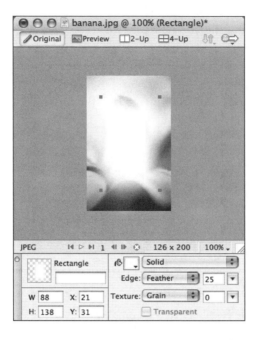

5. Switch to the Pointer tool. Hold down the Shift key, and click the banana photo.

At this point, both the rectangle and the photo should be selected. Verify that both are selected, or the next step won't work. You should see a blue outline surrounding the banana photo, and the four corners of the rectangle should also be highlighted in blue.

6. Choose Modify > Mask > Group as Mask.

The rectangle now reveals the banana photo wherever it overlaps the photo.

> **Tip** *Fireworks lets you create vector or bitmap masks. This is a vector mask, because the masking object is a vector rectangle. However, you can create dramatic mask effects by using one bitmap to mask another. Since Fireworks has 256 shades of masking, a bitmap used as a mask can create interesting compositional effects.*

The background now has a checkerboard pattern, which indicates a transparent background. You want a white background, however.

7. Choose Select > Deselect. In the Property inspector, use the Canvas Color box to change the canvas color from transparent (red slash) to white.

The checkerboard pattern disappears, and the background is now white.

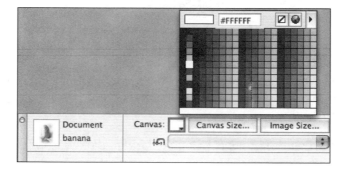

8. Click to select the mask, and use the Property inspector to lower its opacity to 75 percent.

By lowering the mask's opacity, you further fade the banana photo into the background.

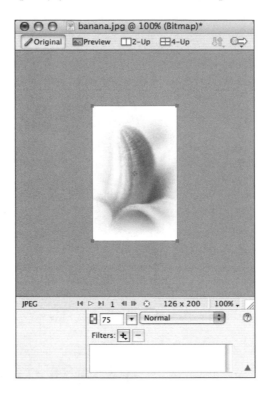

9. Press and hold the mouse button over the Blur tool, until a submenu appears. From this submenu, select the Dodge tool. In the Property inspector, change the Size setting to 26.

> **Tip** Use the keyboard shortcut R to toggle through the group of tools that contains the Dodge tool.

The Dodge tool is a bitmap editing tool that lets you "paint" pixels lighter. You'll use the Dodge tool to fade the banana a little more, without further degrading the quality of the photograph.

The default size, 13, is a little too small. By increasing the brush size to 26, you'll be able to apply the effect quickly and evenly.

10. Press and drag across the image, until it has lightened a small amount.

When you're finished, the banana photograph will be faded a little more—enough that text can be legibly layered over it. Although it's not as colorful as the original, the banana still has appeal.

Applying the Type

Now that the banana photograph has been fully prepared as a background graphic, you can now start adding and formatting the type.

1. Select the Text tool. Use the Property inspector to set the Font to Arial Narrow, the Size to 14, and the text Color to black (hexadecimal #000000).

Bold, italics, and underline should all be toggled off.

2. Click anywhere in the Document window, and type the following: *Organically Grown Fruits and Vegetables: The FRESH taste you will never forget*.

As you type, the text scrolls off the right edge of the canvas, where you can't see it.

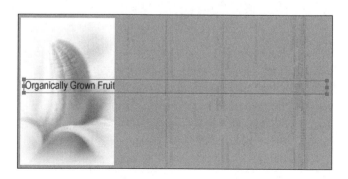

3. Press and drag the control handle in the lower-right corner of the text box down and to the left, until the text block is about the same size as the one shown in the figure.

Fireworks text boxes automatically expand when you start typing. In this step, you're defining a fixed width. Fireworks will wrap the text and extend this box downward, as needed, to accommodate more text.

4. With the text box still selected, specify right alignment (the default is left). Also, change the Leading to **32** px (pixels).

Note *If your text looks bunched together, you probably forgot to change from percent to pixels.*

Leading (pronounced "ledding") refers to the amount of space between lines of text. In most cases, paragraph text leading is about 20 percent larger than the font size. Therefore, a size 10 font often has a 12-point leading. The number you enter here, 32 pixels, is quite a bit higher than 20 percent. It calls attention to the text, and makes it more readable—exactly what you want in an advertisement.

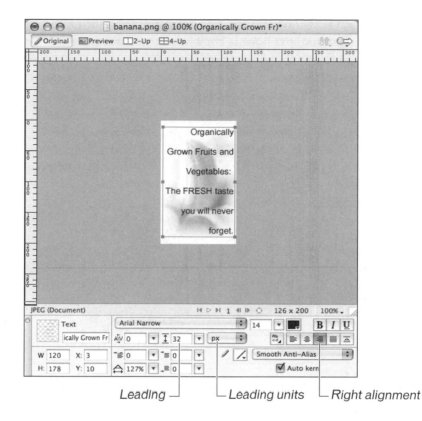

Leading —   └ Leading units   └ Right alignment

5. Using the Text tool, drag to select the word *Organically*. Use the Property inspector to change the color to a deep green (hexadecimal **#669900**). Increase the size to **16**.

Making key words stand out is another useful design technique for ads.

6. Drag to select the word *FRESH*, and use the Property inspector to increase its size to **16** and change its color to a deep red (hexadecimal **#993333**).

Now the two most important words in the ad stand out.

7. Resize the text box, if necessary, and press Enter/Return after the colon (if necessary) to make the text flow as shown in the figure.

The ad is finished.

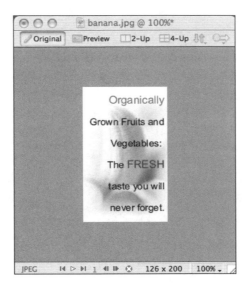

8. Choose File > Save As and save the file as banana.png. Close the file.

As you complete this step, you may see a dialog inquiring whether you should Save JPEG (which would save the present file on top of the original banana.jpg, making the file uneditable) or Save Fireworks PNG (which creates a new Fireworks PNG file, which will remain fully editable in the future).

As with logo.png, you'll optimize and export this file for the Web in Lesson 3.

Applying Type Effects

In this lesson's final task, you'll use one of Fireworks' special filters to add a drop shadow to the letters *J* and *V* in the original logo graphic. Filters are fun features available in Fireworks. They can be applied to both vector and bitmap objects. You can add instant effects with filters, like shadows, glows, bevels (for button effects), embossing, and much more. Better still, you have considerable control over how they are applied. Even better, filters can always be modified or removed; they do not permanently alter anything in your image.

1. Open logo.png.

This file contains the Jade Valley logo.

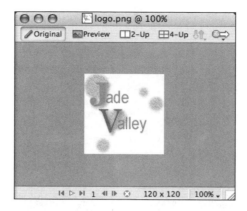

2. Use the Pointer tool to select the *J*. Click Filters or Choose a Preset (+) button in the Property inspector.

A pop-up menu appears that lists several categories of filters.

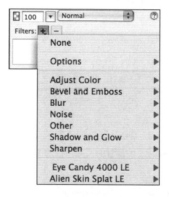

3. From this menu, choose Shadow and Glow › Drop Shadow. In the pop-up that appears, change the Distance from 7 (the default) to 5, and change the Color to the same as the letter *J* (hexadecimal #FF9900). Click anywhere on the canvas to apply the changes.

Distance ⎯

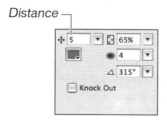

When you're finished, the *J* has an orange shadow, which gives it some additional interest.

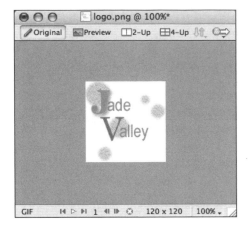

Also notice that the Filters section of the Property inspector now displays Drop Shadow. Whenever you apply a filter, it's listed in the Property inspector. Note that you can apply multiple filters to the same object, and when you do, all the filters will be listed in the order in which they were applied.

To remove a filter, select the filter in the Property inspector, and click the Delete the Current Selected Filter (–) button. To edit an existing filter (for instance, say you wanted to change the drop shadow's color back to black), double-click the name of the filter.

4. Use the Pointer tool to select the *V*. As before, add a Drop Shadow filter to it. Set its Distance to 5 as well, and set the Color to the same shade of green as the *V* (hexadecimal #669900).

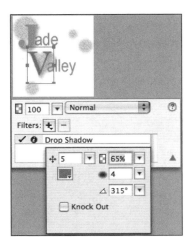

Filters are powerful and fun. Take a few minutes to experiment with some of the different filters and their settings.

5. Save and close logo.png.

What You Have Learned

In this lesson, you have:

- Drawn, scaled, and positioned vector paths (pages 5–13)
- Applied fills, strokes, and textures to vector paths (pages 14–18)
- Typed and formatted text (pages 18–21)
- Applied a mask to a bitmap graphic (pages 21–27)
- Used the Dodge tool to lighten a bitmap graphic (pages 26–27)
- Modified text box boundaries and adjusted leading (pages 27–30)
- Applied and customized Filters (pages 30–33)

2 Designing a Page Interface

Most Web pages are composed of multiple elements, such as logos, navigation systems, text, images, multimedia, and forms. Designers often attempt to design page layouts in Dreamweaver. While there is nothing wrong with using Dreamweaver for page layout, the intrinsic limitation of standard HTML code can hinder design decisions and experimentation.

Macromedia Fireworks is a natural alternative for designing layouts. Thanks to its vector tools, layers, guides, and rulers, Fireworks is a great tool for entire page layouts. Fireworks' vector content is always editable, so you are never trapped with a bad decision or an experiment gone wrong. Also, because every graphic element sits on the canvas independent of all other objects, it's easy to arrange and rearrange content quickly and precisely. Creating quick variations on a theme for a picky client couldn't be easier. Throw in Fireworks' robust optimization interface and diverse HTML export features, and it's clear that Fireworks is an ideal environment in which to create page layouts.

Designing the whole page layout in Fireworks implies a certain workflow. You start the page-design process by assembling different elements in a Fireworks document. Next,

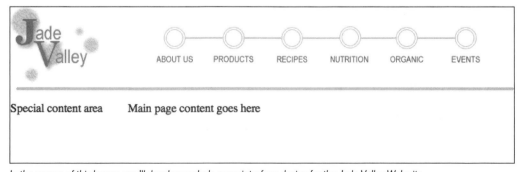

In the course of this lesson, you'll develop a whole-page interface design for the Jade Valley Web site.

you slice the page into individual pieces: banner, navigation, main content area, and so on. Then, you optimize each piece to achieve the twin goals of high-quality appearance and small file size. Finally, you export the page and all its parts to reassemble in Dreamweaver.

In this lesson, you'll begin this process, although you won't complete the process until Lesson 4, *Preparing a New Site*. You'll develop a whole-page design in Fireworks, complete with a logo, a navigation system, a banner, a main content area, an additional navigation aid, and a footer area. You'll also design a slicing scheme in preparation for the optimization and export processes, which are covered in the lessons that follow.

What You Will Learn

In this lesson, you will:

- Design a whole-page layout in Fireworks
- Use the Button Symbol editor to develop and program button states
- Work with the Library
- Understand hotspots and slices
- Develop a slicing scheme
- Make the page accessible to visitors using screen readers

Approximate Time

This lesson takes approximately 90 minutes to complete.

Lesson Files

Starting Files:

Lesson02/Start/banana.png
Lesson02/Start/logo.png
Lesson02/Start/interface.png
Lesson02/Start/red_onion.png

Completed Files:

Lesson02/Completed/banana.png
Lesson02/Completed/button.png
Lesson02/Completed/interface.png
Lesson02/Completed/interface_slices.png
Lesson02/Completed/red_onion.png

Creating Buttons

In this task, you'll create a button using Fireworks' Button Symbol editor. Before you start creating buttons for the Web, you should understand how button symbols work in Fireworks.

On the Web, the appearance of navigation buttons often changes depending on user actions. Actions such as clicking a button, rolling over a button, and moving the mouse away from a button can change the button's appearance. For example, when you mouse over a button, it may light up. To achieve this effect, designers have to create separate graphics to represent each of the different ways the button will appear.

Fireworks calls the various appearances of a button states. Fireworks buttons have the following four button states:

- **Up.** The Up state is the default, at-rest appearance of the button—the version that most commonly appears when a page loads.

- **Over.** The Over state appears when the mouse rolls over the button's active area. Many of the navigation buttons you see on Web sites have only the Up and Over states.

- **Down.** The Down state is the appearance of the button after a user clicks it. This state is typically displayed on the destination Web page, to indicate which page the user is currently on (or, for larger sites, the section the user is viewing).

- **Over While Down.** The Over While Down state is the appearance of the Down state button when the cursor is moved over it.

The following figure shows an example of the two most common states of a button: the Up state and the Over state. The Up state is the normal state of a button, and is displayed when the Web page first loads. The Over state is displayed when the mouse hovers over the button.

To create a button, you must create a separate graphic for each state you want to capture. But that's not all. You also need a script to instruct the browser to display the correct button graphic, depending on the user's activity. The script is usually written in JavaScript, a scripting language used for controlling the browser. This script has to account for each of the button graphics (which represent states) and respond to appropriate user events. It may sound complicated, especially for a nonprogrammer, but fortunately, Fireworks does just about all the work for you.

All you have to do to create a functional button is build a button symbol in Fireworks' Button Symbol editor. Once you've created it, Fireworks stores the button symbol in the Library. You can then create as many instances (that is, copies of the original button symbol) as you need.

Note *The Library is discussed in more detail later in this lesson.*

Designating the button as a symbol has the following advantages:

- Fireworks saves the button symbol in the Library, so you can reuse its instances as often as you like. Reusing symbols boosts productivity and ensures consistency.
- Fireworks' Button Symbol editor contains a four-state environment in which you can use various vector and text tools to easily develop and modify the button's appearance in different states.
- Fireworks automatically exports the necessary HTML and JavaScript to accompany the different states of the button to ensure that the button effect functions properly and that each state is correctly referred to in the scripts.

Now that you have a basic understanding of how Fireworks handles buttons, we can return to the task at hand: creating the button's Up state. The button symbol you will be creating for Jade Valley's navigation system contains only two states: Up and Over. You'll start with the Up state. In the process, you'll get a hands-on review of what you learned from Lesson 1: drawing vector graphics, creating and formatting text, and sizing and positioning objects with numeric precision.

You'll begin by creating a new document.

1. Open Fireworks, and choose File › New from the main menu.

Alternatively, you can use the keyboard shortcut Ctrl+N (Windows) or Command+N (Mac).

2. In the New Document dialog, specify 200 as the Width and 200 as the Height. Leave the Resolution at 72 Pixels/Inch (the default) and the Canvas Color as white (the default). Click OK.

We need a canvas that is big enough to accommodate the final size of the button. In fact, the button you'll create is smaller than the canvas, but you can resize it later. It's better to have a little too much room than not quite enough.

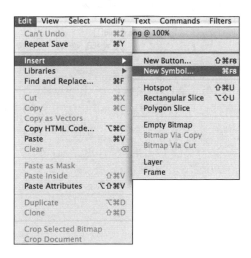

3. Choose File › Save and save the new file on your hard disk as *button.png*.

As always, remember to save early and often.

Although buttons are eventually output using several files (one graphic for each state, as well as an HTML file with the requisite JavaScript), Fireworks encapsulates them all in the button symbol. Therefore, you can create all the button assets in a single document.

4. Choose Edit › Insert › New Symbol to create a symbol on the Document window.

Fireworks offers two ways to create symbols: converting existing graphics to symbols and creating symbols from scratch. Because you need a custom-design graphic for the Jade Valley navigation system, you will use the second method.

Tip | *In addition to using the main menu to create a symbol, you can use Ctrl+F8 (Windows)/Command+F8 (Mac) or choose New Symbol from the Library panel's Options menu.*

5. In the Symbol Properties dialog, name the new symbol *nutrition* and select Button as its type.

We need to designate the new symbol as a button symbol in order to develop two states using the Button Symbol editor.

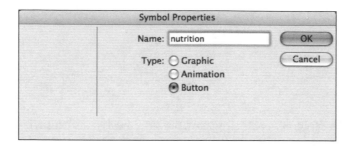

6. Click OK to complete the button symbol creation process.

When you click OK, Fireworks automatically opens the Button Symbol editor. This editor enables you to create the different button states. In addition, Fireworks adds this new symbol to the Library. You can see the button by choosing Windows > Library to open the Library panel, where the new button is listed.

7. Select the Ellipse tool in the Tools panel and hold down the Shift key to draw a perfect circle on the canvas. Don't worry about the size and location at this point.

> **Note** *The Ellipse tool is located in the same group as the Rectangle tool, and it might not be visible. To select it, press and hold the Rectangle tool until a pop-up menu appears, displaying all the hidden tools.*

This step is a review of drawing vector graphics, which you learned in Lesson 1, *Preparing Graphics*. You'll customize the exact size and location of the circle in the next step.

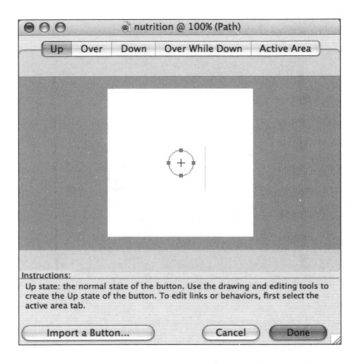

8. Use the numerical sizing in the Property inspector to further format the size and location of this circle. For the W, H, X, and Y coordinates, use **24, 24, −12, and −12**, respectively. The Fill should be set to white (#FFFFFF), and the Stroke Color set to light gray (#CCCCCC).

The numeric settings do two things: ensure that the circle is exactly 24 pixels in diameter, and ensure that the circle is centered on the canvas. The X and Y coordinates represent the distance in pixels from the top-left corner of the graphic from the center of the canvas. Thus, to ensure that the graphic is centered on the canvas, half its pixels need to be above the center (−12), and half need to be to the left of the center (−12).

Fireworks' Property inspector is context sensitive; because you just drew an ellipse, the Property inspector updates to provide several options for formatting this new shape.

9. In the Property inspector, select Stroke Options from the Stroke category. In the Stroke option dialog, choose Pencil as the Stroke type, 1-Pixel Soft as the Stroke name, and 1 as the Tip size.

This sets the stroke to 1 pixel wide, with a soft, smooth edge.

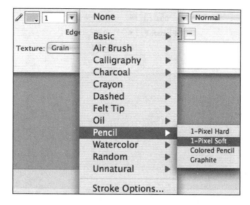

10. Follow the steps above to draw a bigger circle alongside the first one (but not touching it).

The stroke options of this new circle should be the same as those of the one you just drew.

Don't worry about the location of the new circle in relation to the smaller one. In the next step you'll use the Align panel to align both circles properly in the Document window.

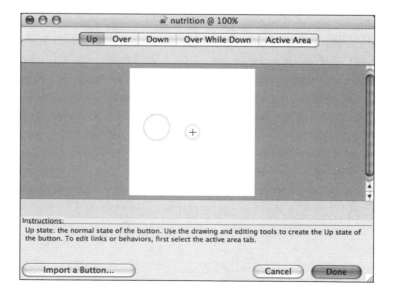

11. Open the Align panel by choosing Window › Align.

The Align panel enables you to align objects with precision on the canvas.

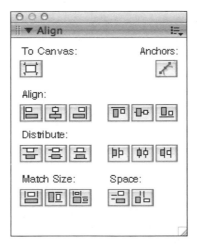

12. Select both circles by choosing Select › Select All. With both circles selected, click Align Horizontal Center and then Align Vertical Center to align the two circles.

You will notice that the smaller circle disappears after you align the two circles. That's because the fill of both circles is set to white, so that the more recently drawn circle obscures the original circle.

13. Use the Pointer tool to click on a blank area of the canvas to deselect both circles. Then click the larger circle to select it, and choose Modify › Arrange › Send to Back.

You just used the Align panel's controls for aligning objects on the canvas. These alignment controls make it possible to precisely align as many objects as you want on the canvas. Now you're ready to resize and reposition the second circle.

14. Set the W, H, X, and Y coordinates of the larger circle to 30, 30, –15, and –15, respectively.

Because you are creating only one of the six buttons that make up the Jade Valley Web site's navigation system, resizing and repositioning is necessary so all the buttons look consistent. In the next step, you'll complete the development of the button Up state by giving it a label.

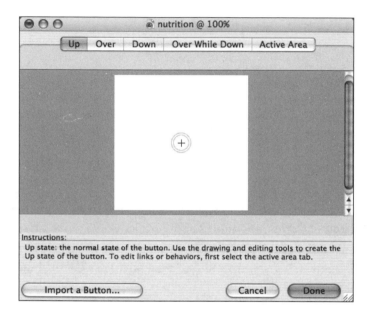

15. Use the Text tool and type *NUTRITION* under the two circles. In the Property inspector, choose Arial Narrow as the Font, 12 as the font Size, #666666 as the font Color, and Center-alignment for the button label. Finally, set the text block's X and Y coordinates to 31 and 22, respectively.

This completes the button Up state development process, including how the button will look when it is first loaded on the page. Fortunately, creating the remaining states will be much easier, since you can reuse much of your work.

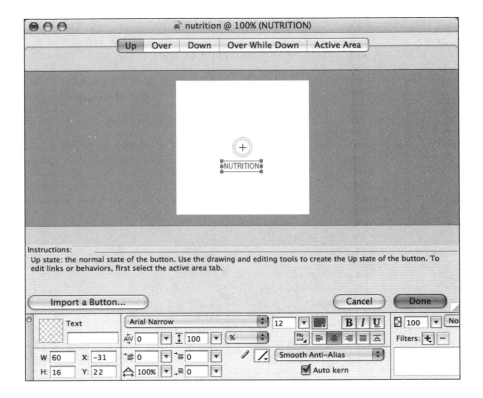

Creating Button Over States

At this point you've created the default state of the button, the Up state. You'll develop the Over state of the button in the following task. The Over state appears when the mouse is hovering over the button.

The Over state will have the same look and feel as the Up state—the differences will lie in the size of the circles and the additional bitmap image you'll import to fill the inner circle. Your goal is to maintain consistency for the overall navigation system, while introducing a different look to make the Over state stand out.

1. Open red_onion.png in Lesson 2's Start folder.

You'll use this stock photograph to create a mask. As you learned in Lesson 1, the outline of a mask is the frame through which you see the bitmap image. When the mouse is hovering over the button on the Jade Valley Web site (the Over state), you want the photo of the red onion to be revealed. This makes the navigation system of the site more interesting, and gives visitors a sense of the types of products Jade Valley offers.

2. Select the Ellipse tool in the Tools panel. Use the Property inspector to set the Stroke and the Fill to none. Holding down the Shift key, draw a small circle on top of the onion photograph that fits within the confines of the photo.

After you've converted the circle to a mask, neither the stroke nor the fill color of the circle will be visible. Setting both stroke and fill to none makes it easier to see what you're doing.

The circle's path will eventually cover exactly the area you want to reveal; thus it is only the outline of the circle that matters. When the effect is finished, the onion photo in a circle will replace the Up state's plain smaller circle when the mouse rolls over the button.

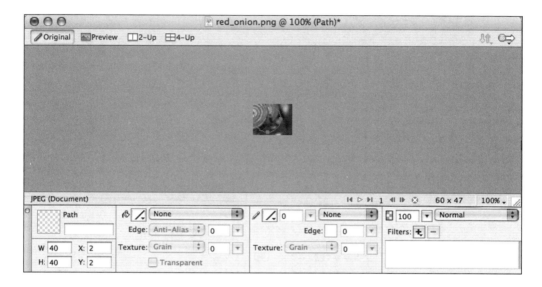

3. With the circle still selected, use the Property inspector to change the W, H, X, and Y coordinates to 36, 36, 1, and 1, respectively.

In the previous task, you created the nutrition button's Up state by drawing two circles and aligning them using the Align panel. The masked onion will need to fit into the inner circle, so you'll need to resize the masking circle.

4. Switch to the Pointer tool. Holding down the Shift key, select both the circle and the red onion photo. Choose Modify > Mask > Group as Mask. In the Layers panel, click the mask (right-hand) thumbnail in the mask layer. In the Property inspector, set the Mask type to Path Outline (not Grayscale).

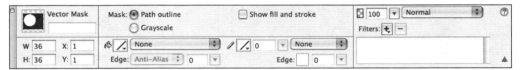

The circle now reveals the red onion photo wherever it overlaps the photo.

The Path Outline setting instructs Fireworks to disregard the stroke and fill of the circle and refer only to the outline of the shape itself. In effect, the masking object crops the masked object. Use the alternative setting, Grayscale, when you want to blend two objects together in a mask, rather than using one to crop the other.

5. From the main menu, choose Select > Deselect. In the Property inspector, press the Fit Canvas button. Then save red_onion.png and close the file.

This makes the circled onion mask fit perfectly on the canvas without any extra space.

6. Return to button.png and double-click the Up state of the button you created earlier to open the Button Symbol editor. Click the Over tab to access the button Over state's development environment.

In the Button Symbol editor, the Document window shows the button canvas, which is blank as soon as you choose the Over tab. The crosshair symbol you see denotes the center of the button.

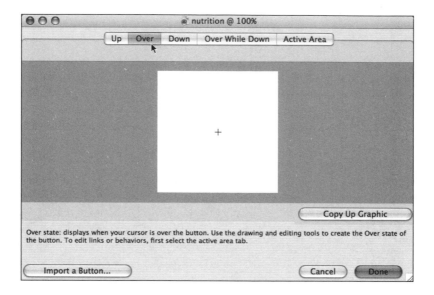

7. Click the Copy Up Graphic button.

Because most button states are variations of button Up, the Copy Up Graphic button is a convenient way to automatically copy the button Up state and place it into the Over state's canvas in the same position.

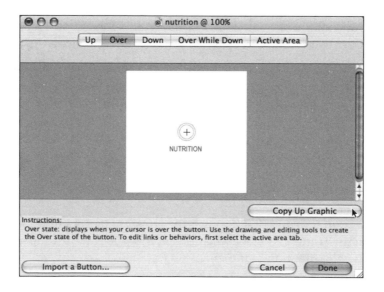

Next, you need to modify the Over state to distinguish it from the Up state.

8. Select the outer circle and use the Property inspector to change the W, H, X, and Y coordinates to 42, 42, −21, and −21, respectively. Then select the inner circle and use the Property inspector to change the W, H, X, and Y coordinates to 36, 36, −18, and −18, respectively.

The Over state needs to be slightly different from the Up state, so you'll enlarge it in this step to make room for the onion mask you created earlier.

9. Choose File › Import to import red_onion.png. After the file is on the canvas (denoted by the L-shaped cursor), place the red onion mask inside the inner circle.

Note *You can use the arrow keys on your keyboard or the X and Y settings of the Property inspector to help you precisely position the mask.*

Now that the red onion mask is placed inside the inner circle, the red onion is revealed in the inner circle when the mouse hovers over the button.

10. Select the Type tool in the Tools panel and change the color of the button label, **NUTRITION,** to blue-green (#009966). Click Done to close the Button Symbol editor.

Changing the button's color will further distinguish the Over state from the Up state.

You have successfully created the button's Up and Over states.

11. In button.png, click the Preview tab at the top of the Document window, and roll the cursor over the button to preview both the Up and Over states. Then save button.png and close the file.

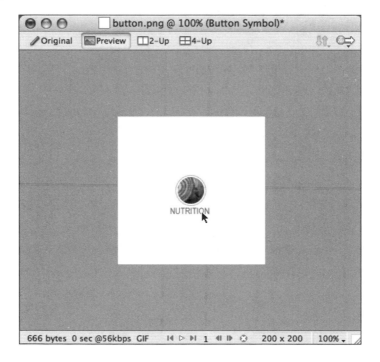

The Preview tab provides a quick and easy way to preview your work throughout the development process.

Tip *Another, more reliable, way to test Fireworks documents is to press F12. Fireworks generates a temporary Web page complete with all the necessary graphics and JavaScript, enabling you test the page in an actual browser.*

Working with the Library

Fireworks' Library lets you store, share, and reuse assets throughout the development process. The Library makes it possible for developers to improve productivity, maintain consistency, as well as streamline animation and interactivity production.

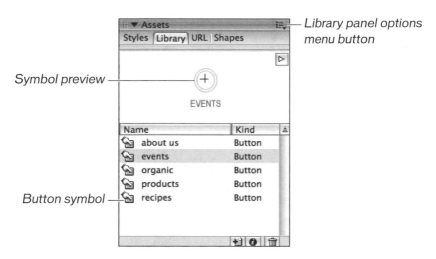

Library panel options menu button

Symbol preview

Button symbol

You can drag and drop symbols from the Library onto the canvas. You're not dragging the original symbol to the canvas; rather, you're placing a copy of the symbol there. Remember, this copy is called an instance. When you modify a symbol, all instances of this symbol are changed automatically, no matter where they're placed. Because the Library lets you drag many copies of the same symbol onto the canvas, you can eliminate repetitive work and errors during production if you need several copies of the same asset.

Tip *During the development process—especially if a lot of developers are involved— one effective workflow is to develop all graphic, button, and animation assets in a single Fireworks PNG file. Once that file is completed, any team member can retrieve any asset by importing the appropriate symbol into a file's Library. And because Fireworks maintains the link between symbols and instances, any time a developer changes a symbol, all instances of this symbol can be updated in all the files where the instances are used.*

In this task, you'll learn how to use the Library to create a navigation bar for the Jade Valley Web site. You'll find a list of premade button symbols in the Library of the file that you'll be working on: "interface.png." In the process, you'll also learn how to import a button symbol and position and align instances on the canvas.

1. Open interface.png from this lesson's Start files and, if necessary, choose
Window > Library.

You can open the Library of any Fireworks file by choosing Window > Library or using the
keyboard shortcut F11. There are five button symbols in this file's Library: about us, events,
organic, products, and recipes. You'll place all five button symbols alongside the nutrition
button you created earlier to build the navigation bar for the Jade Valley Web site.

Take a few moments to explore the Library. To preview a symbol in the Library, first select
the symbol by clicking it. You can change the order of the symbols in the Library by using
the Toggle Sorting tool, which is located under the Symbol Preview pane on the right-hand
side (the triangle with the arrow pointing to the top or bottom). You can also use the Play
control (the triangle pointing to the right, above the Toggle Sorting tool) to preview
different states of a button symbol or an animation.

2. Open the Library panel's Options menu and select Import Symbols. In the Open
window, navigate to button.png and click the Open button. Next, in the Import
Symbols dialog, select the Nutrition button symbol (if it is not already highlighted)
and click Import.

The Library panel's Options menu contains several commands pertaining to symbol-related tasks: creating, editing, duplicating, deleting, and exporting symbols, among others. You created the Nutrition button symbol in a separate PNG file earlier, so you need to import the Nutrition symbol as an independent symbol Library item into the current file, interface.png.

When you choose Import from the Library panel's Options menu, an Open dialog appears, enabling you to search for PNG files that contain any files with symbols.

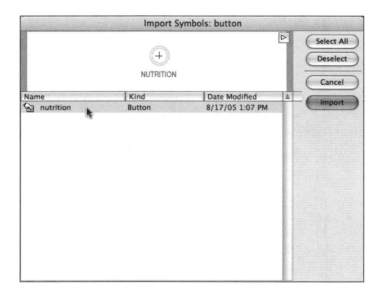

Note *If you choose a PNG file that doesn't contain any symbols, Fireworks bypasses the Import Symbols dialog and first converts the contents of the file to a group and then converts that group to a graphic symbol and places the symbol in the Library.*

In the Library, Fireworks marks imported symbols as "imported" to distinguish them from native symbols.

3. Drag an instance of the following six button symbols from the Library to the canvas, from left to right, and in the following order: ABOUT US, PRODUCTS, RECIPES, NUTRITION, ORGANIC, and EVENTS.

As stated earlier, items in the Fireworks Library can be dragged to the canvas to eliminate repetitive work. Just select a symbol in the Library and drag it directly from the Symbol Preview pane to the canvas.

4. Reposition all six button instances using the Property inspector of each one, according to the following specs: ABOUT US (X: 200, Y: 20), PRODUCTS (X: 278, Y: 20), RECIPES (X: 364, Y: 20), NUTRITION (X: 439, Y: 20), ORGANIC (X: 523, Y: 20), and EVENTS (X: 604, Y: 20).

All six button instances have the same Y coordinate. These six buttons make up the navigation bar and need to be in the same position vertically in relation to the top-right corner of the canvas.

5. In turn, select each button instance and use the Property inspector to give it a descriptive name: *about, products, recipes, nutrition, organic,* **and** *events.*

Naming each button slice makes the resulting HTML code and exported image assets more self-evident.

5. Use the Line tool to draw a straight line that connects all six button instances, starting at the center of the ABOUT US button and ending at the center of the EVENTS button. Hold down the Shift key while you draw the line. This line should have the following specs: W 400; H 1; X 225; Y 42; Stroke Color light gray (#CCCCCC); Tip size 2; and Stroke category Pencil, 1-Pixel Hard.

Holding down Shift constrains the drawing to 45-degree increments, making it easy to get the line perfectly horizontal.

For aesthetic and design reasons, you need to draw this gray line to visibly group all six buttons into a navigation bar for the Jade Valley Web site.

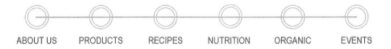

6. With the line still selected, choose Modify > Arrange > Send to Back to hide the gray line behind the buttons.

The navigation bar doesn't look very attractive with a line across it, so use the Arrange feature to neatly tuck the line behind all the buttons, while still visually connecting them.

7. Save interface.png.

You're finished working on the navigation bar for now. Later in the lesson you'll continue developing the Jade Valley Web site banner by combining the navigation bar with the logo you created in Lesson 1.

Developing a Site Banner

Now that you've successfully created the navigation bar for the Jade Valley Web site, your next task is to develop a site banner that consists of both the navigation bar and the Jade Valley logo. Let's get started.

1. Still in interface.png, choose File > Import to import logo.png from Lesson 2's Start folder to interface.png.

Because of their high quality, PNG files are good for sharing graphics for the Web or screen (but not for printing). The graphic looks as good here as it did when you first created it. The same cannot always be said of GIF and JPEG files.

2. With every element of the file logo.png still selected, choose Modify › Group to group them into one entity.

When you first import the logo each of the elements within the larger graphic is separate (see the figure on the left), making it difficult to keep the logo together as a unit. To avoid missing any elements of the logo when you relocate it, it's best to group all the elements together into one (see the figure on the right).

After you group all the elements of the logo, you'll see four handles in the corners of the logo. The handles indicate that the elements have been grouped into one entity.

Note *The grouping action you just performed affects only the file you imported; the original is not changed. Groups are flexible. You can group groups, creating nested groups. And you can ungroup graphics at any time.*

3. Select the Jade Valley Web site logo and use the arrow keys on your keyboard to move the logo to the top-left corner of the canvas. The final X and Y coordinates of the logo should be 2 and 2.

Because the navigation bar takes up the top-right portion of the canvas, we will place the logo at the top-left corner to complete the banner for the Jade Valley Web site, leaving only a 2-pixel border around it.

4. Select the Line tool in the Tools panel. Holding down the Shift key, draw a horizontal line just below the logo and the navigation buttons.

The horizontal line creates a visual division between the site banner and the content area.

5. With the line still selected, use the Property inspector to format this line. Set the W, H, X, and Y coordinates to 680, 1, 10, and 113, respectively. Change the stroke thickness to 4 pixels.

With the line's width set to 4 pixels, you now have a horizontal bar as the divider.

6. With the bar selected, use the Property inspector to further format the divider, and make the Fill Color #CCCCCC with No stroke.

To be consistent throughout the interface, you'll make the divider a light gray color—the same color (#CCCCCC) used in the navigation buttons' outlines.

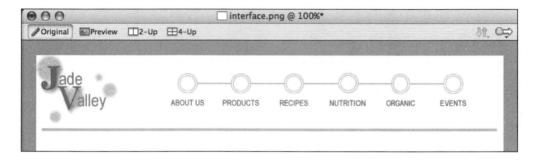

7. Save interface.png.

Finalizing the Whole-Page Design

Now that the banner for the Jade Valley Web site has been developed, you can start adding other elements to the interface and finalize the whole-page design.

1. Select the Rectangle tool in the Tools panel. Use the Property inspector to set the Stroke to 1-Pixel Hard and the Size to 1.

We need to further divide the main content area into two columns: $^{21}/_{43}$ on the right for page content and $^{11}/_{43}$ on the left for special events, advertisements, or other promotional materials.

2. Click and draw a rectangle anywhere in the Document window. Don't worry about the size and placement of the rectangle when you first draw it. When you're finished, use the Property inspector to set the W, H, X, and Y coordinates to 680, 415, 10, and 121, respectively.

The rectangle you just drew is the content area for the Jade Valley Web site.

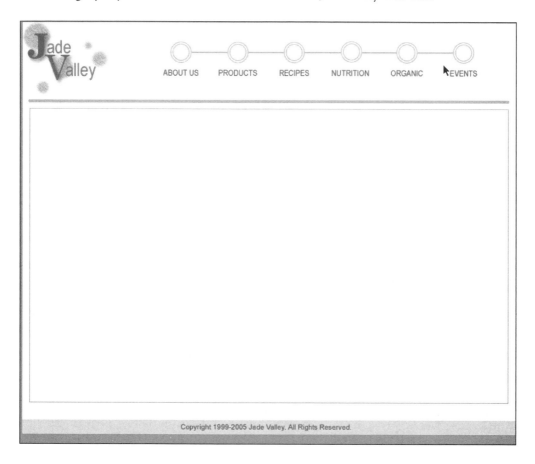

3. Select the Line tool and draw a line from the top of the rectangle down to the bottom. Use the Property inspector to set the X value of the line to 160.

The line you just drew serves as a visual divider to separate the special events area and the page content space.

4. Select the Rectangle tool. Use the Property inspector to set the Fill Color to bright yellow (#EBCF10) with No stroke. Then click and draw a rectangle at the top of the left segment of the content area. Once you've drawn a rectangle on the canvas, use the Property inspector to set the W, H, X, and Y coordinates to 150, 24, 11, and 122, respectively.

To improve usability, the yellow rectangle will be another indicator for visitors to know where they are on the Jade Valley Web site.

5. Using the Text tool, type the word *PRODUCT* in all capital letters. Use the Property inspector to change the font Color to white (#FFFFFF). Use Arial Narrow for the Font, 14 for the font Size, and Bold type for the text, and set the alignment to Right-aligned. Finally, the X and Y coordinates of the word PRODUCT should be 74 and 123, respectively.

With the completion of this yellow indicator, you've provided one more way for your visitors to go through the Jade Valley Web site.

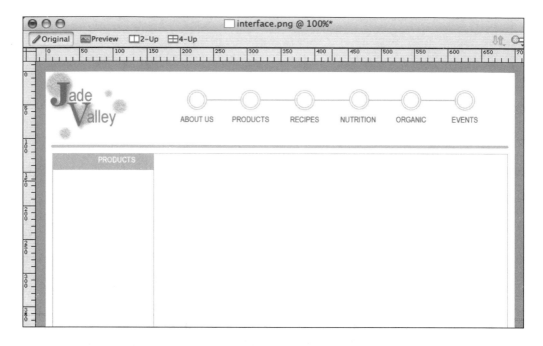

6. Choose File > Import and select banana.png from the Start folder of this lesson. Place the file underneath the yellow indicator.

As explained earlier, the left segment of the content area is reserved for marketing, promotional events, or other such elements (depending on which page you're on in the Web site). You've imported the file banana.png as a placeholder for the special element.

7. With all the elements of the file banana.png still selected, choose Modify › Group to group the background banana image and the text in the foreground into one entity.

The banana photo and the text are separate, so it's difficult to move both at the same time. Grouping them makes it easier to move both elements without damaging an element while you position it or moving one element but not the other.

The placeholder is now finished.

8. Select the Text tool and use the Property Inspector to set the Font to Arial, Size to 10, Color to charcoal (#333333), and alignment to Center. Then type, using all capital letters, *ABOUT US | PRODUCTS | RECIPES | NUTRITION | ORGANIC | EVENTS* right above the gray horizontal bar (where the copyright information is located):

To help make the Jade Valley Web site more user-friendly, this step provides another way for visitors to navigate through the site. When visitors reach the end of a lengthy page, they won't have to scroll all the way up to the navigation bar in order to move to a different page. The text-based navigation in the footer area of every page makes it easy for visitors to move beyond the current page.

9. Choose File › Save to save the file.

We will develop the page-slicing scheme in the next section.

Developing the Page-Slicing Scheme

If you've ever developed a Web page in Dreamweaver or by hand-coding some HTML, you know that most pages contain dozens or even hundreds of elements. The browser reads the HTML code that describes the elements, and does its best to render them. Looking over your Fireworks document, you can see dozens of objects laid out in various places on the page. Somehow, the elements in the Fireworks document need to be converted to HTML code.

Fireworks is fully capable of converting a complex page layout such as ours into HTML, but it needs our help. Specifically, Fireworks needs to know where to separate elements. For instance, we know that the lower-right $21/43$ of the page is eventually supposed to be the main content area. We also know that it is distinct from the footer and the navigation bar. We need to communicate these divisions to Fireworks.

To do so, we'll use the Slice tool. With the Slice tool, we draw regions on top of our layout, and Fireworks uses these regions as a guide to cut up the layout and to write the HTML we need to reconstruct the Web page. Slices have uses above and beyond indicating where to cut up the document; you can also use slices to optimize a complex graphic, designate an area that responds to the mouse, trigger an interactive element, and so on. In fact, interface.png already has numerous slices; a slice is created automatically for each button symbol instance placed on the canvas.

Upon export, each slice is by default converted to an HTML table cell. The complete collection of slices is exported as an HTML table. Any graphic contained within that slice is also exported, usually as a GIF or JPEG file. By default, if you draw a slice anywhere in a document, even if you do not explicitly draw slices over the remaining areas, Fireworks slices them upon export. Because of changes in Web standards over the years, HTML tables are no longer the preferred method for laying out page content; instead, Web designers are encouraged to use CSS layers. You'll use CSS layers to lay out the main regions of the page, which is possible thanks to Fireworks' ability to export slices as CSS layers as an alternative to HTML table cells.

> **Note** *Slices are often confused with hotspots. Whereas slices actually cut a Fireworks document into several pieces and reassembles those pieces in an HTML table, hotspots are exported as image maps. You can think of image maps as invisible layers hovering over a given image. An image map generally contains a series of hotspots that respond to a user's actions. Image maps don't interact with or affect the underlying images; the original images are not altered because of the hotspots you place on them. Hotspots are typically used to add hyperlinks to image regions.*

The whole-page design you just completed contains regular images (e.g., the Jade Valley logo and the yellow indicator), interactive graphic elements (e.g., the navigation buttons), and text areas (e.g., the main content area and the special content segment), rather than using hotspots. You will develop a slicing scheme to export the whole-page design. Fireworks slices make it possible for you to retain the functionality of each of your design elements.

To prepare the whole-page design, you'll first remove many of the design elements. The more complex the design, the harder it is to slice and export it out of Fireworks into Dreamweaver. When the design is too complicated, the slicing scheme can become too convoluted and can result in overly complex and fragile HTML code. In addition, depending on the nature and functionality of the elements, it makes more sense to reconstruct some of them (e.g., the footer) in Dreamweaver.

Note | *Although the whole-page design you created needs to be stripped down for slicing purposes in this section of the lesson, your effort in creating the more elaborate design was not wasted. It's helpful to put all the necessary elements together and visually explore where they need to go. In addition, the design will come in handy as a blueprint when you reconstruct the design in Dreamweaver in later chapters.*

1. With interface.png still open, choose File > Save As and save the file as *interface_slices.png*.

The original interface.png file will remain intact so that you have something to compare when you reconstruct the file. You will use the new file interface_slices.png to develop the slicing scheme to export the whole-page design.

2. Using the Crop tool, drag a region around the logo and the navigation bar, including but not exceeding the gray line underneath them.

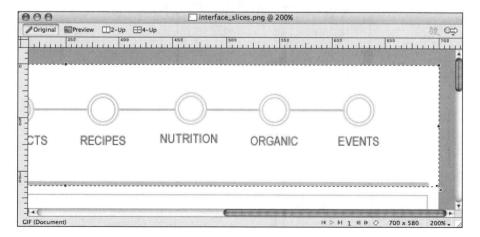

Use the Zoom tool to ensure that the crop region includes all the gray bar, but no white pixels beneath it.

You're removing the parts of the page that will hold the main page content as well as the footer. You'll add these sections back in Dreamweaver. For now, you're preparing the document to export the page banner (the logo and the navigation bar).

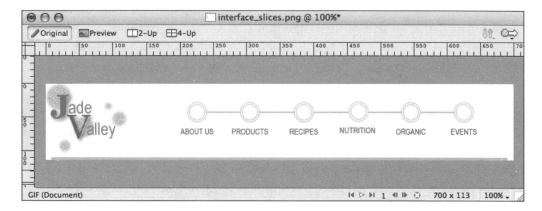

3. Select the Slice tool in the Tools panel and draw a rectangle slice over the Jade Valley Web site logo.

After you draw a slice object over an image in Fireworks, the image turns neon green.

You can customize the slice color by using the color swatch in the Property inspector when the slice is selected.

4. With the slice still selected, go to the Property inspector, type *logo* as the name of the slice, and verify that Image is the specified Slice Type. Apply the following settings: **W 161; H 115; X 0; Y 0.**

It's a good habit to name all your slices; doing so makes it a lot easier to troubleshoot problems in the HTML code if the need arises.

Notice that the slice inherits the default export option, which is GIF WebSnap 128. Keep the default setting for now. You'll change it in the next lesson.

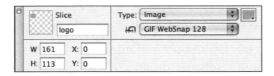

Slicing the navigation bar will require a little more work; you'll deal with that in the next lesson.

5. Preview your work and save the file.

Enhancing Site Accessibility

Accessibility refers to the availability of page assets, including interfaces, images, sounds, multimedia elements, and all other forms of information. This information should be available to anyone, regardless of how they access site content. For example, visitors with visual disabilities can access your site with a screen reader, which is a program that reads page content aloud. Screen readers are great for text, but how can a screen reader summarize the contents of an image? Built into HTML is the ability to provide caption-like text alternatives for images, so when a screen reader encounters a graphic, it can convey its content or meaning to the user. It is up to the site developer/owner to provide this content.

In HTML, alternate text descriptions are added via the alt attribute of the <img> tag. The <img> tag is used to insert images into a page, as the following basic example shows:

```
<img src="images/pantheon.jpg">
```

This code provides enough information for a browser to retrieve the correct file and display it in a page. But it does not provide any useful information to a screen reader. As a result, a user accessing your site through a screen reader would access less content than a user with Internet Explorer or Netscape. If you add the alt attribute, everyone can access your site's content.

```
<img src="images/pantheon.jpg" alt="The granite columns of Rome's Pantheon
dominate the Piazza Della Rotunda.">
```

To learn more about accessibility, including Web developers' legal obligations, available technical solutions, and achieving accessibility goals with Macromedia tools, check out the following resources:

- U. S. Section 508 Guidelines (www.section508.gov)
- Web Accessibility Initiatives (www.w3.org/WAI/Resources)
- Macromedia Accessibility (www.macromedia.com/resources/accessibility/)

In Fireworks, the easiest way to enter alt information for images is to slice them and use the Property inspector to add captions. You already have your slices, so now it's just a matter of selecting each one and entering an alternate text description for it in the Property inspector.

Note *You can automate the process of adding alt descriptions using two commands available at the Macromedia Exchange. (The Macromedia Exchange is a resource containing hundreds of installable features that you can add to Macromedia products. It can be found at www.macromedia.com/exchange/.) The commands are Select Blank ALT Tags, which selects all hotspots and slices that do not have alternate text, and Set Blank ALT Tag, which enables designers and developers to provide a single description for all images that do not have alternate text.*

1. Open interface_slices.png

As a first step to make the Jade Valley Web site accessible, you will specify alternate text for all the slices you created earlier.

2. Select the logo slice on the left side of the document. In the Property inspector, enter *Jade Valley Logo.* in the Alt field as the alt text for the logo slice.

To specify alternate text for a selected slice, all you have to do is type the text in the Alt field in the Property inspector. Make sure the alt text is meaningful and that it accurately conveys the function of the graphics.

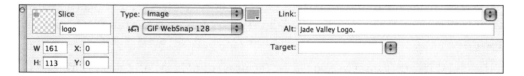

Tip *When entering alt text for your graphics, make sure you include a period at the end of the alternative text, so that the screen reader knows it's the end of the description of a graphic.*

3. Select the ABOUT US navigation button. In the Property inspector, enter *Go to About Us page section.* in the Alt field as the alt text for the ABOUT US button.

Because all of the navigation buttons are images, you'll need to provide alternative text for each of them.

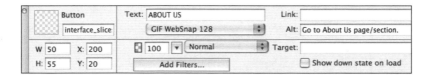

4. Repeat Step 3 and provide alt text for the other five navigation buttons.

In general, alternative text either describes the graphic (for example, Jade Valley Logo.) or indicates the graphic's functionality (for example, Go to About Us page/section.). Of course, you can enter both a visual description and a functional description. Alternate descriptions can be up to 1,024 characters in length.

5. Save and close interface_slices.png.

What You Have Learned

In this lesson, you have:

- Learned about the four button states in Fireworks (pages 37–38)
- Created the Up and Over states for a button (pages 37–50)
- Learned how to streamline the development process by working with the Library and button symbols in Fireworks (pages 51–55)
- Developed a site banner using different graphic elements (pages 55–57)
- Created a whole-page design (pages 57–61)
- Developed a slicing scheme for the whole-page design (pages 62–65)
- Learned how to make Web sites and graphic elements accessible to people with disabilities (pages 65–67)

3 Exporting a Site Design

After you create and finalize the whole-page design and determine the slicing scheme, you can turn your attention to moving the design from Macromedia Fireworks to Macromedia Dreamweaver. Moving the design is a two-step process: image optimization and file export. Image optimization is the process of converting the high-quality Fireworks PNG file's graphics to low-bandwidth Web graphics, usually in GIF or JPEG format. More specifically, optimization refers to finding the balance between image quality and the shortest download time for your graphics. High-quality images generally include a lot of detailed information, and that information results in large file sizes. Your goal is to reduce file sizes (and hence remove or compress some of that information) without compromising the quality of your images. Although optimization is a complex task, Fireworks offers a unique set of tools to make it easy.

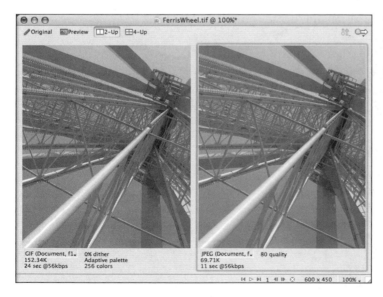

In the course of this lesson, you'll work with Fireworks' 2-Up (shown) and 4-Up Preview panes to find the optimal balance of file size and image quality. The image on the left is a much larger file—and longer download—and yet actually looks worse than the image on the right.

When the graphics are optimized, you're ready to export them. In Fireworks, exporting generally occurs in two steps. In the first step, the graphics in each slice (except HTML slices) are exported according to their optimization settings; that is, Fireworks creates a new GIF or JPEG file for that region of the overall layout. In the second step, Fireworks generates an HTML file to reconstruct the individually exported graphics into a page layout. Fortunately, Fireworks and Dreamweaver work seamlessly together, so it's easy to reconstruct the Fireworks design in Dreamweaver and start developing pages right away.

In this lesson, you'll concentrate on learning the techniques to optimize graphics. In addition, you'll work with various export settings to prepare the Fireworks document for export. In the process, you'll become familiar with Fireworks' Optimize panel and the Export HTML setup process, mastering the techniques used to find the best optimization and export settings for your original design.

What You Will Learn

In this lesson, you will:

- Optimize graphics for small file size and high quality
- Specify export settings and output the files
- View output pages in a browser

Approximate Time

This lesson takes approximately 50 minutes to complete.

Lesson Files

Starting Files:

Lesson03/Start/interface_slices.png

Completed Files:

Lesson03/Complete/jade_valley
Lesson03/Complete/interface_slices.png
Lesson03/Complete/interface_layers.png
Lesson03/Complete/interface_navbar.png

Optimizing the Logo

The goal of optimizing Web graphics is to avoid long download times by limiting the file size. The challenge is to limit the page size in such a way that image quality is not sacrificed along the way. In other words, to optimize a graphic, you need to balance the file size and image quality. However, the many factors involved often complicate the optimization process.

You'll find the optimization process easier if you understand some basics about the different graphic file types, including their distinct advantages, disadvantages, and unique capabilities. In general, for screen-viewing purposes, you have a choice of three viable formats: GIF, JPEG, and PNG. The PNG (Portable Network Graphic) file format, although a flexible and compact format, is unfortunately only partially supported by most browsers. As a result, it's best not to publish PNG files directly to the Web (though it's an ideal format for sending graphics to other applications, such as Flash).

Note *Don't confuse Fireworks PNG files with standard PNGs. The Fireworks PNG contains proprietary data that can only be fully read by Macromedia Fireworks. The standard PNG is an open-source alternative to the GIF format that can be read by many applications. One feature of standard PNG files is that they enable developers to store proprietary data about the file, so strictly speaking, a Fireworks PNG file is a standard PNG. However, it's more useful to think of Fireworks PNG files the way you think of a Photoshop PSD or a Microsoft Word DOC file—that is, as a file that can only be read fully in its native application, and not as a file you share with other applications.*

Note *The TIFF file format, which is another common graphics format that you may have used in other applications, is not a good format for the Web because of its large file sizes and lack of support in browsers.*

Because PNG files are not ideal for Web publishing, you have two choices for exporting most graphics for use on the Web: GIF and JPEG. Let's look at each.

In general, images with limited colors, distinct edges, and large areas of solid colors work well as GIF (CompuServe Graphics Interchange Format) files. Logos (as shown in the following figure), charts, vector graphics, diagrams, and text are best compressed as GIFs.

In many respects, JPEG (Joint Photographic Expert Group) is the opposite of GIF. JPEGs excel at representing millions of colors, as is often the case in digital photography (as shown in the following figure). As a result, you should choose JPEG as your compression format for digital photos, images with millions of colors, complex images that do not have wide areas of single colors, and images that have subtle transitions and gradations of color. JPEGs do not support animation or transparency. In general, you should avoid using JPEGs with text, graphics with sharp edges, or logos.

Now let's return to our first task: optimizing the Jade Valley Web site logo. You'll first need to decide which file format to choose (a decision that Fireworks can help you make). After you've made that decision, you'll need to provide additional information specific to the chosen file format, while balancing image size and quality.

Let's get started!

1. Open Fireworks, and open interface_slices.png in the Lesson 3 Start folder.

This is the file you completed in Lesson 2, *Designing a Page Interface*. Because you finalized the whole-page design at the end of the last lesson, you'll use it to optimize all the graphic slices and export the design.

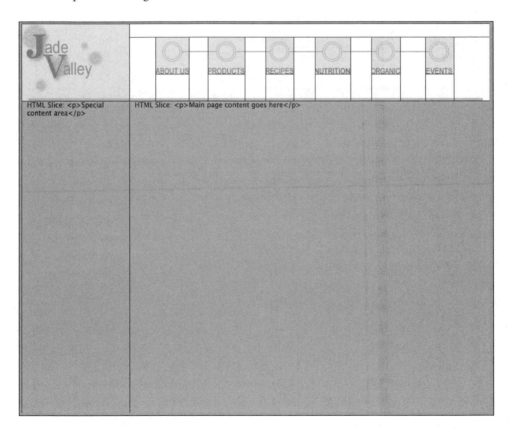

2. With the file open, click the 4-Up View button.

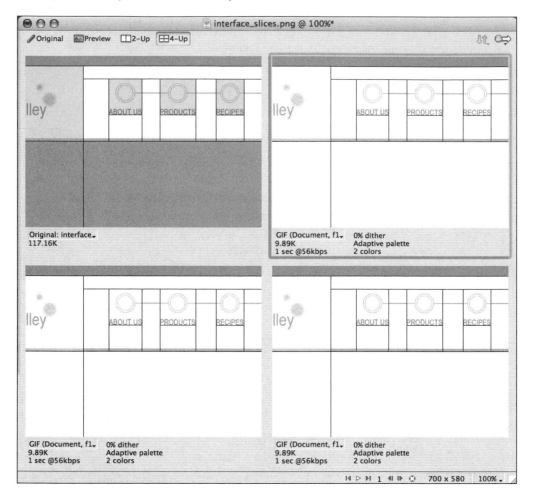

Fireworks provides two environments for graphic optimization: one is the Export Preview dialog and the other is a combination of the three Preview tabs (Preview, 2-Up, and 4-Up) and the Optimize panel. The most challenging task when optimizing graphics is walking the fine line between file size and image quality; therefore, the Preview-tab environment is especially helpful because you can experiment with different settings and compare their size and quality with ease.

When you click the 4-Up View button, the original file appears in the top-left corner, and you can compare three optimized preview panes simultaneously. In addition to letting you compare image quality, all preview tabs provide useful information such as export type, export options, estimated file size, estimated download time on a 56K modem, and so on.

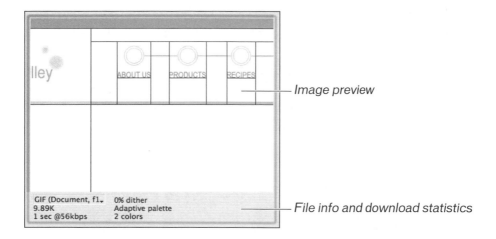

Image preview

File info and download statistics

3. Select the Hand tool in the Tools panel and drag the original file interface_slices.png to the top-left corner of the Document window so you can see the entire Jade Valley Web site logo and make sure it's in focus.

The whole-page design contains many slices. Each slice will be exported as a different graphic, which means that you can optimize each slice according to its own needs, without regard for the optimization settings associated with other slices.

The Hand tool works well to help bring the slice into focus so that you can see the slice you're trying to optimize. Notice that when you drag the original file, the images in the surrounding panes move as well.

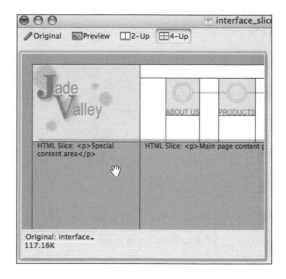

4. Switch to the Pointer tool in the Tools panel and select the logo slice. To show the Optimize panel, if necessary, choose Windows > Optimize (or press the F6 key on your keyboard).

The other part of the combined optimization environment is the Optimize panel. This panel provides convenient access to all the settings you need in order to optimize the graphics. As the following figures show, the Optimize panel has different settings for GIF and JPEG, reflecting the nature of the file formats.

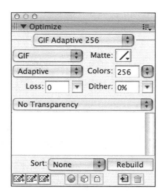 

Note *You might be tempted to use the optimization settings in the Property inspector to optimize the graphic, but you should avoid the temptation. The Property inspector provides access to only a handful of optimization presets; it does not provide access to individual settings.*

5. Click the logo slice in the lower-left pane in the Document window to activate it. In the Optimize panel, select JPEG - Better Quality from the Saved settings drop-down list.

As mentioned earlier, optimization is a two-stage process; in the first stage, you choose a file type, typically GIF or JPEG. In the second stage, you enter settings appropriate to the selected file type. In this step, you begin the process of identifying which file type is more appropriate for this file. You've selected JPEG as your exported file format for the lower-left pane, and in a moment, you will enter other possible file types in the other two panes, and then compare the three results.

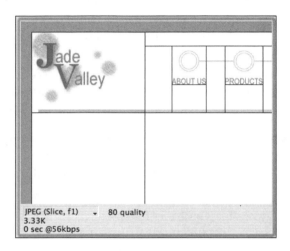

Notice that the JPEG – Better Quality setting results in an estimated 3.33K file size, and would take approximately 0 seconds (which really means "under 1 second") to download the Jade Valley logo on a 56K modem.

Optionally, take a moment to experiment with other setting options in the Optimize panel. For example, drag the Quality slider lower than 80 and see how it affects the estimated file size and the image quality. When you're finished, make sure you set the slider back to 80.

6. Click the logo slice in the upper-right pane of the Document window. In the Optimize panel, choose GIF Web 216 from the Saved settings drop-down list.

This time, you've chosen GIF as the output file type. Unlike JPEG, GIF lacks a Quality slider. Instead, to control the file size and image quality of a GIF, you must work with its color palette. Every GIF has a color palette of 256 colors or fewer. Many images have more than 256 colors, so GIF has to represent all the colors as best as it can with the limited colors available to its palette. For example, if the original image has 2,500 colors, 90 percent of those colors will be dropped from the file, and the pixels that used those colors will use the nearest available color. So how does Fireworks determine which colors are in the color palette, and which ones are thrown out?

With the exception of special palettes, such as grayscale palettes that use only black, white, and gray pixels, Fireworks does its best to represent all the original colors, taking into account two conflicting considerations:

- **Color fidelity:** Fireworks tries to pick colors that best represent the colors in the original image.

- **Conformance to the Web Safe palette:** In the early 1990s, 8-bit video cards displayed 256 colors. Windows and Macintosh systems use 40 colors for system menus, and the remaining 216 colors are available on all monitors with 8-bit color or higher. In the mid-1990s, designers tried to stick to these 216 colors, to ensure that everyone could see what they designed. For almost a decade, most computers have shipped with video cards capable of displaying 16.7 million colors or even more. Thus, the Web Safe palette is quickly becoming an obsolete concept.

The color palette you chose in this step, GIF Web 216, forces Fireworks to use colors in that 216-color Web Safe palette. As a result, color shifting occurs, and the logo doesn't look like it did before. We can get a much better representation of our file using GIF, but not with this palette.

The GIF Web 216 setting produces a smaller file size (e.g., 2.60K), compared to the JPEG – Better Quality setting. As with the JPEG setting, the GIF Web 216 setting will take less than a second to download on a 56K modem. If file size is all you care about, then this setting is a better choice. But file size isn't everything; the image looks awful.

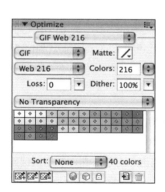
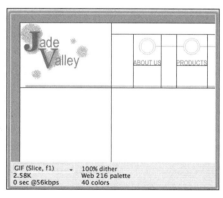

Tip *The hexadecimal values for the Web Safe palette are in the following pairs: 00, 33, 66, 99, CC, FF. For example, #66CCFF, which is a shade of teal, is a Web Safe color, but #B32600, which is a shade of orange-red, is not.*

You should think twice before choosing Web 216 as the optimization setting. For example, in an effort to create branding, corporate logos generally contain official colors (e.g., the yellow in McDonalds' arch or the bright red in the Coca Cola logo). If your company's logo has an official color, and you choose Web 216 as the optimizing setting for the logo, you're likely to end up with a different color!

7. Click the logo slice in the lower-right pane of the Document window. In the Optimize panel, choose GIF Adaptive 256 from the Saved settings drop-down list.

Whereas GIF Web 216 prioritized Web Safe color way above color fidelity (and the file shifted color accordingly), GIF Adaptive is the other extreme; all it cares about is color fidelity, and it doesn't take the Web Safe palette into consideration. Of the three, this version of the logo probably looks the best, although it's also the largest.

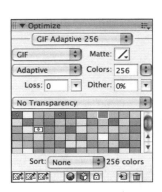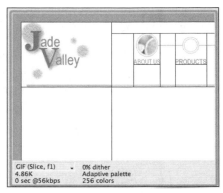

Note *Web Snap 128 (or 256) is another common GIF setting. This setting is the middle ground of the two extremes of GIF Adaptive 256 and Web 216. The Web Snap setting uses Web Safe color where doing so results in only subtle color shifts. If a color in the original is just too far from a Web Safe color, it uses a non-Web Safe color. Thus, the palette is part Adaptive, and part Web Safe. Web Snap is Fireworks' default palette for GIFs. For most situations, we recommend using Adaptive, rather than Web Snap.*

8. Choose the GIF Adaptive 256 setting as the final optimization setting by making sure the logo slice in the lower-right pane is selected. Click the Original button in the Document window to return to the interface_slices.png file.

GIF Adaptive 256 should be the chosen optimization setting in the Optimize panel.

You chose GIF Adaptive 256 as the final optimization setting for the logo slice because it was best looking of the three choices. It has better color fidelity than the Web Safe version, and the edges of the text are clearer than those of the JPEG, which look slightly blurry. And although it's also the largest file, it's still only 4K, which takes less than a second to download, so the difference in download time is negligible.

Optimizing the Navigation Bar

At this point you've optimized the logo slice, and with some optimization knowledge and experience under your belt, you're ready to dive into another task: optimizing the navigation bar for the Jade Valley Web site.

1. Click the 2-Up Preview View button. Select the Hand tool and drag the original file interface_slices.png (i.e., the left pane of the Document window) so that the ABOUT US button of the navigation bar is in focus and you can see it in its entirety. Switch to the Pointer tool in the Tools panel and click the ABOUT US button slice to select it.

There are six navigation buttons, and you'll need to optimize them one at a time. The good news is that once you find the best optimization setting for the first button, you can reuse that setting for the remaining five buttons.

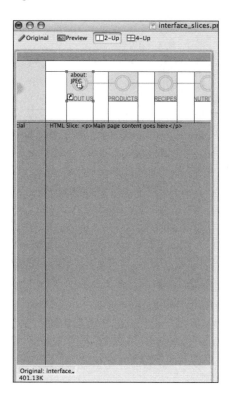

2. With the ABOUT US button slice selected, toggle the Original to Image Preview mode. In the Optimize panel, select GIF Adaptive 256 from the Saved settings drop-down list.

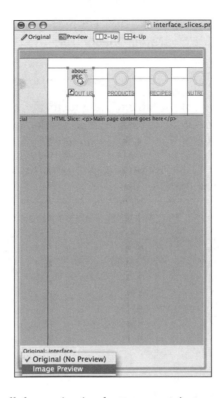

Recall from Lesson 2 that all the navigation buttons contain two states: the Up state (simple text and vector drawing) and the Over state (text, vector drawing, and a digital photo within a vector graphic). The challenge of optimizing these navigation buttons is to find a setting that best translates both the simple vector graphics and the more complex digital images. In this step, you'll experiment with the GIF Adaptive 256 setting, which results in an estimated 681 bytes (.6 K) file with a 0-second download time using a 56K modem.

To see both states of the button, you need to set Fireworks to preview it, which is why you toggled to Image Preview mode. Mouse over the ABOUT US button and take a look at how this setting affects the lemon image in the Over state.

3. Use the Pointer tool to click the **ABOUT US** button in the right pane. In the Optimize panel, choose JPEG - Better Quality from the Saved settings drop-down list.

Do not click any other slice, or you will select (and optimize) the wrong slice!

Because the Over state of the button contains a digital image, in this step you'll choose JPEG – Better Quality as the optimizing setting. This results in an estimated 1.03K file size with a 0-second download time on a 56K modem.

Again, mouse over the ABOUT US button and see how this setting affects the vector circles and the button label below it.

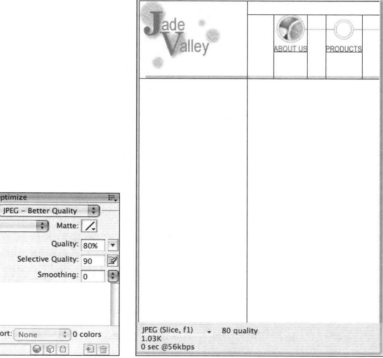

4. Use the Zoom drop-down in the lower-right corner of the Document window to raise the resolution to 200% or higher, and review both panes side by side. Compare the two settings for file size, estimated download time, and visual image quality.

You're dealing with small graphics, so it's helpful to zoom in.

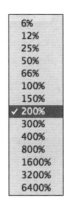

	6%
	12%
	25%
	50%
	66%
	100%
	150%
✓	200%
	300%
	400%
	800%
	1600%
	3200%
	6400%

5. With the Pointer tool, click to select the ABOUT US button in the left pane.

The Optimize panel once again displays the settings for GIF Adaptive 256, which means that you have effectively chosen GIF Adaptive 256 as your final optimization setting.

This setting makes sense because its download time is shorter than that of the JPEG, and yet it looks as good as or better than the JPEG version. While JPEG is generally a better setting for digital images, and the bitmap graphic within the Over state's circle is very small, using GIF Adaptive 256 doesn't sacrifice the image quality noticeably. Because the Up state contains only vector circles and text, which compress better as GIF, GIF is ultimately the best choice.

6. Click the Original button to return to the image in Authoring mode.

You can apply optimization to slices in Original mode as well, but you can't preview them. You don't need to preview the remaining buttons. In Original mode, you can select button slices and their buttons won't disappear.

7. Hold down the Shift key and use the Pointer tool to select the remaining button slices. Change the optimizing setting to GIF Adaptive 256.

The remaining buttons need to be optimized, but you can be confident that the same setting—GIF Adaptive 256—will work for them.

8. Save the file.

Fireworks saves optimization information as a part of the PNG. In the future, if you want to export or re-export the graphic, it will always be properly optimized.

At this point, you've optimized all the slices with content. There are more than a dozen rectangular regions without content on the page that don't have slices drawn over them. However, for our design to work, Fireworks will create graphics for them as well. Because we haven't specified otherwise, these slices will use the document default, which is Web Snap 128 (all these slices have only white pixels, so the color palette doesn't matter much). You can leave these slices alone.

Exporting Fireworks Slices as CSS Layers

With all the graphic slices optimized, you're ready to tackle the next major task: exporting a Fireworks document. As you learned in Lesson 2, *Designing a Page Interface*, every Fireworks slice by default becomes an HTML table cell upon export. However, we want to use the newer, standards-compliant layout mechanism: CSS layers. You can export slices to XHTML standards-compliant CSS layers, instead of HTML table cells (which is the good news), but doing so disables all your buttons, including the slices and scripts that enable them to function as buttons (which is the bad news).

Because you cannot get standards-compliant XHTML and working buttons at the same time, you'll use a workaround method to export your design. You'll export your design two times, each time with its own procedures and purposes:

* You'll first export the overall page layout as CSS layers
* Then you'll export the functional navigation bar as nested tables

After the two export processes have been completed, you'll reassemble the full page in Dreamweaver in Lesson 4.

In this section, you'll export the page layout as CSS layers.

1. Save interface_slices.png as interface_layers.png.

You'll use this file to export the overall page layout. Some of the changes you'll make to it in preparation for export will be destructive, so to protect your earlier work you'll save this version under a different file name.

2. On your Desktop, create a folder named jade_valley. Make sure the name of the folder is in lowercase letters.

This folder is going to be the root for the site. In other words, all the site assets—all HTML files, graphic files, and so on—will be stored in this folder.

As you know, when you go through the export process, Fireworks will generate an HMTL document (with layers) and an image for each of the slices. You want all those files to go into this folder.

Note | *The folder doesn't have to be on the Desktop; it can be anywhere that's accessible to your computer, including the My Documents folder (Windows) or the Documents folder (Macintosh). Just make sure you don't forget where you put the folder. Also, be aware that the steps in this book will assume the folder is on the Desktop.*

3. With the ABOUT US button slice selected, choose Modify › Symbol › Break Apart. Perform the same procedure on all the other button slices.

You'll export the navigation bar separately later, so at this point you'll need to remove all behaviors that are attached to the slices in order to prepare for the export of the page architecture.

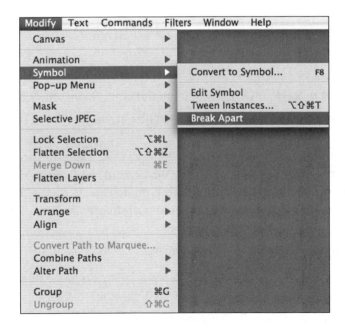

4. Use the Slice tool to draw a slice over the navigation bar area. Name it navbar.

This allows the entire navigation area to be treated as one entity during export.

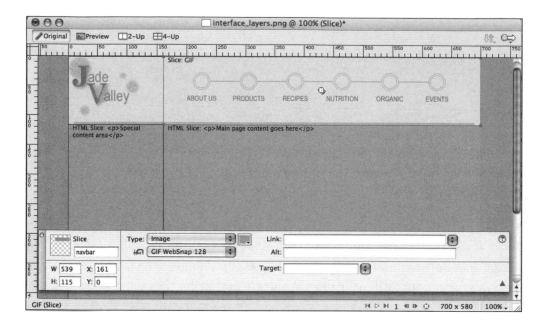

5. With interface_layers.png open, choose File › Export.

This step accesses the Export dialog.

6. In the Save As drop-down list, navigate to the jade_valley folder on your desktop.

You need to direct Fireworks to save all exported files in the designated folder.

7. Type *template.htm* in the Save As field. Select CSS Layers from the Export drop-down menu, and choose Fireworks Slices from the Source drop-down menu. Make sure the checkbox next to the Trim Images is not selected. Finally, check the box next to Put Images in Subfolder and verify the word 'images" appears to the right of the Browse button.

You've done a lot in this step. Let's take a moment to discuss each of these options.

You named the new HTML file template.htm. You'll base your template on this file when you use Dreamweaver to build the Jade Valley Web site in later lessons.

The Export drop-down menu tells Fireworks how to export your design. The CSS Layers option exports the page architecture into CSS layers that reconstruct the original design.

The Put Images in Subfolder choice ensures that the generated GIF and JPEG images get saved in the right place. In most Web sites, images are stored in a centralized folder—often called images—separate from the HTML files. By checking this box, Fireworks automatically creates an images subfolder within the Save In folder you specified earlier.

8. Click Export to export the template.htm file.

Fireworks exports all the images, according to your export criteria, as well as the HTML needed to create the page.

9. Launch a Web browser and review the exported template.htm file by choosing File > Open File. Navigate to the jade_valley folder on your Desktop. Select template.htm and click Open.

You've optimized and exported the interface design for the Jade Valley Web site, and as a result you have all the graphic and HTML files that are needed to reconstruct the

Fireworks design. Before you import this design into Dreamweaver for further work, you should review the exported HTML file in a browser. After you're satisfied with the results, you can begin reconstructing the design and creating the template in Dreamweaver. By reviewing the file, you'll be able to detect any problems that appeared during the export process and resolve them before investing time and effort on something that's not right.

Mouse over the navigation bar to make sure all the buttons function properly. Because the roll-over behavior was removed prior to the export, the navigation bar does not work.

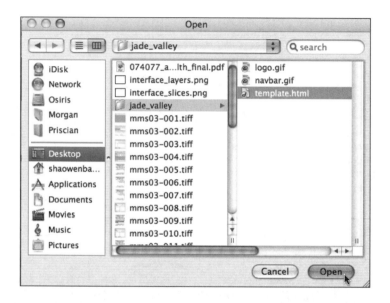

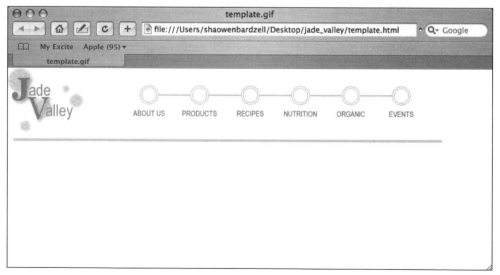

10. Choose View > View Source to review the source code.

Notice the <div> tags in the source code. You've successfully exported the page architecture as CSS layers.

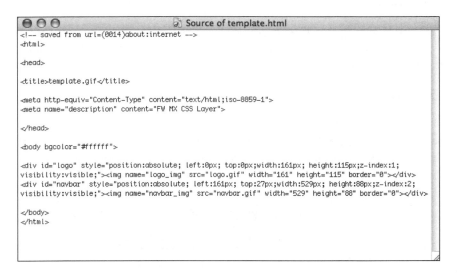

11. Save and close interface_layers.png.

You've exported the Jade Valley Web site design. Next, you'll need to export the navigation bar.

Exporting Fireworks Slices as Tables

In this section, you'll export the navigation slice as HTML tables so that you can reassemble all the page layout elements in Dreamweaver.

1. In Fireworks, reopen interface_slices.png. Save the file as interface_navbar.png.

You'll use this file to export the navigation bar. As before, you'll be making destructive changes to the file, which is why you should return to the original version of the file (interface_slices.png) and then save it under a new name.

Note   *The file you need in this step is the original interface_slices, not interface_layers, which you used in the previous section to export the page architecture.*

2. Use the Crop tool to remove everything except the navigation bar area. The resulting canvas size for the navigation bar slice should equal the W, H, X, and Y coordinates for the navigation slice from interface_layers.png, which are 539, 115, 161, and 0, respectively.

> **Tip** *The easiest way to complete this step is to use the Crop tool to draw a crop rectangle of any size anywhere on the canvas, and then enter the numbers given in this step in the Property inspector.*

Because you need to export just the navigation bar this time, you'll need to remove all the other elements in the design prior to the export.

It's important to make sure the exported navigation slice is the same size as the one from interface_layers.png, so that you can assemble all the pieces in Dreamweaver in the coming lessons.

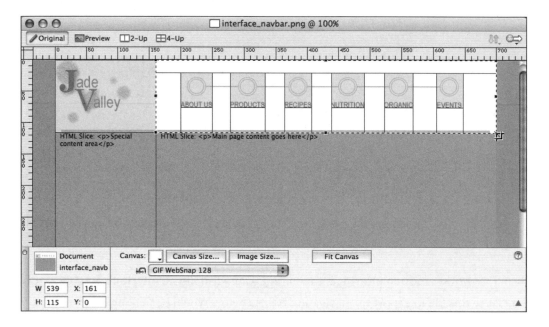

3. Double-click anywhere inside the selection area to remove everything except the navigation bar.

This step preserves the navigation bar and removes all the other elements, such as the logo, the left content area, and the main content area of the original design.

4. With interface_navbar.png open, choose File › Export.

This step brings up the Export dialog.

5. In the Save As drop-down list, navigate to the jade_valley folder on your Desktop.

You need to direct Fireworks to save all exported files in the designated folder.

6. Type *navbar.htm* in the Save As field. Select HTML and Images from the Export drop-down menu, and choose Export HTML File from the Source drop-down menu. Select Export Slices from the Slices drop-down menu. Make sure the checkbox next to Include Areas without Slices is checked. Finally, check the box next to Put Images in Subfolder.

The navigation bar export process is similar to the one performed earlier during the page architecture export. Rather than choosing CSS Layers as the export option, here you'll choose HTML and Images to generate a new HTML file that will reconstruct the original navigation bar, this time using a Fireworks-button-friendly HTML table.

In this dialog, you can also control how Fireworks handles slices. The Export Slices option exports slices with their specific behaviors, URLs, and so on. Because your intention is to export the entire design (text and graphics) of the navigation bar, you need to check the

Include Areas Without Slices option, which ensures that those plain-white areas without slices are exported as well.

7. Click the Options button on the right side of the Export dialog.

This step brings up the HTML Setup dialog, where you'll give Fireworks further directions on how the HTML code should be generated.

8. In the HTML Setup dialog, switch to the Table tab, and select Nested Tables – No Spacers from the Space With drop-down.

The Space With drop-down of the Table tab enables you to specify exactly how Fireworks codes HTML tables. The default option, one-pixel transparent spacer, is generally the most reliable at reproducing the exact look of the Fireworks file in HTML; however, it also creates a lot of extra code and—fatally for us—adds a one-pixel buffer around the table. If we left the table at the default setting, this extra one pixel would have caused the table not to line up properly when we reunited the navigation bar with the main page in Dreamweaver. The option Nested Tables – No Spacers does not add that one-pixel buffer, so we can be confident that the two HTML files will align correctly when they're recombined.

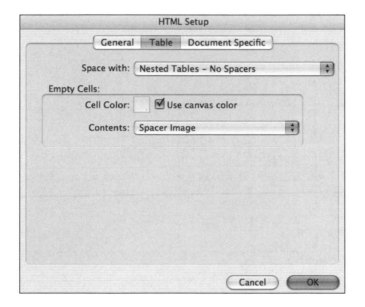

9. Click Export to export the navigation bar to the jade_valley folder on your Desktop. Save and close interface_navbar.png.

You've exported the Jade Valley Web site navigation bar. In the next step, you'll review the output page in a browser.

10. Repeat the steps in the previous section to view the file, navbar.html, in a Web browser. Mouse over the navigation bar to make sure all the buttons are working properly.

The Over states of all the buttons should be presented correctly. If you followed every step accurately during export, all your navigation buttons should respond to the mouse as expected when you test them in your browser.

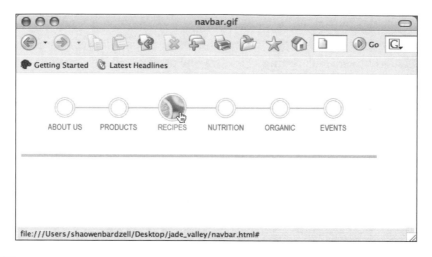

Note *Don't bother clicking any of the buttons. They don't do anything yet, because you didn't associate URLs with the buttons in Fireworks. While Fireworks does enable you to attach links to buttons, you'll take care of that in Dreamweaver.*

11. Close navbar.html.

If you've followed these instructions carefully, the navigation bar tests out fine in the browser. You'll reconstruct the design in Lesson 4.

What You Have Learned

In this lesson, you have:

- Learned the different graphic file types (pages 71–73)
- Decided whether to use GIF or JPEG for graphics (pages 71–79)
- Tested different GIF and JPEG settings (pages 80–84)
- Specified CSS Layers and HTML export settings (pages 84–89)
- Previewed exported files in a browser (pages 89–94)

Project 1: The Jade Valley Web Site

Part 2: Dreamweaver

4 Preparing a New Site

Macromedia Dreamweaver 8 is an HTML editor that lets you create Web pages and work with images or multimedia assets in a visual and/or code environment. In addition to its page development capabilities, Dreamweaver also provides tools to manage and maintain Web sites.

One of the greatest challenges of authoring content in HTML—where files, graphics, and other assets can quickly grow into the hundreds or thousands—is file management. Even a minor organizational slipup can cause your pages to go awry, with missing images and broken links, and can result in a lot of wasted time hunting around for files and fixing bad code. Dreamweaver comes with a powerful site manager that's designed to help you keep your site organization sound.

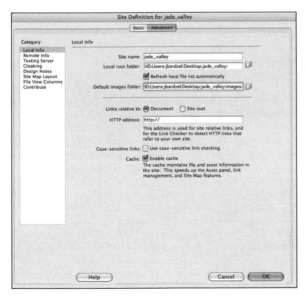

Dreamweaver's Site Definition dialog not only configures a site for development, but it also enables Dreamweaver's site management features and even Web publishing features.

Dreamweaver 8 is also able to work with assets developed in Fireworks. The Fireworks HTML you exported in Lesson 3, for example, can be imported into a Dreamweaver document with just a click of a button.

In this lesson, you'll set up a site in accordance with the site plan and your authoring preferences. Once the site is set up, you'll create a generic page that you can use as a template in Lesson 5, *Developing a Page Template*, for all your subsequent pages. In the process, you'll learn the basics of page production in Dreamweaver 8 and become familiar with its interface and tools. In addition, you'll work with the Extension Manager, downloading, installing, and using a Dreamweaver extension. Extensions are additional features, developed by Macromedia or third-party developers, that you can install to add functionality to Dreamweaver.

What You Will Learn

In this lesson, you will:

- Define a static site in Dreamweaver
- Open a new HTML page
- Import Fireworks HTML into Dreamweaver
- Search for Dreamweaver extensions
- Work with Dreamweaver's Extension Manager
- Insert placeholder text
- Reconstruct the original interface design
- Insert images
- Make images accessible

Approximate Time

This lesson takes approximately 75 minutes to complete.

Lesson Files

Starting Files:

Lesson04/Start/jade_valley/images/banana.jpg
Lesson04/Start/jade_valley/images/label_products.gif
Lesson04/Start/jade_valley/template.htm
Lesson04/Start/jade_valley/navbar.htm

Completed Files:

Lesson04/Complete/jade_valley/jadevalley_template.htm

Defining a Static Site in Dreamweaver

In this task, you'll define the site in Dreamweaver's Site Manager. Now that your page design has been exported out of Fireworks, you'll need to reconstruct the full design (remember, the sliced file you exported was simplified somewhat) and start building individual pages for the Jade Valley Web site.

1. Copy all the files in the Lesson04/Start/jade_valley folder to your Desktop. Allow your files to be overwritten to use ours, or disallow overwriting to use your own.

This folder contains several new files that are needed to complete this and later lessons. If you like, you can use your version of template.html and all the GIF files you exported from Fireworks; alternatively, you can use the ones included in the Start folder. In either case, be sure all the new files and folders—most of which you haven't yet seen—are in your working directory.

2. Open Dreamweaver. From the main menu, choose Site > Manage Sites.

When you launch Dreamweaver, you'll see the Start page, which enables you to easily and quickly open a recent document, create a new document, or create a document from sample pages. In addition, you can also take a quick tour of the program, go through the tutorial, or access Dreamweaver Exchange.

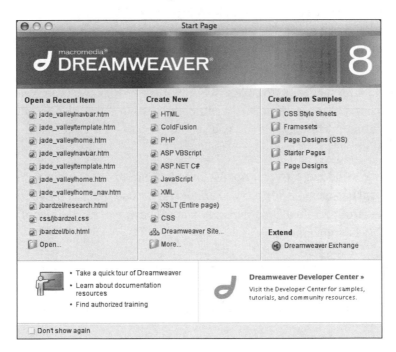

Choosing Manage Sites brings up the Manage Sites dialog, which lists all the currently defined sites as well as a series of options. If this is your first time in Dreamweaver, no sites are listed.

When you define a site, Dreamweaver remembers the site's root folder (the folder that contains all the files within the site) and defines every asset within the site (including the assets nested in folders) relative to the root folder. Defining a site is critical, because it activates Dreamweaver's site management features.

As with Windows Explorer or Macintosh Finder, you can create, move, and delete files in Dreamweaver's Site Manager. Unlike Windows Explorer or Macintosh Finder, Dreamweaver helps ensure that if you move files around, links in other documents are updated accordingly. Another nice feature of the Site Manager is that you can use it to check for broken links sitewide.

As a custom tool for managing complex Web sites, the Site Manager is a powerful ally in site development. Dreamweaver makes it comparatively hard to work on individual HTML files without defining sites, and you should always define a site before you start working on a file.

Tip *Neither Windows Explorer nor Macintosh Finder has features to maintain the integrity of links within a site, so you should never use them to move, rename, or delete files from within a Dreamweaver site. Always move, rename, or delete files from within Dreamweaver.*

3. Click New in the Manage Site dialog, and select Site from the drop-down.

You use this dialog to manage whole sites, as opposed to files within sites, which you do with the Site Manager. From this dialog, you can create new sites or edit, duplicate, or remove existing sites.

Note *Removing sites does not affect the site files on your hard drive; it just means that Dreamweaver no longer tracks them as sites.*

4. Click to select the Advanced tab in the Site Definition dialog.

The default Basic tab is a little more wizard-like, but you have more options available using the Advanced tab.

5. In the Local Info category of the Site Definition dialog, name the site *jade_valley*. Next to the Local root folder field, click the folder button to browse to the jade_valley folder. Navigate to the image subfolder in the jade_valley folder and select it as the Default images folder. Leave the remaining options at their defaults.

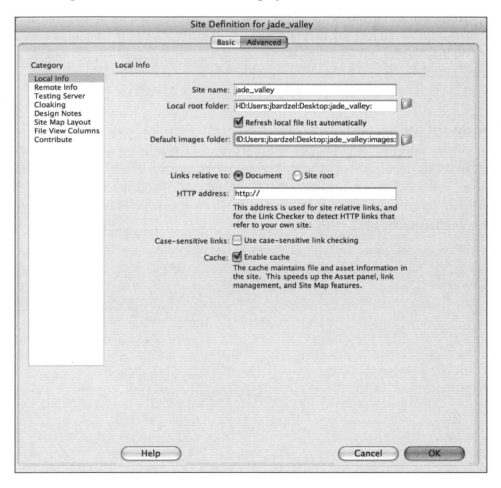

In this step, you're naming your site. This name can be anything you like, and will not affect the site in any way; it's used by Dreamweaver to identify and track your site. However, try to give the site a meaningful name, so that you know what it is when, for example, eight months from now you need to update the site.

The root folder is an important concept. All site files are located inside this folder (possibly in subfolders) and are defined in relation to this folder. This relative addressing is important, because when the site is uploaded to a Web server, the location of the folder in relation to the server is likely to be different from what it is on your hard drive. But all the files inside the root folder will be in the same place in the folder as they are in the folder on your hard drive, which means that no matter where you copy this folder on any workstation or server, the links will always work.

Designating a default image folder is also important when you first set up your site in Dreamweaver. By so doing, not only are the files and assets of your site better organized based on their nature and functions, but Dreamweaver will also make copies of the images that are not currently in the default image folder and save them in this folder to prevent broken image links when you upload your site to the hosting Web server.

6. In the left pane of the Category list, click the Remote Info category.

You enter the information Dreamweaver needs to access the remote site in the Remote Info category—that is, the actual Web server where this site will be published. You choose an access method, including network, FTP, SFTP, and so on, in the Access drop-down menu. This information, which your server administrator or Internet host can give you, greatly facilitates uploading the files.

You will not be uploading the Jade Valley site, so you can leave this setting at the default: None.

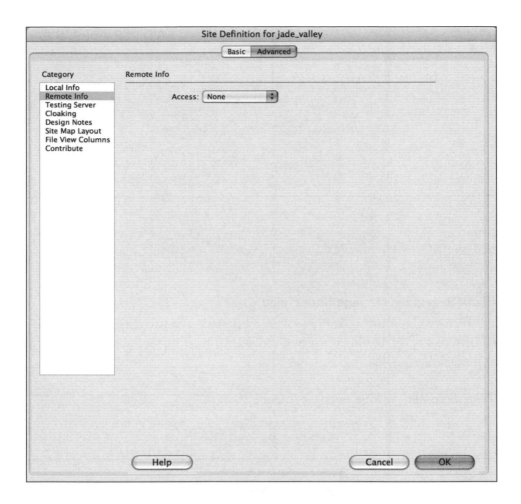

7. Click OK at the bottom of the Site Definition dialog.

You've defined the local root folder. By clicking the OK button, Dreamweaver creates a site cache for your site. In other words, Dreamweaver creates a file containing information about the names and locations of your files and folders, and also tracks the links within those files.

After the file is created, you're returned to the Manage Sites dialog, with the new site highlighted.

8. **Click Done in the Manage Sites dialog.**

When you click Done, you're sent back to the Start page, with your site visible in the Files panel. The Files panel should display by default, but if you don't see it, you can access it by choosing Window > Files.

9. **Take a moment to look over the folder structure.**

When you begin a large project, you should make sure that your structure is flexible enough so the site can grow without becoming unmanageable. When creating a new site, you should create folders to hold different types of content; images, CSS, Flash, and more. When creating a site, build a comprehensive structure even if you don't initially have assets planned for all the folders. For example, the flash folder for this project is currently empty, but if you add a Flash movie later on, you'll have a place to put it.

The images folder is an old standby; most sites use this folder. You should place all your production GIFs and JPEGs there. In addition to the images folder, there's also a fireworks_source folder where you should put all the original Fireworks PNG files. It's helpful to put the source Fireworks PNG files in the local version of the site, because doing so enables certain features of Fireworks–Dreamweaver integration. You should keep the Fireworks PNGs files in a separate folder from the production images (that is, not in the images folder), though, so that they're all in one place so they don't get accidentally uploaded. In the same vein, the text_files folder contains source scripts. These text files can be any content written in a word processor that needs to be converted to HTML, Flash, or whatever format is appropriate. In this book, the folder contains the text for pages you'll be creating.

The css folder is used for the site's style sheet(s). In large sites, you might have many style sheets—if you have different sections or themes, for example—and keeping them all in one folder simplifies organization.

What should be clear from this structure is that each folder contains a type of asset: image, HTML file, cascading style sheet, and so on. All files of one type are stored in one folder. You will not find GIFs anywhere but the images folder, for example. Sticking to this scheme saves production time as you develop the site, and, perhaps more importantly, it vastly simplifies long-term site maintenance, a need often neglected in the early design stage.

Opening a New HTML Page

At this point you've defined the Jade Valley Web site in Dreamweaver. The next step is creating a new HTML page in Dreamweaver.

1. Choose File > New to create a new HTML document in Dreamweaver.

You can also use the Start page to create a new HTML document (choose HTML under the Create New section).

2. In the New Document dialog, select Basic page as the document category from the Category list on the left. Select HTML as the document type from the Basic page list on the right. Verify that the Document Type (DTD) drop-down is set to XHTML 1.0 Transitional. Click Create to create a new HTML document.

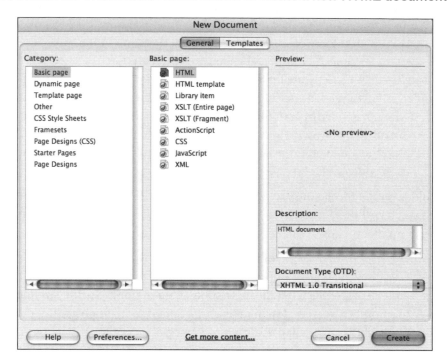

Tip *Another way to create a new page is to click the HTML link in the Create New section of the Start page.*

The New Document dialog enables you to easily and quickly create new documents in Dreamweaver. You can create a new page based on the nature of the page (e.g., basic page, dynamic page, frameset, page designs, and so on) or based on an existing template from other sites. The list on the right changes based on the document category of your choice. A description and a preview of the selected document type (for most categories) are available upon selection.

XHTML (Extensible Hypertext Markup Language) is a reformulation of HTML so it's compliant with XML syntax. In general, using XHTML ensures the backward and future compatibility of your Web pages. HTML is a relatively loose and forgiving language, whereas XML is more strict. In the long run, this strictness actually makes it easier to ensure consistency.

For the most part, the difference between XHTML and HTML is that XHTML is a little more structured about the way it's written. For example, both HTML and XHTML have a tag used for marking up paragraphs. In HTML, both <P> and <p> are acceptable ways of writing this tag. But in XHTML, only <p> is acceptable because uppercase tags are forbidden in XML. Another difference is that all tags in XML must be closed. Certain HTML tags are open tags; for example, the <hr> (horizontal rule),
 (line break), and <img> (image) tags do not need a corresponding close tag (</hr>, for example). In XHTML, these tags are <hr />, <br />, and <img />. This convention both opens and closes the tags; basically, it's equivalent to <hr></hr>,
</br>, and <img></img>. A further discussion of XHTML is beyond the scope of this book, but as long as you understand that XHTML is essentially HTML written to be in compliance with XML, that is sufficient.

Tip *To make an existing HTML document XHTML-compliant, you need to open the document and select File > Convert > XHTML.*

3. **Take a moment to explore the Dreamweaver work environment.**

Before developing the HTML pages for the Jade Valley Web site, take a few minutes to become familiar with Dreamweaver's work environment. You will notice that Dreamweaver provides many panels, inspectors, and windows, which is quite different from, say, a word processor's workspace. To open any Dreamweaver panel, inspector, or window, use the Window menu.

Below is an overview of Dreamweaver's tools and panels:

The Insert bar contains buttons for inserting various types of objects, such as images, tables, and layers, into a document. Each object is a piece of HTML code that enables you to set various attributes as you insert the object. For example, you can insert an email link by clicking the Email link button in the Common category of the Insert bar. Alternatively, you can insert objects using the Insert menu.

The Document toolbar contains buttons that provide options for different views of the Document window (such as Design view, Code view, and Split view), various viewing options, and common operations such as previewing in a browser. In addition, you can title the HTML document by typing in the Title text field in the Document toolbar.

The Document window displays the document you're currently working on.

The Property inspector, as in other Macromedia applications, lets you view and change a variety of properties for the selected object or text. Each object has different properties.

The Tag selector in the status bar, at the bottom of the Document window, shows the hierarchy of tags surrounding the current selection. Clicking any tag in the hierarchy enables you to select that tag and all its contents. Right-clicking (Windows) or Control-clicking (Macintosh) tags yields several additional commands and options.

Panel groups are sets of related panels that are grouped together under one heading. To expand a panel group, click the expander arrow at the left of the group's name; to undock a panel group, drag the gripper at the left edge of the group's title bar.

The Files panel enables you to manage your files and folders, whether they're part of a Dreamweaver site or on a remote server. The Files panel also enables you to access all the files on your local hard drive, much like Windows Explorer (Windows) or the Finder (Macintosh).

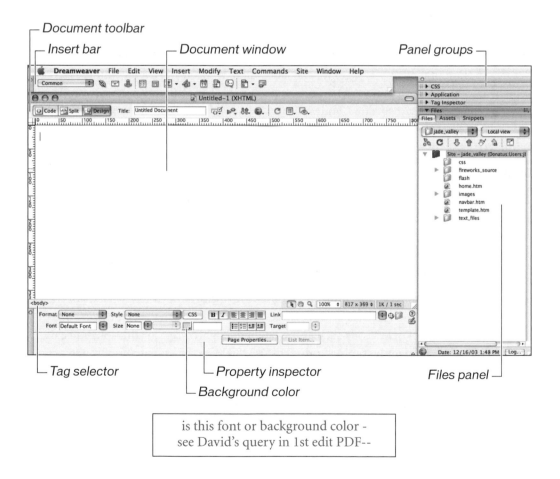

is this font or background color -
see David's query in 1st edit PDF--

Now that you've learned how to create a new document and explored Dreamweaver's workspace, let's close the document and get to work on the template you're creating.

4. Close this document without saving. Choose File › Open and select template.htm. Choose File › Save As, and name it *jadevalley_template.html***. In the Document Toolbar, rename the default title from template.gif (which Fireworks erroneously named the file) to** *Jade Valley Template***.**

The title appears in the title bar of the Document window in Dreamweaver, as well as in the browser's title bar when you view the page in most browsers. The title appears in the results page of many search engines as well. It's a good habit to specify a descriptive page title for all your pages.

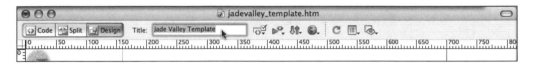

Tip *To modify a page title, enter a new title for the page in the Title text box in the Document toolbar. You can also change the title using the Page Properties dialog (Modify › Page Properties).*

Unfortunately, titling the document template.gif isn't the only oddity of exporting CSS Layers from Fireworks. Fireworks also fails to insert the proper document-type information. Earlier in this task, when you created a new Dreamweaver file, you made sure that XHTML Transitional was selected as the document type. Doing so inserts a couple lines of code at the top of the document, which is invisible in Dreamweaver's design view and in a browser, but which browsers use to understand what kind of a document (e.g., HTML, XML) the page is. The exported Fireworks HTML file lacks this information, so you'll need to reinsert it.

5. To see the code, click the Code View button on the left side of the Document toolbar.

Dreamweaver switches to code view, which displays the HTML code of the document. You can return to the visual design view by clicking the Design View button in the Document Toolbar. Also of note is the Split View button, which enables you to see a split screen revealing both the code and the visual design. Leave it in code view for a moment.

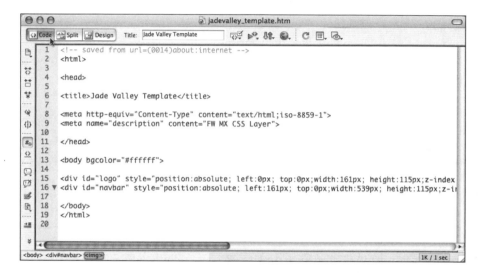

6. If necessary, go to the top of the document and select and delete the comment line (the line that begins `<!-- saved from url`).

A comment, which in HTML is surrounded by `<!--` and `-->` markup, is disregarded by the browser, but is often used by developers to make comments on their pages to help them while they're coding. Aside from contributing a small amount to the file size, comments do no harm. We're not certain why Fireworks inserts this comment, but it's of no use in the Jade Valley site, so you can delete it.

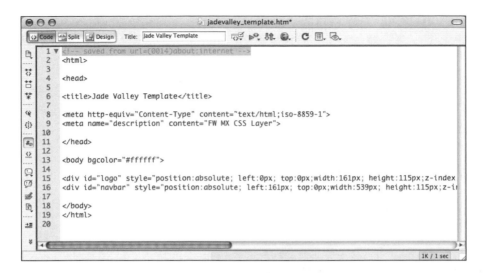

At this point, you're ready to insert the proper document type information at the beginning of the document.

7. Still in code view, choose File › Convert › XHTML 1.0 Transitional.

This inserts the correct document type at the beginning of the document (visible only in code view).

As you complete this step, you'll see a warning dialog indicating that two images (the logo and navigation bar) lack alt attributes. You'll fix that in a moment, so just click OK for now.

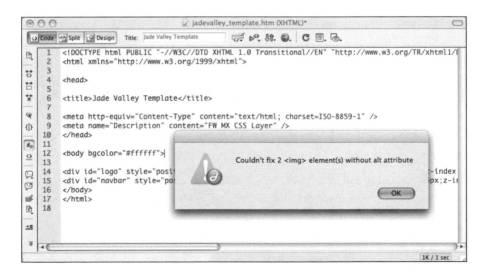

8. Click the Design View button in the Document Toolbar to return to design view. Click the Jade Valley logo graphic to select it. In the Property inspector's Alt field, type *Jade Valley logo*.

With the alt attribute, the logo is now more accessible than it was before.

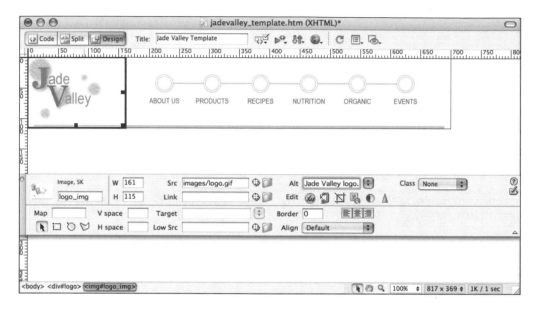

You don't need to add an alt attribute to the navbar graphic on the right, because you'll be deleting it soon and replacing it with the real navigation bar.

9. Save jadevalley_template.html.

After cleaning up the file, you're now ready to insert the navigation bar.

Importing Fireworks HTML into Dreamweaver

The export process in Fireworks allows you to export and save optimized images and HTML files to a designated location (often a folder). You can then import the HTML file into Dreamweaver.

Dreamweaver has two ways to import Fireworks HTML. In one approach, you can open the Fireworks HTML document directly in Dreamweaver and start editing, which is what you just did with template.htm.

The other approach to importing Fireworks content is to insert Fireworks-generated HTML code, with associated images, slices, and JavaScript, into an open document.

Dreamweaver detects and resolves conflicts (for example, the Fireworks and Dreamweaver HTML files will have their own <html>, <head>, and <body> tags), and inserts the appropriate code from the Fireworks file into the location of the insertion point in Dreamweaver. In this task, you'll insert the navigation bar into the template file.

1. If necessary, open jadevalley_template.html.

You'll use the second approach mentioned in the preceding paragraph, and import the Fireworks HTML file into the file you just created and titled.

2. Click to select the graphic depicting the navigation bar. Press Delete.

The layer (represented as a blue rectangle) that contained the image is now empty. You can see the cursor blinking on the left side of the layer.

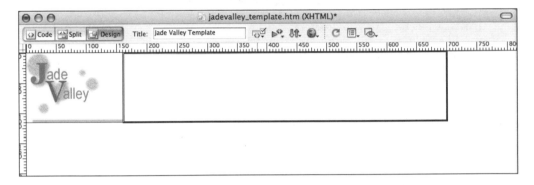

You're ready to insert the functioning navigation bar.

3. Choose Insert > Image Objects > Fireworks HTML.

You can also use the Insert bar to insert Fireworks HTML into a HTML page in Dreamweaver. In the Common category of the Insert bar, choose Images > Fireworks HTML.

Either method will bring up the Insert Fireworks HTML dialog.

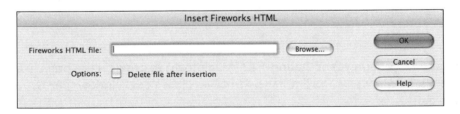

4. In the Insert Fireworks HTML dialog, click Browse, select navbar.htm, and then click Open. Do not check the Delete File After Insertion option.

Remember, navbar.htm is the file you exported from Fireworks. It contains functioning buttons, which make up the navigation bar. In Lesson 3, when you prepared these files, you created slices to ensure that the functioning navigation bar in navbar.htm was the exact size of the layer you created in interface_layers.png.

If you select the "Delete file after insertion" option, the original Fireworks HTML file will be moved to the Recycle Bin (Windows) or Trash (Macintosh) when the process is complete. Use this option only when you're certain that you no longer need the Fireworks HTML file after inserting it in Dreamweaver. If you delete the file and later discover that you need it after all, you can always re-export it from Fireworks.

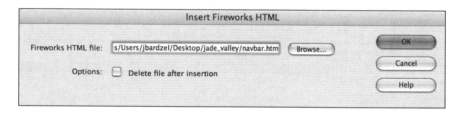

5. Click OK to insert the Fireworks HTML code.

This command enables Dreamweaver to insert the Fireworks HTML code, complete with its associated images, slices, and JavaScript, into the document in Dreamweaver.

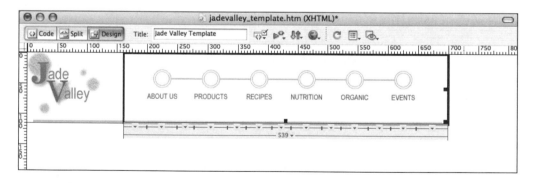

6. Press F12 (Windows) or Option+F12 (Macintosh) to preview the page in a browser. If Dreamweaver prompts you to save, click Yes (Windows) or Save (Macintosh).

Take a few moments to review the page in the browser. It should be identical to the exported Fireworks HTML, with the Jade Valley logo and a partially functional navigation bar (the buttons change when the mouse rolls over them, but nothing happens when you click them).

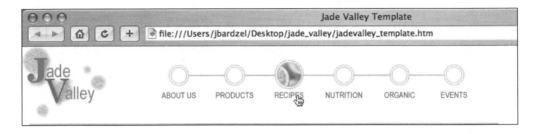

7. Save jadevalley_template.html.

You've finished inserting the Fireworks HTML. Now you can start reconstructing the original design and dropping in placeholders.

Creating CSS Layers in Dreamweaver

The template is coming together. You've reconstructed much of the original design from Fireworks, and the hardest part is behind you. As you'll recall from the original design, below the logo and navigation bar there should be two regions on the page. On the left is a special content area, while on the right is the main content area. Each of these regions will be enclosed in its own CSS layer. In this task, you'll create both of these layers.

1. In the Insert Bar, choose the Layout category.

By default, the Common category is selected.

The Layout category contains tools that enable you to insert HTML objects that control page layout, including HTML tables, CSS layers, and framesets. As you know, the preferred way to handle page layout needs is with CSS layers.

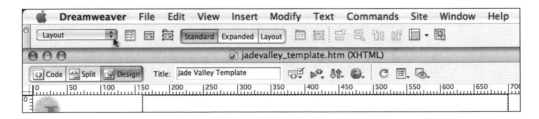

2. In the Insert Bar, click to activate the Draw Layer button. On the screen, somewhere below the navigation bar, draw a rectangle.

Don't worry about the size just yet.

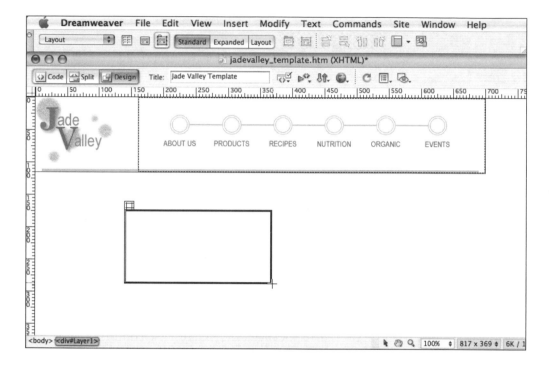

3. Click once on the # icon in the top-left corner of the new layer to select it. In the Property inspector, name the layer *special_content*.

Here, you're giving your new layer a unique ID. This ID is invaluable, because it makes it possible for you to use CSS to format the layer.

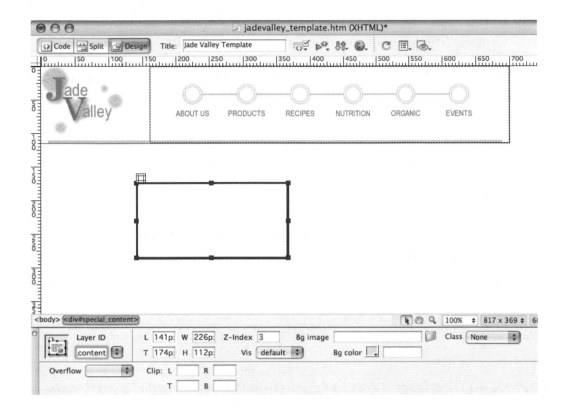

4. Still in the Property inspector, specify the layer's positioning as follows:

L: 0px

T: 115px

W: 161px

H: 25px

Where did these numbers come from? L is the distance from the left, so it's set to 0 to move the layer all the way to the left edge. T is the distance from the top, and the logo layer above it is 115 pixels tall; thus, by setting this layer's distance from the top to 115, you ensure that it lines up perfectly below the logo layer. The width of the logo layer is 161, so you're setting this layer's width to the same value. The height doesn't need (and should ordinarily have) a value. You specified 25 pixels, because if you had not, the layer might collapse down so small that you wouldn't be able to put anything in it! After you put content in the layer, you will eliminate this value, so that the layer stretches to accommodate its contents, which is the behavior you want.

> **Note** *Don't forget to specify the px after each of the number values. Some browsers, including Dreamweaver's design view, will display the layers correctly. Others, however, will not be smart enough to guess that by 161 you mean 161 pixels, and they will simply ignore the properties altogether.*

5. **Repeat steps 2–4 to create another layer, with the following properties:**

Layer ID: main_content

L: 161px

T: 115px

W: 539px

H: 25px

Again, don't forget the px after each of the numbers. Also, as before, the 25 pixel H value is a temporary trick to make it easier to work with the layers.

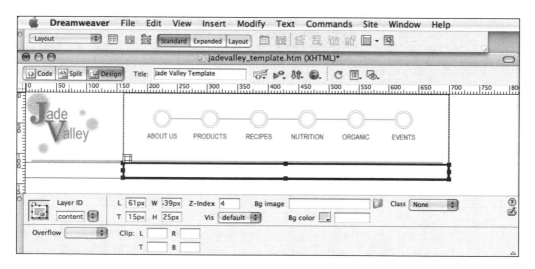

6. Position the insertion point inside the special_content layer. Type *Special content goes here*. In the main_content layer, type *Main content goes here*. In turn, select each of these layers, and use the Property inspector to remove the H attribute.

The layers are now ready for use.

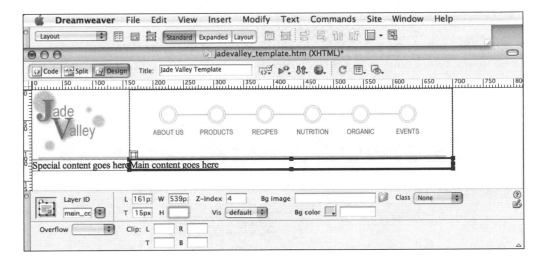

7. Save jadevalley_template.html.

Inserting Placeholder Text

During the design phase of a Web project, it's often helpful to work with placeholder content rather than actual content. Your goal during the design phase is not to worry about the message of the content, but rather to decide how you want to format the assets and text you import before you begin working on them.

One technique designers use for placeholder text is the fake Latin *Lorem Ipsum* text. This text is nonsense, and yet it looks enough like regular English to be a serviceable stand-in for real content. Dreamweaver lacks a tool that enables you to pour in a specified amount of Lorem Ipsum text; however, an extension for Dreamweaver lets you add this functionality. When run from within Dreamweaver, this extension prompts you for the number of characters or paragraphs you need, and dumps in the requested amount of placeholder text at the active insertion point.

Before you can use the Lorem Ipsum Generator extension, you'll have to download and install it using the Macromedia Extension Manager, a program that installs automatically with any Studio 8 product. Most extensions are available at Macromedia's Web site. While many of them are freeware, some require payment to download.

In this task, you'll learn to search for, download, install, and use the Lorem Ipsum Generator extension.

1. With jadevalley_template.html open, choose Insert > Get More Objects.

This takes you to the Dreamweaver Exchange page at Macromedia.com.

2. Click Search Exchanges at the top-right corner of the page. When the search page loads, type *Lorem* in the Search box and click the Search button.

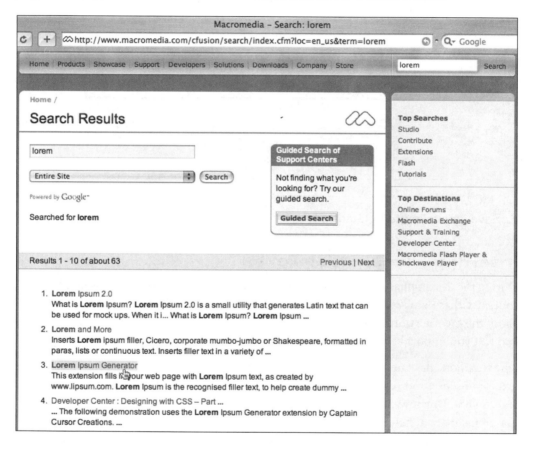

Because the Lorem Ipsum extension was not displayed on the Dreamweaver Exchange page, you'll need to search for it.

3. Click the Download icon next to the Lorem Ipsum Generator extension.

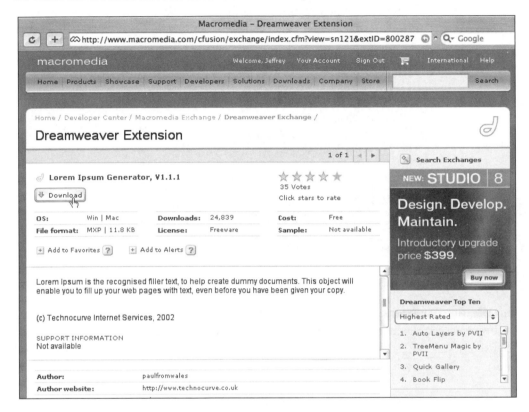

When you click the Download icon, the Macromedia Web site will prompt you to either sign in or create a profile before downloading the extension. Follow the onscreen directions to sign in or register.

Save the extension on your Desktop.

4. Open the extension on the Desktop. Click Accept in the Extension Disclaimer.

When you click the Accept button, the Extension Manager automatically installs the extension into Dreamweaver. When it's finished, a dialog appears, confirming the success of the installation.

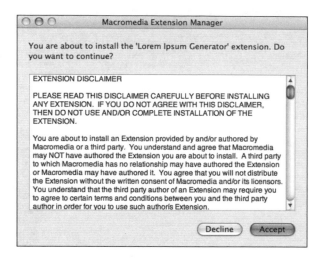

The Macromedia Extension Manager indicates that the Lorem Ipsum Generator extension has been successfully installed and that you need to restart Dreamweaver in order for the extension to take effect. It also tells you how to access the new extension you just installed: Insert > Technocurve > Lorem Ipsum.

5. Save your file if prompted, close, and restart Dreamweaver.

This time, the new feature will appear in the Insert menu.

6. In the Files panel, double-click jadevalley_template.html to open it.

You will again use jadevalley_template.html to insert the Latin text to mock up the page.

7. In the Document window, position your cursor after "Main page content goes here." The insertion point should be at the very top of the content area of the page. Choose Insert > Technocurve > Lorem Ipsum.

You can also select the Lorem Ipsum option from the Common category in the Insert bar.

This command brings up the Lorem Ipsum dialog.

8. In the Lorem Ipsum dialog, choose 3 from the Paragraph quantity drop-down menu.

Three paragraphs of Latin words will give you enough text to mock up this page.

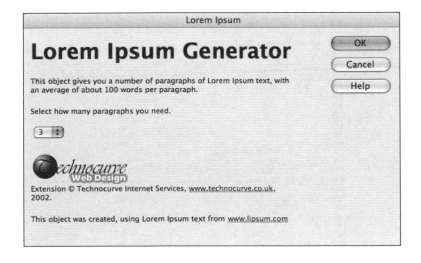

9. Click OK to insert the Latin text. Scroll back up to the top and delete "Main content goes here."

This command inserts three paragraphs of dummy text for the page mockup.

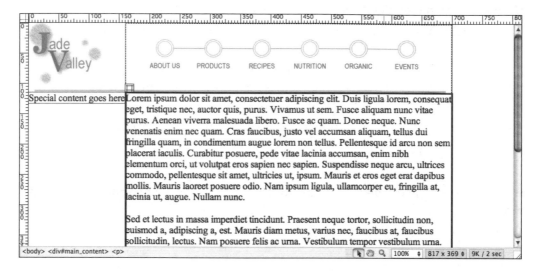

10. Save your file.

Now that the Lorem Ipsum Generator extension has been successfully added to Dreamweaver, you can use this extension to quickly mock up a page while you're waiting for page content.

Adding the Footer and Basic Navigation

In this task, you'll continue reconstructing the original page design in Dreamweaver. You'll add the footer, which contains both a text-based navigation bar and some copyright information. You'll also set up the hyperlinks, to ensure that the template is functional.

1. Position the cursor at the end of the dummy Latin text, and press Enter/Return. Type _ABOUT US | PRODUCTS | RECIPES | NUTRITION | ORGANIC | EVENTS_.

You created a text-based navigation aid at the bottom of the original design, so that visitors to the Jade Valley Web site don't have to scroll to the top of the page to use the navigation bar to visit a different page. This part of the design was eliminated from the Fireworks version, and you eliminated it because it will download much faster as plain text than it would as graphic images of text.

Don't worry about formatting the text just yet, including its alignment (it should eventually be center-aligned). In Lesson 5, you'll use a style sheet to format all the text on the Jade Valley Web site.

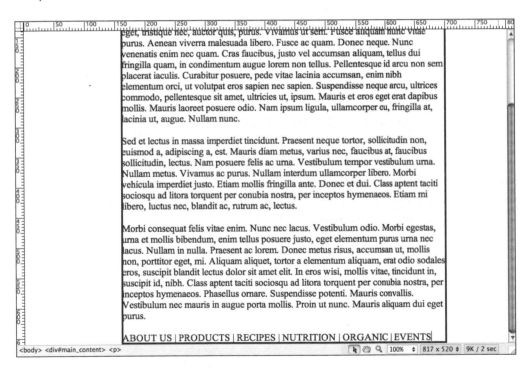

2. At the end of the text navigation bar line, press Enter/Return again to create a new line, and type *Copyright 1999-2006 Jade Valley. All Rights Reserved.*

Again, don't worry about the formatting, because you'll use CSS to format the text in the next lesson.

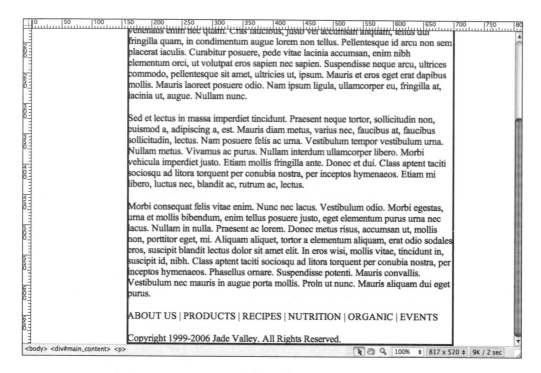

You're almost finished working with the HTML in this page (although you have a lot of work to do yet to format it using CSS). However, one significant aspect of the page is still incomplete. The graphic navigation bar at the top and the text navigation bar at the bottom don't actually link to anything.

You'll start at the bottom.

3. Drag to select the words ABOUT US. In the Link field of the Property inspector, type *about.htm* and press the Tab key.

Dreamweaver adds a hyperlink to the words, which also become underlined and turn blue. Of course, about.htm doesn't even exist yet (you'll create it in Lesson 6). The blue color of the hyperlink may not be attractive for this design, but you'll change that using CSS in the next lesson.

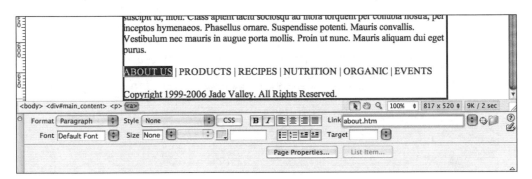

4. Repeat Step 3 and associate each navigation item with a page in the eventual site: link PRODUCTS to products.htm; RECIPES to recipes.htm; NUTRITION to nutrition.htm; ORGANIC to organic.htm; and EVENTS to events.htm.

If those pages actually existed, the navigation bar would be fully functional. If you tested the page now, without the existing pages, you'd get a The Page Cannot Be Displayed (or similar) error.

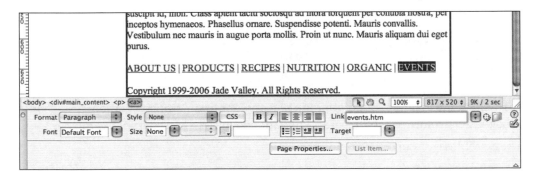

Now that the lower navigation bar is in place, you can set up the graphic navigation bar at the top of the page.

5. In the graphic navigation bar at the top of the page, click the circle above **ABOUT US**. In the Property inspector's Link field, type *about.htm*.

You apply hyperlinks to graphics the same way you do to text: via the Property inspector's Link field.

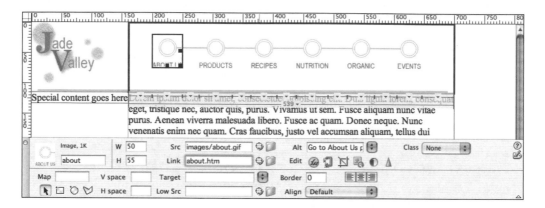

6. Repeat Step 5 and associate each navigation button with a page in the eventual site: link **PRODUCTS** to products.htm; **RECIPES** to recipes.htm; **NUTRITION** to nutrition.htm; **ORGANIC** to organic.htm; and **EVENTS** to events.htm.

The navigation bars at the top and bottom of the page are now functional (the absence of actual pages to point to notwithstanding).

7. Save the page.

Inserting Images

In this lesson's final task, you'll add some images to the page template.

1. Position the insertion point after the placeholder text, "Special content area," and press Enter/Return to create a new line. Choose Insert › Image from the main menu.

The Select Image Source dialog appears.

2. In the Select Image Source dialog, browse to the images folder within the jade_valley site folder. Select label_products.gif and click OK (Windows) or Choose (Macintosh).

This graphic was exported from the original (simplified) Fireworks design, and was placed inside the images folder for you. Now it appears at the top of the left column.

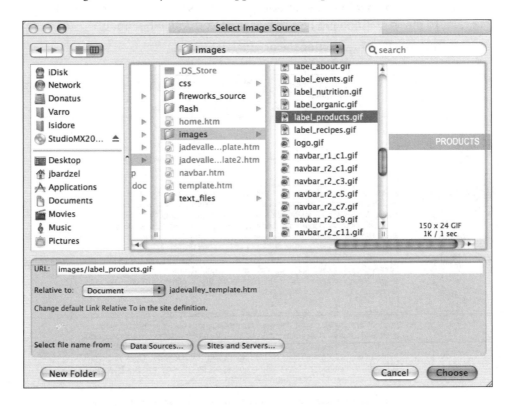

3. In the Image Tag Accessibility Attributes dialog that appears, enter *Jade Valley Products.* as the Alternate text. Click OK.

This dialog appears by default to help ensure that you don't forget to add the alt attribute to any images.

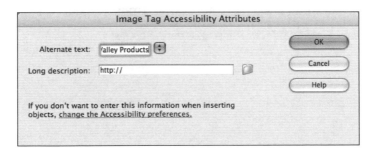

4. Delete the "Special content goes here" text. Click the yellow PRODUCTS graphic. Press the right arrow key once and then the Enter/Return key to move the insertion point below the label image you just inserted. Repeat Steps 1 and 2 in this task to insert banana.jpg just below the Products label image.

You're almost finished reconstructing the original design.

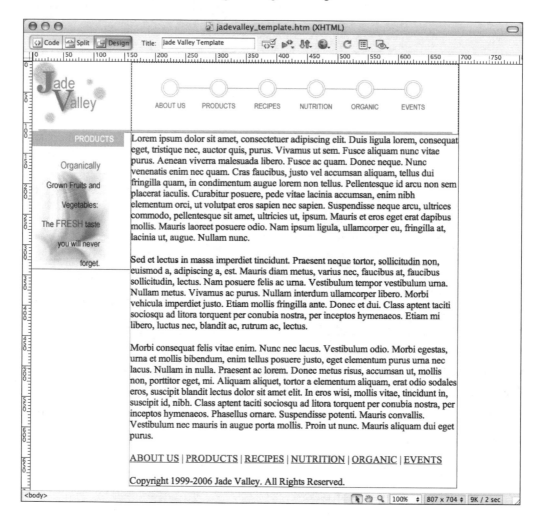

5. In the accessibility dialog, enter *Ad for organically grown fruits and vegetables.* as the Alternate text. Click OK.

Once again, you're providing a meaningful summary of the graphic for those visitors who can't see the graphic.

The graphics may appear misaligned; you'll fix that problem using CSS in the next lesson.

6. Save and close the file.

In the next lesson, you'll develop a style sheet and create a template for the Jade Valley Web site based on this page.

What You Have Learned

In this lesson, you have:

- Defined a static site in Dreamweaver 8 (pages 99–105)
- Opened a new HTML document (pages 105–112)
- Imported Fireworks HTML into an existing Dreamweaver document (pages 112–115)
- Created CSS layers in Dreamweaver (pages 115–119)
- Searched for a Dreamweaver extension for page mockup (pages 119–121)
- Worked with the Extension Manager to install and use the extension (pages 119–124)
- Reconstructed the original interface design using HTML tables (pages 125–128)
- Inserted images into the document (pages 128–131)

5 Developing a Page Template

In this lesson, you'll work with two powerful Macromedia Dreamweaver site-development tools: cascading style sheets and Dreamweaver templates. Both are efficient production-streamlining tools that automate the development and maintenance of Web pages. In addition, they ensure design consistency across pages.

A cascading style sheet (CSS) is a collection of text and layout formatting rules that control the appearance of content on one or more Web pages. CSS have considerably more formatting options—from numerous font settings to layout, spacing, and border controls—than traditional (and now discouraged) HTML-only alternatives, such as the `<font>` tag or the `align` attribute of many tags. Using CSS, you can achieve a better design than you could in the past. Because multiple pages can point to a single cascading style sheet, you can have consistency across your site and make extensive design changes with minimal effort.

In the course of this lesson, you'll create a cascading style sheet for the Jade Valley Web site to ensure consistent content formatting.

A Dreamweaver template is a Dreamweaver-only feature that applies the same concept of style sheets to the document's overall layout and repeating elements (such as navigation bars). To use templates, you design a generic page layout, complete with graphics, navigation bars, footers, and placeholder text, and save the generic version as a template. You can later generate new pages based on the template. Templates ensure that you don't accidentally make a page look different from other pages in your site. Also, all the pages based on the template remain connected in Dreamweaver's memory; thus, if you change a template (change a color, add a new button to the navigation bar, or change the date in the footer, for example), Dreamweaver can automatically update all the pages that are based on that template.

The workflow, then, is to create a nearly perfect generic page that you can use as the basis for any number of new pages (and templates, if you wish). You've already created the basic HTML layout. Now you'll format it with CSS, ultimately reproducing the original design created in Fireworks. Finally, when you're satisfied with this page you'll save it as a template and use it to create the actual pages of the site in Lesson 6, *Developing Site Content*.

What You Will Learn

In this lesson, you will:

- Learn how a cascading style sheet works
- Design a cascading style sheet
- Redefine HTML tags and add custom classes
- Apply CSS styles
- Enhance page accessibility
- Convert a page to a Dreamweaver template
- Designate editable regions

Approximate Time

This lesson takes approximately 90 minutes to complete.

Lesson Files

Starting Files:

Lesson05/Start/jade_valley/jadevalley_template.htm

Completed Files:

Lesson05/Complete/jade_valley/zz_archive/jadevalley_template.htm
Lesson05/Complete/jade_valley/css/jadevalley.css
Lesson05/Complete/jade_valley/Templates/jadevalley_template.dwt

Introducing Cascading Style Sheets

Cascading style sheets are collections of style and formatting information that you can apply consistently to multiple elements and across multiple pages. CSS can do much more than apply italics and right-align text. For example, you can assign a colored border to a single table cell in an otherwise borderless table using CSS styles, which is not possible using traditional HTML. You can also control the positioning of block-level elements in a Web page. For example, you can set margins, padding, and so on.

A CSS style rule contains two parts: the selector and the declaration. The selector is the name of the style (such as h2 for level 2 headings, or p for body-text paragraphs), and the declaration defines the style elements' changes. The declaration consists of two parts: the property (such as font-size or background-color), and the property's value (such as 10 points to indicate a font size, or #000099 to specify a blue color).

The word "cascading" refers to the built-in inheritance of CSS. As you know, HTML elements are nested inside one another. At the outside—the beginning and the end of an HTML document—are the <html> tags, and inside these tags are the <head> and <body> tags. Inside the <body> tag, if you use a CSS layers-based layout, you'll have <div> tags before you get to the first text element, which might be an <h1> heading tag. CSS takes advantage of this nested hierarchy by enabling formatting information to pass through this hierarchy. This cascading effect is illustrated in the following figure.

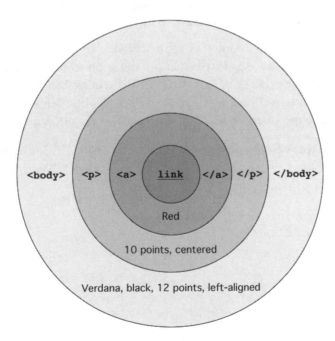

This figure shows the nesting of tags. It represents the tag hierarchy of a typical hyperlink. Hyperlinks are created with the <a> tag, and are often found inside <p> (paragraph text) tags. On the outside is the <body> tag (the figure does not show the <html> tag outside the <body> tag). For the sake of argument, let's assume that this hyperlink is inside the footer, which is a specially formatted paragraph, different from regular paragraph text. Each of these elements might be formatted as follows:

- <body>: Verdana, black, 12 points, left-aligned
- <p.footer>: 10 points, center-aligned
- <a>: Red

How would the link be formatted? Based on the principles of inheritance, it would be in the Verdana font (from the <body> tag), 10 points in size and center-aligned (from the p.footer style), and red (from the <a> tag).

A major advantage of CSS styles is that you can make sweeping changes to the site quickly and easily. When you update a CSS style, the formatting in all the documents that use that style are automatically updated to the new style, without you having to modify their HTML or even re-upload the changes to the server.

In addition to associating formatting with built-in HTML tags (<body>, <p>, and so on), you can create custom CSS styles that you can apply to any portion of the document's content, whether it's only one portion of an existing tag or spans multiple tags. Dreamweaver refers to associating styles with built-in tags as redefining HTML tags.

In Dreamweaver, you can also use another approach, which is to create custom CSS classes. A CSS class is a custom collection of styles that you can apply to an existing HTML tag, such as a <p> tag. You can use either or both approaches to defining CSS, based on the needs of your Web site. In general, you'll want to redefine HTML tags first before developing custom CSS styles to avoid unnecessary code. You'll work with both approaches in this lesson.

Tip *Dreamweaver's Reference panel contains an online CSS reference. To display the CSS reference, choose Help > Reference and select O'Reilly CSS Reference from the pop-up menu in the Reference panel.*

Redefining HTML Tags

The interface design for the Jade Valley Web site is colorful and warm; the designer conveys the spirit of Jade Valley through a carefully chosen color scheme of yellow, green, and orange. The challenging task now is to develop a cascading style sheet that creates harmony with the existing color scheme.

In this task, you'll redefine five HTML tags to make the color scheme consistent throughout the site and make sure that the fonts you choose are easy for visitors to read online. The five HTML tags whose formatting you'll redefine with CSS are <body>, <p>, <a>, <h1>, and <h2>. You'll save the formatting for these styles in a separate file and folder in the site, making the definitions universally available to everything in the site, rather than just the file that's open when you create it.

1. Open Dreamweaver, and choose jadevalley_template.htm from the Files panel.

Because most of the page elements have been reconstructed on this page, this page is a good candidate to use for developing a cascading style sheet for the Jade Valley Web site.

2. Select Window > CSS Styles. In the CSS Styles panel, click the New CSS Style button.

You can author new CSS styles or edit existing styles using the New CSS Style panel.

Notice that the panel is not empty; it already lists three styles. These were created earlier as a result of your work on creating CSS layers. You'll return to these styles later in this lesson.

3. In the New CSS Style dialog, choose Tag (which redefines the look of a specific tag) and select the body element from the Tag drop-down menu. Select (New Style Sheet File) in the Define In option. Click OK.

Depending on the chosen Selector Type, the drop-down Tag menu changes. The HTML <body> tag is one of the tags you need to redefine in this task.

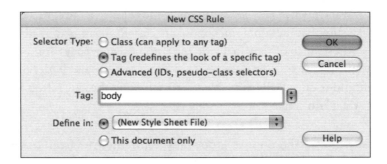

4. In the Save Style Sheet File As dialog, navigate to the css folder within the jade_valley folder. Name the new style sheet *jadevalley.css* and save it in the css folder.

Although you won't do so in these lessons, it's possible to have multiple cascading style sheets in your site. For this reason, it's often easiest to have a css folder in your site's root folder, where you can put all your CSS files.

Note that all style sheets end with the extension .css.

After you click the Save button, the "CSS Rule Definition for body in the jadevalley.css" dialog appears.

5. In the dialog, select the Type Category and choose Arial, Helvetica, sans-serif as the Font and 12 pixels as the Size. Click Apply and then OK to finish redefining the body element.

As a rule, you should use only sans-serif fonts for screen-based content, because they're easier to read onscreen than serif fonts. By specifying multiple sans-serif fonts (Arial, Helvetica, sans-serif), a user's browser will try each font in turn until it finds one of the specified fonts.

Note *By specifying sans-serif at the end, you include a catch-all in case a user's computer doesn't have any of the other fonts installed.*

Although you can specify a different measurement for the font size, the most common options are points or pixels. In this task, you'll use pixels as the measurement for all text formatting.

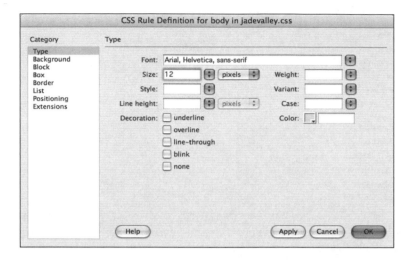

6. Click the New CSS Style button in the CSS Styles panel again. If necessary, select Tag as the Selector Type and choose the p element from the Tag drop-down menu. Verify that jadevalley.css is selected in the Define In option. Click OK.

As before, you're preparing to use CSS to redefine how the browser renders an HTML tag (in this case, the <p> tag).

7. In the Type Category of the CSS Style Definition dialog, select Arial, Helvetica, sans-serif as the Font and 12 pixels as the Size. Next, in the Box Category, uncheck the Same for all option under Padding and enter 3 pixels as the amount of padding for Right and Left. Click OK.

You'll notice that the first part of this step is identical to that of the body element redefinition. In theory, the p element should inherit all the formatting of the body element, because it's nested inside and because CSS styles cascade. However, no browser is fully compliant with CSS standards, and some browsers deviate more than others. By duplicating this information, you ensure that all browsers present the text correctly.

You also specify some cell padding around the left and right edges of the text. This creates a margin between the text and the surrounding table cell in which it appears, preventing the text from bumping against the cell border.

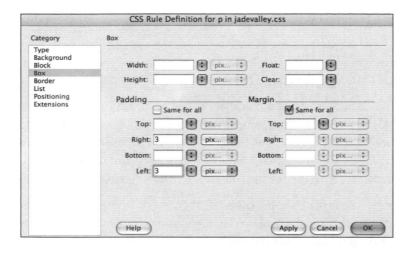

8. Repeat Steps 6 and 7 to redefine the following HTML tags with the specified attributes: the a element (Color: #669900); the h1 element (Font: Geneva, Arial, Helvetica, sans-serif; 18 pixels; Color: #852112; Padding: Right and Left both 3 pixels); and the h2 element (Font: Geneva, Arial, Helvetica, sans-serif; 16 pixels; Color: #C27C44; Padding: Right and Left both 3 pixels).

These attributes were chosen based on the following factors:

- Easy reading onscreen
- Consistency with the original design's color scheme
- The need for a small amount of white space between the text content and the border surrounding the content

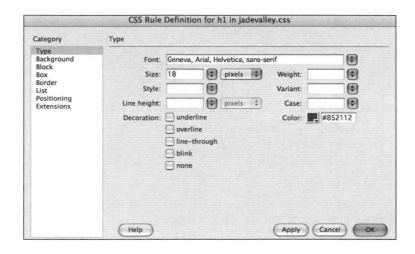

Adding Custom Classes

At this point, you've redefined five HTML tags to automate text formatting. However, there are still areas of content on the Jade Valley Web site that need special formatting for which there are no HTML tags. You'll need to create a custom CSS class instead.

In general, you want to create custom classes as one of the CSS styles in the style sheets to format special content areas. For example, you generally want the text in the footer area to be smaller than your regular content, but HTML has no <footer> tag that you can format for this purpose. Instead, you have to use a regular <p> tag, but create a special .footer class that you can apply to the <p> tag you want to use as the footer.

In this task, you'll create five custom classes: .footer, .text_nav, .copyright, .content_main, and .content_special. You'll use these classes to format four special areas: the footer, the copyright line of the footer, the text-based navigation bar at the bottom of the page, and the two table cells that hold the two main content areas. You'll begin with the footer.

1. Select the New CSS Style button from the CSS Styles panel.

Again, you will use the CSS Styles panel to create custom classes.

2. In the New CSS Style dialog, select Class (this can apply to any tag), and then in the Name text box, type .footer and click OK.

Custom class names must begin with a period and can contain any combination of letters and numbers.

> **Note**   If you don't enter a period before the name of the custom class, Dreamweaver automatically enters it for you.

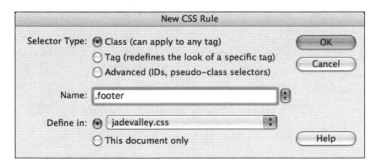

3. In the CSS Style Definition dialog, switch to the Block Category and set Text Align to Center. In the Box Category, set both the Top and Bottom Padding to **4** pixels.

Remember that elements inherit formatting from elements in which they are nested. The footer will apply to a <div> tag at the bottom of the main_content layer, and even though you will apply the .footer custom class to a <div> tag, it will inherit all the formatting of the base <div> tag, except those attributes (such as size) that you explicitly changed in the definition of the .footer class. As a result, you don't have to specify a font face when you create the .footer class.

The 4-pixel top and bottom cell padding you specified creates extra space above and below the text block, so that it doesn't run into the edges of its cell.

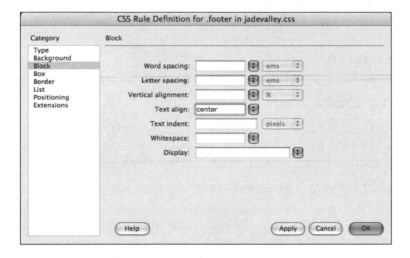

4. Repeat Steps 1–3 above to create the .text_nav custom class, with the following attributes: Font Size: 11 pixels; Color: #666666; Text Align: Center; Padding: Top and Bottom both **6** pixels.

As before, these settings can be found in different categories of the CSS Style Definition dialog: Type, Block, and Box.

The .text_nav custom class is similar to the .footer custom class in many ways. The only difference is the text color, the larger font size, and increased cell padding.

5. Repeat Steps 1–3 above to create the .copyright custom class, with the following attributes: Font Size: 9 pixels; Background Color: #CCCCCC.

The Background Color setting can be found in the Background category.

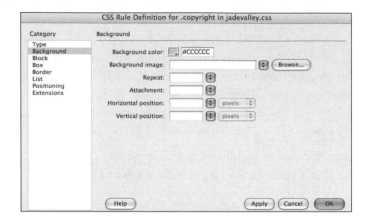

6. Save jadevalley_template.htm.

Applying CSS Styles

As you're about to see, applying CSS styles is very easy, especially given how much work the styles do. The only catch, as noted below, is that you have to be sure to attach a style to the correct page element. Knowing a bit of HTML can come in handy.

CSS styles must be applied to an existing HTML tag. It's possible to apply a CSS style to any one of several tags, including paragraphs, hyperlinks, and table cells, and therein lies the problem. A given block of text can appear inside a hyperlink, which is itself inside a paragraph, which is inside a table cell. In such situations, it's hard for Dreamweaver to guess which tag it should attach the style to. The following technique ensures that you give Dreamweaver the information it needs to apply the style to the right tag every time.

Because you've redefined several HTML tags, Dreamweaver automatically formats the content that's within the <p> tags. In this task, you'll learn how to format content using other redefined HTML tags such as <h1>, <h2>, <a>, and custom classes.

1. If it isn't already open, open jadevalley_template.html. Position the cursor before the word Lorem in the first paragraph on the main page and press Enter/Return to create a new paragraph. Type *Main Heading* and press Enter/Return. Then type *Sub-heading* and press Enter/Return again.

We're creating descriptive text to which Dreamweaver will apply the styles. At this point, these two new paragraphs are formatted as body paragraphs, using the <p> tag.

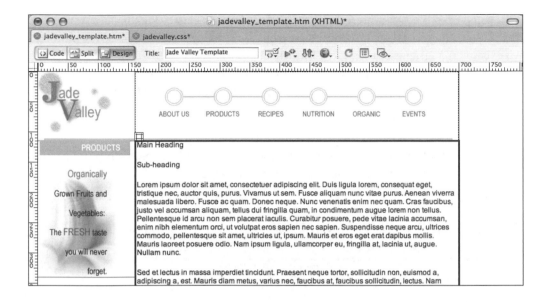

2. Click anywhere in the Main Heading line and choose Heading 1 from the Format selector in the Property inspector. Next, click anywhere in the Sub-heading line and choose Heading 2 from the Format selector in the Property inspector.

Changing the formatting to Heading 1 adds <h1> tags around the text. You redefined the attributes of both the <h1> and <h2> tags using CSS, so Dreamweaver automatically applies the formatting you specified as soon as you change them to headings.

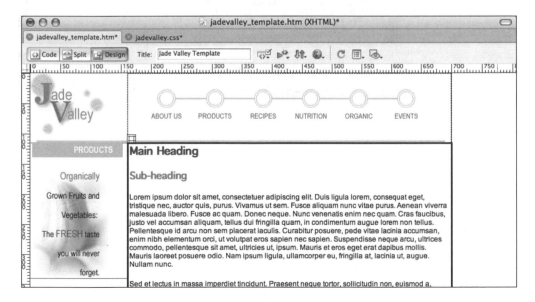

Next, you'll prep the footer area. You defined three custom classes for this: `.footer`, `.text_nav`, and `.copyright`. Obviously, `.text_nav` and `.copyright` map clearly onto the two existing paragraphs of the footer. But what about `.footer` itself? That style is meant to apply to both of the lines in the footer. What you need to do, then, is to wrap both of those lines in a new tag—once again a `<div>` tag—and apply the `.footer` style to it.

You'll start with the `<div>` tag.

3. Drag to select the text navigation bar and the copyright lines. Using the Layout category of the Insert menu, click the Insert Div Tag button.

This button enables you to insert a `<div>` wrapped around the current selection.

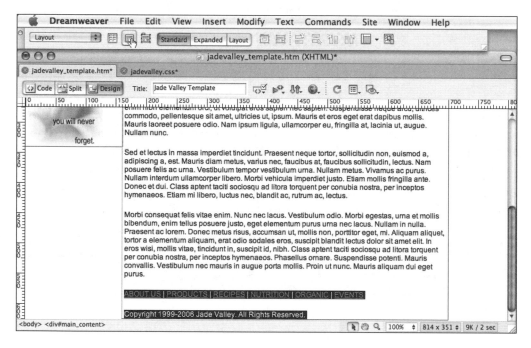

After you click the button, a small dialog appears.

4. In the Insert Div Tag dialog, make sure that Wrap Around Selection is selected in the Insert option. In the Class option, specify footer. Leave ID blank. Click OK.

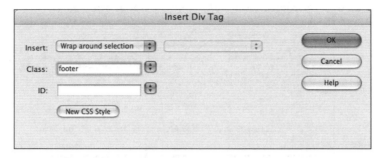

The two footer lines are separated from the rest of the main_content `<div>`. The lines are still inside that `<div>` tag, so they inherit its properties, except where explicitly overridden. In this case, the alignment is overridden (the two lines are center-aligned).

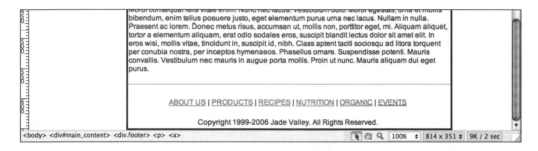

5. Click anywhere in the text nav bar line. Right-click the `<p>` tag in the Tag Selector, and choose Set Class > text_nav.

This applies the `.text_nav` class to the whole paragraph, effectively shrinking the font.

6. Click anywhere in the copyright line. Right-click the **<p>** tag in the Tag Selector, and choose **Set Class > copyright**.

When you're finished, the footer should look like the one in the figure.

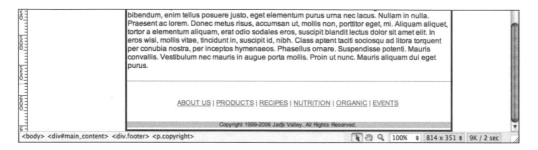

7. Save your file.

Finalizing the Layout

The layout is looking pretty good. You'll need to tweak it a bit, but there's a more substantive task ahead, which involves optimizing the code. As you know, <div> tags in combination with CSS are used to create layout regions called layers. To create layers, you attach CSS to <div> tags using one of the following methods:

- You can apply CSS as an inline style. That is, when you create a <div> tag, you can use its optional style attribute to apply CSS to it.

- You can apply CSS as an embedded style. With this technique, you write the CSS definition at the top of the document, and you associate a collection of rules with an ID. When you create the <div> tag, you give it that ID, and the collection of rules immediately applies to it.

- You apply the CSS from an external style sheet using an ID. This method is the same as the previous one, except that rather than storing the CSS styles inside the HTML document, you store them in an external style sheet.

At this point in the lesson, you've created an external style sheet (jadevalley.css). However, all the style descriptions for your four CSS layers are stored in the local document. Two of them (the settings for the navbar and logo layers) use inline styles. The other two (the styles for the special_content and main_content layers) use embedded styles. The former two were exported from Fireworks, while the latter two were created in Dreamweaver.

As a rule of thumb, it's generally better to have layer styles defined in an external style sheet, so that multiple pages can use them, rather than inline or embedded styles, which can be used only on the page in which they appear. In this task, you'll move the layer styles out of jadevalley_template.htm and into jadevalley.css. After the move is complete, you'll add further styles to some of the layers to finish their formatting.

The workflow will be as follows. You'll convert the two layers with inline styles to embedded styles. Then you'll move all the embedded styles to your external style sheet. Finally, you'll modify these styles to complete the design.

1. Click once on the logo at the top of the page. Select <div#logo> in the Tag Selector. Switch to code view.

Inside the <div> tag, look for the style attribute; that's what needs to be moved out of this line and up to the top of the code.

Note *In the figure, line wrapping is toggled on (View › Code View Options › Word Wrap).*

2. Select the entire style attribute, and choose Edit > Cut. Scroll up near the top of the page, and paste the code just before the closing **</style>** tag.

```
55
56 ▼ <div id="logo" style="position:absolute; left:0px; top:0px;width:161px; height:115px;z-index:1;
     ▲ visibility:visible;"><img src="images/logo.gif" alt="Jade Valley logo." name="logo_img" width="161"
       height="115" border="0" id="logo_img" /></div>
```

The attribute is not yet formatted correctly, but at least it's in the right place.

```
 7    <meta name="Description" content="FW MX CSS Layer />
 8    <style type="text/css">
 9    td img {display: block;}
10    #special_content {
11        position:absolute;
12        left:0px;
13        top:115px;
14        width:161px;
15        z-index:3;
16    }
17    #main_content {
18        position:absolute;
19        left:161px;
20        top:115px;
21        width:539px;
22        z-index:4;
23    }
24
25 ▼  style="position:absolute; left:0px; top:0px;width:161px; height:115px;z-index:1; visibility:visible;"
26
27    </style>
28    <script type="text/JavaScript">
```

```
9K / 2 sec
```

3. Reformat the code so that it reads as follows:

```
#logo {
  position:absolute;
  left:0px;
  top:0px;
  width:161px;
  height:115px;
  z-index:1;
  visibility:visible;
}
```

The #logo is the identifier. Any element that has the #logo ID will be assigned this collection of styles. the <div> from which you took these styles has an id="logo" attribute, which ensures that these styles will be attached to it.

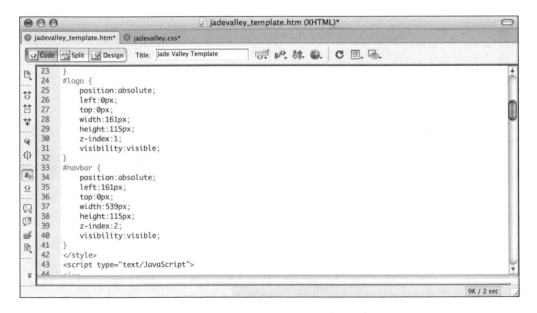

```
    14    width:161px;
    15        z-index:3;
    16    }
    17    #main_content {
    18        position:absolute;
    19        left:161px;
    20        top:115px;
    21        width:539px;
    22        z-index:4;
    23    }
    24  ▼ #logo {
    25        position:absolute;
    26        left:0px;
    27        top:0px;
    28        width:161px;
    29        height:115px;
    30        z-index:1;
    31        visibility:visible;
    32  ▲ }
    33    </style>
    34    <script type="text/JavaScript">
    35    <!--
```

4. Repeat steps 1-3 to move the inline styles associated with the navbar `<div>` into the `<style>` tag near the top of the code.

If you switch back to design view, you'll see that the page looks exactly the same as it did before. Now, however, you at least have all your layer styles in one place.

```
    23    }
    24    #logo {
    25        position:absolute;
    26        left:0px;
    27        top:0px;
    28        width:161px;
    29        height:115px;
    30        z-index:1;
    31        visibility:visible;
    32    }
    33    #navbar {
    34        position:absolute;
    35        left:161px;
    36        top:0px;
    37        width:539px;
    38        height:115px;
    39        z-index:2;
    40        visibility:visible;
    41    }
    42    </style>
    43    <script type="text/JavaScript">
    44    <!--
```

The next step is to move those styles out of this document and into your external CSS file.

5. Still in code view, drag to select all four of the CSS blocks for each of the layers (from `#special_content {` down to and including the closing curly brace of the #navbar block). Choose Edit > Cut.

All that's left of the `<style>` tag is the `td img` line that was inserted by Fireworks.

```
5    <title>Jade Valley Template</title>
6    <meta http-equiv="Content-Type" content="text/html; charset=ISO-8859-1" />
7    <meta name="Description" content="FW MX CSS Layer" />
8    <style type="text/css">
9    td img {display: block;}
10   </style>
11   <script type="text/JavaScript">
12   <!--
13   function MM_swapImgRestore() { //v3.0
14     var i,x,a=document.MM_sr; for(i=0;a&&i<a.length&&(x=a[i])&&x.oSrc;i++) x.src=x.oSrc;
15   }
16
```

6. Open jadevalley.css. Scroll to the bottom of the code, and paste in the four blocks you just cut.

```
36   }
37   h2 {
38       font-family: Geneva, Arial, Helvetica, sans-serif;
39       font-size: 16px;
40       color: #C27C44;
41       padding-right: 3px;
42       padding-left: 3px;
43   }
44   #special_content {
45       position:absolute;
46       left:0px;
47       top:115px;
48       width:161px;
49       z-index:3;
50   }
51   #main_content {
52       position:absolute;
53       left:161px;
54       top:115px;
55       width:539px;
56       z-index:4;
```

```
2K / 1 sec
```

The file jadvalley.css has been open during this lesson. Whenever you work on the file, even if only through the CSS panel, Dreamweaver opens a copy of the file.

At this point, the styles are now all external to the HTML document. If you look at jadevalley_template.htm in design view, the file looks the same as it did before.

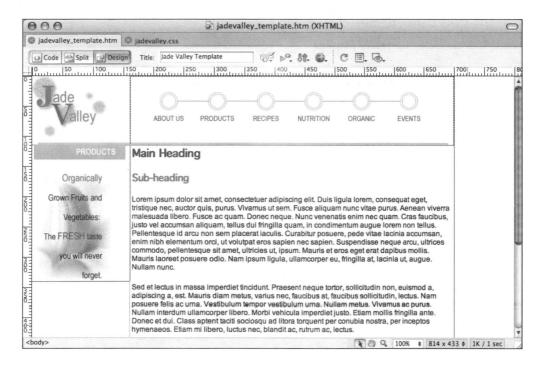

If you look in the CSS panel, you'll see the four layer styles listed at the bottom.

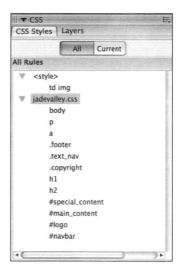

A couple of tweaks remain. You want to right-align the contents of the special_content layer, and you want to put silver borders around the special_content and main_content layers. Both tasks can easily be accomplished by modifying the CSS descriptions.

7. In the CSS panel, double-click to edit #main_content.

The CSS Rule Definition dialog opens.

8. In the Border category, specify the following settings. Click OK.

Style: (Same for all) solid

Width: (Same for all) thin

Color: (Same for all) #CCCCCC

These changes add a silver border around all sides of the main content area, reproducing the original design.

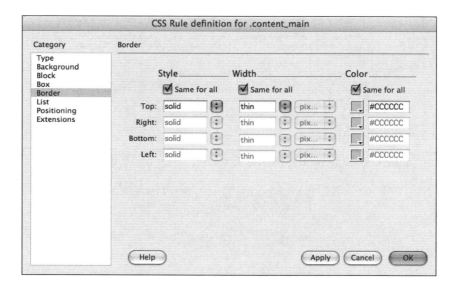

9. Repeat steps 7 and 8 above to create the #special_content, with the following attributes, all found in the Border Category. Also, in the Block Category, set the Text Align option to Right. Click OK.

Style: (Top, Bottom, and Left) solid; (Right) none

Width: (Same for all) thin

Color: (Same for all) #CCCCCC

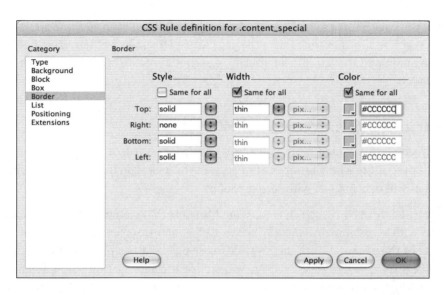

This style is identical to the one in the preceding step, with the exception that the right edge has no border. This is because #special_content already has a border, thanks to the left border of #main_content . The Text Align option not only aligns text, but images as well; the PRODUCTS and banana graphics are now right-aligned inside the layer.

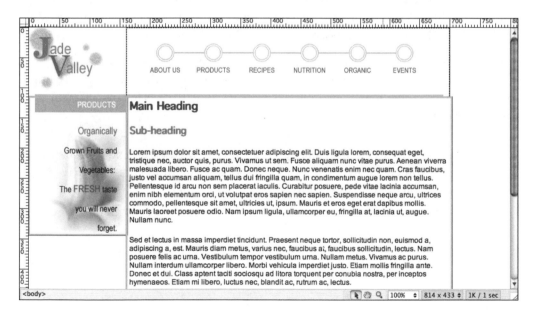

10. Save the file.

Now that the page has the same look and feel as the original design, and the appropriate CSS styles, you're almost ready to turn the page into a Dreamweaver template. Before you finalize the page and convert it to a template, you should make sure it is accessible to screen readers.

Enhancing Site Accessibility

You've already implemented some accessibility features to the Jade Valley Web site by adding alt descriptions for a number of images. In this task, you'll add an accessibility feature that will benefit users with screen readers.

As you learned in Lesson 2, screen readers are browsers that read page contents aloud, so that users with visual impairments can access Web content. Screen readers start at the beginning of the page and work their way down, which creates a problem for pages with layouts like ours, which begin every page with an identical navigation bar and banner. This means that screen readers will read the navigation bar, along with all its hotspots, over and over again throughout the site.

In this task, you'll implement an easy solution to overcome this problem: you'll create a tiny, invisible graphic at the beginning of the first page that jumps over the logo and navigation bar, sending users directly to that page's main content. Because the graphic that triggers this behavior is invisible and only a fraction of an inch in size, users accessing your site through traditional browsers won't even know this feature exists.

To implement this feature, you'll insert a 1-by-1-pixel graphic and add a link that skips to a named anchor (a link target in the middle of a page) next to the main page heading. You'll place this graphic at the top of the <body> element, so that it's the first element a screen reader encounters.

1. With jadevalley_template.htm still open, switch to code view, and (if necessary) add a few empty lines below the opening <body> tag but above the first <div> tag. Leave the insertion point in the empty space you just created.

You're ensuring that the invisible graphic you're about to insert is the first thing on the page.

```
30
31    function MM_swapImage() { //v3.0
32      var i,j=0,x,a=MM_swapImage.arguments; document.MM_sr=new Array; for(i=0;i<(a.length-2);i+=3)
33        if ((x=MM_findObj(a[i]))!=null){document.MM_sr[j++]=x; if(!x.oSrc) x.oSrc=x.src; x.src=a[i+2];}
34    }
35    //-->
36    </script>
37    <link href="css/jadevalley.css" rel="stylesheet" type="text/css" />
38    </head>
39
40    <body bgcolor="#ffffff" onload="MM_preloadImages('images/about_f2.gif','images/products_f2.gif','images/re
41
42    |
43
44
45    <div id="logo"><img src="images/logo.gif" alt="Jade Valley logo." name="logo_img" width="161" height="115"
46    <div id="navbar">
47      <table border="0" cellpadding="0" cellspacing="0" width="539">
48        <!-- fwtable fwsrc="interface_navbar.png" fwbase="navbar.gif" fwstyle="Dreamweaver" fwdocid = "7423080
49        <tr>
50          <td colspan="13"><img name="navbar_r1_c1" src="images/navbar_r1_c1.gif" width="539" height="20" bord
51        </tr>
52        <tr>
53          <td rowspan="2"><img name="navbar_r2_c1" src="images/navbar_r2_c1.gif" width="39" height="95" border
54          <td><a href="about.htm" onmouseout="MM_swapImgRestore()" onmouseover="MM_swapImage('about','','image
55          <td rowspan="2"><img name="navbar_r2_c3" src="images/navbar_r2_c3.gif" width="28" height="95" border
56          <td><a href="products.htm" onmouseout="MM_swapImgRestore()" onmouseover="MM_swapImage('products','',
```

```
                                                          1K / 1 sec
```

2. Switch back to design view. From the main menu, choose Insert > Image. Browse to spacer.gif in the images folder, and click OK. In the accessibility dialog that appears, type *Skip to main page content.* as the Alternate Text. Click OK.

The spacer.gif file is only 1 pixel wide and 1 pixel high, which makes it a fast download. In addition, the GIF file is set to 100% transparency, so that it's invisible in a traditional graphic browser. A screen reader can see it, however, which is what you want. The spacer.gif has the two features you need most: the ability to add a hyperlink, and the ability to add an alt description.

3. Without clicking, go immediately to the Property inspector, which still shows the properties of the invisible image you just inserted. In the Link field, type *#top*.

In a moment, you'll create a named anchor—that is, a within-the-page hyperlink target—for this link to point to. Named anchors are always preceded with a pound sign (#).

It's important that you create the hyperlink target before clicking elsewhere, because the image is practically invisible in Dreamweaver, making it almost impossible to find in design view.

Tip *In the event you* did *click before you added the hyperlink, the easiest way to find the image again is to switch to code view and find the <img> tag between the <body> and first <div> tags. Position the cursor anywhere in the tag, and the Property inspector will once again display its properties.*

Now that the graphic is in place and linked, you need to add the target.

4. Position the insertion point just to the left of the Main Heading text at the top of the main_content layer. Choose Insert > Named Anchor. In the Named Anchor dialog, name it *top*, and click OK.

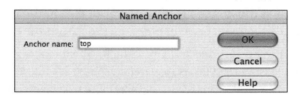

Dreamweaver inserts the anchor in the code. Depending on your view settings, you might also see a yellow anchor icon next to the main heading. This icon is a Dreamweaver visual aid only; it will not appear in a browser.

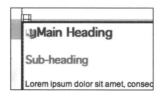

Tip *You can toggle these invisible icons on or off by checking or unchecking View > Visual Aids > Invisible Elements.*

5. Save jadevalley_template.html.

You're ready to convert this file to a Dreamweaver template.

Converting the Page to a Dreamweaver Template

To develop the rest of the Web pages for the Jade Valley Web site, you could open a new page and start designing. In the long run, however, this is not the most efficient way to proceed. It's much more effective to create a template that includes the page layout, navigation bar, attached CSS styles, the accessibility feature, and the footer.

Setting up templates has three distinct advantages:

- Templates decrease authoring time
- They help ensure design consistency across pages
- They enable you to easily update multiple pages

In creating a page template, you spare yourself the redundant task of reconstructing the basic and common page elements every time you want to create a new page. In addition, any HTML document that is created based on the template remains associated to that template (although you can disassociate, or "detach," a document from its template). If you modify the template, you can instantaneously update all the documents based on that template to reflect your changes.

In Dreamweaver, you can create a template based on an existing document, or you can develop a template from a new, blank document. After the template is created, you can specify different template regions that can be modified by the template users.

In the final two tasks of this lesson, you will first convert an existing HTML document to a Dreamweaver template and define editable regions.

1. With jadevalley_template.htm open, select File-> Save as Template.

The file jadevalley_template.htm contains all the information you need in a template: the logo, site navigation, standard CSS styles, and footer information, which are all common page elements for all the HTML pages you'll need to develop for the Jade Valley Web site.

2. In the Save As Template dialog, select jade_valley from the Site drop-down menu. In the Save as text box, enter *jadevalley_template* and click Save. When the Update Links dialog appears, choose Yes.

Dreamweaver saves template files in a special folder, and when it moves the template file into that folder, it effectively breaks all the relative links inside the file. Fortunately, Dreamweaver's link checker catches the change and offers to fix the links for you.

You can create multiple templates for a site. To differentiate the current template from other templates you might create for the site in the future, make sure you give the template a meaningful name.

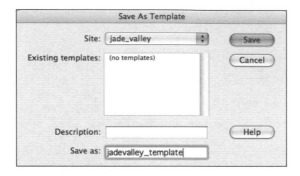

3. In the Files panel, click the + (Windows) or arrow (Macintosh) icon next to the Template folder. You should see a file called jadevalley_template.dwt in that folder.

Dreamweaver saves the template file in the site's Templates folder (which is created automatically by Dreamweaver as soon as you create a template for a site), with a .dwt file extension.

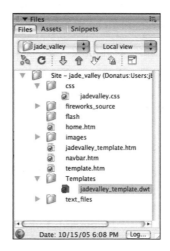

Tip *Never move your templates out of the Templates folder or put any non-template files in the Templates folder. Remember not to move the Templates folder out of the local root folder, so that links won't be broken.*

4. Archive the following files: jadevalley_template.htm, template.htm, and navbar.htm.

Now that the official template for the Jade Valley Web site is created, you should archive the now obsolete files to prevent confusion. You can create a special folder on your computer to store these two files in case you need them in the future. They don't need to be kept in your site file any more. Most developers find that unneeded files clutter the workspace and sometimes lead to errors.

Designating Editable Regions

In this final task, you'll specify editable regions on the template you just created for the Jade Valley Web site. An editable region refers to the areas on the template in which users can edit and modify content. All other areas in a document are locked, and users can't change them. Dreamweaver automatically locks the whole document when you first save an HTML document as a template, you need to go back and make some regions editable.

You can create an editable region anywhere in the template document. For the template to be effective, you want to make the content areas editable, so that you can easily and quickly create all the pages for the site.

1. Open jadevalley_template.dwt in split view. In the design half of split view, click to select the yellow Named Anchor Link icon. Then in the code half of split view, drag the entire block of highlighted code for the named anchor link to the left of the opening <h1> tag, as shown in the figure.

As you know, the anchor link was created to enhance accessibility, and you don't want anyone to edit it or accidentally delete it. As a result, you need to keep the named anchor as part of the locked region, so that anyone using the template can't accidentally remove it. But you don't want Main Heading to be the heading of every page! The main heading must be editable, while the image must not. Therefore, you'll have to move the image outside the <h1> tag.

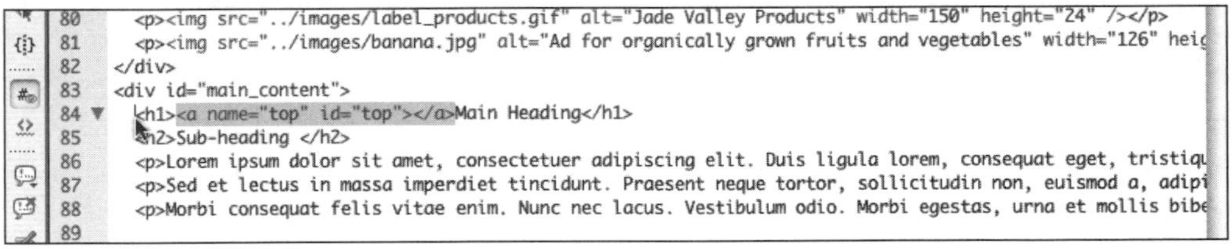

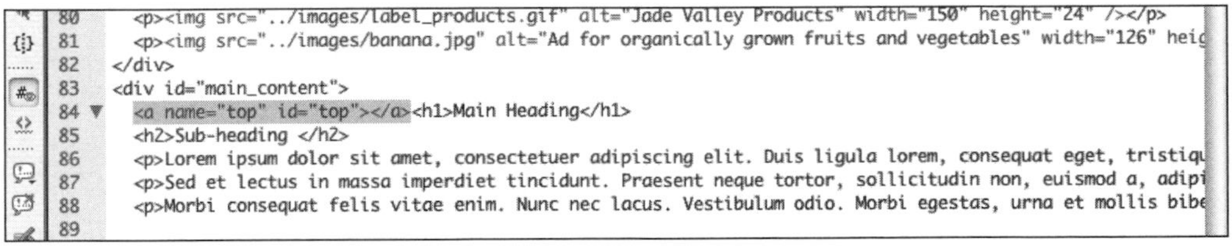

```
80    <p><img src="../images/label_products.gif" alt="Jade Valley Products" width="150" height="24" /></p>
81    <p><img src="../images/banana.jpg" alt="Ad for organically grown fruits and vegetables" width="126" heig
82    </div>
83    <div id="main_content">
84 ▼  <h1><a name="top" id="top"></a>Main Heading</h1>
85    <h2>Sub-heading </h2>
86    <p>Lorem ipsum dolor sit amet, consectetuer adipiscing elit. Duis ligula lorem, consequat eget, tristiqu
87    <p>Sed et lectus in massa imperdiet tincidunt. Praesent neque tortor, sollicitudin non, euismod a, adipi
88    <p>Morbi consequat felis vitae enim. Nunc nec lacus. Vestibulum odio. Morbi egestas, urna et mollis bibe
89
```

```
80    <p><img src="../images/label_products.gif" alt="Jade Valley Products" width="150" height="24" /></p>
81    <p><img src="../images/banana.jpg" alt="Ad for organically grown fruits and vegetables" width="126" heig
82    </div>
83    <div id="main_content">
84 ▼  <a name="top" id="top"></a><h1>Main Heading</h1>
85    <h2>Sub-heading </h2>
86    <p>Lorem ipsum dolor sit amet, consectetuer adipiscing elit. Duis ligula lorem, consequat eget, tristiqu
87    <p>Sed et lectus in massa imperdiet tincidunt. Praesent neque tortor, sollicitudin non, euismod a, adipi
88    <p>Morbi consequat felis vitae enim. Nunc nec lacus. Vestibulum odio. Morbi egestas, urna et mollis bibe
89
```

2. Return to design view, position the cursor before the Main Heading text block, and drag to select everything on the column except the yellow named anchor link icon (at the top) and the footer section (at the bottom).

All the highlighted text is placeholder content. The whole point of creating a template is to replace placeholder text with real content, which isn't possible if it's locked.

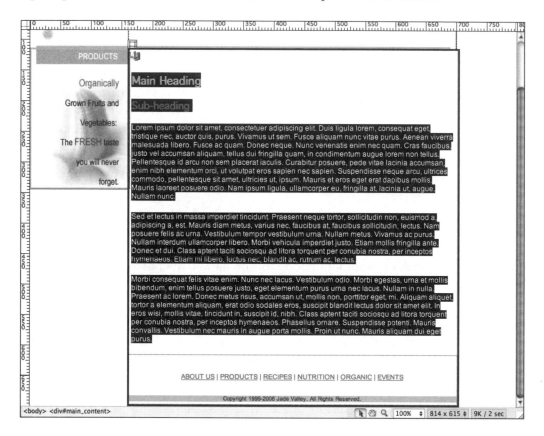

3. Select Insert > Template Objects > Editable Region. The Editable Region dialog appears. Enter *content_main* in the Name field and click OK to create the editable region.

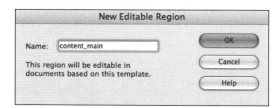

Always use a unique and descriptive name for the editable region. Because a template can have multiple editable regions, you can't use the same name for more than one editable region in a page template.

After you designate an editable region, Dreamweaver encloses the area in a highlighted box in the template. The tab at the upper-left corner of the region shows the name of that editable region. The tab is for identification only; it doesn't appear in browsers.

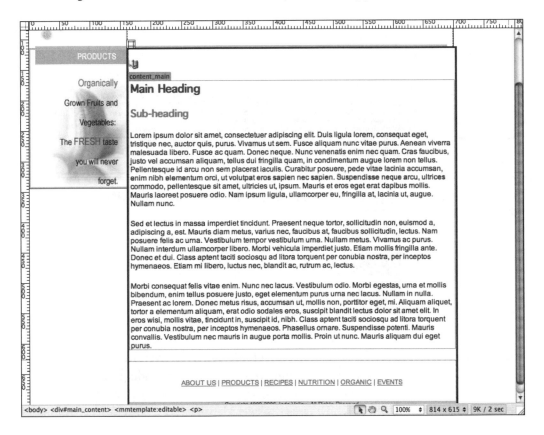

4. Position the cursor in the left column of the page. Select <div#special_content> from the Tag selector. In the Common category of the Insert bar, choose the Template drop-down and select Editable Region.

The entire left column is reserved for special content. You want the entire section to be editable, so you can bring in unique content for different parts of the Jade Valley Web site. By selecting <td.content_left> from the Tag selector, you ensure that the entire cell is editable.

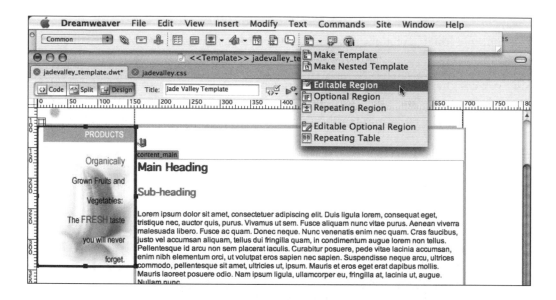

5. In the New Editable Region dialog, type *content_special*. Click OK to create this editable region.

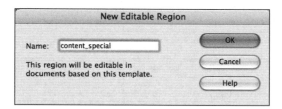

Unfortunately, Dreamweaver provides no visual feedback that this entire layer is editable. However, you can verify that it is by switching to code view. Surrounding the `<div id= "special_content">` tag is an HTML comment: `<!-- TemplateBeginEditable name= "content_special" -->`, which is how Dreamweaver identifies editable template regions.

6. Save and close jadevalley_template_main.dwt.

The template is ready to use. In the next lesson, you'll use it to create the entire Jade Vallley site.

What You Have Learned

In this lesson, you have:

- Developed a cascading style sheet (pages 135–136)
- Redefined HTML tags (pages 137–141)
- Created custom tags (pages 142–144)
- Used CSS styles to format text (pages 144–156)
- Created a hidden link to enhance accessibility for users with screen readers (pages 156–158)
- Saved an existing page as a template (pages 159–161)
- Specified editable regions to unlock portions of a template (pages 161–164)

6 Developing Site Content

You've completed five lessons, but you haven't yet finalized the seven pages in the Jade Valley site. By the end of this lesson, with the exception of a Flash animation, the entire site will be complete. By front-loading the creation of a layout and assets, such as templates and cascading style sheets, you can rapidly develop and maintain large and frequently changing Web sites.

In this lesson, you will create pages in Macromedia Dreamweaver, using the assets you've prepared. You will work with a number of common Web page elements. You'll create hyperlinks; insert a table to organize content; insert images for alignment and accessibility; create a bullet list; and add line breaks for spacing.

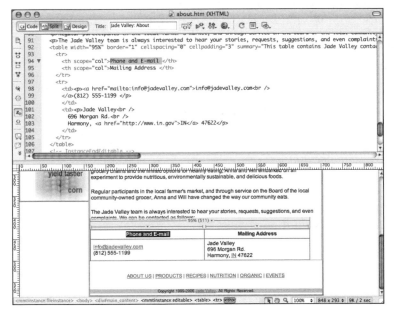

In the course of this lesson, you will create a table to organize the contact information for Jade Valley's Web site.

In the process, you'll become familiar with how the templates interact with the pages they build, and you'll see how your work thus far automates production.

What You Will Learn

In this lesson, you will:

- Create three HTML pages based on a template
- Add and format text
- Create hyperlinks
- Insert and lay out images
- Insert a table
- Modify a template and update all its child pages

Approximate Time

This lesson takes approximately 90 minutes to complete.

Lesson Files

Starting Files:

Lesson06/Start/jade_valley/Templates/jadevalley_template.dwt
Lesson06/Start/jade_valley/events.htm
Lesson06/Start/jade_valley/home.htm
Lesson06/Start/jade_valley/nutrition.htm
Lesson06/Start/jade_valley/organic.htm

Completed Files:

Lesson06/Complete/jade_valley/Templates/jadevalley_template.dwt
Lesson06/Complete/jade_valley/about.htm
Lesson06/Complete/jade_valley/events.htm
Lesson06/Complete/jade_valley/home.htm
Lesson06/Complete/jade_valley/nutrition.htm
Lesson06/Complete/jade_valley/organic.htm
Lesson06/Complete/jade_valley/products.htm
Lesson06/Complete/jade_valley/recipes.htm

Building the Site Using a Template

Using your template, you'll build the pages you need to complete the Jade Valley Web site. In this task, you'll create three pages based on the template you created in Lesson 5, *Developing a Page Template*, and populate the content by importing prewritten content from several text files. To save typing time, we've included the text for the three pages in the text_files subfolder within the jade_valley site. It's accessible from within Dreamweaver.

The remaining pages for the site have been created for you. You will bring them into your Web folder later in this task.

1. Open Dreamweaver and select File > New. In the New Document dialog, click the Templates tab. In the Templates for list, select the jade_valley site and then choose the jadevalley_template_main template from the list on the right. Click Create to create a new document based on the chosen template.

The New Document dialog provides a convenient way to create a new page based on a template from any of your sites.

Take a few moments to examine the new document that's now available in the Document window. Try clicking the navigation bar, the logo, the yellow anchor link icon, the text-based navigation aid, and the footer. You'll notice that you can't select or modify them; these elements are in the template's locked region and can't be altered on any page. The only sections you can modify are the areas of the template you designated as editable regions: the two content columns on the page. Later in this lesson you'll learn how to change page elements that are in the locked regions.

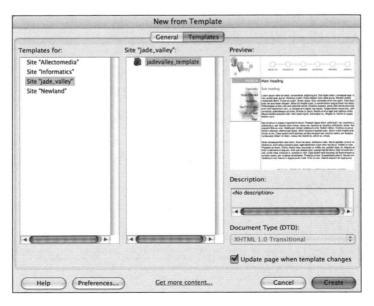

Note *Dreamweaver displays the template file in a box with a yellow border. A light-blue box with a blue label at the top-left corner surrounds the editable regions. You can customize these colors by choosing Edit › Preferences › Highlighting.*

2. In the Title box, delete Jade Valley Website Template and enter *Jade Valley: About* **as the page title.**

Even though the title of the page doesn't appear anywhere in the document area, it's important. It gives the page an identity, and appears in the browser title bar, search engine listings, and on pages you print.

3. In Dreamweaver's Files panel, open the text_files folder, and double-click to open about.txt.

About.txt is a plain text file, without formatting applied, such as bold, italics, or special font colors. When you copy and paste the file into Dreamweaver, all the word processor formatting is lost anyway. The figure shows the text as it appears in Notepad, the minimalist word processor that ships with Windows.

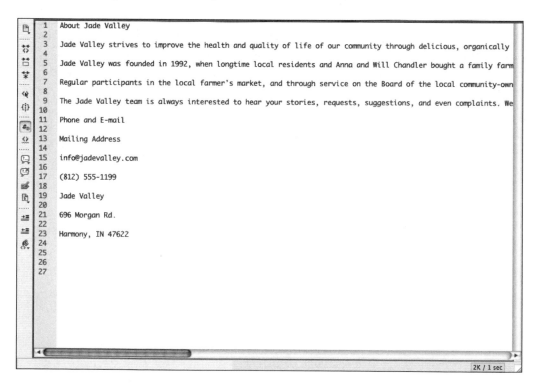

4. **Choose Edit > Select All, and then choose Edit > Copy.**

In this step, you're copying all the text to the Clipboard, making it available to paste into Dreamweaver.

5. **With the newly created page open in Dreamweaver, select the placeholder heading and subheading as well as all the Latin placeholder text.**

You're about to replace all the placeholder text with the text on the Clipboard.

6. **Choose Edit > Paste.**

The text appears in Dreamweaver. If you click inside each line and look in the Tag selector, you will see that each paragraph has been marked with the <p> tag.

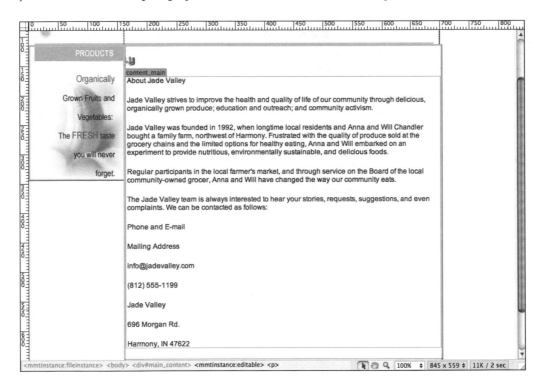

7. **Click anywhere in the page heading "About Jade Valley" and select Heading 1 from the Format drop-down menu in the Property inspector.**

Selecting Heading 1 from the Property inspector replaces the default <p> tag with an <h1> tag, which you can see if you look in the code. Changing the markup to <h1> makes the heading more prominent. Because the <h1> tag has been redefined in the cascading style sheet (CSS), it becomes large and red.

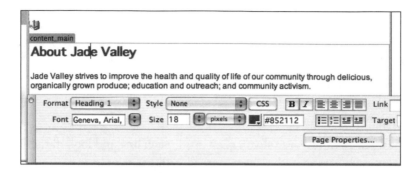

8. Choose File › Save and save the new document. In the Save As dialog, choose jade_valley as the designated site in the Save in drop-down menu. Enter *about.htm* as the file name. Click Save to save the file.

> **Note** *By default, Dreamweaver may try to append .html rather than .htm. The navigation bar you created in Fireworks used .htm, rather than .html, so make sure you stick with .htm.*

The new about.htm page now appears in the Files panel.

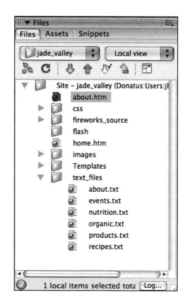

9. Repeat Steps 1–8 to create two more new pages: products.htm (using text from products.txt) and recipes.htm (using text from recipes.txt). In recipes.htm, apply Heading 2 (<h2>) to the text "Cinnamon Baked Apples."

You now have three new pages for the Jade Valley Web site. The site actually has seven pages, including the home page. In the next step, you'll copy the other three premade pages from the Start folder to your folder.

Tip | *In addition to using the New Document dialog to create a new document based on a template, you can also use the Assets panel. In the Assets panel (Window ›Assets), click the Templates icon on the left to view the list of templates in your site. Right-click (Windows) or Control-click (Macintosh) the template you want to use as the source for the new document, and from the context menu, choose New from Template.*

10. In Windows Explorer or Macintosh Finder, browse to the Lesson06/Start/jade_valley folder on the CD. Press Ctrl (Windows) or Command (Macintosh) and click to select nutrition.htm, organic.htm, and events.htm. Choose Edit › Copy. Paste the three documents into the jade_valley folder on your hard drive.

You now have all six pages needed for the Jade Valley Web site. Click the Refresh button in the Site folder if necessary to see the files.

These three predeveloped pages contain all the necessary images and content for a particular section of the Web site. Take a few minutes to explore these new additions and learn more about the site you're developing.

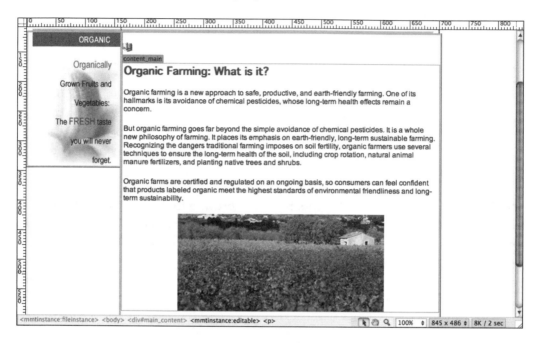

11. **Save and close all files, including, if necessary, jade_valley.css.**

When you work on a CSS file using the CSS Styles panel, Dreamweaver opens it in the background, providing you direct access to its code. You didn't work on its code directly; you modified it through Dreamweaver's interface.

Adding Hyperlinks

Now that you have all the pages for your site (although some are not yet completed), you can start linking them to other resources. Using hyperlinks, you can link pages to other pages within your site, to pages in other sites, to other file types (such as images or PDFs), and even to email. After all, links are what make the World Wide Web a web. In HTML, regardless of the type of link, all links are created with the anchor tag pairing: <a></a>. For example, to create a link on your Web page to Peachpit's Web site, use the following HTML:

```
<a href="http://www.peachpit.com/index.asp">Peachpit Press</a>
```

In this example, the words between the two tags, Peachpit Press, would appear (by default) underlined and colored. The resource (in this case, a Web page) link is specified in the href attribute.

In Dreamweaver, you can easily create different types of links for your Web site: links to pages within the site, links to a different site, email links, anchor links, and so on. In this task, you'll create links to pages within the site, links to external sites, and email links. And don't forget that in Lesson 4, *Preparing a New Site*, you created a within-page link for accessibility purposes.

1. Open about.htm. Drag to select the word "outreach" in the second line of the first paragraph.

The outreach page will link to events.htm.

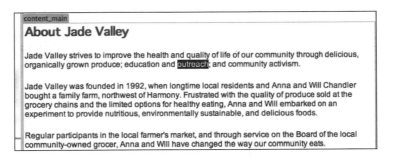

2. In the Property inspector's Link field, press and drag the Point to File icon to events.htm in the Files panel.

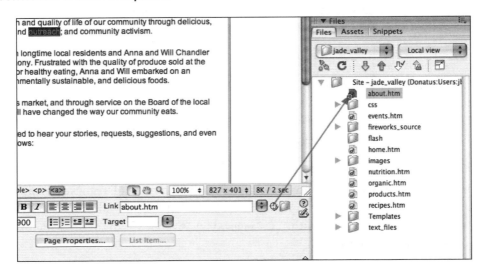

When you click outside the paragraph, you'll see that the word "outreach" is underlined and in green, the color you designated as the link color when you redefined the <a> tag in the previous lesson.

You just successfully created one type of hyperlink: linking an existing page to another page on your local site. When linking to pages within your site, you use relative URLs, which are partial URLs that indicate files located in the same folder tree as the file pointing to it. If you look at the Link text field when you return to the page window, you will see that instead of a full URL (like the http://www.peachpit.com/index.asp URL you saw earlier), the link contains about.htm. In the absence of additional information (including the http:// part and the domain), the browser looks for the file in the same folder as the source file.

The alternative to relative URLs is absolute URLs. As you have seen, absolute URLs contain the full URL, including the protocol (for example, http://), the server (for example, www.peachpit.com) and the file name (for example, index.asp). For local files, you shouldn't use absolute URLs because your local machine and the server probably have different directory structures.

3. **Return to the Document window. Near the bottom of the page, drag to select info@jadevalley.com. Choose Insert > Email Link. In the Email Link dialog, make sure the text info@jadevalley.com is in both the Text and Email text boxes. Click OK to create the email link.**

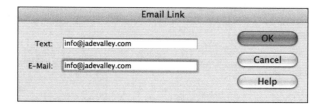

You've just created an email link. When users click email links, their default email editor (such as Outlook Express) opens with the correct email address specified in the To line. These email addresses also use the <a> tag, but they place the prefix `mailto:` before the email address. The code Dreamweaver writes for you during this step is as follows:

```
<a href="mailto:info@jadevalley.com">info@jadevalley.com</a>
```

By going through the main menu to establish the email link, you let Dreamweaver write the code for you. The text block you selected now looks just like a link, but when clicked, it opens the default email editor with `info@jadevalley.com` already in the To field, rather than opening a new Web page.

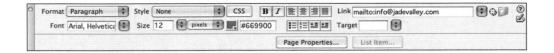

4. At the bottom of the page, drag to select the state initials **IN**, just before the **ZIP** code. In the Property inspector Link field, enter the following URL: http://www.in.gov.

This is a link to the official government Web site of the State of Indiana.

This is an absolute URL, easily recognizable because it specifies the protocol and domain. Interestingly, it does not specify a file name; that is, you don't see index.htm or home.htm at the end of the URL. Nearly all Web sites have a default home page that appears when users send requests with only the domain name.

5. Save about.htm.

You've added some links, but you're not yet finished with the file. In the next task, you'll lay out the contact information inside an HTML table.

Working with Tables

HTML tables were originally created as a means of presenting tabular data. However, in the early days of HTML development, designers had few options for creating page layouts, and as a result tables suddenly became the primary paradigm for Web layouts. Recently, CSS layers have replaced HTML tables as the preferred technology for page layouts; however, there's nothing wrong with using tables for their original purpose: laying out data.

Tables are created in HTML by means of one optional and three required tags. The required <table> tag encloses all the rows and cells within the table. Each row is created with the <tr> (table row) tag, and can contain one or more cells. Each table cell is marked with the <td> tag. The optional <th> (table header) tag can replace a <td> tag to create a header row or column. The following code is an example of a simple HTML table.

```
<table border="1">
  <tr>
    <td><p>Row 1, Column 1</p></td>
    <td><p>Row 1, Column 2</p></td>
  </tr>
  <tr>
    <td><p>Row 2, Column 1</p></td>
    <td><p>Row 2, Column 2</p></td>
  </tr>
</table>
```

This code produces the following table, as displayed in a browser.

Row 1, Column 1	Row 1, Column 2
Row 2, Column 1	Row 2, Column 2

After you've compared the code with the rendered table, notice two other things about the code. First, no tags exist to specify table columns. Rather, columns are built out of the <td> cells in each row; if each row has three <td> cells, then the table has three columns. In addition, notice that the only tag that has any output content is the <td> tag. The <table> and <tr> tags do not have any paragraphs or images.

Now that you understand the HTML code for tables, you can return to the Jade Valley Web site. In this task, you will create a table to better organize Jade Valley's contact information, so it will be easier to read. This figure shows the final table you'll be creating:

The Jade Valley team is always interested to hear your stories, requests, suggestions, and even complaints. We can be contacted as follows:

Phone and E-mail	Mailing Address
info@jadevalley.com (812) 555-1199	Jade Valley 696 Morgan Rd. Harmony, IN 47622

1. With about.htm open, position the insertion point right before the Phone and Email text, and press Enter/Return. Use the Up arrow to move the insertion point one line above the text block.

The new table will be placed where the insertion point is positioned on the document.

2. In the Common category of the Insert bar, click the Table button. The Table dialog appears.

Alternatively, you can insert a table using the Insert > Table command from the main menu.

3. Complete the Table dialog with the following settings: Rows: 2; Columns: 2; Table width: 95 percent; Border thickness: 1 pixel; Cell padding: 3; Cell spacing: 0; Header: Top; Summary: *This table contains Jade Valley contact information*. Click OK.

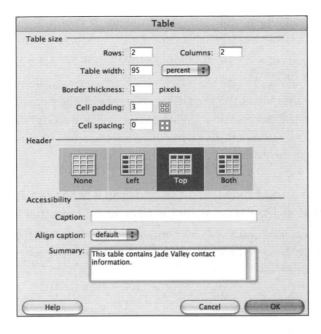

Most of the settings are self-explanatory, such as the number of rows and columns. A few might need further explanation.

The Table width can be measured in pixels (fixed width) or percentage (flexible width). If you know exactly how wide you want the table, choose fixed width. If you want the table to stretch to accommodate the screen, use a flexible width. You're specifying a flexible width in this case, but it won't really stretch to fill the screen, because this table is nested inside the layout table for this page, and the layout table uses fixed width.

The table's Border thickness is measured in pixels. The setting you're using, 1 pixel, creates a thin border around each of the cells.

Tip *To make the table appear without borders, set the thickness to 0. At the other extreme, if you increase the width of the border to a larger amount, say 6 or 12, the border is thicker and displays a 3-D bevel effect.*

Cell padding defines, in pixels, the amount of space between the content of the cell (such as text and images) and the edges of the cell. Designating a cell padding of 3 pixels prevents the contents of the cell from bumping up against the cell borders.

Cell spacing defines, in pixels, the amount of space that separates each cell from neighboring cells. A Cell spacing setting of 0 places the cells right next to one another. Any higher setting creates a gutter between the cells.

The table Header creates the optional (but recommended) `<th>` tags discussed earlier. The information placed in table headers helps visitors with all types of browsers, including screen readers, identify the content within the table. You can specify four types of table headers: None, Left, Top, or Both.

The table Summary lets you add an accessibility feature for your table. You can also use a Caption to enhance table accessibility. Unlike the Summary, the Caption appears in the document as a separate paragraph-like element before the table. Because you don't want a caption to appear in the document, leave the Caption blank.

4. Select the Phone and Email text block and drag it to the top-left cell of the table you just created. Do the same for the Mailing Address text block.

Because these two text blocks are table headers, as soon as you move them into the header cells their formatting changes (they will be centered and bold) to make them stand out as header text in the table.

Phone and E-mail	Mailing Address

5. Move the email address and the phone number to the cell below the Phone and Email header cell, and move the Jade Valley address to the cell below the Mailing Address header cell.

The content is now in the appropriate cells, but at this point still needs some formatting. Notice the extra line space between each line in the address. Each line is considered its own paragraph (`<p>`), which in HTML is considered a block-level element. Most browsers render block-level elements with some white space above and below them.

complaints, we can be contacted as follows: 95% (511) ▾

Phone and E-mail	Mailing Address
info@jadevalley.com (812) 555-1199	Jade Valley 696 Morgan Rd. Harmony, IN 47622

To resolve this problem, you need to strip the paragraph tags from all the lines after the first one. Then, you'll move the contents into the first line and separate them with a line break (`<br />`) character, which is not a block-level element.

6. Position the insertion point just before the (812) in the phone number line, and press Backspace (Windows) or Delete (Macintosh). Press Shift+Enter/Return.

Shift+Enter/Return creates a line break (<br />) character, moving the phone number to the line just below the email address.

Phone and E-mail	Mailing Address
info@jadevalley.com (812) 555-1199	Jade Valley 696 Morgan Rd. Harmony, IN 47622

7. Replace the paragraphs in the mailing address with line breaks to make that portion of the table appear as it does in the figure.

You're finished with the table.

Phone and E-mail	Mailing Address
info@jadevalley.com (812) 555-1199	Jade Valley 696 Morgan Rd. Harmony, IN 47622

8. Save the file.

Remember, if you want to preview the file in a browser, just press F12 (Windows) or Option+F12 (Macintosh).

Insert and Align Graphics

In this task, you'll insert a number of images into three pages in the site, and then format the images. Some of the pages have images in the main content area, and all the pages have images in the left column (Products, About, and so on).

In HTML code, images are inserted using the <img> tag, as shown in the following example:

```
<img src="foldername/filename.jpg" alt="This is a description or caption for the
image" />
```

The <img> tag has a number of attributes, but you'll only need to use two for every image: the src and alt attributes. The src attribute specifies the location of the graphic on the server, relative to the file into which it's inserted. The alt attribute, as you've seen in previous lessons, provides a textual description of the image, useful for users who access Web pages with nongraphical browsers, including screen readers.

Note *The <img> tag is known as an empty tag. That is, it does not have an opening and closing tag, as does, for example, the <p> </p> tag pairing. In the latest version of the HTML standard, XHTML, empty tags are not allowed. To close these empty elements, add a space and a slash before the closing angle bracket, as in the following examples: <img />, <br />, and <hr />.*

Dreamweaver writes all this code for you when you insert an image. Nevertheless, it's a good idea to maintain at least a working familiarity with HTML, even if you're using a visual editor such as Dreamweaver.

1. With about.htm open, in the left column of the page, select and delete both the PRODUCTS label and the banana image right below it.

You inserted these two images as placeholders when you created the template in the previous lesson. Now that you're working on about.htm, the first thing you need to do is remove the placeholders and replace them with the appropriate graphics for this page.

You can remove and insert any content (whether text or images) freely because you designated this area as an editable region when you set up the template.

2. Position the cursor at the top of the left column. In the Common category of the Insert menu, choose Image from the Images button's drop-down menu.

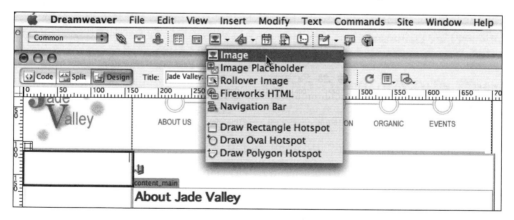

The Insert menu contains dozens of prebuilt HTML objects. They are stored in different categories, and Common is the default. Other categories include Layout (tables and layers), Forms (forms, text fields, and Submit buttons), and Text (text formatting features such as bolding, as well as special characters such as © and ™).

Tip *Most elements in the Insert bar can also be found in the Insert menu. For example, you can insert an image from the main menu by choosing Insert > Image.*

3. In the Select Image Source dialog, navigate to label_about.gif in the images folder. Click Select (Windows) or Choose (Macintosh). In the accessibility dialog that pops up, enter *Jade Valley: About.* as the Alternate text.

Use the Insert Image Source dialog to locate the image you need for the page. Check the Preview Images checkbox to preview the image you want to insert. Notice that the URL we have is a relative URL; it specifies the location of the file relative to the page in which it's inserted.

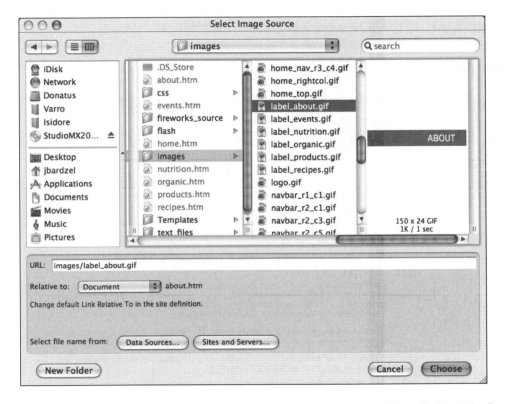

The image appears in the page and is right-aligned, as was the image it's replacing. That's the alignment you want for this image, so leave it as is.

4. Use the Right arrow to move the cursor to the right of the ABOUT label, and press Enter. Repeat Steps 2 and 3 to insert corn.jpg just below the label. Enter *Ad: Natural growing methods yield tastier corn.* as the alternate text.

The look of the template is preserved, but you've given the page a new identity by replacing these two graphics.

5. To view the page in a browser, click anywhere in the page and press F12 (Windows) or Option+F12 (Macintosh). When you're finished, return to Dreamweaver and save and close about.htm.

The file about.htm is finished. In the process of developing this page, you've built a new page based on a template, worked with text, established various types of hyperlinks, created and formatted a table, and inserted and aligned images. These are core Dreamweaver skills that you'll use over and over again.

Even though about.htm is finished, two more pages still need changes.

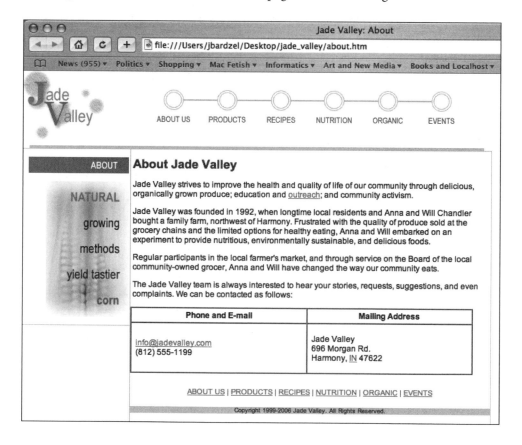

6. Open products.htm. Remove the banana photo in the promotional column and replace it with peppers.jpg. Enter *Ad: From our fields to your table within a day.* as the alternate text.

You don't need to replace the page graphic—PRODUCTS—because the correct one for this page was used in the template and already appears.

7. Position the cursor after the word "slimming" at the end of the last paragraph, and press Enter/Return once. Insert bread_girl.jpg. After the new image is in place, click the Align Center button in the Property inspector, and enter *Girl with bread.* as the alternate text.

You can't center-align an image left-to-right in HTML using the <img> tag alone, because its align attribute doesn't include horizontal centering. However, if the image is inside a <p> tag, you can apply centering to the <p> tag, and if that <p> tag contains only an image (as in this case), then the image is center-aligned.

> **Note** *You can also align objects with CSS. In fact, the alignment options are much more robust in CSS than they are in HTML. The only downside to aligning objects in CSS is that it takes an extra step up front. The extra setup is usually worth it, especially for large sites. Because this site is small, you can stick to the Property inspector, which aligns using HTML.*

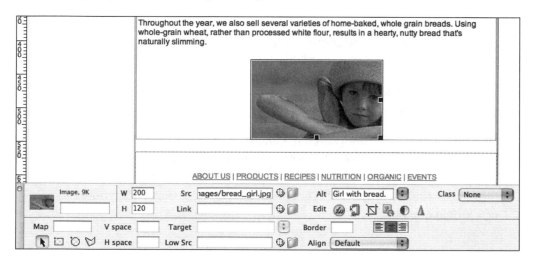

8. Move the cursor to the left of the first word of the first paragraph in the main content section (just before "Jade Valley grows plants..."). Insert zucchini.jpg into the page. Enter *Summer squash.* as the alternate text.

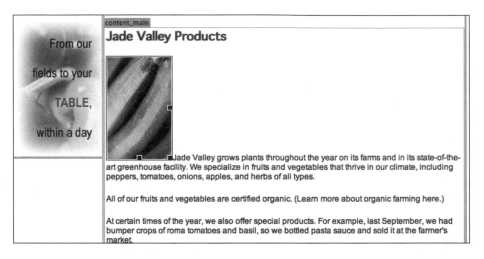

The image appears above the content block, right below the page heading. The alignment leaves something to be desired. By default, text doesn't wrap around images, wasting considerable screen space and pushing your content offscreen.

Note *While most users tolerate some vertical scrolling in Web pages, usability tests have shown that any content that must be scrolled to be seen is much more likely to be overlooked or ignored than content that appears without scrolling.*

It's not always possible to prevent pages from scrolling, but you can wrap text around images to make better use of screen space

Tip *Designers use the phrase "below the fold" to refer to offscreen content that can only be seen if the user scrolls down the page. The phrase is a reference to traditional newspapers, where the day's most important content is placed above the fold on the first page—the portion of a newspaper visible from newsstands or vending machines.*

9. With the cucumber image still selected (click to select it, if necessary), choose Right from the Align drop-down menu in the Property inspector.

The Align drop-down menu provides access to all the values of the <img> tag's align attribute. Many options are available. Two of the options, Left and Right, enable text wrapping.

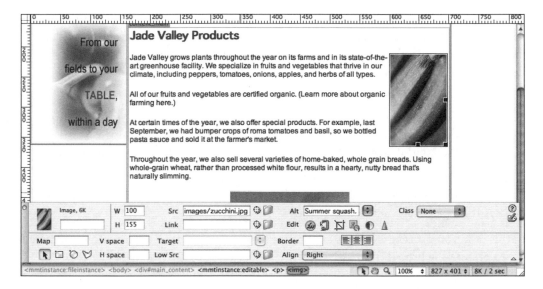

10. Select the word "here" at the end of second paragraph and create a hyperlink to organic.htm in the site.

You can use any method you learned earlier to create this link. This step completes the development of products.htm.

11. Press F12 (Windows) or Option+F12 (Macintosh) to preview the page. Return to Dreamweaver. Save and close the document.

Click the hyperlink you created in Step 10. It should take you to organic.htm, where visitors can learn more about Jade Valley's organic farming approach.

Creating List Items

HTML gives you the ability to create different types of lists. You can create numbered lists (known in HTML as ordered lists) or bullet lists (known in HTML as unordered lists) to organize content. You can even create lists inside of other lists—but we won't do so in this lesson.

All lists are constructed from two sets of tags. First, the entire list is enclosed inside an <ol> (ordered list) or <ul> (unordered list) tag. Then, each item inside the list is enclosed inside a <li> (list item) tag. Most lists have multiple <li> tags, because they have multiple items. The following code sample shows a basic bullet list.

```
<ul>
  <li>Bullet point 1</li>
  <li>Bullet point 2</li>
  <li>Bullet point 3</li>
</ul>
```

To convert this bullet list into a numbered list, simply replace <ul> and </ul> with <ol> and </ol>, respectively.

In this task, you'll format the steps for a recipe for cinnamon baked apples into a numbered list to present the procedures more clearly.

1. Open recipes.htm. Select the text block from "Preheat oven to 350° F or 175° C" to the text block "Bake apples in oven for 15 minutes, until golden brown."

1 teaspoon ground cinnamon

Directions

Preheat oven to 350° F or 175° C

Core, but do not slice, apples.

Melt butter in microwave.

Mix brown sugar and cinnamon with butter.

Brush cinnamon mixture onto each apple.

Bake apples in oven for 15 minutes, until golden brown

Variation: Try substituting tart Granny Smith apples instead.

The first step in turning any existing text into a numbered or bulleted list is to make certain that each text element is in its own paragraph.

Conveniently, when you copied and pasted the content into this page earlier in the lesson, the baking procedures were already in their own separate paragraphs, so you don't have to do anything additional to get ready for the list creation.

2. In the Property inspector, click the Ordered List button. You can also choose Text › List › Ordered List.

Dreamweaver automatically formats the selected text block into a numbered list. Behind the scenes, it creates both the <ol> tag and a series of <li> elements.

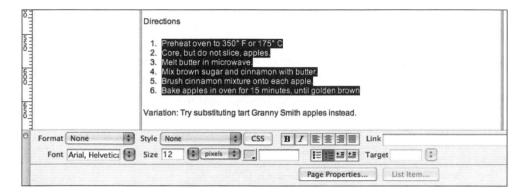

Tip *You can use the List Properties dialog (Text › List › Properties) to specify the numbering system you want to use for your ordered list or the symbols to use for the unordered lists. This system is especially handy when you need nested ordered lists or unordered lists and you need to distinguish the main list from the nested list. For more advanced list formatting, you can use the List category of the CSS Style Definition dialog, where you can specify bullet size, type, and position, or even use a custom image for the bullets.*

3. In split view, examine the HTML code to see the ordered list you just created.

As shown in the figure, the list items are enclosed in the open and closing <ol> tags, with an <li> tag in front of each list item and an </li> tag after each list item.

```
95    <p>1 teaspoon ground cinnamon </p>
96    <p>Directions</p>
97    <ol>
98      <li>Preheat oven to 350&deg; F or 175&deg; C </li>
99      <li>Core, but do not slice, apples. </li>
100     <li>Melt butter in microwave. </li>
101     <li>Mix brown sugar and cinnamon with butter.</li>
102     <li>Brush cinnamon mixture onto each apple. </li>
103     <li>Bake apples in oven for 15 minutes, until golden brown</li>
104   </ol>
105   <p>Variation: Try substituting tart Granny Smith apples instead.</p>
106   <p>If you have a recipe that you'd like to share, please contact us! </p>
107   <!-- InstanceEndEditable -->
```

4. Save the document.

You still have a few more things to do to finish recipes.htm.

Finishing the Recipes Page

You were exposed to line breaks earlier in this lesson, when you formatted Jade Valley's contact information in the table cell on about.htm. In HTML, line breaks are created with the <br /> tag. In this task, you'll reformat the ingredients for the Cinnamon Baked Apples recipe, so that they're listed one after the other. To do this, you'll replace the paragraphs tags and separate the lines using <br /> tags.

1. Position the insertion point just before "2 tablespoons butter." Press Backspace/Delete. Press Shift+Enter/Return to create a line break.

As before, you're collapsing two paragraphs into one, and then inserting a line break between them.

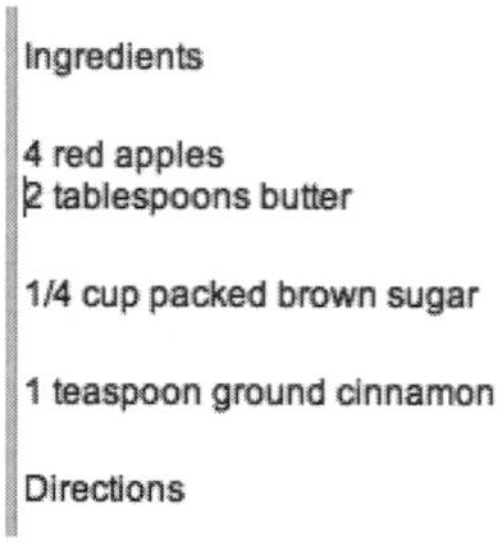

Ingredients

4 red apples
2 tablespoons butter

1/4 cup packed brown sugar

1 teaspoon ground cinnamon

Directions

2. Reformat the next two lines (sugar and cinnamon) in the same way.

The ingredients should now appear as shown in the figure, which is displayed in split view so you can also see the HTML code for the list.

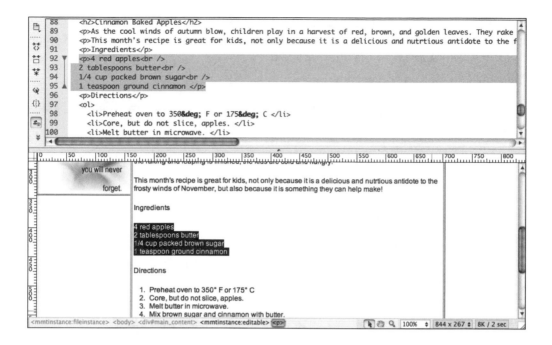

```
88    <h2>Cinnamon Baked Apples</h2>
89    <p>As the cool winds of autumn blow, children play in a harvest of red, brown, and golden leaves. They rake
90    <p>This month's recipe is great for kids, not only because it is a delicious and nutrtious antidote to the f
91    <p>Ingredients</p>
92    <p>4 red apples<br />
93    2 tablespoons butter<br />
94    1/4 cup packed brown sugar<br />
95    1 teaspoon ground cinnamon </p>
96    <p>Directions</p>
97    <ol>
98       <li>Preheat oven to 350&deg; F or 175&deg; C </li>
99       <li>Core, but do not slice, apples. </li>
100      <li>Melt butter in microwave. </li>
```

you will never
forget.

This month's recipe is great for kids, not only because it is a delicious and nutrtious antidote to the frosty winds of November, but also because it is something they can help make!

Ingredients

4 red apples
2 tablespoons butter
1/4 cup packed brown sugar
1 teaspoon ground cinnamon

Directions

1. Preheat oven to 350° F or 175° C
2. Core, but do not slice, apples.
3. Melt butter in microwave.
4. Mix brown sugar and cinnamon with butter.

`<mmtinstance:fileinstance> <body> <div#main_content> <mmtinstance:editable> <p>`   100%   844 x 267   8K / 2 sec

3. Press and drag to select "Ingredients," and make it Bold in the Property inspector. Make the same formatting changes for "Directions."

At this point, you need to fine-tune the overall presentation of the recipes.htm page by formatting these three text elements on the page. The new formatting attributes make these elements stand out, which makes the document easier to read.

4. Select the word "contact" at the end of the content and create a hyperlink to about.htm.

You're getting close to finishing the development of this page. By creating a hyperlink to about.htm, you're making it easy for users who visit Jade Valley's Web site to immediately go to the section they need without using the navigation bar at the top of the page

5. Remove the PRODUCTS label and the banana photo and replace them with label_recipes.gif and apples.jpg. Enter *Jade Valley Recipes.* and *Fall harvest apples make delicious snacks.* as the alternate text, respectively.

You've performed this task on several occasions. Refer to the steps earlier in the lesson if you need help.

6. Position the cursor just before the word "Ingredients." Insert the image green_apple.jpg at the top of the main content column of the page and Right-align it. Enter *Green Apples.* as the alternate text.

This concludes the development of recipes.htm.

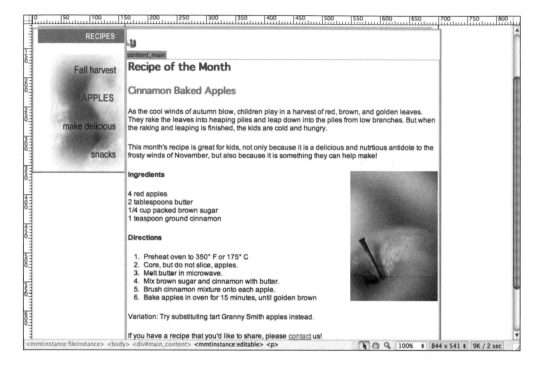

7. Press F12 (Windows) or Option+F12 (Macintosh) to preview the page in a browser. Return to Dreamweaver. Save and close recipes.htm.

Modifying Templates

All the pages for the Jade Valley site are created, and you're almost ready to launch the site! But—as so often happens—at the last minute you realize that you need to make a few improvements to the site as a whole.

- The Jade Valley logo at the top does not link to the home page

- You want to add a hyperlink to the words "Jade Valley" in the footer, which will take visitors back to the home page.

If you have a page open, you'll notice that none of these changes is in an editable region of the page; they're all locked. Actually, this is good news; it means that after you make the changes to the template itself, the changes will ripple through all the pages based on the template. You won't need to go through every page and make each change one at a time—a tedious and time-consuming job that's likely to create errors.

1. Open jadevalley_template.dwt.

Remember, jadevalley_template_main.dwt is located in the Templates folder, which you can access via the Files panel.

2. Select the Jade Valley logo at the top-left corner. Use the Property inspector's Link field to create a hyperlink to home.htm.

The hyperlink makes it possible for visitors to return to the home page of the site with a simple mouse click. Linking the logos on Web pages helps both usability (users expect this functionality) and branding.

3. Choose File › Save. In the Update Template Files dialog that appears, click Update. When the Update Pages dialog appears, click Close.

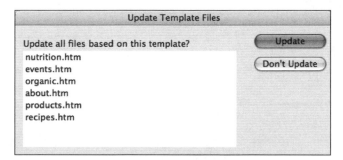

Any time you change a template, Dreamweaver prompts you to update all the pages based on the template. By clicking Update, Dreamweaver automatically rewrites the code behind the scenes of all the dependent HTML files.

Once Dreamweaver has completed the updates, it displays the Update Pages dialog, which summarizes the changes and the affected files. Use this dialog to verify that all the pages you want to update were updated. This dialog is especially useful if you have a site that uses multiple templates.

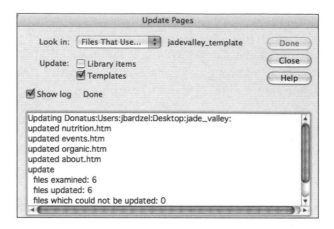

4. Open any page in the Files panel. Press F12 (Windows) or Option+F12 (Macintosh) to preview the page in a browser. Click the logo to test the change you made in the template.

When you click the logo, you should be taken to home.htm.

5. Back in Dreamweaver, with the template open, select the text "Jade Valley" in the footer and link it to home.htm as well.

This link also enhances branding, because, among other things, the hyperlink underlines and displays the company name in a bright color.

ABOUT US | PRODUCTS | RECIPES | NUTRITION | ORGANIC | EVENTS

Copyright 1999-2006 Jade Valley. All Rights Reserved.

6. Choose File > Save and save the document. Click Update to apply all the changes you made to the template to the rest of the site.

Again, the documents based on a template are not updated until you save the template.

7. Open any page from the Files panel and preview the page in a browser. Explore the site in its complete form.

The benefit of the workflow you used for these six lessons are now visible. You created the original design in Fireworks, because Fireworks is an ideal application for creative problem-solving, thanks to its always editable vector graphics. When you were happy with the design, you optimized it (in more ways than one) for export to HTML. You then reconstructed the design in Dreamweaver, cleaning up the HTML and perfecting the basic document. With the HTML document in place, you finalized the design using the flexible and powerful CSS. You created a Dreamweaver template to stabilize the design. With these assets in place, as you've seen in this lesson, it takes just minutes to create new pages and make sitewide changes. Better still, the site is now easily maintained, whether you need to change the text or the look of the content within a page, or want to give the whole site a face-lift.

Integrating Macromedia Fireworks, Macromedia Dreamweaver, and CSS has numerous advantages, ranging from initial development to long-term maintenance. The key is using each application/technology in a way that plays to its strengths. Fireworks is great for design and fair at generating HTML. Dreamweaver is outstanding at working with HTML, but as a design tool it's less robust than Fireworks. Both Fireworks' and Dreamweaver's design features typically affect only the active document, whereas CSS can be used for formatting content across an entire site. But designing CSS is often an abstract and piecemeal process; designing CSS works better when you know in advance how you want the site to look. The workflow you've used in the book thus far lets you take advantage of each application's strengths and minimize its native limitations.

What You Have Learned

In this lesson, you have:

- Created HTML pages based on an existing template (pages 169–174)
- Established three types of hyperlinks on a page: email links, links to a page within a site, and links to an outside site (pages 174–177)
- Created and formatted an HTML table (pages 177–181)
- Inserted and aligned graphic assets (pages 181–187)
- Learned the difference between ordered and unordered lists (pages 188–189)
- Created an ordered list (pages 188–189)
- Added line breaks (pages 190–192)
- Updated multiple pages simultaneously by modifying their parent template (pages 192–195)

Project 1: The Jade Valley Web Site

Part 3: Flash

7 Creating a Flash Movie

Macromedia Flash 8 is a powerful authoring tool in which you can create simple Web animations, Web-based software applications, multimedia experiences, and business applications that work on- or offline. Flash's capabilities are deep and diverse; fortunately, it's not too hard to get started with simple Flash projects.

Flash provides easy-to-use vector drawing tools for creating graphics. You can integrate these vector graphics with video, bitmaps, and sounds created in other applications.

Perhaps the easiest starting point in Flash development is the creation of animations. With Flash, you can create the illusion of motion by placing content in successive frames, which pass by so quickly that the eye perceives motion. Flash's authoring environment is based on the metaphor of frames in a movie reel; you place content in each frame, and when the Flash movie plays back, it proceeds through the frames until it reaches the end.

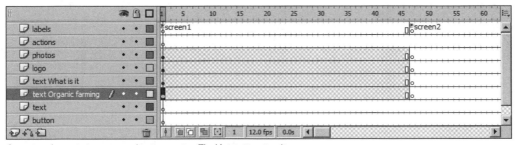

Organize elements in space and in time, using Flash's intuitive timeline.

Sometimes you'll want the user to have some control over the content. That is, rather than having the user sit passively and watch an animation, you might want the user to click buttons, drag objects, or interact with the keyboard—and have the Flash movie react to these actions. Flash comes with a powerful scripting language called ActionScript, which can be used to give the user control over the movie.

In this and the next lesson, you'll explore the capabilities of Flash by creating a simple three-screen Flash movie. It will incorporate a handful of animations as well as simple interactivity. Along the way, you'll work with vector art, text, and imported bitmaps.

What You Will Learn

In this lesson, you will:

- Create new layers in the timeline
- Insert new frames and keyframes
- Move text and graphic objects to appropriate layers
- Become familiar with the Library
- Import bitmap graphics to the Library
- Convert an existing graphic to a button symbol

Approximate Time

This lesson takes approximately 90 minutes to complete.

Lesson Files

Starting Files:

Lesson07/Start/logo.tif
Lesson07/Start/mushrooms.jpg
Lesson07/Start/peppers.jpg
Lesson07/Start/pg2.txt
Lesson07/Start/pg3.txt
Lesson07/Start/squash.jpg

Completed Files:

Lesson07/Complete/organic_farming.fla

Introducing Flash's Workspace

Although much of Flash's interface is similar to that of Fireworks or Freehand—a Document window, Property inspector, Tools panel, and a group of panels on the right—some new Flash users complain that Flash's interface overwhelms them. Taking a moment now to glance over the interface can help clarify what each part does.

1. Open Macromedia Flash 8.

Flash opens, and the Start page appears by default.

2. In the Start page's Create New category, click the Flash Document link.

A blank document with an empty timeline opens.

3. Take a few moments to explore the interface.

Notice that clicking a panel name (for example, Actions or Components) expands or collapses that panel. Notice also that as you roll the mouse over certain elements, a Tooltip pops up after a moment, indicating the name of the element (for example, if you roll over the "A" in the Tools panel, you'll see "Text tool (T)" appear in a Tooltip).

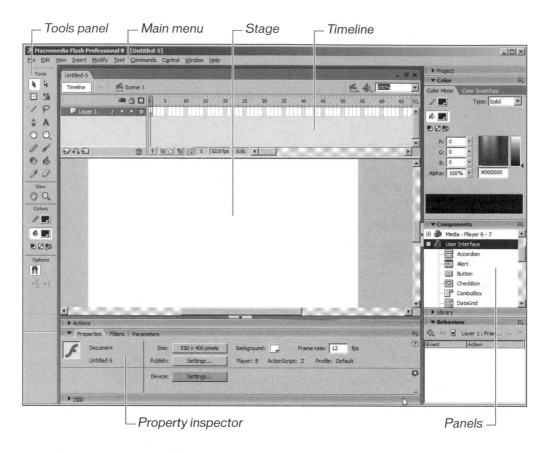

The following list summarizes the main components of the Flash authoring environment.

- **Main menu:** Located across the top in the workspace, the main menu contains most of the commands used in Flash.

- **Tools panel:** The Tools panel contains a set of tools used to create and edit vector art and other screen elements. Located on the left side of the workspace, the Tools panel is divided in to four sections: Tools, View, Color, and Options.

- **Property inspector:** The Property inspector provides context-sensitive information and options for the active tool or interface element. You can access and change the most commonly used attributes of a document in the Property inspector.

- **Timeline:** The timeline is a vital organizational tool in Flash. The timeline organizes and controls a movie's content over time. The passage of time is measured in frames (the small rectangles that fill the timeline), while the stacking order of screen objects is controlled by the layers within the timeline (only one layer appears in the timeline in the figure).

- **Stage:** All the graphic elements that make up the movie are placed and displayed on the stage. The stage represents the appearance of the movie within a given frame. You can control the size and the color of the stage using the Property inspector.

- **Panels:** Located by default on the right side of the workspace, panels provide interfaces for handling specific tasks, such as mixing colors or aligning screen elements. You can find a complete list of panels in the Window menu.

Introducing Basic Flash Architecture

Before you jump in and start building Flash movies, you should think ahead and try to anticipate how you want to structure, or architect, a movie.

Note *You might find it helpful to view the completed version of the Flash movie that you'll be working on in this and the next lesson. Doing so should give you a clearer idea of the different elements, as well as the timing of different animations and the functionality of the buttons. You can see the final version of the Flash movie by double-clicking organic_farming.swf in the Lesson08/Complete folder.*

A completed Flash document typically has the following elements:

- **Timeline:** The sequence of frames in which you specify how the stage should look at any given moment

- **Layer stack:** Virtually all graphic applications organize the stacking order of screen elements using layers, and Flash is no exception. But Flash handles layers in a slightly unusual way: layers are a part of the timeline. This timeline enables developers to handle various screen elements differently as they change over time.

- **The Library, symbols, and instances:** As in Fireworks, Flash symbols are reusable elements, often with special capabilities. Flash symbols include static graphics, buttons, and movie clips. Symbols are stored in the Library, and when you place a symbol on the stage, you're creating an instance of that symbol.

While it's often impossible to know in advance exactly how the timeline, layer stack, and Library will look at the end of the project, you can and should try to anticipate how they'll look. Architectural decisions are usually made at the beginning of a project, and a bad decision can have long-term consequences.

Our project will contain three screens, so you can probably guess that these screens, representing different states of the Flash movie over time, will somehow be tracked using the timeline. Some of the graphic elements appear on more than one screen; that is, they are reused. And when something is reused, you should be thinking about the Library. If you are totally new to Flash, you might not be able to anticipate more, and that's OK. The important thing is that you start thinking about how Flash organizes content differently than print layout tools. Whereas print uses a page-based structure, Flash uses a more sophisticated timeline structure.

In the upcoming tasks, you'll prepare the Flash stage and timeline in preparation for importing various graphic elements into a layer stack that makes sense for the content. In this lesson, all the graphic elements will remain static; that is, you will not add any animation or interactivity to your Flash document. You'll add animation and interactivity to your Flash movie in Lesson 8, *Creating Animation and Interactivity*.

Preparing the Stage

As with any authoring tool, setting up the page to suit the task is important. Before you begin working with the new Flash document, you'll need to specify the size of your stage so that it fits in the Organic Farming page in the Jade Valley Web site.

1. Check the size of your stage in the Property inspector.

Note *If you don't see the Property inspector, choose Window > Properties, and it will appear below the stage.*

The size of the stage is shown in the Property inspector. You can see the pixel dimensions of the stage in the Size button. The factory-set default for new documents is 550 by 400 pixels, which is what you want in this case, so you can keep this setting. If you see a different size, click the Size button and enter 550 pixels as the width and 400 pixels as the height in the Document Properties dialog.

Working with the Timeline

As you create the new Flash document, you'll work with the timeline to organize the various elements of the document and plan the content changes over time to create a movie. First, you'll need to organize the project so that you can identify the individual components more easily and work with each discrete element independently to animate them.

If you're new to Flash, you should think of it like any film you might watch. The individual rectangles in the timeline represent frames, and each frame contains information about the appearance of the movie for the instant the frame is active. Then Flash moves on to the next frame and shows its content, and so on, until it gets through the movie.

Flash has two kinds of frames: static frames and keyframes. A keyframe is a frame in which content is able to change. Something can move, be added to, removed from, or change appearance on the stage in a keyframe. In fact, one of the most important things to understand about working in Flash is this axiom: "All changes occur in keyframes." The first frame of every layer in the timeline is a keyframe. A static frame is a frame whose contents are the same as the content in the preceding keyframe (that is, the closest keyframe to its left).

Consider this example. Imagine you wanted a circle to suddenly appear in an animation, but after it appeared, it would just sit on the stage. To make the circle appear, you would create a keyframe and draw a circle on the stage. Now remember, each frame—even keyframes—last only a fraction of a second, before Flash moves on. But you want that circle to last for several seconds. The solution is to add a couple dozen static frames after the keyframe, all of which would show the circle. Now imagine that after these seconds expire, you want the circle to disappear. You could achieve this by creating another keyframe and deleting the circle from the stage.

The following figures show the timeline and stage with two different frames selected: Frame 1 and Frame 12. What do you think the stage would look like with Frame 48 selected?

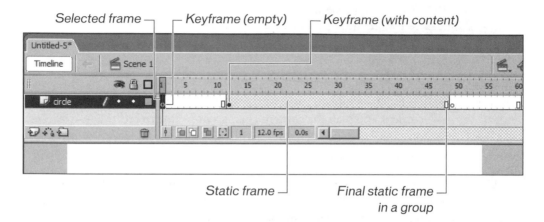

Selected frame — ┌─ Keyframe (empty) ┌─ Keyframe (with content)

Static frame ┘   Final static frame ┘
                      in a group

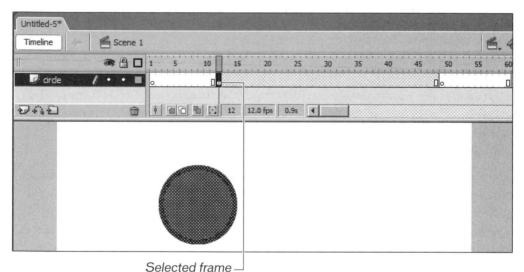

Selected frame ┘

The major components of the timeline are layers, frames, and the frame indicator. One way to think of layers is to imagine multiple filmstrips stacked on top of each other, each containing a different image that appears on the stage. Like films, Flash movies divide lengths of time into frames. The frame indicator is the red rectangle above the timeline that represents the active frame. You can drag the frame indicator back and forth to preview an animation.

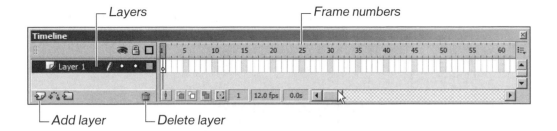

Layers

Frame numbers

Add layer

Delete layer

This timeline reveals that the document so far has only one layer, named Layer 1. Clicking any frame in the timeline takes you directly to that frame and displays its contents on the stage.

As mentioned earlier, layers allow developers to specify the layer stacking order, which determines the visibility of elements relative to one another. Specifically, if two opaque elements overlap, the one on the higher layer will obscure the one on the lower layer. In addition, isolating elements by organizing them into separate layers is critical when it comes to animating the elements independently.

Clearly, one layer isn't going to be enough. You'll need to add some new layers. After the new layers are created, you'll move elements out of their current layer—Layer 1—and into one of the new ones.

1. Click the Insert Layer button on the bottom of the timeline to create a new layer.

This step adds a new layer directly above the selected layer (Layer 1 in this case). When you click the button, you see a new layer with a default layer name (most likely Layer 2) appear above Layer 1.

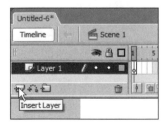

Notice that the new layer has only an empty keyframe in Frame 1.

2. Add six more new layers above Layer 2.

You'll need nine layers in this timeline to create the Organic Farming Flash movie. You already have two layers (Layer 1 and Layer 2) in the timeline, so you need to add six more. You'll then have layers from Layer 1 to Layer 8.

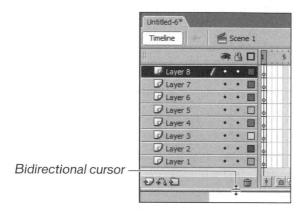

Bidirectional cursor

The names of layers are currently not very descriptive. You can rename them so that you can tell which content will go to which layer.

3. **One at a time, double-click each layer name, type in a new name (see the following), and press Enter or Return. Rename the new layers so that they read as follows from top to bottom:**

labels

actions

photos

logo

text What is it

text Organic farming

text

button

The layer names are descriptive enough that you understand which elements will go where. Some of the layers—in particular the actions and labels layers—might not have an immediately obvious purpose now. As you'll see later, the actions layer will be used to hold the ActionScript that will make the button functional. The labels layer will hold bookmark-like frame labels, which will make it easier to write the ActionScript for the button.

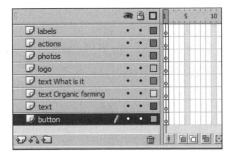

4. Choose File > Save in the main menu to save the file. Browse to the jade_valley/ flash folder in the Jade Valley Web site. Name the file *organic_farming.fla*. Click Save.

The file is saved as a Flash FLA (pronounced "flahh") file.

One aspect of Flash that confuses new users is that two different file types are associated with Flash: the FLA and the SWF file formats. Flash authoring files (FLA files) are used when you're working on the files in Macromedia Flash. When you choose File > Save, Flash will save your document in this file format, adding the extension name, FLA. Flash documents, which have the FLA filename extension, contain all the information required to develop, design, and test interactive content. To open a FLA, you must have Macromedia Flash. You've been working in a FLA ever since you opened Flash and chose Create New Flash document.

Flash Player files (SWF files, pronounced "swiff") are the output files for the free Flash Player that the end user actually sees, often (but not necessarily) in a Web browser. In other words, you work on FLA files, and when you're finished, you publish and distribute them as SWF files.

Lengthening a Movie with Static Frames

To plan for the changes of the movie over time, you need to add frames. Before adding frames, you at least need an estimate of the total run time of the movie (the time it takes for the movie to run from Frame 1 to the last frame in the timeline). By default, Flash plays 12 frames per second, or fps; therefore, if you want to create a movie that runs for 5 seconds, you'll need approximately 60 frames in the timeline. The movie as it stands is one frame long; the movie would take about .08 seconds to play through.

Tip *You can change a movie's frame rate by choosing Modify > Document from the main menu. The default rate of 12 is a good bet for most Web animations, though.*

The Organic Farming Flash movie doesn't have an exact estimate of the running time, because it will stop for the user to press the Next button before it moves on to the next page. But it does have some animations, so you can estimate the length of the animations in seconds, multiply the number of seconds you want the movie to run by 12, and create that many new frames. The length of the animations will be about 8 seconds, so go ahead and add 93 more frames to the movie.

1. Verify that you can see all eight layers in the timeline.

Remember, you can always drag the divider between the timeline and the Document window to make extra room.

2. Point the cursor at Frame 96 in the timeline, scrolling to the right if necessary to see it. In a single motion, press and drag to select Frame 96 in all eight layers.

Frame 96 in all eight layers is selected.

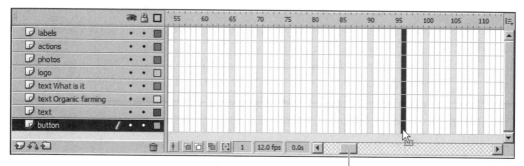

Scroll to view frames offscreen ⌐

3. Choose Insert > Timeline > Frame to insert frames up to and including Frame 96.

This step will insert (static) frames from Frame 2 to Frame 96 in all the layers in the timeline. The frame indicator is now in Frame 96. If any of the earlier keyframes had content, the subsequent static frames would have gray shading. Each of those frames would contain the same content as its preceding keyframe. Static frames that have no content are white.

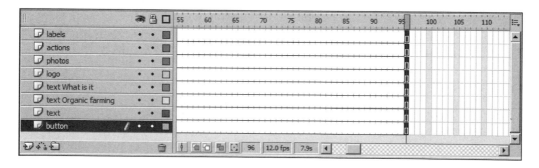

Creating Temporal Structure with Keyframes and Labels

The movie is 96 frames long, and therefore it lasts 8 seconds. Currently the movie doesn't actually do anything. As mentioned earlier, to make things happen in Flash, you create keyframes and change the appearance, location, or presence of the objects within the frames on the stage.

In this task, you'll work on the overall temporal structure of the movie, by making the timeline more clearly reflect the three screens that represent the sections of our movie. As a part of this process, you'll insert two keyframes in the labels layer, which you'll use to create bookmark-like labels to demarcate those portions of the timeline. The first of the two keyframes you'll create will identify the frame where the second screen begins, and the second keyframe you'll create will identify where the third screen begins. You don't have to worry about creating a keyframe for the first screen, because the first frame of every layer is a keyframe.

1. In the timeline, click Frame 47 of the labels layer and choose Insert > Timeline > Keyframe.

Keyframes are represented as a frame with a circle. The circle is hollow as long as the keyframe has no visible content (such as vector art, a digital photograph, or some text). A keyframe without content is called a blank keyframe. A keyframe with content has a solid black circle, and the circle appears against a shaded background.

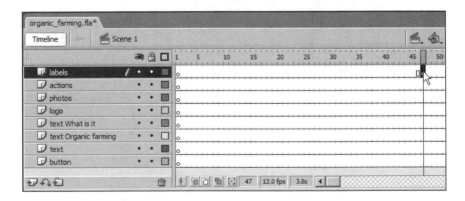

You add a keyframe to Frame 47 because an animation is going to separate the first and second screens, and it will take almost 4 seconds.

2. Select Frame 67 of the labels layer and press F6 to insert a new keyframe.

The contents need to change again in Frame 67, at which point the third screen should become active.

In the next lesson, you'll stop this Flash movie after it plays through Frame 47. The movie will also stop in Frame 67, where the third screen appears. To proceed, the user will have to click a button. Giving buttons this functionality requires some scripting. Although the script needed for this kind of interactivity is quite simple, you'll need to specify where the various screens are in the timeline. Because each screen is (or will be) associated with a given keyframe (Frames 1, 47, and 67), you'll need a means of pointing to those frames as having special significance.

You can achieve this goal in Flash by giving the desired frames frame labels, which are like bookmarks that enable Flash to jump to the desired frame. You'll add some frame labels next.

3. Click to select Frame 1 of the labels layer.

The movie has three primary screens, so you'll label each one in turn.

4. In the Frame Label field of the Property inspector, type *screen1* and press Return/Enter.

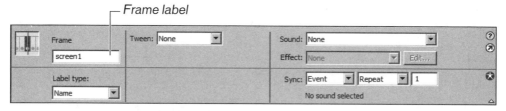

If you can't see the Property inspector, choose Window > Properties.

In the timeline, you'll see a red flag added in Frame 1 of the labels layer, which indicates that this frame is labeled. The red flag is accompanied by the frame label.

5. Repeat Steps 3 and 4 to label Frame 47 *screen2* and Frame 67 *screen3*.

As before, the red flag and label appear in the timeline.

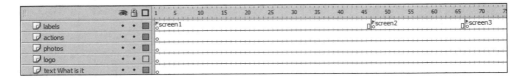

The labels now represent where each of the screens should be.

Adding Content Across Layers

Our movie will consist of a number of graphical and textual elements. Some of these elements should persist across different screens (for example, the Jade Valley logo appears in the top-left corner in the second and third screens); some elements need to be animated (including some of the text elements); others just come and go. Flash makes it possible for you to implement these features and functionalities using the timeline. In this task, you'll move the various elements into their own layers in the timeline, which makes it possible to animate and control each element independently of the others.

1. In the timeline, click Frame 1 of the logo layer. Choose Import > Import to Stage.... Navigate to the Start folder of this lesson, select the file logo.tif from the folder, and click Open to insert the image.

The logo appears on the stage. Notice that the keyframe in Frame 1 of the logo layer is now a solid circle, and that all the static frames that follow it are gray. You know that the logo is in the new layer.

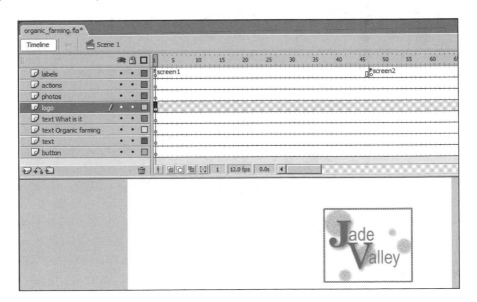

2. With the logo selected, use the Property inspector to set its X value to **390** and its Y value to **265** to position it in the lower-right corner.

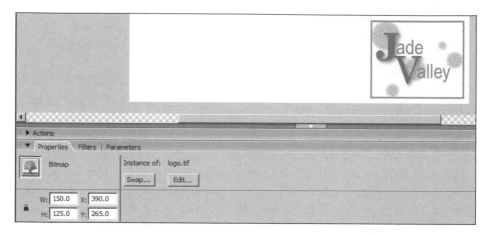

Next, you'll add text for a slogan to the stage. Each text block will be put in its own layer. You can then animate the text block independent of all the other screen elements.

3. In the timeline, click Frame 1 of the text Organic Farming layer. Select the Text tool from the Tools panel. In the Property inspector, select Arial as the Font, style it Bold and Italic, and set the Font Size to 28. Make sure the text is Left-aligned. Next, choose the Text (fill) color tool and set the color value to *#639C00*.

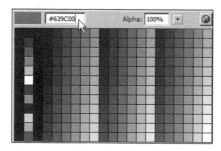

4. Click the middle of the stage and type *Organic Farming*.

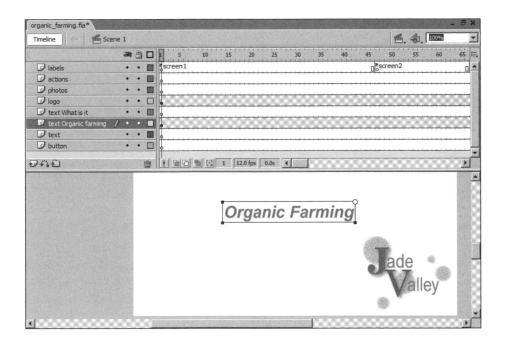

5. Repeat steps 3 and 4 to create another text block, *What is it?* In the timeline, click Frame 1 of the text What is it layer. Give the new text block the following attributes: Arial, Bold, Size 28, Left-aligned and #993300 for the color.

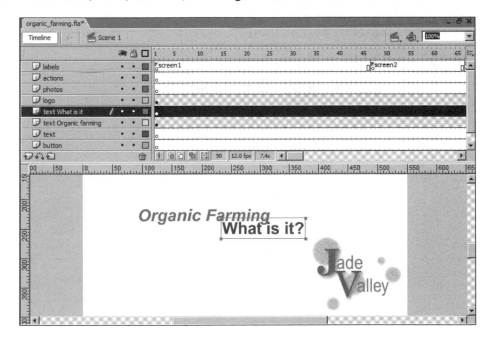

Double-check the timeline to make sure the content ended up in the correct layer; look for a solid-circle keyframe and gray shading in the frames.

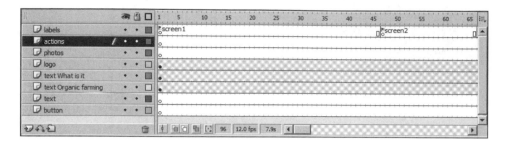

Importing Bitmap Graphics

In this task, you'll learn how to place a bitmap image on the stage and position it. The ability to import both bitmap and vector graphics and incorporate them into Flash movies is very powerful.

1. **Click Frame 1 of the photos layer.**

Any time you import, add, change, or remove content to or from the stage, you must first select the keyframe in which the change is to take place.

2. **Choose File > Import > Import to Stage. Browse to mushrooms.jpg on the CD-ROM in the Lesson07/Start folder. Click Open.**

A digital photograph of mushrooms appears on the stage.

3. Use the Selection (Arrow) tool to drag the mushroom photo to the upper-right corner. If you'd like to place it more precisely, use the Property inspector to set its X value to **240** and its Y value to **10**.

4. Save the file.

Preparing the Second and Third Screens

In this task, you'll import into the proper layers the screen elements common to the second and third screens. The task is more or less a repetition of what you did in the previous task, both in terms of what you're doing and why. The second and third screens share some of the same assets as the first screen: the logo and the slogan, for example. You will again have an image on screens 2 and 3, though with different orientation. In addition, you'll import appropriate text for each screen and insert a gray horizontal line as a visual divider.

1. Click Frame 47 of the photos layer. Choose Modify > Timeline > Convert to Blank Keyframes.

This step inserts a blank keyframe. Remember, use a keyframe any time you want the contents on the stage to change, whether you're adding, relocating, or removing something. By inserting a blank keyframe, you effectively remove any content from this layer that precedes Frame 47, and yet the graphic remains on the stage for Frames 1 through 46, where it belongs.

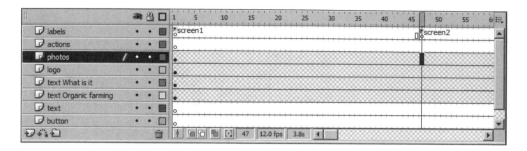

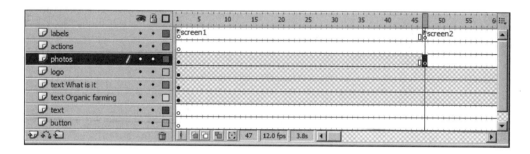

2. Repeat Step 1 to insert blank keyframes into Frame 47 of the logo, text What is it, and text Organic farming layers.

When you're finished with this step, only a blank stage is visible in Frame 47.

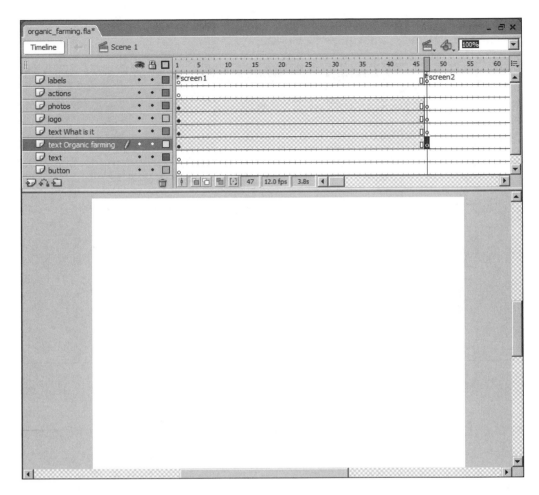

You'll continue to use the logo, Organic Farming text, and What is it? text from the previous screen, but they'll be in different positions on the final two screens. Now that these keyframes are created, you can put the correct content into them.

The Organic Farming and What Is It? text make up Jade Valley's slogan. Rather than recreate them in the second and third screens, we'll simply copy them over from the first screen.

3. Click Frame 1 of the text Organic farming layer. Using the Selection tool, select the Organic Farming text. Choose Edit › Copy.

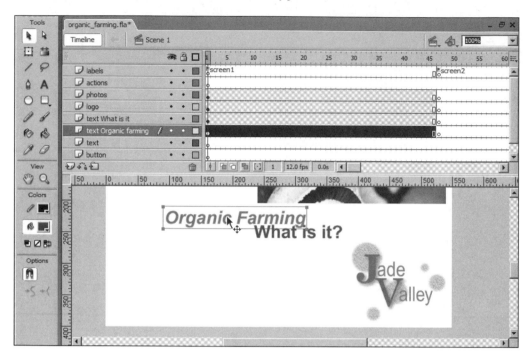

4. Click Frame 47 of the text Organic farming layer. Choose Edit › Paste in Center.

You could also have chosen Paste in Place. It doesn't matter where it's pasted on the stage, as long as it's in the right frame and layer. You'll now reposition it to the upper right-hand corner.

5. Using the Selection tool, click and drag the pasted text to the upper right-hand corner of the screen. If you'd like to place it more precisely, use the Property inspector to set its X value to 252 and its Y value to 10.

Now you can move the What Is It? text. It would have been convenient to just copy the Organic Farming text and the What Is It? text and bring them over together, but they exist on separate layers, so they must be copied separately.

6. Repeat steps 3–5 to copy the contents of Frame 1 of the text What is it layer to Frame 47. Move it to the upper-right corner below and slightly to the left of the Organic Farming text. If you'd like to place it more precisely, use the Property inspector to set its X value to 395 and its Y value to 33.

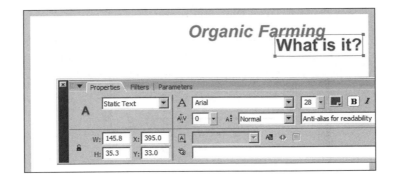

Working with the Library

Every Flash file has a Library, which is a container for all the assets that you can reuse in the movie. These assets can include vector graphics and text; imported bitmaps, sounds, and video; and special Flash objects, such as buttons. The idea behind the Library is a one-to-many concept. That is, one item (in the Library) can be deployed many times on the stage (in one or more frames). The user downloads the item only once, no matter how many times it appears in the movie. And because all the copies on the stage refer to the original version in the Library, if you change the original version in the Library all the copies on the stage are updated instantly.

Flash can store two categories of assets in the Library: imported assets, such as bitmaps, sounds, and video files; and symbols. Symbols in Flash are special kinds of objects, which have unique capabilities. Flash has three types of symbols:

- Graphic symbols are static images that are saved as symbols for reuse in the movie. Graphic symbols are often used when animating an element.
- Button symbols are used to create interactive buttons that respond to mouse clicks, rollovers, and other events. Typically, button symbols are paired with ActionScript, so that the movie can respond to the actions of the user.
- Movie clip symbols are the most powerful of the three symbols. They are essentially Flash movies nested inside the main Flash movie. They have their own timelines, can hold animations, and can be scripted using ActionScript.

The source, or parent, version of an item in the Library is called a symbol. A copy, or child, of that item on the stage is called an instance. Thus, to create an animation of a ball falling, you'll typically create the ball as a symbol and store it in the Library. Then you'll create several instances of the ball on the stage, in different frames, and use them to create the animation.

Now that you understand the underlying architectural benefits of the Library, it's a good time to open it.

1. Choose Window > Library from the main menu.

The Library opens as a panel, usually on the right side of the screen. Although you haven't put anything in the Library, it already contains a couple of items. These were inserted into the Library when you imported the images earlier in this lesson. When you select an item in the Library, a preview is displayed in the top portion of the panel.

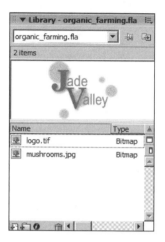

Because your logo is now in the Library, there's no need to import it again for the second and third screens. It's now one of the movie's assets. You'll simply take it from the Library.

2. Click Frame **47** of the logo layer. Click and drag logo.tif from the Library onto the stage. Place it in the upper-left corner of the screen. For precise positioning, you can set both its X and Y value to 5.

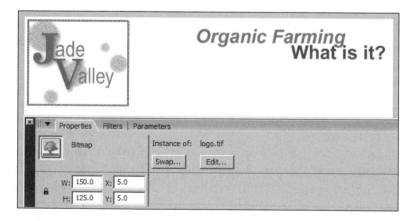

Completing the Basic Layout

Before you leave the logo layer, you'll add one more element to screens 2 and 3. Soon you'll be adding images and text to the lower section of the page. In order to divide the logo and slogan at the top of the page from the content, you'll put in a horizontal line to act as a visual separator.

1. After ensuring that you're in Frame 47 of the logo layer, select the Line tool from the Tools panel. Draw a horizontal line below the "Organic Farming: What is it?" slogan. Hold down the Shift key while you draw to keep the line perfectly horizontal.

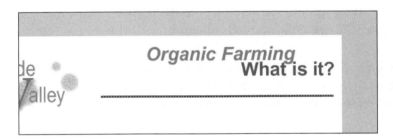

2. With the line still selected, in the Property inspector, set the Stroke height to 2 and the Cap to round. Change the color from black to gray by opening the Stroke Color dialog and setting the Alpha to 30%.

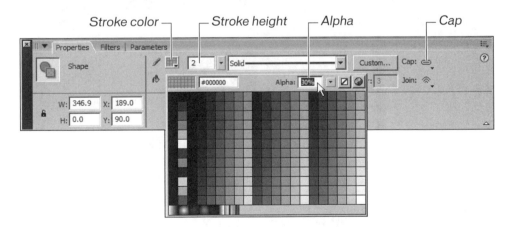

Adding Content to the Second Screen

With the branding of screens 2 and 3 complete, you'll now add the text, images, and navigation to fill out your movie. Each of the screens will have an image and a body of text as well as a uniquely labeled navigational element. As discussed earlier, you insert new keyframes whenever the content or location of content changes in a layer. In this task, you'll fill in these respective content elements for screen 2. You'll add keyframes to the text and button layers. You added the keyframe on the photos layer in a previous exercise.

1. Click Frame 47 of the text layer. Choose Modify > Timeline > Convert to Blank Keyframes. Repeat for the button layer.

Screen 2 uses a vertical photo that you will place in the bottom right-hand corner of the screen and place the text to the left of the photo.

2. Click Frame 47 of the photos layer. Choose File > Import > Import to Stage. Browse to squash.jpg on the CD-ROM in the Lesson07/Start folder. Click Open. Position the image in the bottom-right corner of the screen.

> **Note** In addition to appearing on the screen, squash.jpg also appears in the Library as a new asset of the project.

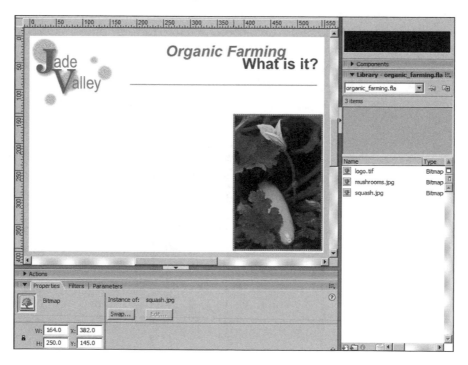

You'll now place text next to the image. You'll copy the text out of a .txt file and paste it into your movie using the Text tool.

3. Navigate to the Lesson07/Start folder on the CD-ROM, and double-click to open the file pg2.txt in the default text editor. Click and drag to select all the text. Choose Edit › Copy.

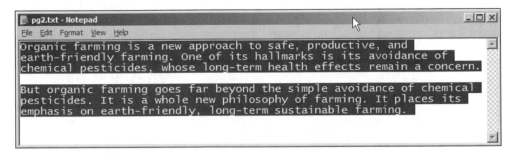

4. Return to Flash and draw a text box next to the image using the Text tool. Choose Edit › Paste Special.... Click OK.

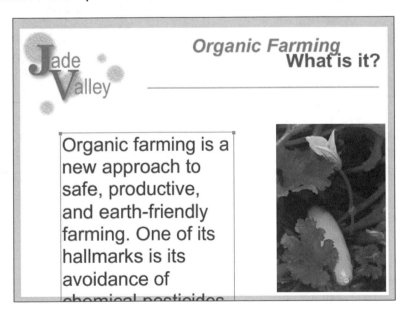

The text from the file spills across your screen in a seemingly unmanageable mess. In all likelihood the Font Size property of your Text tool is still set to 28. You'll correct that and reshape the text box to fit the screen layout.

5. Using the Selection tool, click on the new text box. In the Property inspector, change the Font Size to 12. Press Enter (Return for Macintosh). Move your mouse over a corner of the text box until the cursor turns into a horizontal double-headed arrow. Resize the box horizontally to fit the space next to the picture. Align the top of the box with the top of the photo.

As you resize horizontally, the box will automatically resize vertically until you can fit it all in the space available.

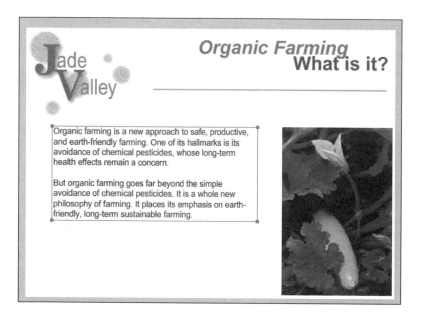

Tip *Should you find that you've placed your text on the wrong layer, you can select the text, choose Edit > Cut, move to the proper layer, and choose Edit > Paste in place. Flash will put the element exactly where it was, but on the correct layer.*

6. Save the file.

Designing a Button Graphic

You'll need a way for users to move between screens, so it's time to create some navigation for the movie. You'll draw an arrow with triangles as a navigation button. The vector drawing tools in Flash are sufficient for the graphics you'll create here. There are a few ways to go about this, and you should experiment.

1. Click Frame 47 of the button layer. Choose the Pencil tool. At the bottom of the Tools panel you'll find the Options for this tool. Choose Object Drawing.

The other option determines what Flash will do with the line you'll draw. Choose straighten. To the right of your squash photo, draw a triangle with one corner pointing to the right. Hold down the Shift key for the vertical line, and Flash will ensure that it's perfectly vertical.

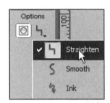

 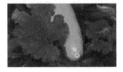

Note *You'll quickly discover that the Object Drawing tool will clean up your work and make a clean shape out of your drawing. It might take a few tries to get it the way you want it. You can turn off Object Drawing, and Flash will still straighten your lines for you.*

2. Choose the Paint Bucket tool. Click the Fill Color in the Colors section of the Tools panel and choose a shade of green. Click your triangle to apply the color to it.

The triangle now has a green fill.

To complete the button graphic, you'll make a duplicate of your triangle. Depending on your method for drawing the triangle, you might have a single element or several. Grouping items holds them together as a single element. You should group your triangle before duplicating it.

3. Using the Selection tool, click and drag a rectangle encompassing the triangle. Release to select the triangle. Choose Modify > Group. Choose Edit > Duplicate to create an identical copy. Use the arrow keys to reposition the second triangle so it covers half the original triangle. If necessary, select both triangles and use the Scale tool to resize them.

The two triangles should look as they do in the following figure.

4. Select the Text tool and type *next* to the left of the two triangles. Use the Property inspector to format the text block's various attributes: Arial, italic, 14, green. Place the text and triangles in the bottom-right corner.

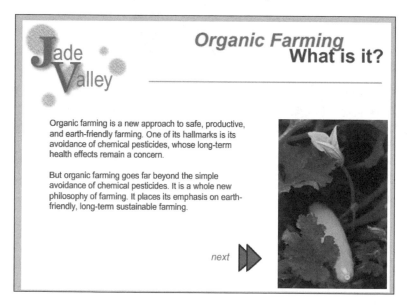

Adding Content to the Third Screen

The third screen closely resembles the second. The image and text are positioned differently, but other than that your steps will closely follow those you used to prepare the second screen.

1. Prepare for the third screen by creating empty keyframes in Frame 67 of the following layers:

photos

text

button

You don't need to add keyframes to the logo, text Organic farming, and text What is it layers, since they don't change from screen 2 to screen 3. When you're done, you should see only the logo/slogan header.

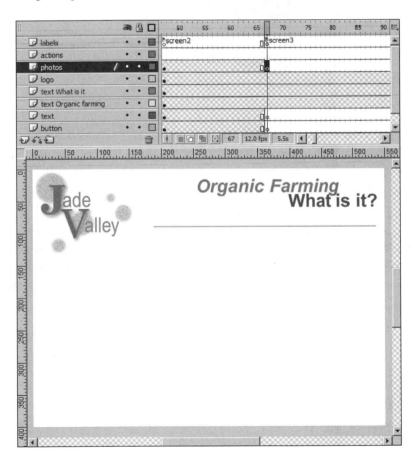

2. Click Frame 67 of the photos layer. Choose File › Import › Import to Stage. Browse to pepper.jpg on the Lesson07/Start folder on the CD-ROM. Click Open.

Center the image at the bottom of the screen.

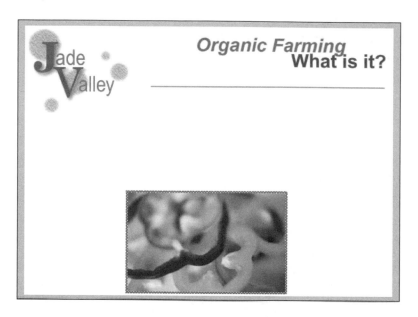

3. Copy the text of the file pg3.txt from the Lesson07/Start folder. Return to Flash and draw a text box above the image using the Text tool. Choose Edit › Paste Special.... Click OK.

Again, the text does not exactly fall into place. It will require resizing and repositioning.

4. Using the Selection tool, click on the new text box. In the Property inspector, change the Font Size to 12. Press Enter (Return for Macintosh). Move your mouse over a corner of the text box until the cursor turns into a horizontal double-headed arrow. Resize the box horizontally to fit above the photo and below the gray line.

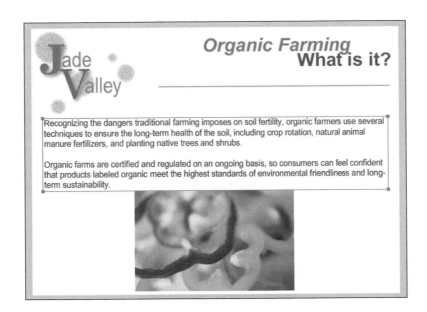

You can reuse the navigation from screen 2, but it will be in a different spot and have different text on screen 3. You'll copy the navigation button and bring it over to the third screen.

5. Click Frame 47 of the button layer. The button and its text should be highlighted. If they're not, choose them with the Selection tool. Choose Edit › Copy.

While the navigation button will suit your need in screen 3, you'll want to modify the text. For this reason, keeping them as separate elements maintains flexibility.

> **Note** *When copying from one frame to another, Flash wants to put the content in the same or nearly the same location as where it originated. It can, of course, be moved after it's on the stage.*

6. Click Frame 67 of the button layer. Choose Edit › Paste in Place.

You won't see anything happen. Don't be alarmed; Flash has pasted the button behind your photo. We'll temporarily suppress visibility of that layer to allow you to see and reposition the button.

> **Note** *It would not have mattered if you chose Paste in Center instead of Paste in Place. Flash would have pasted the button in the vertical center of the page, and it would still have fallen under the photo.*

In the timeline, to the right of the layer names, is an image of an eye. If you click that image it will hide all layers. If you click the dot under the eye corresponding to a given layer, it will hide that layer alone. If you hide the photo layer it will expose the button you just pasted into the stage.

7. Click the black dot to the right of the photo layer label, under the image of the eye.

8. With the Selection tool, drag the button under the text box.

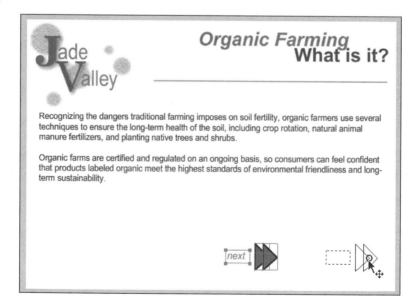

9. Use the Text tool to change the button text to *restart*. Toggle the visibility of the photo layer back on.

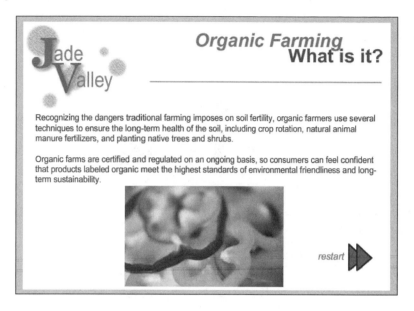

10. Save the file.

Converting Existing Graphics into Symbols

As mentioned earlier, the Flash Library holds imported assets, such as the bitmaps you just imported, and symbols. Symbols are just reusable graphics with special built-in capabilities. In this task, you'll convert a couple of graphics on the stage to a symbol, to take advantage of the symbol's special capabilities when you begin scripting the movie in the next lesson.

1. Click Frame 47 of the button layer. Choose Edit > Deselect All. Holding down the Shift key, click to select each of the two triangle shapes that make up the arrow button.

Although the shapes might look like a button, right now, as far as Flash is concerned, they're just a pair of vector shapes.

2. Choose Modify > Ungroup.

Flash automatically groups all vector graphics imported from Freehand. In the next lesson, you'll need to edit the triangles, and it will be easier if they are not grouped. Notice that their appearance changes after you choose this option; rather than being surrounded by a blue bounding box, they have a crosshatch pattern on them, indicating that they're selected.

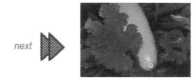

3. Choose Modify > Convert to Symbol. In the Convert to Symbol dialog, name the button *next*, and choose Button as its Behavior. Click OK.

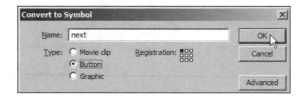

Each symbol must have a unique name, which is how the symbol is tracked in the Library. In addition, all symbols must be one of three types, called Behaviors: movie clip, button, or graphic.

If you look in the Library now, you'll see a button called "next."

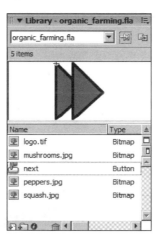

Back on the stage, the two triangles are again surrounded by a blue bounding box, this time indicating that the two triangles are now actually an instance of a symbol, as opposed to simple vector art on the stage.

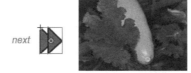

4. Click Frame 67 of the button layer.

The two blue bounding boxes surrounding each of the two triangles indicate that once again, these are a pair of vector graphics, and not a button at all. You already have a button for these in the Library; what's needed here is a new instance of that button.

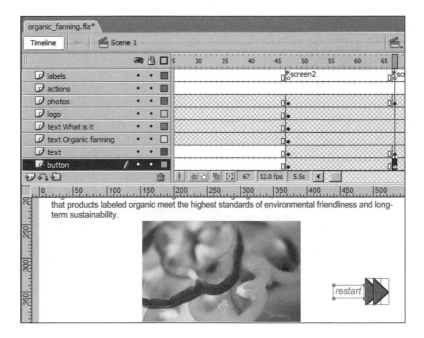

5. Choose Edit > Deselect All. Hold down the Shift key and select each of the two triangles, and then press Delete.

Don't delete the word "Restart"!

You don't need these triangles any more, because you're about to replace them with a button symbol instance.

6. With the Library open (Window > Library), press and drag an instance of the next button out of the Library, and release it on the stage. Use the Arrow tool to position it beside the word Restart.

Creating an instance is a matter of dragging and dropping from the Library. When you complete this step, the movie has two instances of the next button, one in the second screen and one in the third. Although each button has a different label (one says "Next" and the other says "Restart"), both are linked to the parent symbol. Thus, if you update the parent symbol—and you will in the next lesson—you'll update both instances at the same time.

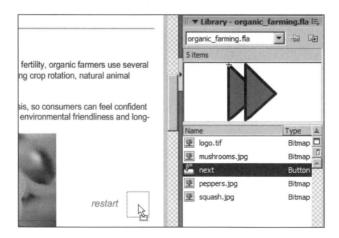

7. Save the file.

You've reached the end of the lesson. You might be surprised that you've spent an hour and a half or so in Flash and still haven't created any animation or interactivity. The ability to create animation or interactivity is dependent on placing the elements in an appropriate architecture: the timeline, layers, keyframes, the Library, and so on. You've done all that in this lesson, and you're finally ready to turn to the fun parts of Flash: animation and interactivity.

What You Have Learned

In this lesson, you have:

- Opened a new Flash document, created new layers in the timeline, and renamed them (pages 201–204)
- Inserted new frames and keyframes in the timeline (pages 205–213)
- Relocated elements into their own layers (pages 213–221)
- Explored the Library (pages 221–222)
- Imported bitmap graphics (pages 223–226)
- Converted existing graphics to symbols (pages 227–237)

8 Creating Animation and Interactivity

In Lesson 7, *Creating a Flash Movie*, you worked with the layout, architecture, and graphic design of the organic farming movie. You didn't work specifically with the movie's behavior, however—that is, what the movie does. Developers primarily turn to Macromedia Flash to create animations and interactivity. In this lesson, you'll upgrade the organic farming movie so that it becomes much more interesting to the user than a static graphic.

Originally intended as an animator's tool, Flash enables developers to create several types of animation. You can make an element move across the stage in a straight line or along a curved path. You can also make an element change its shape or color over time and rotate or spin. You can combine any of these capabilities, along with acceleration and deceleration and nested animations (animations within animations) to create complex motion. Flash provides abundant animation tools, which enable you to automate animation for simple motion or painstakingly plot out an animation one frame at a time. In this lesson, you'll make an element fly across the stage and another element fade in and out over time.

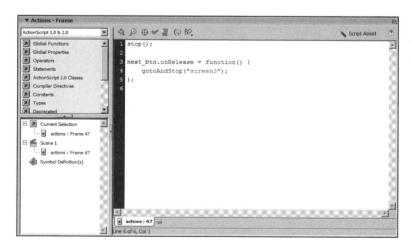

Use the Actions panel to add the scripts that make your movie functional.

Flash also provides developers with a powerful toolset to add interactivity to a Flash movie. At its core is ActionScript, Flash's native scripting language. Using ActionScript, you can change the behavior or appearance of elements within a Flash movie in response to user actions. Whether you want to provide basic VCR-like controls to a long animation, create a nonlinear interaction such as a video game, or collect data from the user via a form, you can achieve it all using ActionScript. Macromedia Flash 8 also offers a number of tools to facilitate using ActionScript, including a visual code editor, complete with code coloring, code hints, and syntax checkers. A useful feature for beginners and non-coders is Behaviors, which is a collection of prewritten ActionScripts that achieve certain common tasks. In this lesson, you'll hand-code a small amount of ActionScript to make the triangle buttons functional.

What You Will Learn

In this lesson, you will:

- Learn three different ways of animating in Flash
- Convert a text box to a graphic symbol and animate it
- Animate fade-ins and fade-outs
- Learn basic ActionScript concepts and syntax
- Add basic actions to stop and play the movie
- Specify a button's appearance in four different states

Approximate Time

This lesson takes approximately 60 minutes to complete.

Lesson Files

Starting Files:

Lesson08/Start/organic_farming.fla
Lesson08/Start/jade_valley/organic.htm

Completed Files:

Lesson08/Complete/organic_farming.fla
Lesson08/Complete/organic_farming.swf
Lesson08/Complete/jade_valley/organic.htm
Lesson08/Complete/jade_valley/flash/organic_farming.swf

Testing Flash Movies

As you turn your attention from the look of the movie in a given frame to the behavior of the movie across frames, you need to be able to see how Flash will play the movie. Flash provides a couple of ways to test the movie, both of which you'll try in this task.

1. Open organic_farming.fla from the end of the last lesson or from the Lesson08/Start folder on the CD-ROM. In the frame numbers just above the timeline, click Frame 1.

This step moves the frame indicator to Frame 1, without selecting any particular layers. The screen also updates to show the frame on the stage as it appears in Frame 1.

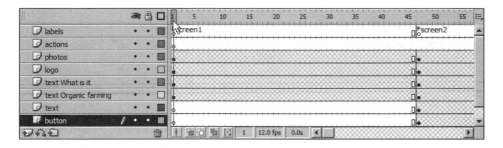

2. Make sure you can see the entire stage (drag the bar between the timeline and Document window, if necessary). From the main menu, choose Control > Play.

The frame indicator plays through the frames at the designated frame rate, which, as you'll recall, is 12 frames per second. The stage updates as the frame indicator moves past the keyframes that change it.

During the playback, you'll see the three screens appear in succession. The first screen shows for nearly 4 seconds; the second and third screens show for less than 2 seconds each. None of these durations should be surprising, given the location of the keyframes in the timeline.

Frame indicator as it plays through timeline

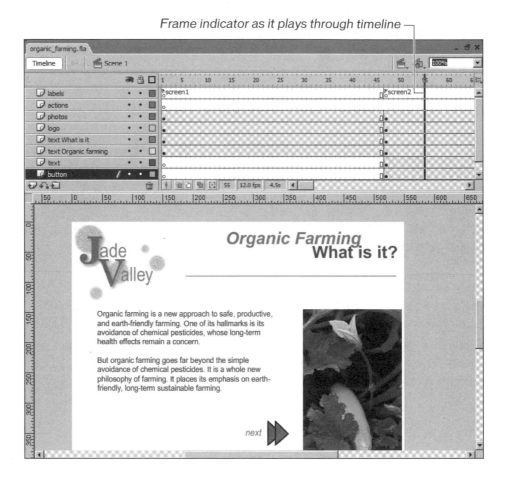

3. From the main menu, choose Control › Test Movie.

Flash opens a new window with a different menu bar and no timeline. The movie plays through, much as it did when you chose Control > Play in the previous step.

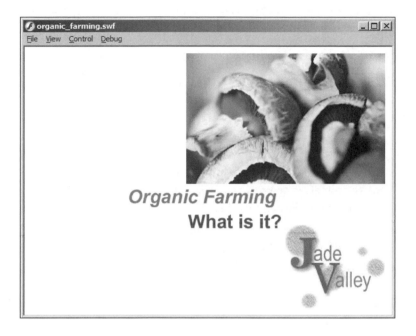

4. Close the test movie document to return to the main movie in the authoring environment.

So what's the difference between the two ways of testing a movie? The first way (Control > Play) previews the playback of the main timeline within the Flash authoring environment. It's a quick and convenient way to test the main timeline, which works fine with simple movies like this one.

The other way, Control > Test Movie, generates a Flash SWF file; it creates the file the end user would see if you published the movie as it currently stands. While slightly more time-consuming than Control > Play, the Control > Test Movie approach has its own benefits. Whereas Control > Play only previews animation in the main timeline, Control > Test Movie previews every feature of Flash, including all ActionScript (most ActionScript is not executed with the Control > Play approach) and nested animations. This movie has neither ActionScript nor nested animations, so at this point there is no benefit to testing the SWF using Control > Test Movie. But after you get beyond the basics, you'll probably use Control > Test Movie exclusively.

Animating Elements

In this task, you'll turn to animation. Flash has several animation tools, but before you learn and start using them you should understand the three primary methods of creating animations in Flash. Each method has its own advantages and disadvantages, so using them correctly can save you a lot of time in the long run.

The three primary methods of creating animation in Flash are as follows:

- **Frame-by-frame animation:** Similar to the traditional form of animation used before the days of computers, frame-by-frame animation simulates motion by changing the contents of the stage in every frame, using a succession of keyframes. In fact, you've already created this type of animation; as you saw in the previous task, the succession of screens you see when you test the movie is an animation of sorts. Frame-by-frame animation is best suited for complex animations, such as facial motion. It's the most labor-intensive animation to create and maintain, and it also yields the largest file size; it should be avoided when possible.

- **Tweens:** Tweens are an animation technique in which developers specify a starting and an ending point of an animation (using a keyframe for each point), and Flash creates a series of incremental changes to that graphic in the intervening static frames. Flash has two different types of tweens. Motion tweens are performed with instances, and are used to change attributes of an instance automatically over time, including location, alpha transparency, size, rotation, and so on. Shape tweens are performed with vector art (not instances), and are typically used to morph shapes.

- **Scripted animation:** You can use ActionScript to control the location, existence, quantity, size, rotation, direction, opacity, and other features of screen elements. This technique is often used in video games, where the animation of screen elements is not predetermined but rather is determined by the user as she or he interacts with the game.

Earlier in the lesson, we mentioned that you want one element to fly across the stage, and another element to fade in and out. Knowing the animations we want, can you guess which of these types would be the best way to achieve the effects?

If you guessed motion tween, you're correct. Because all you're animating is a change of an object's attribute over time—its location and its opacity—a motion tween is the most efficient way to create it. You could create the effect using a frame-by-frame animation, but it would take a lot more effort and would not improve the animation in any way. You could also script these animations, but such an approach would be overkill in this case because you're not trying to give control over each animation to the user.

In this task, you'll create an animation by motion tweening the text elements "Organic Farming" and "What is it?" on the first screen.

1. Place the frame indicator in Frame 1 and select the text box "Organic Farming:" using the Selection tool. Choose Modify › Convert to Symbol in the main menu. Name the symbol *TextOrganicFarming* in the Name field, and select Graphic in the Type group.

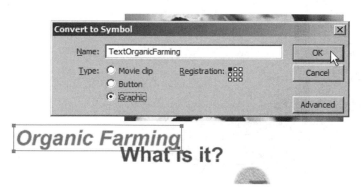

This step converts the text box to a graphic symbol. Motion tweens work only with symbol instances, so you'll have to convert the text to a symbol. You can motion tween any kind of instance, whether it's a graphic, button, or movie clip instance. Because you don't need any of the additional functionality of the latter two symbol types, you should choose graphic.

You can see this Graphic symbol in the Library. In addition, the text on the stage is now changed to an instance of the graphic symbol. If you click the instance of this graphic symbol, you'll see in the Property inspector that its Behavior is set to Graphic, and you'll see a description that the selected object is an instance of the symbol named TextOrganicFarming.

2. Create a new keyframe in Frame 32 of the text Organic farming layer. Select Frame 1 of the text Organic farming layer, and use the Selection tool to drag the graphic symbol up and to the left about an inch or so.

Remember, to create a keyframe, first click the static frame you want to convert, and then choose Modify > Timeline > Convert to Keyframes.

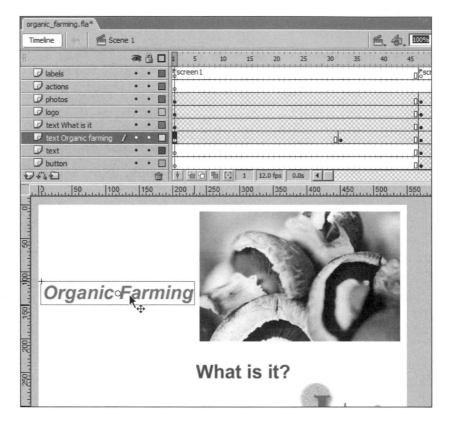

With keyframes in Frames 1 and 32, you now have begin and end points defined for the animation. But until you return to Frame 1 and move the instance up and to the left, both keyframes are the same so there's no animation. After you move the instance in Frame 1, there's an animation in the sense that the text appears in one location for the first 31 frames and then suddenly jerks to a new position in Frame 32 (choose Control > Play to see this in action, if you like).

Of course, you don't want it to jerk into place all at once; you want the text to fly into place over a series of frames. You'll create a motion tween to produce that effect.

3. **Click Frame 1 of the text Organic farming layer. Choose Insert > Timeline > Create Motion Tween.**

This applies a motion tween to this frame segment.

A change in the timeline provides visual feedback regarding the change. A tweened frame segment is colored blue and has an arrow running through it.

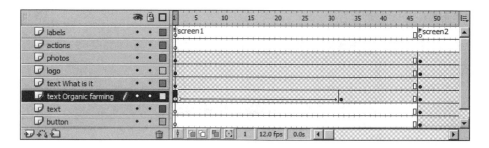

4. **Drag the frame indicator back and forth over the frame segment to preview the tween.**

This process is called scrubbing the timeline. As you scrub the timeline, you'll see the text animate across the screen, from the starting to the ending point. Of course, you can also test this animation using either Control > Play or Control > Test Movie.

As you can see, it's quick and easy to create animations using motion tweens.

Fading Graphics In and Out

Although the name "motion tween" implies that it's used to animate changes in location, a motion tween can be used for much more. More precisely, as mentioned earlier, motion tweens can be used to animate a change in one or more instance attributes, including location, size, rotation, and visibility. In this task, you'll learn how to fade instances in and out using motion tweens.

1. Place the frame indicator in Frame 1 and select the text box What is it?. Convert to it a graphic symbol. Name this symbol *TextWhatIsIt* and select Graphic as the symbol Type.

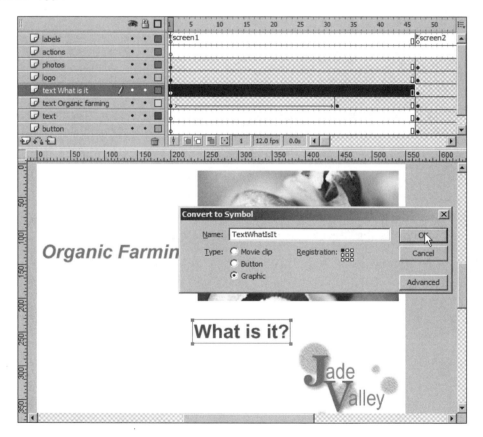

The new graphic symbol now resides in the Library, and the text box on the stage is changed to an instance of this new graphic symbol.

2. Insert a new keyframe in Frame 24 of the text What is it layer. Select Frame 1 of the text What is it layer. Click the instance and choose Alpha from the Color drop-down menu in the Property inspector. Set the Alpha amount to 0%.

In this step, you're creating an end state for the animation by inserting a keyframe in Frame 24. You then redefine the beginning state of the animation by returning to Frame 1 and making the text instance there invisible. After you insert the motion tween, Flash will fade in the text.

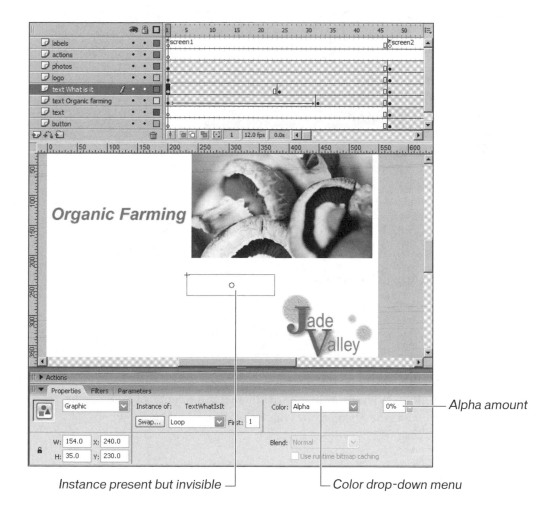

Instance present but invisible ⌐   └*Color drop-down menu*   *Alpha amount*

3. Right-click (Windows) or Control-click (Macintosh) any frame between 1 and 23 of the text What is it layer, and choose Create Motion Tween. Scrub the timeline to preview the tween.

Remember, to scrub the timeline, drag the frame indicator across the desired frames.

The right-click/Control-click shortcut is the same as selecting Frame 1 of the text What is it layer and choosing Insert > Timeline > Create Motion Tween.

Notice as you scrub that the two items of text catch your eye at the same time, competing with each other. A more effective way to animate these items might be to stagger the animations slightly so the eye first perceives one animation and then the other.

4. Click Frame 1 of the text What is it layer. Next, drag this layer over to Frame 5.

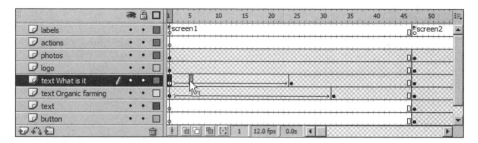

The first keyframe in the layer is now blank, and the text doesn't begin to fade until Frame 5, nearly half a second after the Organic Farming text begins animating.

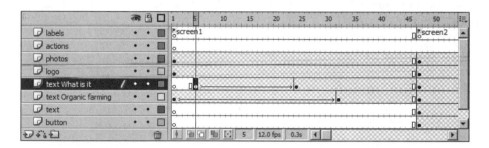

You can scrub the timeline or test the movie to preview the animation, if you like.

Next, you'll make the mushrooms photo fade in and out.

5. Click Frame 1 of the photos layer. Convert the mushrooms photo to a graphic symbol, and call it *mushrooms*.

Remember, to convert something to a symbol, select it and choose Insert > Convert to Symbol.

Even though the mushrooms image is an instance of a bitmap in the Library, it is not properly a symbol. And motion tweens should only be applied to symbol instances. The solution is to convert the mushrooms bitmap instance to a Graphic symbol instance.

6. Insert new keyframes in Frames 25 and 46 of the photos layer.

The mushrooms photo needs to fade in and out, which will require two tweens: one to fade in and one to fade out. The keyframe in Frame 25 will mark the end point of the fade-in and simultaneously the start point of the fade-out. Frames 1 and 46 will both have the mushrooms photo at low opacity.

At this point, all three keyframes still have the exact same content: one instance each of the mushrooms graphic symbol at full opacity.

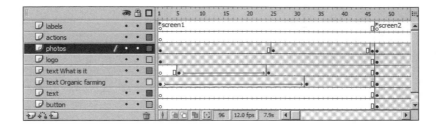

7. Select Frame 1. Select the mushrooms instance and use the Property inspector to apply Alpha color at 20%. Apply a motion tween to the frame segment.

Scrub the timeline to verify that the mushrooms photo animates from 20% to 100% opacity.

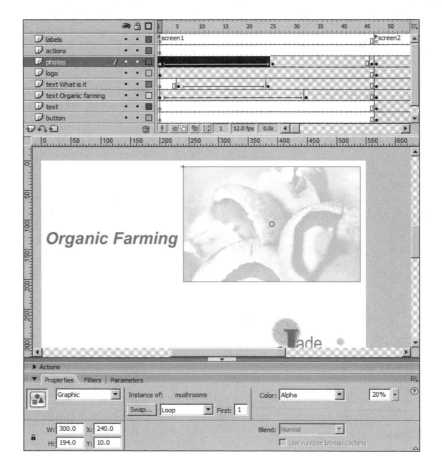

8. Select Frame 46 of the photos layer. Select the mushrooms graphic instance on the stage. In the Property inspector, apply 20% Alpha to the mushrooms instance. Insert a motion tween into this frame segment as well.

You're creating the second half of the tween, where the image fades back out.

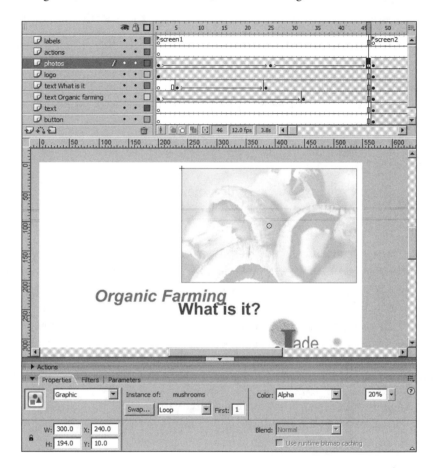

9. Choose Control > Test Movie to test the movie. When you're finished previewing the movie, close the SWF to return to the authoring environment. Save the file.

When you test the movie, you'll see the effects of the three animations. The intro sequence looks pretty good. The problem now is that the Next and Restart buttons don't work and the movie plays back without stopping.

Adding Interactivity to Your Flash Movie

You've added some animations, but the movie still plays back regardless of user interaction. You need to make the movie stop on the second screen (Frame 47) and not advance to the third screen until the user clicks the Next button. Likewise, the movie should stop on the last frame and not loop back to the beginning unless the user clicks the Restart button.

Building interactions requires planning. One of the most basic steps is to outline the two fundamental parts of every interaction: events and behaviors.

- **Events** refer to something that happens when a movie is playing. Events include clicking or rolling over a button, pressing a key on the keyboard, or the frame indicator reaching a given keyframe.
- **Behaviors** refer to statements that instruct a movie to do something in response to a specified event.

For example, imagine you have a movie with a soundtrack playing. You want to give the user the option of turning off the music, so you create a button, which you label "Silence!". When the user clicks the button (the event), the soundtrack stops playing (the behavior).

Creating interactions typically requires graphic interface elements—such as buttons—and ActionScript, which tells the movie what to do. Like other scripting languages, ActionScript follows its own rules of syntax, which is like grammar and punctuation that determine which characters and words are used to create meaning and in which order they can be written. ActionScript is a large and complex language and can take months or years to learn. However, you don't need an in-depth understanding of programming, or even have programming experience, to begin scripting. Flash makes it easy for even beginning programmers to add simple scripts to create an interactive movie.

In this task, you'll script actions that add interactivity to your Flash movie. Scripts, like any other element in Flash, must be added to keyframes or to objects within keyframes that accept ActionScript, such as buttons and movie clips.

1. Choose Window > Actions.

This opens the Actions panel, usually below the stage.

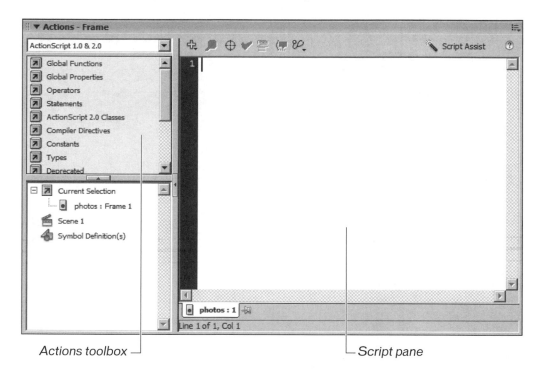

Actions toolbox   *Script pane*

Type your scripts directly in the Script pane. The Actions toolbox provides a comprehensive list of all the language elements of Flash ActionScript, organized hierarchically.

2. In the timeline, insert a new keyframe in Frame **47** of the actions layer. Type the following script in the Script pane in Actions panel:

```
stop();
```

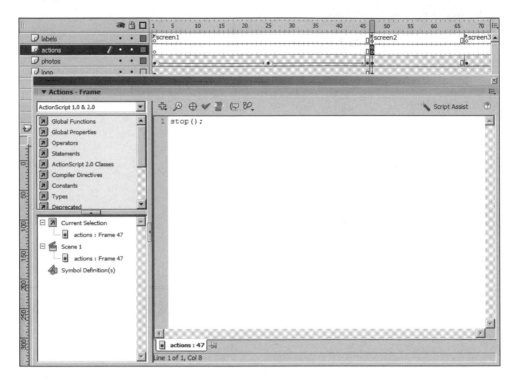

Notice that a small "a" appears in the timeline in the keyframe with the script. This is a visual cue that a script has been attached to the keyframe.

This script makes the movie stop playback in Frame 47. You need to make this movie stop at Frame 47 to allow the user to click the button to move to the next frame.

Earlier we claimed that every script in Flash had both events and behaviors. Here, stop(), which stops the movie in the current frame, is obviously a behavior, but you might be wondering what the event is that triggers it. In this case, although it's implied and unspecified, the event is onEnterFrame. In other words, the event for this script is "as soon as this frame becomes active."

3. Test the movie using Control > Test Movie.

The animations play through, but this time the movie stops on the second screen and you're stuck. The button doesn't work, so there's no way to go forward or backward.

4. Return to the main movie. Select the button instance in Frame 47. In the instance name field in the Property inspector, name the button *next_btn*.

When a user clicks this button, the current frame will jump to Frame 67, where the third screen is located. You'll implement this functionality using ActionScript. But for the ActionScript to work, it has to be able to identify the button instance. In other words, this movie has two button instances—one each in the second and third screens. Each button will do something different, and you'll have to write two short scripts to make them work. To identify each button, you'll give each button a unique identifier by giving it an instance name.

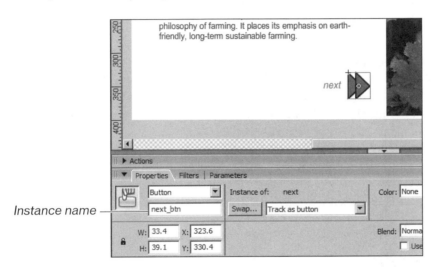

When naming instances, it's a good practice to add certain suffixes to them to make them easier to identify in the code. In this case, you added the _btn suffix to the instance name, making it easier to identify in the script that this instance is a button. Not only is it easier for readers to see that it's a button, but it also tells Flash that it's a button. Using sanctioned suffixes activates code hinting and code completion in the Script pane. Throughout this book, you'll use proper suffixes for all instances so you'll remember them quickly.

5. Return to the Actions panel (Window › Actions or F9). Position the insertion point after the **stop();** line in the script, and enter the following:

```
next_btn.onRelease = function() {
  gotoAndStop("screen3");
};
```

The first and last lines of the script identify the event: next_btn.onRelease. In plain English, this means, "When the user presses and then releases (clicks) the next_btn instance, …" The word function() indicates that you're creating a custom behavior that's supposed to happen when the event is fired. Everything inside the curly braces {} is the behavior itself.

In this case, the behavior is that Flash should skip to the frame labeled "screen3," which is Frame 67. The gotoAndStop() action (or, to use proper programming terminology, method) is built into every Flash timeline. As its name implies, it tells Flash to skip to a certain frame. That frame is spelled out in the parentheses. When you provide additional information to a method, you put it inside the parentheses. Each piece of information you put in the parentheses is called a parameter.

Many, though not all, methods have parameters. For example, the stop() method you used earlier doesn't require parameters; Flash knows where it's supposed to stop, so no additional information is necessary. But the gotoAndStop() method can work only if Flash knows where it's supposed to go to and stop. Sometimes parameters are required, as is the frame parameter of the gotoAndStop() method; other times, parameters are optional.

6. Test the movie, using Control › Test Movie.

This time, click the button when you get to the second screen. When you click the button, you'll go to the third screen. Once again you're stuck, with no way of going backward or forward.

You're ready to set up the second button.

7. Select the button instance in Frame 67. In the Property inspector, give the button the Instance Name *startOver_btn*.

With this identifier, the button instance is made available to, or exposed to, ActionScript.

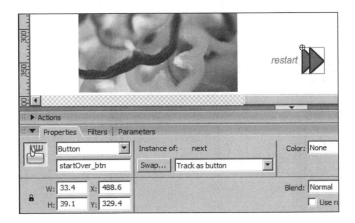

8. Insert a new keyframe in Frame 67 of the actions layer. Open the Actions panel and add the following script:

```
startOver_btn.onRelease = function() {
  gotoAndPlay("screen1");
};
```

The Actions panel is empty, because the script you added earlier was attached to the keyframe in Frame 47. Now that you have a new keyframe active, no script appears in the panel.

As with the previous script you wrote, this one makes it so that when the user clicks the button instance (startOver_btn), the movie is sent to a different frame. In this case, you use gotoAndPlay() rather than gotoAndStop() because you want playback to commence when the movie is in the right frame.

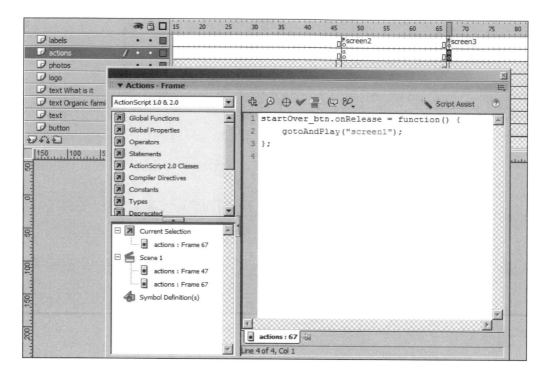

9. Test the movie. When you're finished, close SWF and save the file.

Functionally, the movie is complete at this point. When it first loads, it plays through the animation until it reaches the second screen, at which point it stops and waits for the user to click the Next button. When the user clicks this button, it advances to the third screen and stops again. If the user likes, she or he can click the Restart button and circle back to the beginning.

Adding a Rollover Effect to the Button

The Next and Restart buttons respond to user actions now, but they still don't act like buttons. Most buttons react in some way when the user rolls the mouse over them: they light up, or appear to jump out, or start to glow. This reaction provides important feedback to the user and invites the user to interact with the element. In this task, you'll revisit the button symbol so that it reacts when the mouse rolls over it.

Now that we've established that a button's appearance might change in response to the user, we can take the next step: making buttons respond to users in predictable ways. That is, a button can have one look when it is in its default position—when the movie first loads— and another look when the mouse rolls over it. These conditions (default, rollover) are called button states. Flash recognizes four button states:

- **Up:** A button is in the Up state when the movie first loads, and the user has not yet interacted with it.
- **Over:** The Over state appears when the user rolls the mouse over the button.
- **Down:** In the fraction of a second when the user clicks a button, it's in its Down state.
- **Hit:** This state is a little unusual, in that the user never sees it. The Hit state is used to specify the hot, or clickable, area of a button. In some cases, the button can be different sizes or in different locations across states (it might grow when the mouse rolls over it, for example, or it might move a little down and to the right when in its Down state). Flash needs to know exactly which portions of the button are clickable, and that's specified in the Hit state. If your button doesn't grow or move in any of its states, you usually don't have to worry about the Hit state.

Designing buttons, then, involves putting graphics in each of these four states. As you recall, when you created the buttons in the previous lesson you converted a pair of triangles to a button symbol. When you tested the movie, these triangles didn't seem to react when you rolled the mouse over them. You're now in a position to understand why: no Over, Down, or Hit state has been specified for the button symbol.

1. **Open the Library (Window › Library). Double-click the button icon beside the Next button.**

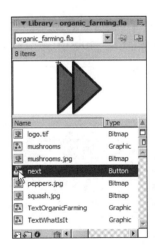

The button opens in Symbol Editing mode. You see its stage and timeline, which are quite different from those of the main timeline and stage. In the button's timeline, you see four frames, named Up, Over, Down, and Hit, representing each of the button's states.

Although the timeline looks a little different, it works just like the main timeline: Before you can edit the Over state, you need to insert a keyframe in the Over frame.

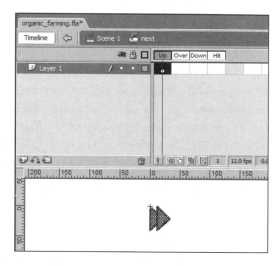

2. Select the Over frame in the timeline, and choose Modify > Timeline > Convert to Keyframes.

This creates a new keyframe in the Over state. You can change the triangles in this keyframe without affecting their appearance in the Up state.

3. In the Colors section of the Tools panel, click the Fill Color box. In the Fill Color pop-up, choose a bright-orange color, such as #FF6600.

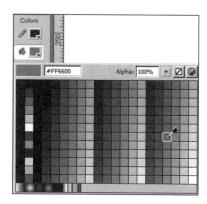

The triangles still have the same black strokes as before, but now the fill color is orange. This color change will make the button appear to light up when the user rolls the mouse over it.

4. Select the Down frame in the timeline and press F6. Use the Tools panel to change their Fill Color to red (#CC0000).

F6 is the keyboard shortcut for Modify > Timeline > Convert to Keyframes. This inserts a new keyframe to the Down frame. The Down state indicates when the button is clicked. The button changes to red while the mouse is pressed while on this button.

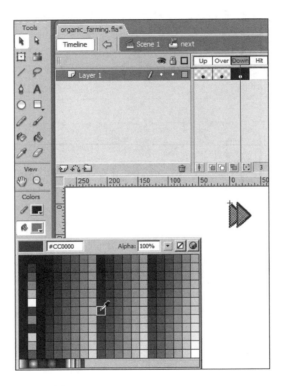

5. Select the Hit frame in the timeline and press F6. To add the Hit state, select the Rectangle tool in the Tools panel and draw a rectangle that covers the area of the button image.

Pressing F6 inserts a new keyframe to the Hit frame. The Hit state of Flash defines the active button area. With the current rollover states, only the triangular areas can be clicked, but the white space between them cannot be clicked. By adding a rectangular area in the Hit state, you make the button a little more forgiving.

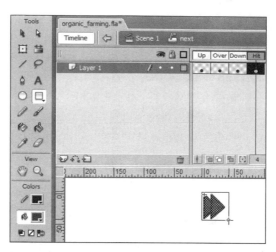

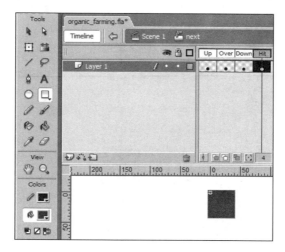

6. Click Scene 1 on the top of the timeline. Choose Control > Test Movie.

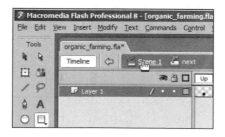

Clicking Scene 1 returns you to the Flash authoring environment. You can't see the button states in this environment, so you'll need to test the movie to see if the button states work correctly. As you can see when you test the movie, the button turns orange when you roll over it, and briefly turns red when you click it. You don't see the rectangle in the Hit state.

Notice that both instances have been updated; that's because they're both instances of the same symbol, and when you edit the symbol you effectively edit all its instances.

Publishing Your Flash Movie

The organic farming movie is complete, and you're ready to publish it on the Web within the Jade Valley site. You'll export your Flash movie as a SWF file and save it in the jade_valley/flash folder within your site. Then you'll replace the static content in organic.htm with the Flash movie that you've developed.

1. Choose File > Export > Export Movie to save the movie in SWF format. Name the file *organic_farming.swf* and save it in the jade_valley/flash folder in your site. Accept the default settings in the Export Flash Player dialog.

You need to save this file as a SWF, because most users have the free Flash Player that displays only SWF files.

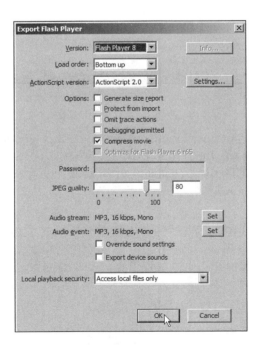

2. Save the file and close Flash.

Your final task is to place the movie in the appropriate page of the Jade Valley site.

3. Launch Dreamweaver and open organic.htm. Delete the existing content in the right column of the page.

You're going to replace the content in the right column of this HTML page with your Flash movie, so remove the content, including the heading, body text, and graphic.

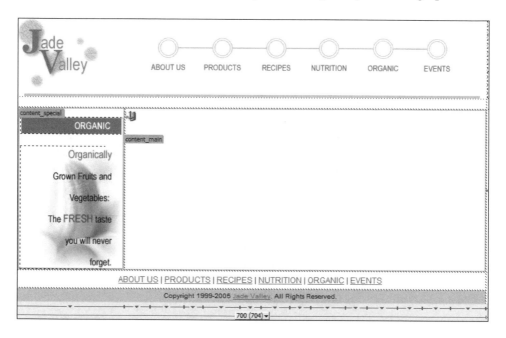

4. With the insertion point positioned in the blank space you just created, choose Insert > Media > Flash in the main menu. Select organic_farming.swf from the flash folder. The Object Tag Accessibility Attributes dialog opens. Enter *Organic Farming* as the Title. Click OK.

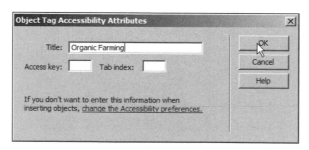

You'll see a large gray box representing the Flash movie in the right column of the page.

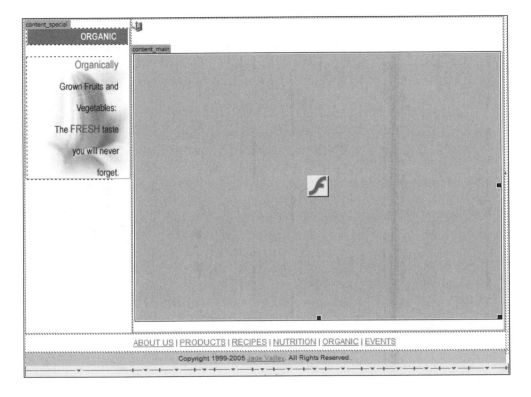

5. Save organic.htm.

You're finished working on the file. All that remains is to test it.

6. Click anywhere in the open document, and press F12 (Windows) or Option+F12 (Macintosh) to open organic.htm in a Web browser.

Notice that the Flash movie is too large for the box it's supposed to go in. The movie is 550 pixels wide, but the layer in which it has been placed is only 539 pixels wide.

7. Return to Dreamweaver. Click to select the Flash placeholder. In the Property inspector, lower the Width to **523** pixels, and the Height to **380** pixels. Save your changes.

This step decreases the display area of the movie by about 5 percent, which is enough to make it fit within the layer. As a vector-based medium, Flash movies scale up and down quite well.

8. Click anywhere in the open document, and press F12 (Windows) or Option+F12 (Macintosh) to open organic.htm in a Web browser.

This time, the entire movie fits neatly inside the layout.

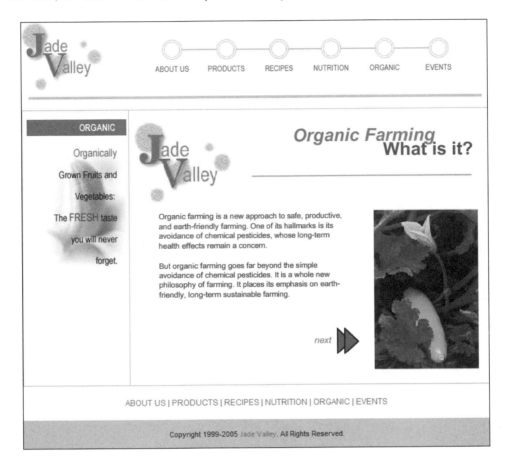

What You Have Learned

In this lesson, you have:

- Animated a text block so that it flew across a portion of the stage (pages 244–247)
- Faded graphic symbols in and out using motion tweens (pages 248–253)
- Used ActionScript to make the buttons functional (pages 254–260)
- Defined the Over, Down, and Hit states of a button (pages 260–265)
- Published your Flash movie (pages 265–269)

9 Flash Video

The basics of working in Flash are now familiar to you: keyframes, tweens, laying out screens, importing digital photos, and some basic scripting. As you'll discover in this lesson, working with video in Flash is somewhat different from working with bitmaps, because there's more to video.

Specifically, video contains a sequence of bitmap images, rather than a single image; a video file also may include one or more audio tracks; and the video file may be encoded using special compression algorithms. In addition, video files tend to be massive by

In this lesson you'll start with a QuickTime video file, import it into Flash, and publish it on a page in the Jade Valley Web site.

Web standards (and arguably by any standards). Each of these characteristics of video has implications for how you deploy it. For example, because of its large file size, Web users might require a minute or potentially much longer to download a video. As a result, you must decide whether to stream the video or force the user to download the entire movie first; each option has its pros and cons.

When you import video into Flash, these issues don't go away—at least for you, the developer. Flash can't shrink the video to a tiny file size. The audio and video tracks are still there, and they still have to be synchronized with each other. But if you do your part right, the problems are greatly minimized for the viewer, because the Flash player ensures that users can see the video and that it plays back as you specified it should.

What You Will Learn

In this lesson, you will:

- Create a new movie to host a video
- Convert a QuickTime video to the native Flash FLV video format
- Learn basic Flash video concepts
- Test and publish the Flash video in a Web page

Approximate Time

This lesson takes approximately 30 minutes to complete.

Lesson Files

Starting Files:

Lesson09/Start/FarmersMarketVideo.mov
Lesson09/Start/farmers_bkg.jpg
Lesson09/Start/jade_valley/events.htm

Completed Files:

Lesson09/Complete/jade_valley/events.htm
Lesson09/Complete/jade_valley/flash/farmers_market.fla
Lesson09/Complete/jade_valley/flash/farmers_market.swf
Lesson09/Complete/jade_valley/flash/FarmersMarketVideo.flv
Lesson09/Start/jade_valley/MojaveExternalPlaySeekMute.swf

Preparing the Movie

In this task, you'll prepare the Flash movie so that it's ready for the video. The techniques should already be familiar from earlier lessons, and will become second nature over time as you use them frequently in your Flash development workflow.

1. Open Flash 8. From the main menu, choose File › New. In the New Document dialog, choose Flash Document and click OK.

An untitled movie opens, whose dimensions are by default 550 pixels wide by 400 pixels tall.

Note *You can see the movie dimensions in the Property inspector; if they are other than 550 × 400, click the Document Properties button in the Property inspector (the button with the pixel dimensions in it) and make the change.*

2. With nothing selected, click the Document Properties button (which indicates 550 × 400 as the present pixel dimensions). In the Document Properties dialog, change the pixel dimensions to 500 × 350.

The video itself is only 320 × 240 pixels, so creating a 550 × 400 stage would create a lot of wasted space, rather than the tasteful frame that you want.

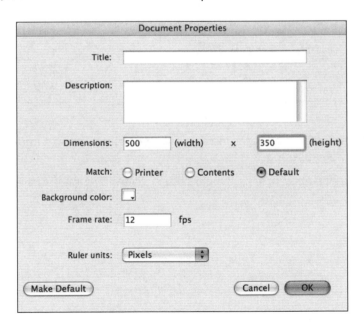

3. In the timeline, click the Insert Layer button to add a new layer.

You'll place a background in the lower layer, and you'll put the video in the upper layer.

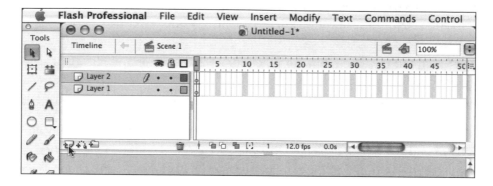

4. One at a time, double-click each layer name and rename it, naming the lower layer *background* and the upper layer *video*.

Naming your layers meaningfully makes them much easier to use in the long run.

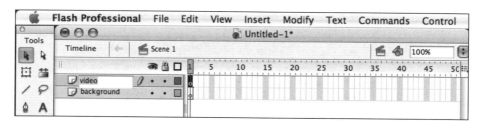

5. Select Frame 1 of the background layer. Select File > Import > Import to Stage, and import farmers_bkg.jpg.

A digital photo appears on the stage. It looks blurry because it's simply a background photo.

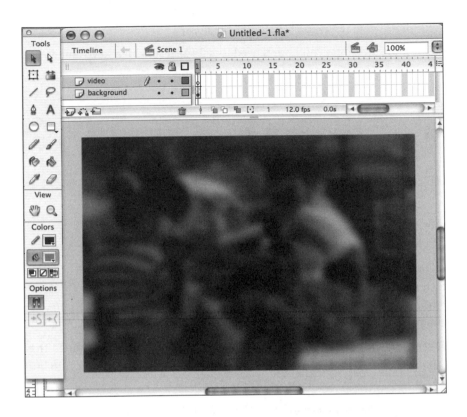

6. Save the file, naming it *farmers_market.fla*, in the Jade Valley flash folder.

Converting Video to the FLV Format

From the standpoint of the interface, converting non-Flash video (such as QuickTime or AVI video) to the Flash-friendly FLV format is quite easy. Flash has an importer that does just about all the work. The challenging part isn't working through a complex set of steps, but rather in making educated decisions as you work through the import wizard.

In this task, you'll import a QuickTime video that has been provided for you. To do so, you'll work through Flash's video import wizard. As you go through the screens in the wizard, you'll accept most of the defaults. However, we'll explore the options anyway, so you understand *why* you're accepting the defaults and, more importantly, so you know when you should choose other options.

1. In the timeline, select Frame 1 of the video layer.

Before you import anything, you always need to tell Flash in which keyframe you want the item to appear, whether it's a video, image, or sound file.

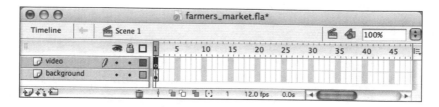

2. From the main menu, choose File > Import > Import Video.

The Import Video wizard appears, with the Select Video screen active.

3. Click the Browse or Choose button and navigate to the FarmersMarketVideo.mov file, which is provided on the CD-ROM in this lesson's Start folder. Click Continue.

Immediately, you're faced with a decision concerning the location of the file. If the file is on your local computer, as it is in this case, select the On Your Computer radio button and browse to the file. If the file is already on a server, provide its address here.

> **Note** Different kinds of servers host video in different ways. If the file is sitting on a regular Web server, it's treated much like any other file. However, video-streaming servers, such as Flash Communications Server, offer special features. Note that you're not limited to http:// when specifying video URLs; you can also use the Flash Media Server rtmp:// protocol.

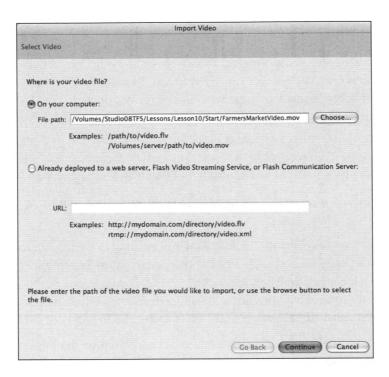

4. In the Deployment screen of the Import Video wizard, leave the default set to Progressive Download From a Web Server. Click Continue.

Flash can work with video in a number of different ways, and this screen presents perhaps the most important decision that you'll make. The deployment methods are as follows:

- Progressive download from a Web server. The video is converted to an FLV file and stored outside of the Flash SWF in which it appears, and it is streamed into Flash over standard HTTP. User interface and scripting controls in the SWF file itself control the user experience. This option requires the Flash 7 player, which was released in 2003, or higher.

- Stream from Flash Video Streaming Service. The Flash Video Streaming Service is a hosted Flash Media Server account. It offers improved features and functionality over standard HTTP video streams, but you have to pay for the service.

- Stream from Flash Media Server. This option is very similar to the previous one, the main difference being that you're hosting the Flash Media Server yourself, rather than working through a third party. Again, it's more expensive than the Progressive download option, and it is more full-featured.

- Embed video in SWF and play in timeline. This option is the most intuitive, and yet is probably the worst choice. The video is actually imported into the SWF itself and plays on the timeline, just like any other Flash asset (such as an image or a graphic symbol). However, video is not like any other Flash asset, and introduces problems, such as bloated SWF file size, sound synchronization issues, and other performance problems. This option is generally not recommended, unless the video is very short (say, a few seconds), it doesn't contain a soundtrack, and/or you're limited to the Flash 6 or earlier.

• Linked QuickTime video for publishing to QuickTime. This is a legacy option, which is available only if you're publishing to the antiquated Flash 3, 4, or 5 players. It lets you export the Flash content in the QuickTime MOV format, which is playable in the QuickTime player with the added benefit of Flash features, such as basic interactivity.

In most situations, if you use video sparingly, Progressive download is the option you should use.

If you're using video heavily, you should consider upgrading to a Flash Media Server, either through an external hosting solution such as Flash Video Streaming Service, or by hosting your own copy of the Flash Media Server. Flash Media Server enables faster startup; far better control over the video, including deep interactivity with the video; live video; improved seek and navigation; and even tracking and logging capabilities.

Avoid embedding video unless it is only a few seconds in duration, has no sound, and is targeted to older Flash players.

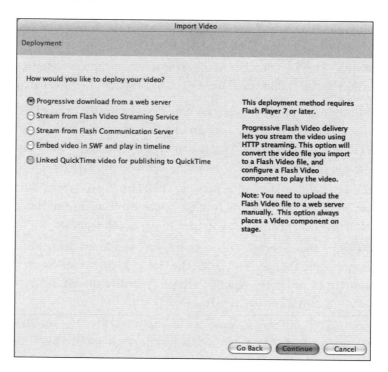

5. In the Encoding screen, click **Show Advanced Settings**. View the various options, returning to the default (Flash 8 – Medium Quality 400kbps). Then, at the bottom of Encode Audio section, change the Data Rate setting to **64 kbps (mono)**. Click **Continue**.

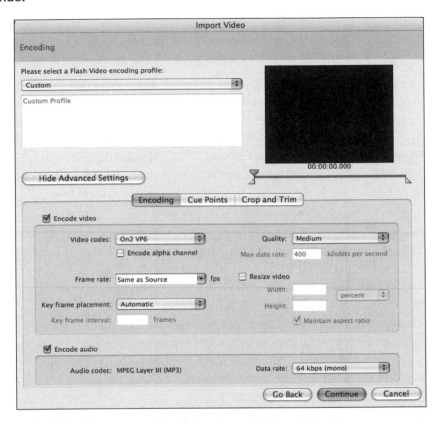

The decisions you make on this screen have two primary consequences: file size and compatibility. The usual tradeoffs are in full force: video quality, file size, and compatibility. You can usually prioritize any two of these, but at the expense of the third.

For example, by sticking with the default you'll obtain the highest possible quality and lowest file size by using the latest codec; in doing so, however, you sacrifice compatibility, because some visitors might have older Flash players that lack the latest codec. You can switch to an older codec, thereby increasing compatibility, but because its coding algorithms aren't as good, the file size is likely to be larger and/or the image quality is likely to be lower.

The term *codec* stands for code-decode, and is the algorithm (computerized sequence of steps) used to compress and then decompress the video for playback. When publishing to the Flash 8 player, use the default On2 VP6 codec, which is superior to the older Sorenson Spark codec but is available only in Flash 8. If you want to include Flash 7 players, you should use the Sorenson Spark codec.

After you've chosen a codec, you can configure several of its characteristics (displayed in the Advanced settings in the lower half of the window). These include the following:

- **Frame rate:** Higher frame rates render the original video more faithfully but increase the file size. Because external (progressive or streamed) video can have different frame rates than the parent SWF, you can make your decision without regard for the rest of the SWF. Most SWFs default to a low-quality 12 frames per second, while Hollywood movies are released at 24 frames per second. NTSC (the standard television picture in the United States) is broadcast at just under 30 frames per second. As a rule, you can use lower frame rates for low-action content, such as talking heads, and use higher frame rates for high-action content, such as sports.

- **Key Frame Placement:** A video running at 24 frames per second could theoretically be rendered using a sequence of 24 bitmaps per second. However, the difference between any pair of sequential bitmaps (for example, the difference between image 1 and 2) is likely to be relatively small. Therefore, it's usually more efficient to describe the differences introduced in Frame 2, rather than to download an all-new image. Video compression algorithms, therefore, typically use only one full frame and then follow it with descriptions of the differences. For example, it might provide one full image and then 23 directions before providing a new full image. The full image, of course, is the keyframe, and the more keyframes you have, the higher the fidelity is likely to be—and the larger the file size.

- **Quality:** The quality refers to the amount of data that can be transmitted per second, which has a significant impact on streaming. Higher amounts take longer to download and display; lower amounts are less likely to reproduce the video faithfully.

- **Resize Video:** If your video source is not the size you need, you can resize it. As a rule, decreasing the video size also decreases the file size.

Each of these options only specifies how the video should be compressed. If your source video has one or more audio tracks, you can also specify how they're encoded. As a rule, you'll use the MP3 audio format, and the only setting you can change is the Data rate. As always, higher data rates increase the potential fidelity, while lower ones mean better file size.

You specify 64 kbps (mono) here, because this video was recorded with a handheld camcorder with a mono microphone. There's no need to add the expense of a stereo-quality data rate when the audio track is mono to begin with!

> **Tip** *So far this lesson has a lot of information to digest, and even this is but a sampling of the issues with which you should become familiar. For a jump start into the world of video, check out Macromedia's Flash Video Developer Center at http://www.macromedia.com/devnet/flash/video.html.*

6. In the Skinning screen of the Import Video wizard, select MojaveExternalPlaySeekMute.swf, and click Continue.

Feel free to take a moment to explore different skins. There are four basic designs: Arctic, Clear, Mojave, and Steel. As you can see with some experimentation, a skin is a playback window design. It includes a color scheme and different combinations of button displays. In all cases, the movie will play back in the window the same. The differences, then, are cosmetic. Do you want a blue, brown, or gray player? Which buttons do you want? Where do you want the buttons to appear?

After you're finished experimenting, make sure you select MojaveExternalPlaySeekMute.swf. You chose Mojave because its brown color goes well with the natural and organic themes of the Jade Valley Web site. The distinction between Internal and External has to do with the location of the controls: over the video or outside the video. You chose External so the controls won't block the video, and because there's plenty of room in this design for the video. The remaining variations have to do with which buttons are available. You chose PlaySeekMute because they are all buttons that function in a progressive video. Had you chosen All, two more buttons—seek forward and seek backward—would have appeared; however, these buttons won't function correctly unless you're streaming video from Flash Media Server or Flash Video Streaming Service.

If you've designed your own skin you can use it, provided that it's published on a server. In that case, enter the server location in the URL field, instead of choosing a skin.

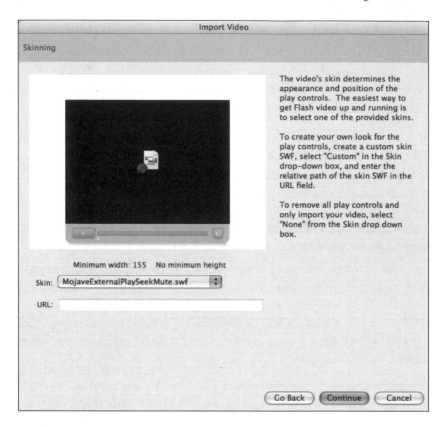

7. Click Finish.

The final screen lets you review your selections and go back and make corrections before you start the process of converting the video to the FLV format.

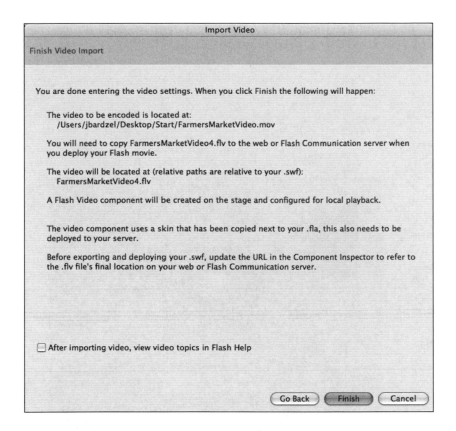

Import Video

Finish Video Import

You are done entering the video settings. When you click Finish the following will happen:

The video to be encoded is located at:
/Users/jbardzel/Desktop/Start/FarmersMarketVideo.mov

You will need to copy FarmersMarketVideo4.flv to the web or Flash Communication server when you deploy your Flash movie.

The video will be located at (relative paths are relative to your .swf):
FarmersMarketVideo4.flv

A Flash Video component will be created on the stage and configured for local playback.

The video component uses a skin that has been copied next to your .fla, this also needs to be deployed to your server.

Before exporting and deploying your .swf, update the URL in the Component Inspector to refer to the .flv file's final location on your web or Flash Communication server.

☐ After importing video, view video topics in Flash Help

(Go Back)   (Finish)   (Cancel)

8. Save the file as *farmer's market.fla* inside the flash folder of the Jade Valley Web site.

After you click Save, Flash initiates the process of converting the video to the FLV format, attaching the selected skin to the video, and so on. Once begun, the process may take a while. (On a dual-processor Macintosh G5, for example, the whole process took over 4 minutes. On a laptop, it will likely take much longer.)

When the import is finished, an instance of the FLVPlayback component appears on your screen.

9. Adjust the position of the FLVPlayback component, as appropriate. Then test the movie by pressing Ctrl+Enter/Command+Enter.

The movie plays back inside the component.

Publishing the Flash Video

You've now done the hard part, which is getting video into Flash. Actually, doing so is quite easy now, thanks to the combination of the FLVPlayback component and the Import Video wizard. The final remaining issue is to put it in your site.

1. Save and close the movie in Flash. Open Dreamweaver 8.

Publishing the movie at this point is pretty much the same as publishing any Flash SWF in a Web page, with a couple of exceptions that you'll work through here.

2. Open events.htm. Position the insertion point just before the "A Harmony tradition" paragraph, and press Enter/Return once to create an empty paragraph.

You're creating the space in which you'll put the new Flash movie.

Jade Valley Events

The town of Harmony, Indiana, and its surrounding region hosts events throughout the year. Jade Valley is proud to participate in and in some cases co-sponsor these events.

Every Memorial Day weekend, Harmony hosts the **Strawberry Festival**. Children from all around come to Jade Valley and other farms to pick strawberries from green fields. Later, the town comes together on Main Street for live music, bar-be-que, and (of course!) strawberry pie.

Jade Valley is always well represented at the **Farmer's Market**. Held every Saturday morning, the Farmer's Market has dozens of stalls with fresh fruits and vegetables, flowers, popcorn, and crafts from throughout the area. Look for the Jade Valley stall each week, where we bring the best of the season directly to you.

A Harmony tradition, **Picnic in the Park** is an event that takes place every year in Columbus park on the last Saturday of September. Join us as we say goodbye to the hot nights of summer and welcome the equinox and the autumn harvest that follows on its heels.

In addition to these major events, look for Jade Valley staff at Green Grocer-sponsored events (such as the semi-annual Truckload Sale), the annual 10K Run/Walk for the Cure, and Shakespeare in the Park.

ABOUT US | PRODUCTS | RECIPES | NUTRITION | ORGANIC | EVENTS

---

3. Choose Insert > Media > Flash. Select farmers_market.swf in the site's flash folder and click OK/Choose. In the accessibility dialog that appears, enter *Sights and sounds of the farmer's market.* as the Title and click OK.

When you're finished, a gray box representing the Flash movie appears in the page.

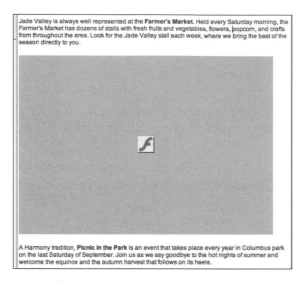

4. Press F12 (Windows) or Option+F12 (Macintosh) to preview the page in a browser, saving the file at the prompt.

The good news is that the Flash movie appears and the video starts playing. However, the Mojave controls do not appear.

The problem is that the Mojave skin, which is called MojavePlaySeekMute.swf, needs to be in the same directory as the HTML page that calls the Flash movie to load properly. However, it too has been saved in the flash folder, along with farmers_market.swf and FarmersMarketVideo.flv.

5. In Dreamweaver's Site panel, locate MojavePlaySeekMute.swf in the flash folder. Press and drag the file until it's in the parent (root) directory. When the dialog appears asking to update the links, click Update.

When you're finished with this step, the skin file is located in the root directory, at the same level as events.htm.

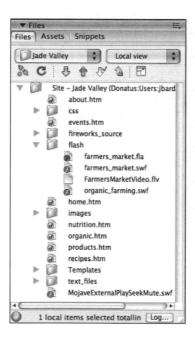

6. Press F12 (Windows) or Option+F12 (Mac) to test the page again.

This time it works!

What You Have Learned

In this lesson, you have:

- Prepared a Flash movie to hold and play back a video file (pages 273–275)
- Converted a QuickTime movie to a Flash FLV (pages 275–284)
- Learned the basics of video compression and optimization (pages 275–281)
- Published the Flash video in an HTML page (pages 285–288)

Project 2: A Class on Dante

Part 4: Dreamweaver and Flash

10 Preparing the Dante Site

This lesson marks a significant turning point in the book. Until now, you've worked on the Jade Valley Web site, learning how to integrate Macromedia Fireworks, Macromedia Dreamweaver, and Macromedia Flash to create a visually appealing static Web site. In the second half of the book, you'll learn how to create sites that *do* something. You'll create Flash movies with sophisticated interactive interfaces. You'll harness the power of Macromedia ColdFusion to enable Web pages to interact with databases, showing live data on the fly; capture data your users enter into forms; and save the data to a database. In Lessons 15, *A Component-based Flash Quiz*, and Lesson 16, *Flash, ColdFusion, and the Database*, you'll put it all together by creating a Flash-based quiz, whose data is sent to a database.

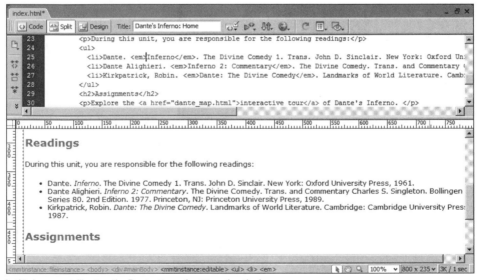

In this lesson you'll set up the Dante site and put together the home page.

The project you'll complete is for a class on the medieval poet Dante. You'll create an interactive map of his *Inferno*, a description of the peoples and places of Hell. Users will be able to click different elements in the map to learn more, and they'll even be able to play a drag-and-drop monsters game. You'll also create a page that shows basic information about all the students in the class.

In this lesson, you'll set the project in motion by defining the new site in Dreamweaver and using a template, which we've provided, to create all the pages that will eventually be in the site. You'll populate those pages with real content over the remainder of the book. Right now, you're just preparing the site for what's to come.

What You Will Learn

In this lesson, you will:

- Define the new Dante site
- Create several placeholder pages based on a Dreamweaver template
- Format text and insert an image to create the site's home page
- Familiarize yourself with the eventual plan for the site

Approximate Time

This lesson takes approximately 30 minutes to complete.

Lesson Files

Starting Files:

Lesson10/Start/dante/Templates/dante_template.dwt

Completed Files:

Lesson10/Complete/dante/dante_admin.html
Lesson10/Complete/dante/dante_map.html
Lesson10/Complete/dante/dante_quiz_login.html
Lesson10/Complete/dante/dante_quiz_questions.html
Lesson10/Complete/dante/dante_quiz_results.html
Lesson10/Complete/dante/index.html

Defining the Dante Site

In this task, you'll copy the files from the CD-ROM included with the book to your hard drive and define the site in Dreamweaver.

1. Copy the entire dante folder from the Lesson10/Start folder on the CD to your hard drive.

You can put the folder on your Desktop, in your Documents or Sites folders (Macintosh) or the My Documents folder (Windows), or anywhere you want, as long as you remember where you put it.

2. Open Dreamweaver. Choose Site › Manage Sites. Click New and choose Site from the pop-up.

The Site Definition dialog appears.

The Advanced tab should be active, but if it is not, click the tab so that you can define the site in advanced mode.

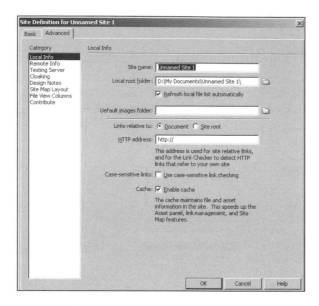

3. In the Local Info category, name the site *dante*. In the Local Root Folder field, browse to the dante folder you just copied to your hard drive.

You can leave all the other options at their defaults.

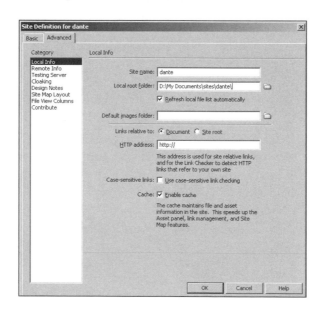

4. Click OK to finish defining the site. Return to the Manage Sites dialog and click Done.

For now, you're defining the site as a static site; you're not configuring the site to work with ColdFusion or a database just yet. In Lesson 13, *Dynamic, Data-Driven Sites*, you'll return to this dialog and redefine the site so that it can access a ColdFusion-enabled Web server.

The Files panel lists the folders and files in the site. No HTML files yet exist, but there is a template in the Templates folder, which you'll use to create each of the site's files. In addition, a cascading style sheet, stored in the css folder, has already been created and applied to the template file.

Two of the folders won't be used directly in the site: the Fireworks Source and Text Source folders. The Fireworks Source folder contains the Fireworks PNG file that has the layout for the Dante site, and is included in case you want to explore it. The Text Source folder contains some of the text that will be used in the site; it's included to save you some typing.

Creating the Placeholder Pages

Different developers have different workflows for creating Web sites. Some developers like to create and develop pages one at a time, as they build the site, while others like to create placeholder pages in advance and then go back and fill in the content. You'll use the second approach in this lesson. One benefit of creating placeholder pages in advance is that you can then take advantage of Dreamweaver's site and link management features.

The process is somewhat repetitive, since you'll be doing the same three tasks over and over: creating a new page based on the template, changing the page title and header, and saving the file.

1. Choose File > New. Click the Templates tab. In the Templates for column, choose Site "dante," if it's not already selected. Verify that the dante_template is selected and check the Update page when the template changes. Click Create.

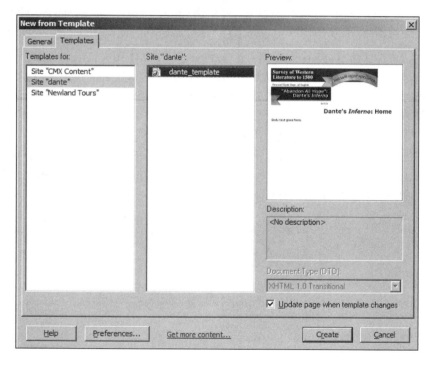

When you're finished, a page with two editable regions appears. One region is for the page heading, which is set to Home by default. The other region is for the main page contents.

Note *Actually, there's a third editable region on the page, although you can't see it right away. The* <title> *element inside the* <head> *tag is also editable.*

Note *The benefits of templates were discussed earlier, in Lesson 5,* Developing a Page Template.

Note *The image of the template in the preview window might appear misaligned. You can disregard that.*

2. In the Title field in the Document toolbar, change the title to *Dante's Inferno: Home.*

Remember, the title is not displayed in the body of the document. It's shown in the browser title bar and is used by search engines. It's important to name each page descriptively.

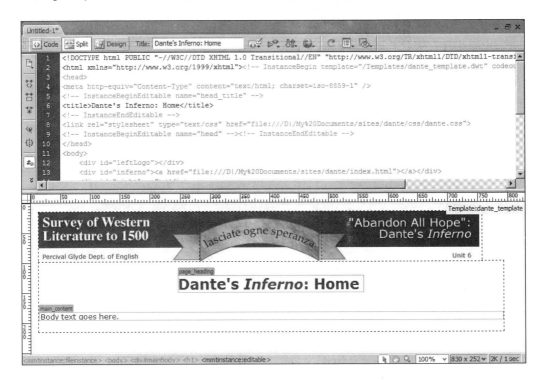

Normally, the next step would be to change the page heading, but it already says Home, which is what we want.

3. Save the file as *index.html* and close it.

You're going to do more to this page in the next task, but for now, the page at least exists.

4. Repeat Steps 1–3 to create five more pages, using the information in the following table as a guide.

File Name	Page Title and Heading
dante_admin.html	Dante's Inferno: Admin
dante_map.html	Dante's Inferno: Interactive Map
dante_quiz_login.html	Dante's Inferno: Quiz Login
dante_quiz_questions.html	Dante's Inferno: Quiz Questions
dante_quiz_results.html	Dante's Inferno: Quiz Results

In each case, you can leave the "Body text goes here" placeholder alone. You'll fix that later.

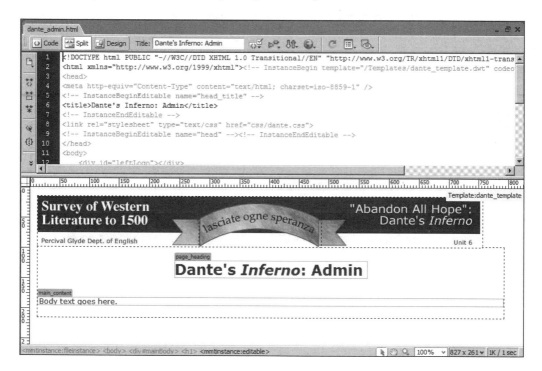

When you're finished with this step, the Files panel should list six HTML files in the root directory.

As mentioned earlier, the final version of this site will have three major components: an interactive map of the *Inferno*, an administrative area where users can see information about all the students in the class, and a quiz. You can see how these six pages represent the three components.

Formatting the Home Page

As far as Dreamweaver's Files panel and site manager are concerned, you're already finished with the site. In reality, you still have a lot of work to do, but Dreamweaver is now tracking each of the files that you'll use for the remainder of the project. As a result, you can add hyperlinks using Dreamweaver tools such as Point to File, and be certain that no links are broken.

In this task, you'll assemble the home page, which links to each of the site's three main components.

1. Open index.html, the file you just saved.

At this point, index.html has only a page title and the placeholder text, "Body text goes here."

2. In the Files panel, double-click the Text Source folder icon, and open index.txt.

A plain text document opens in Dreamweaver.

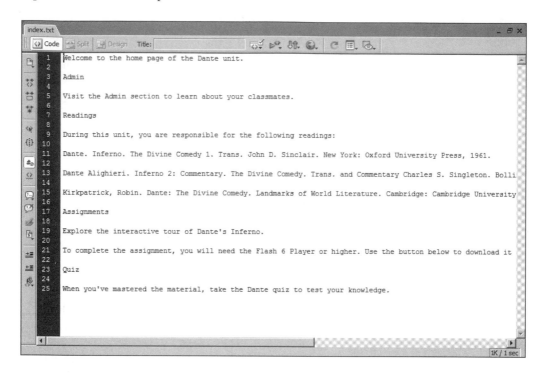

3. Click anywhere in the text, and choose Edit > Select All and then Edit > Copy. Close the text file and return to index.html. Drag to select "Body text goes here" in the design half of split view, and choose Edit > Paste Special.... Choose Text with structure and click OK.

The text is pasted into the document. Dreamweaver creates <p> tag paragraphs for each of the paragraphs in the original text. If Dreamweaver does not create paragraphs, click at the end of each line in the Design pane and press Enter/Return. Some of the paragraphs should actually be headings, but this is a start.

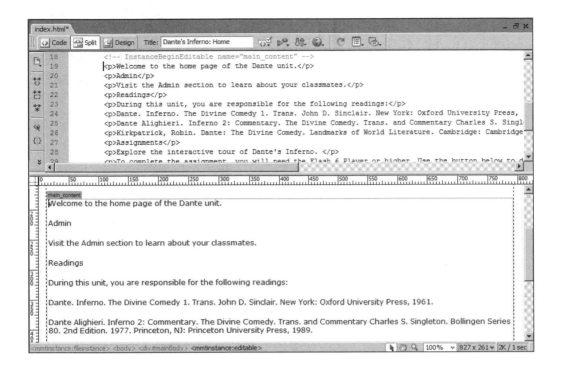

4. In the design half of split view, click once inside each of the following paragraphs and use the Format drop-down of the Property inspector to set each of the following to Heading 2.

Admin

Readings

Assignments

Quiz

You've replaced the <p> tag wrapping each of these paragraphs with an <h2> tag.

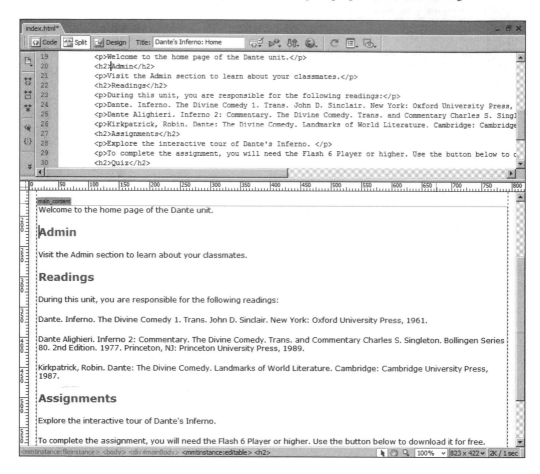

Each of these headings appears gray, because the <h2> tag has been redefined using CSS to be gray. Later, you'll see that all the hyperlinks are red; again, this setting was achieved using CSS.

5. Still in design view, select the word "Admin" in the body section beneath the Admin heading, and link it to dante_admin.html in the Property inspector.

To link Admin, you can use the Point to File tool in the Property inspector, you can browse to the file by clicking the folder next to the Link field in the Property inspector, or you can type the name manually.

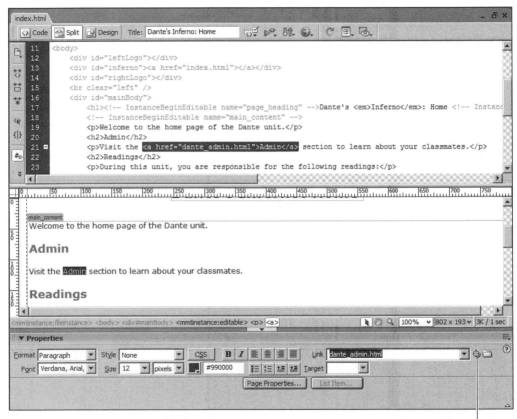

Point to File

6. Repeat Step 5 to link the words "interactive tour" (in the Assignments section) to dante_map.html, and the words "take the Dante quiz" (in the Quiz section) to dante_quiz_login.html.

The home page now works as a navigation interface.

You still need to put some finishing touches on the page.

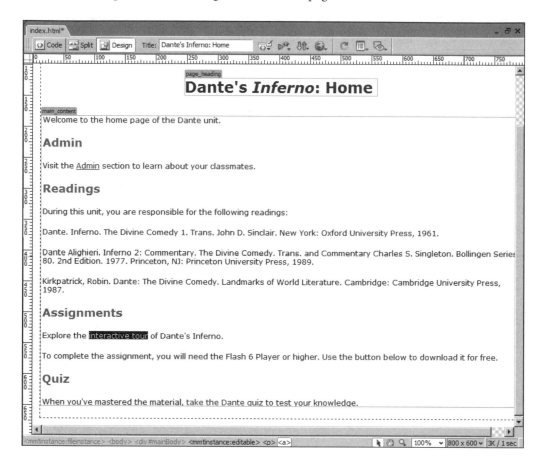

7. Select the three books listed in the Readings section, and use the Property inspector to apply an unordered list.

Use unordered lists for lists that do not imply any sort of sequence.

Each item in the list is wrapped inside an <li> (list item) tag, while all the items as a group are wrapped inside a <ul> (unordered list) tag.

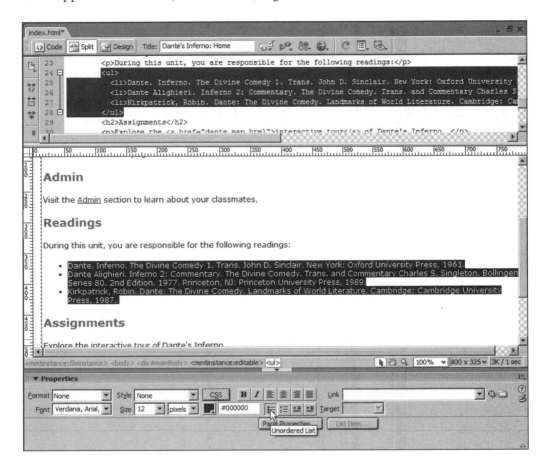

8. Use the Property inspector to apply italics to each of the three book titles listed below.

Inferno

Inferno 2: Commentary

Dante: The Divine Comedy

Use the <em> (emphasis) tag to add italics.

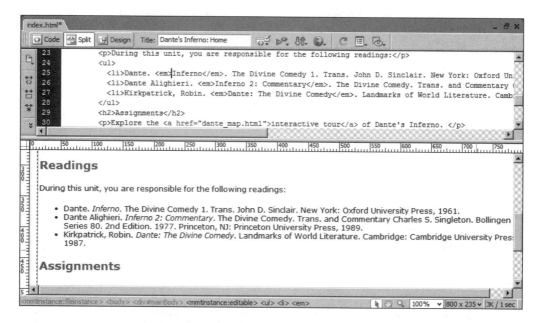

At this point, you're only missing the button in the line that begins "To complete the assignment," in the Assignments section.

9. Place the insertion point at the end of the line that begins "To complete the assignment," and press Enter/Return.

This creates an empty paragraph just above the Quiz heading.

10. Choose Insert > Image from the main menu, browse to the site's images folder, and insert get_flashplayer.gif.

11. The Image Tag Accessibility Attributes dialog box appears. Type *Download the Flash Player.* in the Alternate text box.

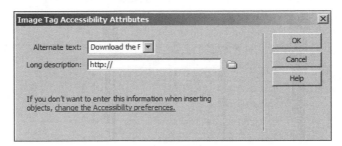

The image appears in the document, but it is not yet linked to Macromedia's site, where users can download the Flash Player.

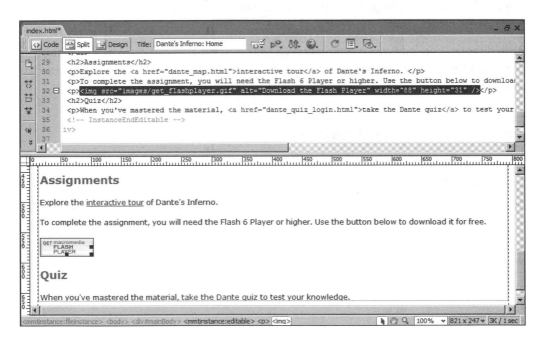

12. With the image selected, enter the following URL in the Link field of the Property inspector.

```
http://www.macromedia.com/go/getflashplayer/
```

Because this link points outside of the Dante site, you'll need to use an absolute URL. As discussed in Lesson 6, *Developing Site Content*, absolute URLs need to be complete, starting with http:// and containing the full path to the desired page or other resource.

13. Save and close index.html.

You're finished preparing the site. In subsequent lessons, you'll add several interesting pieces of functionality using Flash and ColdFusion.

As you develop sites in Dreamweaver, you'll repeat the tasks from this lesson many times, until doing so becomes nearly automatic. The key is to use reusable page elements, in particular Dreamweaver templates and CSS styles. With the templates and CSS styles in place, it's easy to mock up the basics of even large sites very quickly.

What You Have Learned

In this lesson, you have:

- Defined the Dante site (pages 293–295)
- Used a Dreamweaver template to create placeholder pages for each page needed in the final version of the site (pages 296–299)
- Created and formatted items in a list (pages 299–308)
- Formatted the home page (pages 299–306)
- Inserted an image with a hyperlink (pages 306–308)

11 Nonlinear Flash Interactions

One of the advantages of multimedia is that you can pack a lot more information in the same amount of space as a traditional printed page. In the project you'll begin in this lesson, an interactive map of Dante's *Inferno*, the text presented is three pages, single spaced, and yet all the text appears in only two Macromedia Flash screens, using about 20 percent of the space on each screen. This efficiency is possible because only a certain portion of the text—the text that the user actually needs—is showing at one time.

Determining which pieces of text the user needs is easy. When she or he clicks on an object, the descriptive text for that object should appear. Before the user clicks an object, a generic set of directions appears, telling the user what to click, roll over, or drag.

Making the movie this responsive by changing the text on the fly, depending on the user's actions, is possible with dynamic text. To create a dynamic text region, you set

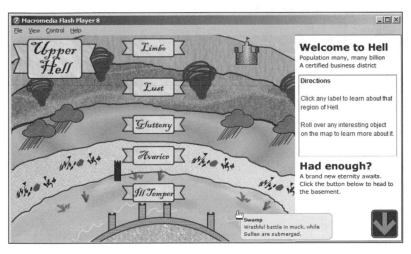

Both the text in the Swamp pop-up window and the main text in the scrollbar box are set dynamically, depending on what the user is doing.

up a text field, just as you would for static text, but you designate it as dynamic text in the Property inspector. You then dynamically change the text through ActionScript. In this lesson, you 'll explore many of the possibilities of user-controlled dynamic text.

The resulting movie is nonlinear; users can access content in any order they want, skip content, and see content as many times as they like. Creating this open-ended Flash experience is best with a different movie architecture from the linear, timeline-based movies you made in the previous lessons. Nonlinear, interactive movies rely on a low number of keyframes—often just one or two—and lots of ActionScript. Fortunately, as you'll soon see, the ActionScript needed to power the dynamic text in the interactive map of Dante's *Inferno* is simple.

What You Will Learn

In this lesson, you will:

- Learn about Flash objects and how they're accessed and manipulated using ActionScript
- Control the visibility of movie clip instances
- Create and position Tooltips using a movie clip, dynamic text, and mouse positioning
- Format dynamic text with HTML tags
- Use `onRollOver` and `onRollOut` event handlers
- Implement a scrollable TextArea component

Approximate Time

This lesson takes approximately 90 minutes to complete.

Lesson Files

Starting Files:

Lesson11/Start/dante/flash/dante.fla
Lesson11/Start/dante/flash/dante_complete.swf
Lesson11/Start/dante/Text Source/script_inferno_html.txt

Completed Files:

Lesson11/Complete/dante/flash/dante.fla

An Interactive Map of Dante's *Inferno*

Before beginning this lesson, you'll take a look at the finished project in Lesson 12, *Drag-and-Drop Interactions*. When developing any sophisticated multimedia asset, you should have a clear road map of what you're trying to build. It might include a text description, some notes scribbled on paper, line drawings, and so on. But before you begin the development process, you should know exactly what you're trying to build. In this task, you'll look at the finished map to get a firm idea of where you're headed in these two lessons.

The Dante file you'll work with has two keyframes, each representing one half of a map of Hell, as depicted in Dante's *Inferno*. In this lesson, you'll build most of the first keyframe—the upper half of the map. In Lesson 12, which focuses on creating drag-and-drop interactivity, you'll build the lower half of the map.

As you work through the steps in this first task, take your time and explore the movie. As you do so, be sure to notice how the upper half of the Inferno map works, because that's what you'll be building in this lesson.

1. Open dante_complete.swf in the Lesson11/Start/dante/flash folder.

This entire project is an interactive map. The maps and all the graphic assets were created with Macromedia Fireworks, and imported into the file as flat PNG bitmaps. All the interactivity is layered on top of the map using invisible Flash buttons, which act like hotspots.

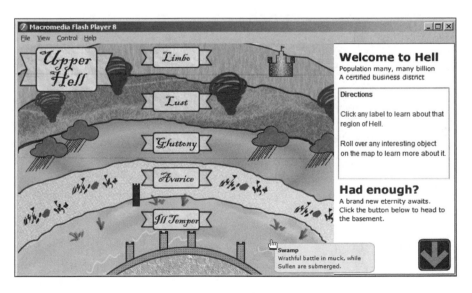

2. Roll over the objects depicted in each circle, including the tempests, storm clouds, castle, and city.

As you roll over each object, a Tooltip appears, telling you about each screen element. Although it might seem that the movie has lots of these hidden tips that pop up when the mouse rolls over them, in fact, the movie has only one. The Tooltip is a movie clip instance, whose visibility is toggled on and off when the user rolls over hot areas of the map. In addition, each time the Tooltip is activated, it's dynamically positioned via ActionScript and its text is dynamically populated.

3. Click each of the parchment labels, including Upper Hell, Limbo, Lust, and so on.

As you click each label, the text displayed in the right text area changes. This, too, is dynamic text. The scrollbar allows text fields of different lengths to fit in the same-sized window. Thanks to scrollable text areas like this one, you can edit for content, rather than editing for fit—that is, trying to squeeze text into a given space.

4. Click the Down button to enter Lower Hell.

When you click the Down button, the second map appears. This map is on the second keyframe of the movie.

5. Explore the second movie by clicking the parchment labels and dragging the monsters to target areas.

You'll build this file in the next lesson, so for now just get a sense of how it works.

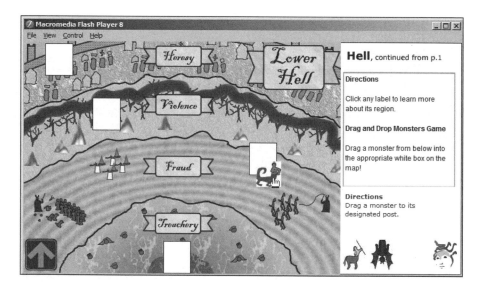

6. Close the movie and the SWF player.

The preview is finished, and now it's time to start building your own Inferno.

Introducing Flash Objects

In this lesson, you'll deploy a number of different types of Flash objects and manipulate them via ActionScript. You'll implement text fields, movie clips, buttons, and a TextArea component, which automates the process of creating scrollable text fields. While it's possible to simply dive in and start using these objects, it's best if you understand what's happening behind the scenes. In the long run, you'll have a clearer idea about how Flash works, and writing ActionScript will become much easier.

Anatomy of an Object

As Flash continues to evolve, it has become increasingly object-oriented in nature. Object-oriented programming (also known as OOP) is a large and intimidating topic for nonprogrammers. However, even if you understand only the gist of the theory behind it, many once-mysterious aspects of Flash become more comprehensible. You've made use of objects every time you've worked in Flash, whether or not you did any scripting. Flash's interface—timeline, Library, stage, tools, and many panels—provides a visual environment for implementing and manipulating the underlying objects that make Flash what it is.

You can think of objects of as a cluster of information and capabilities residing in a single entity, which can be reused in many different ways. Think for a moment about buttons in Flash. All the buttons have four states (Up, Over, Down, and Hit). All the buttons notify Flash when they're being clicked, rolled over, or dragged. All are capable of causing something else to happen (for example, triggering a `gotoAndStop()` action). Flash has an underlying `Button` object with all these features built in. Each time you create a new button, you configure various parameters (such as the size and color of its Up state), and you make use of—but cannot change—its built-in capabilities.

> **Note** *Strictly speaking, you can change Flash objects' built-in capabilities. You can often extend them—that is, add new capabilities and features to the objects. However, that's an advanced topic that requires advanced programming. The potential to extend existing objects notwithstanding, you still cannot remove their built-in capabilities and features.*

Objects—in Flash or elsewhere—are complex entities, which comprise a combination of several different parts. Broadly speaking, these parts can be divided into three categories.

- **Events:** Notifications that something has happened with or to the object. For example, button events include pressing, releasing, and dragging over the button. A frame event occurs every time Flash enters a new frame, notifying Flash that a new frame has loaded. Events are often used to trigger some other action.

- **Properties:** Variable pieces of information. A button has both height and width properties. Every button has a height and width, but the values of the height and width vary from button to button. An object's alpha transparency and location on stage are also stored as properties.

- **Methods:** Behaviors that the object can do. You use methods to make a timeline play or stop. The now familiar `stop()` and `gotoAndPlay()` are both methods of the `MovieClip` class.

Any object can have any combination of parts in any of these categories. An object might have five built-in properties, two methods, and no events, or just about any other combination. A large part—if not the majority—of learning ActionScript is learning about the different objects available in Flash, and learning how to take advantage of their built-in events, properties, and methods.

Scripting with Flash Objects

To make use of an object, you must create an instance of it, often referred to as instantiating the object. Once it's instantiated, you can take advantage of an object's events, properties, and methods. Obviously, you can't specify a button's height and width unless the button exists. Thus, objects exist at two levels: in an abstract level where events, methods, and properties are defined but don't have any values (think of human DNA); and a concrete level of an individual instance of that object, with fully defined values (think of an actual person). Objects at the abstract level are called classes or object classes, while concrete versions are called instances, or often just objects.

Flash offers different ways of instantiating classes. When you create a new movie clip (Insert > New Symbol), you create a movie clip object based on the `MovieClip` class. When you put the movie clip on the stage, you instantiate it further. Notice that there are different levels of instantiation. A movie clip symbol in the Library is an instance of the `MovieClip` class, while an instance of a movie clip symbol on the stage instantiates the movie clip symbol. Some types of objects don't require this two-level instantiation; for example, text fields don't need to be placed in the Library before they can be deployed on the stage.

Now that you have an idea of what's going on underneath the interface, you can probably see that you can often accomplish the same task either visually in the Flash interface or via ActionScript. For example, you can create a movie clip instance by dragging an instance of a movie clip symbol out of the Library and onto the stage. Another way to create a movie clip is to use the `attachMovie()` method of the `MovieClip` object, which creates an instance of a movie clip symbol residing in the Library and places it on the stage. Either way, the result is the same: a movie clip instance is placed on the stage.

Regardless of how they're created, all objects need unique identifiers. In Flash, these unique identifiers are called instance names. Visible objects on the stage, such as buttons and text fields, can be given instance names in the Property inspector. If you create an instance using ActionScript, you usually give the instance an ID when you create it. After it has an instance name, Flash ActionScript can see it, which means that you can manipulate the movie clip and learn about it (such as whether a user is dragging it, and if so, where) via ActionScript.

> **Note** *Not all objects are visible. For example, Flash's LoadVars class, when deployed, is an invisible data holder. This class's built-in methods enable developers to send and load data to and from a server script, such as a ColdFusion, ASP, or PHP script. It also has built-in events that notify Flash when a given piece of requested data is fully loaded. This object has no visual representation in Flash.*

To summarize, using Flash objects usually follows a general sequence:

1. The object is created, often in the form of a symbol or component. Some objects are built-in, such as the MovieClip class and Flash components (like the TextArea component), while others can be user-defined.

2. The object is instantiated (that is, a copy of it is generated and deployed) on the stage, where it also receives specific attributes (such as location, height, visibility, and so on).

3. The object is given a unique ID, called an instance name.

4. The object is controlled, manipulated, or read via ActionScript.

Programming the Down Button

In this task, you'll program the button that enables users to access the lower half of the Inferno map. You'll use a script much like the ones you learned to create in Lesson 8, Creating Animation and Interactivity. As you program the button this time, keep the preceding discussion in mind.

1. Open dante.fla from the dante/flash/folder in your local site.

This file is already partially built, with the graphics in place to enable you to focus on the architectural and scripting aspects of the movie.

2. Click the red button with the down-pointing arrow in the lower-right corner to select it.

This button was created for you in advance. Its purpose is to enable the user to access Lower Hell. Currently, it lacks an instance name, and no script has been written to do anything with the button.

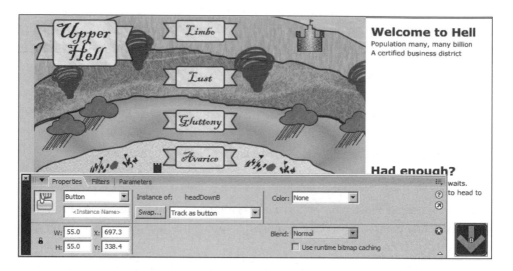

3. Use the Property inspector to give it an instance name of down_btn.

The instance name exposes the button to ActionScript.

4. Click Frame 1 of the actions layer, and press F9 to open the Actions panel.

The panel currently has only a stop() action.

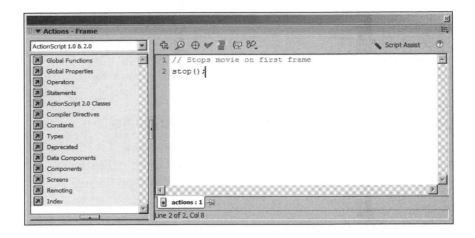

5. Beneath the existing script, add the following code:

```
// Powers the Down button
down_btn.onRelease = function() {
gotoAndStop("lower");
};
```

The ActionScript tells Flash that whenever a user clicks the down_btn instance, the timeline should skip to the frame label called "lower." onRelease is an event handler that's built into all button instances. gotoAndStop() is a method that's built into all timelines.

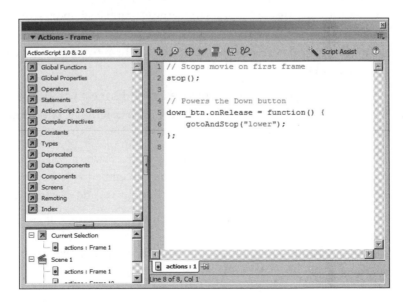

6. Test the movie by pressing Ctrl+Enter (Windows) or Command+Return (Macintosh). Click the button and make sure that Lower Hell appears.

Lower Hell has an up-pointing button that returns the user to Upper Hell. This button has already been programmed, so you should be able to go back and forth.

Preparing for the Quicktip Interactions

In this task, you'll build two nonlinear groups of interactions. One is the Tooltip-like interaction, in which users roll over screen elements. The second is the scrolling text area, which provides information when a user clicks one of the labels on the map.

You'll build the quicktip interactions first. These interactions are typical of the way Flash objects can be integrated to create nonlinear interactivity with a minimum of ActionScript. Each interaction will make use of three objects: a button, a movie clip, and a dynamic text field. More specifically, the movie will have many buttons—one for each hotspot/quicktip you want to create—but only one movie clip and one text field. The text field will be nested inside the movie clip.

You worked with buttons in Lesson 10, *Preparing the Dante Site*. You might have less experience working with movie clips and dynamic text fields.

Introducing Movie Clips

Movie clips are one of the three types of Flash symbols, the other two being graphic and button symbols. Movie clips are created the same way as graphic symbols (you can go through Insert > New Symbol or convert an existing element to a movie clip symbol), they reside in the Library, and you can create instances of them by dragging the symbol from the Library to the stage.

Of the three types of Flash symbols, movie clips are by far the most powerful, flexible, and interesting. You can think of a movie clip as an entire Flash movie encapsulated inside another Flash movie. A movie clip has the following key features:

- **Its own timeline and stage.** Anything you can put in a Flash movie, you can put in a movie clip (including other movie clips). You can embed video, create lengthy animations, or create complex ActionScript functionality inside movie clips.

- **Timeline independence.** Movie clip timelines run independently of all other timelines. So if a movie clip with a 100-frame animation is inside Frame 1 of the main timeline, for example, and the main timeline is stopped in Frame 1, the movie clip animation will still play back all 100 frames.

- **Exposure to ActionScript.** Movie clips tap into one of the richest classes in ActionScript, the `MovieClip` class, which has dozens of built-in events, properties, and methods that you can easily take advantage of in ActionScript, even if you are not a programmer.

Movie clips have many other features and capabilities, but these key features provide an idea of the power available to developers.

Introducing Dynamic and Input Text Fields

Now let's take a closer look at dynamic text fields. Flash has three different types of text fields: static, dynamic, and input.

- **Static text fields**—the default—don't do anything and can't change. You type text into the text field and the text stays the same from that point forward, unless you manually change it in the authoring environment.
- **Dynamic text fields** have instance names and therefore are visible, or exposed, to ActionScript. Their contents and even formatting can be changed via ActionScript at runtime. A single text field can display any number of different strings of text.
- **Input text fields** also have instance names, and are typically used for collecting data from the user and submitting the data to ActionScript (and beyond, such as to a database via ColdFusion).

Working with dynamic text is rewarding because it's both powerful and easy. The main thing to keep in mind is that a single text field is a container that can hold many different text strings. When you build dynamic text fields, you should have in mind the nature of the different strings. Are they body text? Headlines? Short, long, or mixed?

The reason you need to ask these questions is that you typically format the text field as soon as you create it. All the strings put in the text field will inherit that formatting, with some flexibility. Generally, if the text field uses Arial size 10, all the text dynamically added to the text field will also be displayed in Arial size 10.

Note *It's possible to radically change the formatting of text in a given dynamic text field, thanks to ActionScript's TextFormat class. However, this requires additional coding and is often easily avoided.*

You create a dynamic text field the same way you create a static text field: you use the Text tool. You then specify what type of text field you want, using the Property inspector's Text Type drop-down, and give the new text field an instance name. At that point, you can control the text field—for example, populate it with actual text—using ActionScript.

Planning the Quicktip Architecture

We've covered a lot of theory up to this point, and now you can start putting it all into action. As mentioned earlier, the quicktip interaction will use button, movie clip, and text field objects.

Here's how it will work. When the movie loads, the movie clip's visibility will be set to off; it will be invisible from the moment the movie loads. Because the text field will be inside the movie clip, it will be invisible as well. When the user rolls over a button, the movie clip's visibility will be toggled on, and the movie clip will be repositioned to appear beside the user's mouse. In addition, the dynamic text field, made visible along with its parent movie clip, will be populated with text that describes the element the user rolls over. When the user rolls away from the button hotspot, the movie clip's visibility will be toggled off.

The key in this architecture is the dynamic text field inside the movie clip. Because you can change the content as often as you like, you don't need to create a separate text field (and by implication a separate movie clip) for each hotspot or Tooltip you want on the map. This one-to-many (one movie clip/text field to many buttons) architecture greatly simplifies production and maintenance. After you've created one hotspot/quicktip combo, you can easily replicate it and create as many other hotspot/Tooltips as you want. And at any point, you can add or remove one without affecting the others.

The start file contains the graphic portions you'll need for this interaction. You'll use the graphic symbol named *hotspot* as the basis for the button, and the graphic symbol named *quickTip* as the basis for the movie clip.

Preparing the Invisible Button Hotspot

In most situations, buttons are a visible interface element that users deliberately click for a given behavior to occur, such as navigating to a different Web page. However, in some cases, you want the button functionality—its ability to trigger behaviors based on user events—without including a visual interface element. The interactive map is a case in point. You want the act of rolling over the tornadoes, storms, wars, and swamps to trigger the quicktip. But these elements, though clearly visible, are actually a part of the background map; they are not button symbols.

The solution is to layer invisible buttons over these map elements. That way, users rely on the visuals of the background map, while they still benefit from the functionality of buttons.

Creating invisible buttons is easy. As you'll recall, buttons have four states: Up, Over, Down, and Hit. The first three enable you to specify the appearance of the button at different times: the default appearance, the look when the user is rolling over the button, and the look when the user is clicking the button. The fourth state, the Hit state, enables you to specify the "hot" area, the area that responds to the mouse.

To create an invisible button, or a hotspot, in Flash, you first draw a shape in a button's Hit state, and leave the remaining states empty. In the Hit state, the shape can be any color, with any fill or stroke you want. As long as the shape is filled, the hotspot will work.

1. Choose Window > Library (or press F11) to open the Library if it's not already open.

The Library contains several elements that you'll use in this and the next lesson. The bitmaps folder contains numerous graphics produced in Fireworks for the map, including the maps themselves. The Library also contains the fiery buttons that enable users to navigate between the two levels of the Inferno. The TextArea is a component that has already been applied to the second screen in the movie. Later in this lesson, you'll apply it to the first screen in the movie as well.

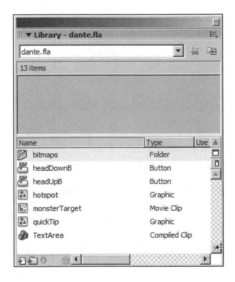

2. Right-click (Windows) or Control-click (Macintosh) the hotspot graphic symbol in the Library. From the contextual menu, choose Type > Button.

This converts the graphic symbol into a Button symbol. Notice that its icon in the Library changes to indicate the new symbol type.

3. Double-click the hotspot Button symbol to open it in Symbol-editing mode.

The stage contains a black square, which will be used to indicate the hotspot of the button. This square is in the Up state, rather than the Hit state. If you deployed the button now, it would appear black on the stage and obscure the map elements you want to make interactive. You'll need to fix that.

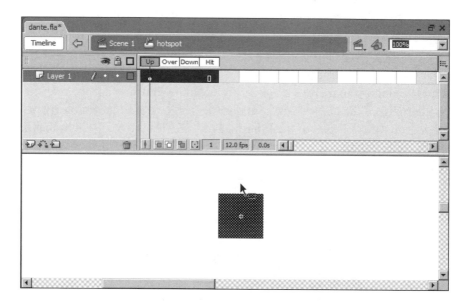

4. Click once in the Up frame within the timeline. Press and drag the keyframe in the Up frame to the Hit frame, and then release.

This transfers the black square keyframe to the Hit state. Notice that the Up, Over, and Down states are all empty at the end of this step.

5. Return to the main timeline by clicking the Scene 1 button in the top-left corner of the Document window.

You're finished editing the button.

6. Select Frame 1 of the buttons layer. Press and drag an instance of the hotspot button from the Library and release it over the tornado just to the right of the Lust label.

You can trigger something to happen when the user rolls over the tornado. Of course, nothing will happen yet, because no script has been associated with this button. You'll do that later in the lesson.

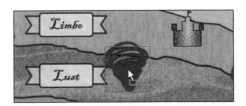

7. With the hotspot instance still selected, name the instance *tempest_1_btn* in the Property inspector.

With an instance name, the button is now exposed to ActionScript, which means you can control its behavior. The button instance is now ready, so let's turn our attention to the other objects in the application: the movie clip and the dynamic text field.

> **Note** *Remember to use the proper suffixes when naming instances in Flash, to enable code hints in ActionScript. Buttons should end in _btn, text fields should end in _txt, and movie clips should end in _mc. A complete list of these suffixes can be found in Flash Help. To access the Help file, press F1 and browse to ActionScript Reference Guide › Writing and Debugging Scripts › Using the ActionScript Editor › Writing code that triggers code hints.*

Preparing the Quicktip Movie Clip and Dynamic Text Field

In this task, you'll prepare the movie clip and dynamic text fields. In the next task, when each element is in place, you'll begin scripting to make them functional.

1. In the Library, right-click (Windows) or Control-click (Macintosh) the quickTip graphic symbol, and choose Type > Movie Clip.

This step converts the graphic symbol to a movie clip symbol. You'll still need to do some work with the graphic symbol, but this change alone opens up a whole new realm of possibility.

The symbol contains only a beige rounded rectangle, which defines the shape of the quicktip.

2. Select Frame 1 of the quickTip layer, and drag an instance of the quickTip symbol anywhere on the stage.

The positioning doesn't matter because this movie clip will be invisible when it's loaded; when it is visible, the same script that makes it visible will also position it correctly.

This small beige rounded rectangle forms the outline of the quicktip pop-up window. Its substance will be provided by text loaded into a dynamic text field. But at the moment, the movie clip has no dynamic text field.

3. Double-click the quickTip instance (it has no instance name yet) to open it in Symbol-editing mode. Select Frame 1 of the text layer. Click on the stage once to set the focus back to the stage. Select the Text tool, and change its settings in the Property inspector to Verdana, Size 11, Black. Also in the Property inspector, set the Text Type to Dynamic Text. Hold down the Shift key, and drag a text field that fits snugly inside the beige rounded rectangle, three lines high.

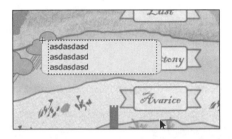

Tip *Insert dummy text, if necessary, to help you position the text correctly.*

Holding down the Shift key ensures that the dynamic text field is exactly tall enough to fit whole lines of text at the specified size.

The first group of text settings—font, size, and so on—is familiar to you, because they are universal to just about any application that handles text. But the most important setting here is unique to Flash: the Dynamic Text setting. By choosing Dynamic Text as the Text Type, you make the text field available to ActionScript.

4. With the text field still selected, in the Property inspector, give the text box an instance name of *quickTip_txt*. Set the Line Type to Multiline. Select the Render Text as HTML option.

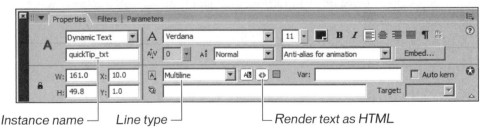

Instance name — Line type — └ Render text as HTML

Again, you use the instance name to identify this text field in ActionScript. As its name suggests, the Multiline setting enables the text inside the text field to wrap.

The other setting, Render Text as HTML, enables Flash to interpret basic HTML tags and format the text accordingly. For example, consider the following text string: my `<b>bold</b>`

text. If Render Text as HTML is toggled off, the dynamic text field displays "my bold text." If Render Text as HTML is toggled on, the Dynamic Text field displays "my **bold** text." In other words, Render Text as HTML enables you to control character-level formatting in Dynamic Text fields.

5. Choose Edit > Edit Document to return to the main document, leaving Symbol-editing mode.

When you leave, the new symbol is saved in the Library, and all placed instances (in this case, just one) are also updated.

6. Select the quickTip instance, and give it an instance name of *quickTip_mc*.

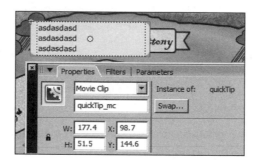

The quickTip_txt dynamic text field is located inside this movie clip instance. When you reference variables inside of movie clips from ActionScript that is outside the movie clip (such as a script on the main timeline), you need to specify which movie clip instance's variable you are setting. To do so, you reference it with its instance name.

In this step, you are creating the instance name that will enable you to change the variable inside the quickTip instance from buttons on the main timeline. You'll actually write such a script in the next task.

Scripting the Quicktip Interaction

Each element is in place: the button, the movie clip, and the dynamic text field inside the movie clip. You're now ready to write the script that makes the interaction work. Before you start, you should plan ahead and spell out what you're trying to do, as well as the role each object will play.

- The three objects you'll use have the following instance names: tempest_1_btn, quickTip_mc, and quickTip_txt. Remember that quickTip_txt is inside quickTip_mc.
- You'll need the script to make quickTip_mc invisible by default.
- You'll need the script to do the following when the user rolls over tempest_1_btn: make quickTip visible, position it near the user's mouse, and populate the Dynamic Text field with the correct text.
- You'll need the script to make quickTip_mc invisible when the user rolls away from it.

It's usually easier to write a script when you know exactly what you're trying to do.

1. Click Frame 1 of the actions layer, and open the Actions panel (F9).

The Actions panel opens, and, as you can see, already contains a small script that stops the movie in the first frame, as well as the script you entered earlier to program the Down button.

You'll add the rest of the scripts for the upper half of the Inferno to this frame.

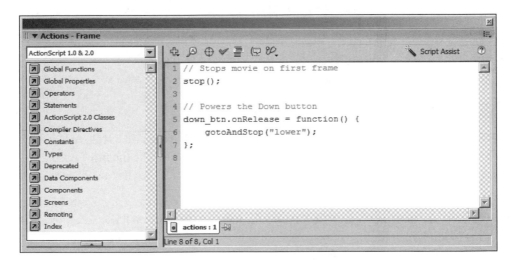

2. Add the following comments to the code, below the existing code, leaving a blank line between each comment.

```
// Initializes quickTip_mc so that it is not visible
// Causes the quick tip to appear when the mouse rolls over tempest_1_btn
// Causes the quick tip to disappear when the mouse rolls away from tempest_1_btn
```

Outlining the code with comments helps you write the code now and also documents the code, which makes it easier to maintain later.

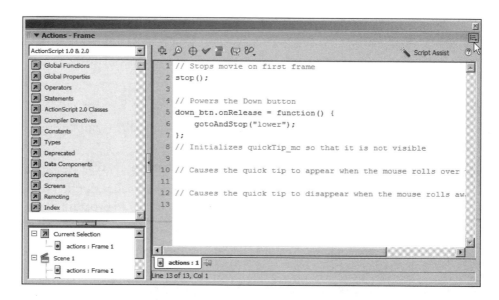

3. Below the first comment, enter the following code block:

```
quickTip_mc._visible = false;
```

Note   *The spacing around the equals sign is optional.*

_visible is a property of all movie clips. It has two settings, true and false. As you have probably guessed, true is the default. By setting it to false, you make the movie clip instance invisible, because this code is executed before the movie clip instance has a chance to display.

The dot (.) between the instance name and its property, called an access operator, implies a relationship: the item on the right belongs to the item on the left. You'll use access operators a lot in ActionScript, because they work almost like an addressing system, enabling you to tell ActionScript where to look for something in the document hierarchy.

The equals sign (=) that separates the two halves of the line is called an assignment operator. Use the equals sign when you want to assign a particular value (in this case, false) to a given object asset (in this case, the quickTip_mc instance's _visible property).

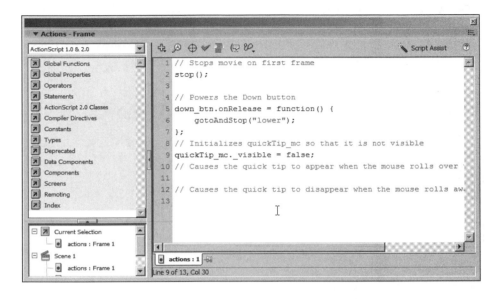

4. Choose Control > Test Movie. Verify that the movie clip instance is not on the stage. Return to the Flash authoring environment.

If the movie clip is not visible on the stage, you know your script is working properly. If it is visible on the stage, make sure the instance name in the Property inspector with the instance selected is spelled exactly the same as the instance name written into the ActionScript.

Any time you add new functionality to a script, you should test the movie to verify that everything went as expected. If you wait and test later, it can be hard to debug if something does go wrong.

5. After the next comment, insert the following code:

```
tempest_1_btn.onRollOver = function() {
  quickTip_mc._visible = true;
  quickTip_mc._x = _xmouse;
  quickTip_mc._y = _ymouse;
  quickTip_mc.quickTip_txt.htmlText = "<b>Tempest</b><br>Those who gave in to
lust swirl around in these.";
};
```

Most of this code block is already familiar to you. You saw how to specify a button event by creating a function literal in Lesson 10 (the `button_btn.onEvent = function() {…};` syntax). Now you're causing a series of actions to occur when the user rolls over the tempest_1_btn instance.

This group of commands is generally easy to read. The first command makes the movie clip instance visible again, since its default state is invisible.

The next two commands, which set the instance's _x and _y properties to _xmouse and _ymouse, have to do with positioning. As you'll recall from the Fireworks lessons at the beginning of the book, every graphic object is positioned relative to the top-left corner of the canvas/stage. This value is stored in its _x (horizontal position) and _y (vertical position) properties. Likewise, Flash stores the current position of the mouse in the built-in _xmouse and _ymouse properties. Thus, in these two lines of code, you're telling Flash to position the top-left corner of the movie clip instance in the same place as the mouse, which ensures that the user easily associates the text in the quicktip with the screen element (in this case, the tornado) that she or he has just rolled over.

In the last statement inside the block, you set the value of the htmlText property of the quickTip_txt Dynamic Text field, which is itself located inside the quickTip_mc instance. Because quickTip_txt is inside quickTip_mc, and because the button (tempest_1_btn) is on the main timeline, outside of quickTip_mc, you must provide directions to Flash to find the text field whose property you want to set. In a way, specifying quickTip_mc is like prefacing a file name with a folder name in a URL; for example, the URL images/mypicture.jpg instructs the browser to first look for an images folder, and then look in that folder for mypicture.jpg. In the same way, quickTip_mc.quickTip_txt tells Flash that it can find the latter inside the former.

As for the htmlText property itself, it holds any HTML-formatted text you want the Dynamic Text field to display. Earlier in the lesson, you clicked the Render Text as HTML button in the Property inspector for the quickTip_txt Dynamic Text field. You did that to enable the possibility of populating the Dynamic Text field with HTML-formatted text. Following the assignment operator is the HTML-formatted string itself, enclosed in quotes.

6. Test the movie again. Roll over the tempest and verify that the movie clip appears and that its text displays. Return to the Flash authoring environment.

So far, so good. The movie clip and text shows up. The only problem is that it never goes away.

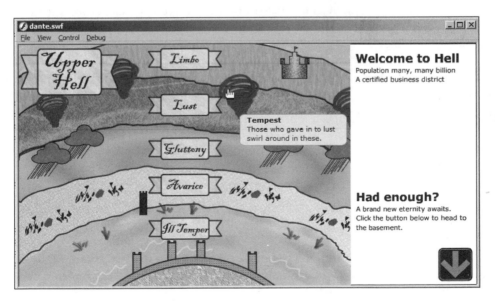

7. After the final comment, insert the following code:

```
tempest_1_btn.onRollOut = function() {
  quickTip_mc._visible = false;
};
```

The meaning of this code block should be obvious. When the user rolls away from the button instance, the movie clip becomes invisible again. You don't need to worry about where it is (_x and _y) or what its text field's htmlText property contains, because the whole movie clip is invisible, and the next time it appears it will have new positioning and htmlText properties specified.

8. Once again, test the movie and verify that the quicktip appears and disappears as expected.

This time, the quicktip disappears when you move away from the button.

9. Copy and paste the hotspot you've been working on so that a hotspot covers each of the remaining tempests on the map. Change the instance name to *tempest_2_btn*, *tempest_3_btn*, and so on, so each is unique.

Because there are multiple tempests on the map, you should make all the buttons pop up the quicktip.

10. Select Frame 1 in the Actions panel, copy and paste the two functions associated with tempest_1_btn, and change the instance name in the ActionScript to *tempest_2_btn* and *tempest_3_btn*.

```
 5  down_btn.onRelease = function() {
 6      gotoAndStop("lower");
 7  };
 8  // Initializes quickTip_mc so that it is not visible
 9  quickTip_mc._visible = false;
10
11  // Causes the quick tip to appear when the mouse rolls over tempest_1_btn
12  tempest_1_btn.onRollOver = function() {
13      quickTip_mc._visible = true;
14      quickTip_mc._x = _xmouse;
15      quickTip_mc._y = _ymouse;
16      quickTip_mc.quickTip_txt.htmlText = "<b>Tempest</b><br>Those who gave in to lust swirl
17  };
18
19  // Causes the quick tip to disappear when the mouse rolls away from tempest_1_btn
20  tempest_1_btn.onRollOut = function() {
21      quickTip_mc._visible = false;
22  };
23
```

```
actions : 1
Line 11 of 23, Col 1
```

```
 5  down_btn.onRelease = function() {
 6      gotoAndStop("lower");
 7  };
 8  // Initializes quickTip_mc so that it is not visible
 9  quickTip_mc._visible = false;
10
11  // Causes the quick tip to appear when the mouse rolls over tempest_1_btn
12  tempest_1_btn.onRollOver = function() {
13      quickTip_mc._visible = true;
14      quickTip_mc._x = _xmouse;
15      quickTip_mc._y = _ymouse;
16      quickTip_mc.quickTip_txt.htmlText = "<b>Tempest</b><br>Those who gave in to lust swirl
17  };
18
19  // Causes the quick tip to disappear when the mouse rolls away from tempest_1_btn
20  tempest_1_btn.onRollOut = function() {
21      quickTip_mc._visible = false;
22  };
23
24  // Causes the quick tip to appear when the mouse rolls over tempest_2_btn
25  tempest_2_btn.onRollOver = function() {
26      quickTip_mc._visible = true;
27      quickTip_mc._x = _xmouse;
28      quickTip_mc._y = _ymouse;
29      quickTip_mc.quickTip_txt.htmlText = "<b>Tempest</b><br>Those who gave in to lust swirl
30  };
31
32  // Causes the quick tip to disappear when the mouse rolls away from tempest_2_btn
33  tempest_2_btn.onRollOut = function() {
34      quickTip_mc._visible = false;
35  };
```

```
actions : 1
Line 45 of 48, Col 78
```

Sometimes multimedia development becomes monotonous. After you make one quicktip functional, it's easy to copy and paste to replicate it. As you do, your main task is the clerical job of copying and pasting instances and ActionScript, changing only instance names as you work.

Tip | *Rather than copy and paste all the comments as well, you might want to simplify the comments so that there's only one comment per group of related hotspots (for example, all the tempest buttons).*

11. Repeat this process to put hotspots over the storms, wars, and swamps, as well as the Castle of Reason and the City of Dis (see the figure for guidance). Then, go into the Actions panel and copy and paste the two button functions for each new hotspot you created, changing the instance names and the text that appears, using text from script_inferno_html.txt.

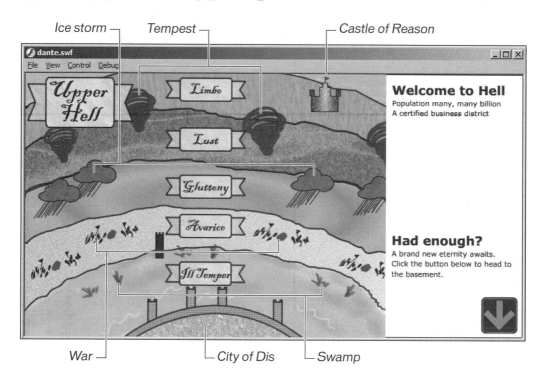

The file script_inferno_html.txt is a text file located in the Text Source folder inside your site. It contains all the text you'll use for the interactive map. The text you should use in this step appears roughly in the middle of the text file.

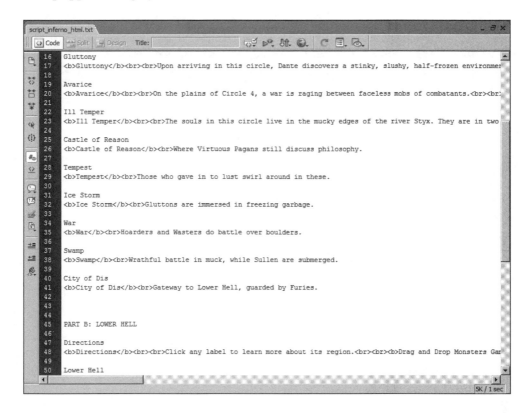

As you place hotspot instances, remember that you can resize them so that they fit better over their intended targets. To resize the hotspots, use the Free Transform tool in the Tools panel to drag the edges.

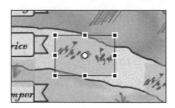

At the end of this step, the script is nearly 200 lines long, although most of it is repetitive. An experienced programmer can remove some of this redundancy using loops and other programming techniques, but that level of code optimization is beyond the scope of this book.

```
 95  storm_4_btn.onRollOver = function() {
 96      quickTip_mc._visible = true;
 97      quickTip_mc._x = _xmouse;
 98      quickTip_mc._y = _ymouse;
 99      quickTip_mc.quickTip_txt.htmlText = "<b>Ice Storm</b><br>Gluttons are immersed in freezi
100  };
101
102  storm_4_btn.onRollOut = function() {
103      quickTip_mc._visible = false;
104  };
105
106  //swamp functions
107
108  swamp_1_btn.onRollOver = function() {
109      quickTip_mc._visible = true;
110      quickTip_mc._x = _xmouse;
111      quickTip_mc._y = _ymouse;
112      quickTip_mc.quickTip_txt.htmlText = "<b>Swamp</b><br>Wrathful battle in muck, while Sull
113  };
114
115  swamp_1_btn.onRollOut = function() {
116      quickTip_mc._visible = false;
117  };
118
119  swamp_2_btn.onRollOver = function() {
120      quickTip_mc._visible = true;
121      quickTip_mc._x = _xmouse;
122      quickTip_mc._y = _ymouse;
123      quickTip_mc.quickTip_txt.htmlText = "<b>Swamp</b><br>Wrathful battle in muck, while Sull
124  };
125
126  swamp_2_btn.onRollOut = function() {
```

actions : 1

Line 54 of 211, Col 93

12. Save and test the file one last time.

The quicktips should pop up for each of the items on the screen.

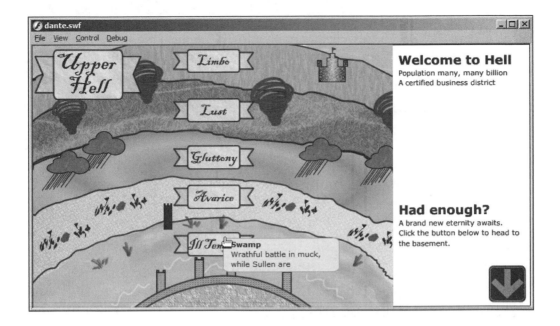

Using a Component to Create a Scrolling Text Area

You've completed the first of the two major features of the upper half of the Inferno map: the quicktips. Now you'll implement the second major feature, which is a scrolling text area that describes each of the five circles as well as the upper half of the Inferno map itself. You'll create the scrolling text area using the TextArea component.

Flash components are ready-made, customizable features that you can drag and drop into your movies. Flash comes with a number of components, including classic form elements such as the CheckBox and RadioButton components, and other useful components such as the ProgressBar component, which creates progress bars that display the loading progress of movies. In this task, you'll work with the TextArea component, which, as its name implies, creates a multiline scrolling text area whose contents you can dynamically populate via ActionScript.

The best part of using components is that they make otherwise difficult tasks quite easy.

1. With the Library panel open, and Frame 1 of the text layer selected, press and drag an instance of a TextArea component onto the stage, in the white space on the right side. Use the Free Transform tool in the Tools panel to enlarge the component, as shown in the figure.

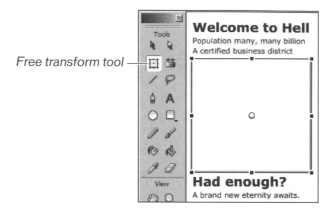

The default instance is quite small, so you'll have to resize it.

2. In the Property inspector, give the new TextArea an instance name of *upperInfo_txt*.

Like other Flash objects, the TextArea has native properties, such as buttons and movie clips. Before you can use any of these objects' properties in ActionScript, you'll have to give the TextArea an instance name.

3. Still in the Property inspector, switch to the Parameters tab, if necessary, and change the Editable setting to False and the HTML setting to True.

Leaving the Editable setting at the default True would enable users to select the text and even modify it. You only want users to be able to read the text, so the Editable setting should be False.

By making the HTML setting True, you enable basic formatting within the text, including line breaks, bolding, and so on.

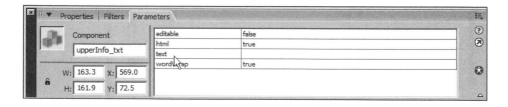

4. Give the TextArea some default text by entering the following in the Property inspector's Text field.

```
<b>Directions</b><br><br>Click any label to learn about that region of
Hell.<br><br>Roll over any interesting object on the map to learn more about it.
```

If you'd rather copy and paste this text, it's available in script_inferno_text.html, under the heading Directions.

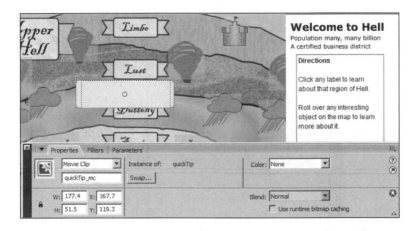

5. Test the movie. When you're satisfied, return to Flash and save the file.

The default text appears in the text area. No scrollbars appear in the text area, because the entire block of text fits. However, if you put in a longer text string, Flash automatically adds scrollbars.

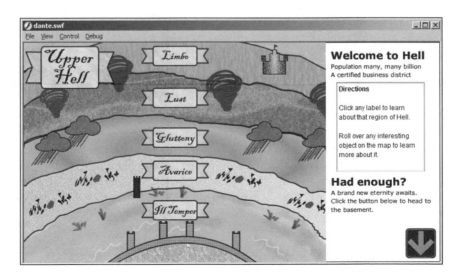

6. With Frame 1 of the buttons layer selected, drag out instances of hotspots, placing and resizing them over the six labels on the page (Upper Hell, Limbo, Lust, and so on). Give each an instance name according to its label, as follows:

upperHell_btn

limbo_btn

lust_btn

gluttony_btn

avarice_btn

illTemper_btn

After the buttons have instance names, they're exposed to ActionScript, and you can write a script that enables the buttons to populate the text area.

| Note | Make sure that no two hotspot buttons overlap each other. Overlapping buttons sometimes behave in unexpected ways.

Dynamically Populating the Text Area

Now that you've created the text area and all the button hotspots, you can write the script that makes the map functional.

1. Select Frame 1 of the actions layer, and open the Actions panel. Add the following script below all the existing script:

```
upperHell_btn.onRelease = function() {
    upperInfo_txt.text="<b>Upper Hell</b><br><br>This map represents the upper
reaches of Hell, where Dante begins his travels.<br><br>The region is bounded by
the gates of Hell at the top and the walls of Dis at the bottom, the city that
contains those damned for the gravest of sins.<br><br>Dante begins in Limbo, the
first circle, where the Virtuous Pagans reside with neither punishment nor hope
of ever seeing God.";
};
```

If you want to copy and paste this text string, it's listed under the heading Upper Hell in script_inferno_html.txt.

```
▼ Actions - Frame
199
200  //city functions
201
202  city_1_btn.onRollOver = function() {
203      quickTip_mc._visible = true;
204      quickTip_mc._x = _xmouse;
205      quickTip_mc._y = _ymouse;
206      quickTip_mc.quickTip_txt.htmlText = "<b>City of Dis</b><br>Gateway to Lower Hell, guarded by Furies.";
207  };
208
209  city_1_btn.onRollOut = function() {
210      quickTip_mc._visible = false;
211  };
212
213  upperHell_btn.onRelease = function() {
214      upperInfo_txt.text="<b>Upper Hell</b><br><br>This map represents the upper reaches of Hell, where Dante beg
215  };
216
actions : 1
Line 214 of 236, Col 417
```

This piece of code changes the Dynamic Text field to show this string of text when the user clicks the Upper Hell label. The original contents of the dynamic text field disappear.

2. Choose Control › Test Movie, and click Upper Hell.

The text string dutifully changes, which is pretty cool. What is even cooler is that Flash automatically adds a scrollbar to accommodate the text that doesn't fit in the text area.

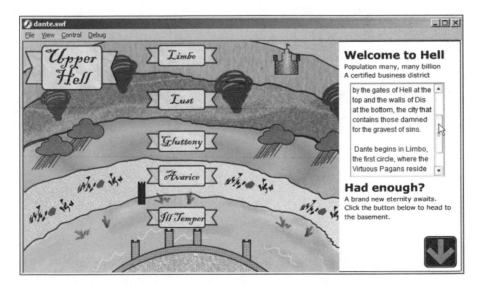

3. Return to the authoring environment, and use the script for upperHell_btn as a model to write five other scripts—one each for the remaining buttons (limbo_btn, lust_btn, and so on). Use the text in script_inferno_html.txt as the source.

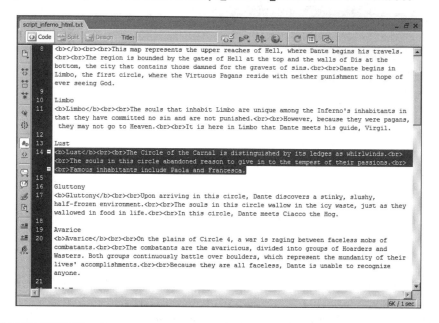

Although this step is somewhat repetitive, bear in mind that you're adding quite a bit of functionality to the movie.

4. Save and test the movie. Click each of the labels to make sure the text area's contents are correctly populated.

As you work through this step, you'll probably notice that if you read one description and scroll down to the bottom, and then click another label, the description remains scrolled to the bottom. It would be more attractive, not to mention usable, if the text area returned to the top every time the user clicked one of the labels.

You can achieve this behavior by adding a simple line of ActionScript to each of the six button functions.

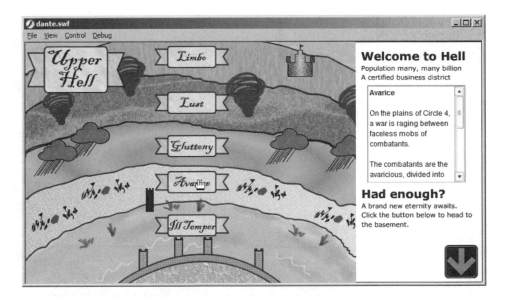

5. Return to the authoring environment. In the Actions panel with Frame 1 of the actions layer in the timeline selected, enter the following script before the line that begins `upperInfo_txt.text` = on each of the buttons.

```
upperInfo_txt.vPosition = 0;
```

The property vPosition is built into the TextArea object. It defines the vertical position of the text. By setting it to 0, you ensure that the first line of text appears at the top of the text area.

```
212
213  upperHell_btn.onRelease = function() {
214      upperInfo_txt.vPosition = 0;
215      upperInfo_txt.text="<b>Upper Hell</b><br><br>This map represents the upper reaches o
216  };
217
218  limbo_btn.onRelease = function() {
219      upperInfo_txt.vPosition = 0;
220      upperInfo_txt.text="<b>Limbo</b><br><br>The souls that inhabit Limbo are unique amor
221  };
222
223  lust_btn.onRelease = function() {
224      upperInfo_txt.vPosition = 0;
225      upperInfo_txt.text="<b>Lust</b><br><br>The Circle of the Carnal is distinguished by
226  };
227
228  gluttony_btn.onRelease = function() {
229      upperInfo_txt.vPosition = 0;
230      upperInfo_txt.text="<b>Gluttony</b><br><br>Upon arriving in this circle, Dante disco
231  };
232
233  avarice_btn.onRelease = function() {
234      upperInfo_txt.vPosition = 0;
235      upperInfo_txt.text="<b>Avarice</b><br><br>On the plains of Circle 4, a war is raging
236  };
237
238  illTemper_btn.onRelease = function() {
239      upperInfo_txt.vPosition = 0;
240      upperInfo_txt.text="<b>Ill Temper</b><br><br>The souls in this circle live in the mu
241  };
242
```

actions : 1

Line 214 of 242, Col 2

6. Save and test the movie.

Try clicking each of the labels and scrolling the text area down to the bottom for each one. Regardless of the current position of the scrollbar, clicking one of the labels should immediately show that label's text, and it should start at the top.

What You Have Learned

In this lesson, you have:

- Learned about objects, properties, methods, and events (pages 313–320)
- Created hotspots using invisible buttons (pages 320–323)
- Used ActionScript to control movie clip visibility and positioning (pages 324–336)
- Dynamically populated text field content using ActionScript (pages 327–336)
- Formatted Dynamic Text fields using basic HTML rendering (pages 337–340)
- Implemented a TextArea component and set its default text (pages 337–340)
- Used ActionScript to dynamically populate a TextArea and set its scroll position (pages 340–344)

12 Drag-and-Drop Interactions

Creating nonlinear, interactive movies gives control to the user. Rather than being compelled to watch the whole movie in a predetermined order—the order of frames in the timeline—users can see what they want when they want. In Lesson 11, *Nonlinear Flash Interactions*, you implemented a nonlinear structure that encourages exploration. In this lesson, you'll extend the movie's interactivity by enabling users to drag and drop objects on the screen. Better still, you'll set up targets for the drag-and-drop objects and provide feedback to users when they drag and drop the objects on the right target.

You'll create drag-and-drop interactions in which the user will put four notorious monsters of the *Inferno*—a snake-haired fury, a centaur, a lizard-man, and Lucifer—in their places. In addition, you'll see how to use these interactions as triggers for other events. That is, the secondary events caused by the drag-and-drop interaction won't be triggered by

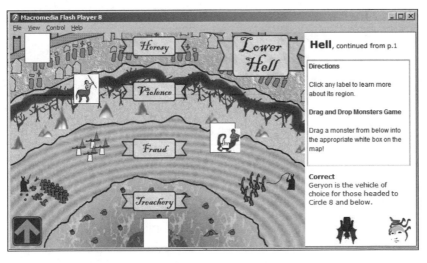

Drag-and-drop interactivity adds a whole new level of user engagement with the content.

traditional Macromedia Flash object events such as `button_btn.onRelease`, but by custom events you program and users trigger as they manipulate the application content.

What You Will Learn

In this lesson, you will:

- Learn how to implement drag-and-drop functionality
- Detect collisions between two movie clips
- Dynamically position movie clips
- Publish the completed project in the Dante site within Dreamweaver

Approximate Time

This lesson takes approximately 60 minutes to complete.

Lesson Files

Starting Files:

Lesson12/Start/dante/flash/dante.fla
Lesson12/Start/dante/flash/dante_complete.swf
Lesson12/Start/dante/Text Source/script_inferno_html.txt

Completed Files:

Lesson12/Complete/dante/flash/dante.fla

Drag and Drop *Inferno*

You already know from Lesson 11, *Nonlinear Flash Interactions*, how the Lower Hell portion of the movie functions. In this quick review, pay close attention to each of the events and what triggers them. Understanding the intended functionality in detail makes scripting much easier.

1. Open dante_complete.swf in this lesson's Start/dante/flash folder. Navigate to Lower Hell by clicking the Down button.

Once again, this is the completed version as it will appear when you've finished this lesson.

To begin with, notice the second set of directions (in blue) that appear at the right side of the screen. When the document first loads, this text reads, "Drag a monster to its designated post."

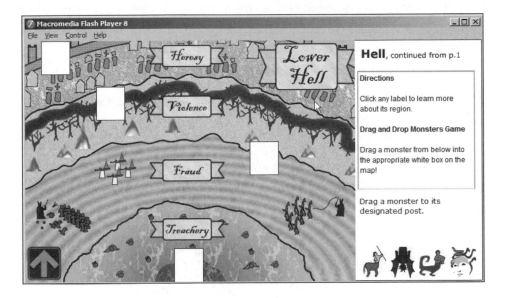

2. Drag Chiron the centaur to the center of the lake of ice at the bottom of Lower Hell and release the mouse button.

This is the incorrect target for the centaur. When you release the mouse button, two things happen. First, the centaur is snapped back to its original location. Second, the drag-and-drop directions now read, "Incorrect. Please try again!"

3. Drag the centaur to the second target from the top, beside the river of blood.

This is the correct target for the centaur. Note that the centaur stuck to its target—in fact, he snapped to his target—and the correct-target feedback now appears where the drag-and-drop directions started.

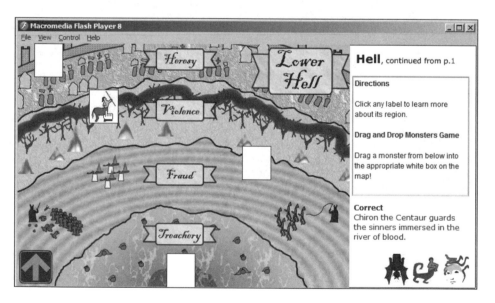

4. Drag the centaur back to its original position.

The centaur snaps back into place and the directions text is reset to "Drag a monster to its designated post."

There are three possibilities for the drag-and-drop object: it can be dropped in the correct position, an incorrect position, or its original position. In all three cases, the object snaps into position and the text directions are updated.

5. Close the SWF.

Now that you've seen a detailed description of how the different user actions work, it's much easier to envision the scripts required to make these actions happen.

Creating Basic Drag-and-Drop Interactivity

Drag-and-drop functionality is made possible by the `startDrag()` and `stopDrag()` methods of movie clips. Because these are movie clip methods, the only objects you can make draggable are, well, movie clips. Remember, just because you have to use a movie clip symbol for something doesn't mean it must include an animation. It could be a single object on a single frame, which is what we'll use in this task.

1. Open dante.fla—either the version you completed from Lesson 11 or the one in this lesson's Start folder. Click Frame 10 in any layer to see the lower half of the Inferno map.

If you take a moment to click on each of the drag-and-drop monsters, you'll see that they're all there, but they're simple bitmap graphics—not movie clips.

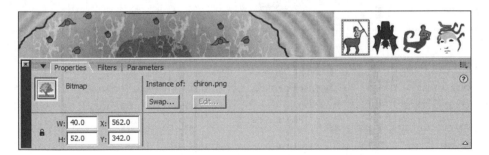

The script for this keyframe has been partially written (look in Frame 10 of the actions layer), so that the invisible buttons over each of the labels are already programmed to send the appropriate explanation text to the text area. The script is the same as the one you wrote in the previous lesson—except for the instance-level specifics (such as the instance name and the text sent to the text area). Likewise, the script has already been written so that the Up button returns the user to the upper half of the Inferno map.

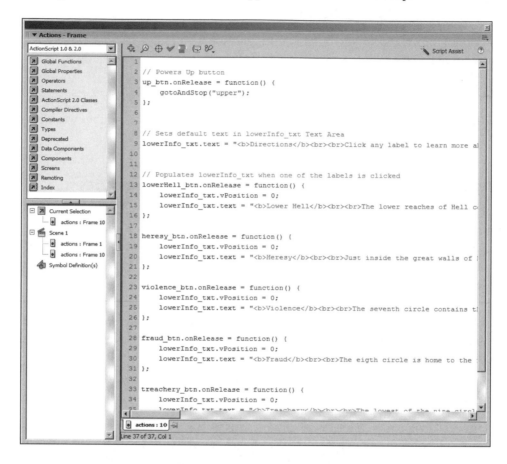

2. Select Chiron the centaur and press F8 to convert the bitmap graphic to a symbol. In the Convert to Symbol dialog, name the symbol *chiron*, set its Behavior to Movie Clip, set its Registration to the top-left corner (if necessary), and click OK.

By converting the bitmap graphic to a movie clip, you enable the drag capability. At this point, you can't drag the movie clip, but the potential is there.

In naming it chiron, remember that you're naming the symbol itself, as it will be listed in the Library. You are not naming the instance, even though the graphic is now in a movie clip instance on the stage.

By setting its registration point to the upper-left corner, you make it easier to position the graphic later.

Registration point set to upper-left corner ⌐

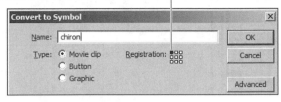

3. Repeat Step 2 for the remaining three monsters. Name the second monster from the left *lucifer*, then *geryon*, and finally *fury*. The Registration for all the monsters should be the upper-left corner.

At this point, you've made it possible for each of the monsters to be dragged.

4. In the Property inspector, give each of the monster movie clips an instance name. Left to right, the instance names should be as follows: *chiron_mc*, *lucifer_mc*, *geryon_mc*, and *fury_mc*.

Giving these movie clips instance names enables you to make them draggable and lets other parts of the movie communicate with each instance.

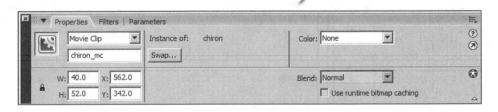

5. Click Frame 10 of the actions layer, press F9 if necessary to open the Actions panel, and add the following code at the bottom of the existing script:

```
// Creates Chiron drag and drop functionality
chiron_mc.onPress = function() {
  this.startDrag();
};
chiron_mc.onRelease = function() {
  this.stopDrag();
};
```

Even if you haven't used the `startDrag()` and `stopDrag()` actions before, you can probably read this script without any trouble. The keyword `this` simply refers to the current timeline—in this case, the chiron_mc movie clip instance. The two event handlers cause the script to activate when the user presses the mouse over the movie clip and then releases the mouse.

```
33 treachery_btn.onRelease = function() {
34     lowerInfo_txt.vPosition = 0;
35     lowerInfo_txt.text = "<b>Treachery</b><br><br>The lowest of the nine circles houses the Tr
36 };
37 // Creates Chiron drag and drop functionality
38 chiron_mc.onPress = function() {
39     this.startDrag();
40 };
41 chiron_mc.onRelease = function() {
42     this.stopDrag();
43 };
44
```

actions : 10

Line 44 of 44, Col 1

6. Press Ctrl+Enter (Windows) or Command+Return (Macintosh) to test the movie. Click the Down button to get to Lower Hell. Try dragging and dropping Chiron.

The script is all you need to make the character fully draggable. At this stage the interaction is primitive, because nothing happens when you drag and drop the character, and there's nowhere special to drop it. Still, you can see how easy it is to add this sort of functionality to a movie clip.

7. Return to the main movie and save your file.

Now it's time to make this simple interaction more meaningful.

For now, don't bother adding the same script for the other three monsters. The script is about to get more complex, so you should wait until you perfect it, and then copy and paste the script to add it to the other monsters. (You'll tweak each copied script to customize it for its specific monster.)

Creating Drag-and-Drop Targets

Drag-and-drop gets a lot more meaningful when users have a target on which to drop the dragged objects. Whether you're building an online shopping cart or creating learning media, targets provide a way for users to trigger events by manipulating onscreen objects so that they interact with each other.

In this task, you'll create drop targets for the monsters. In addition, you'll set up a test to determine whether a user dropped the monster on the correct target. Along the way, you'll learn two new actions: you'll use the hitTest() action to determine whether a monster was released over its target, and you'll use the trace() action to make Macromedia Flash generate feedback to make sure that hitTest() actually worked. After you verify that drag-and-drop works, you'll remove the trace() action and add real code to create the desired behaviors.

1. Select Frame 10 of the monster targets layer in the timeline, and drag an instance of monsterTarget from the Library onto the stage. Use the Property inspector to give it an Instance name of *chiron_targ_mc*. Use the Property inspector to set its X value to 118 and its Y value to 76 to position the instance over the river of blood, to the left of the Violence label.

The monsterTarget movie clip is simply a white rectangle with a black border large enough to enclose each of the monsters. This particular instance is the target for Chiron, hence the instance name chiron_targ_mc. The instance name enables you to write the ActionScript that can compare the _x and _y position attributes of the two objects (the chiron_mc drag object and the chiron_targ_mc target). If these two sets of position coordinates are the same (or close), then the ActionScript knows that Chiron was dropped over its target.

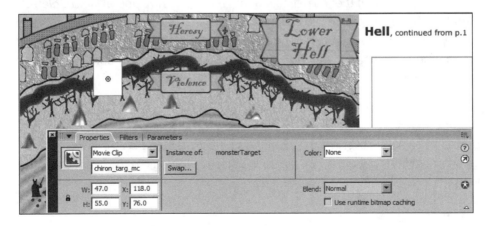

2. Select Frame 10 of the actions layer, return to the Actions panel, and add the following lines of code below the `this.stopDrag();` line:

```
if (this.hitTest(_root.chiron_targ_mc)) {
  trace("Bull's eye!");
} else {
  trace("Nope!");
}
```

```
37  // Creates Chiron drag and drop functionality
38  chiron_mc.onPress = function() {
39      this.startDrag();
40  };
41  chiron_mc.onRelease = function() {
42      this.stopDrag();
43      if (this.hitTest(_root.chiron_targ_mc)) {
44          trace("Bull's eye!");
45      } else {
46          trace("Nope!");
47      }
48  };
```

The `hitTest()` movie clip method evaluates whether the object it's attached to (here, it's this, which refers to chiron_mc) intersects with the object listed as a parameter of the `hitTest()` action (in this case, _root.chiron_targ_mc). The `hitTest()` always returns either true or false. Note that `hitTest()` evaluates whether any pixel of one object is over any pixel of the other. The chiron_mc instance doesn't have to be perfectly positioned inside the chiron target; just a part of it needs to be inside the target.

Note *Remember, parameters are stored in the parentheses, so for `hitTest()` the object being tested is `_root.chiron_targ`. We must use the `_root` prefix, because chiron_targ_mc is on the main timeline, but the `hitTest()` action is associated with the chiron_mc movie clip instance. Because the event specified in this script (chiron_mc.onRelease) refers to one location (the instance chiron_mc), and yet the object it's comparing (chiron_targ_mc) is in a different location (on the main timeline), you must provide explicit addressing.*

The `hitTest()` method is enclosed in an `if` action, which evaluates a condition to see whether it's true or false. In plain terms, the first line of this new block simply says, "if the chiron_mc instance overlaps the chiron_targ_mc instance." Because true or false is exactly what `hitTest()` returns, you don't need to add anything to the `if` action for it to work properly.

Finally, let's take a look at the `trace()` action. The `trace()` action is used for debugging, which refers to the process of troubleshooting scripts. It works by popping up a special debugging window, and displays the message passed as its parameter when it's called. The `trace()` action is very useful for creating a temporary dummy action that you can have fire off only under certain circumstances.

In this case, `trace("Bull's eye!")` executes only if the `if` expression evaluates to `true`. You could have entered real actions in the `if…else` block, but if something were to go wrong you wouldn't know whether the problem was one of the enclosed actions or the block itself. Using `trace()`, you have an easy way to make sure the framework is functioning. If it is, then you can replace `trace()` with real code. The `trace()` commands are temporary, so don't bother putting polished text strings in them.

3. **Press Ctrl+Enter (Windows) or Command+Return (Macintosh) to test the movie. Drag Chiron around, letting him go periodically—sometimes over the target, sometimes away from it.**

As you release Chiron in various places, the Output window pops up and displays the appropriate text string. If you see "Bull's Eye!" or "Nope!" no matter where you drop Chiron, you know something is wrong with your script. Otherwise, the script works, and you'll see a mix of responses.

Notice that if you drop the chiron instance so that it's half in and half out of chiron_targ, the "Bull's eye!" text appears, but the instance remains half in and half out of the target— not very pleasing to the eye.

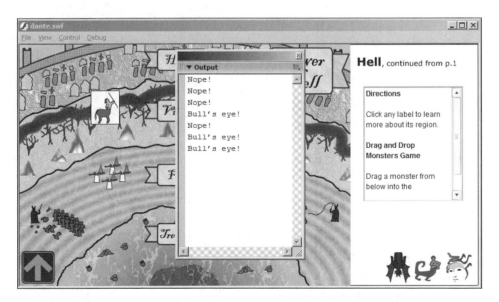

4. Return to the main movie, and in the Actions panel with Frame 10 of the actions layer selected, replace the trace("Bull's Eye!"); line in the Actions panel with the following code:

```
this._x=122;
this._y=78;
```

If these coordinates look familiar, it's because they're just a couple pixels from where you placed the chiron_targ_mc instance in Step 1 of this task. These two lines of code snap the chiron_mc instance into place if the user releases Chiron anywhere over the chiron_targ_mc instance.

5. Replace the trace("Nope!"); line with the following code:

```
this._x=562;
this._y=342;
```

These two lines make the chiron_mc instance snap back to its starting point if it's released anywhere outside the parameters of the chiron_targ_mc instance.

```
37 // Creates Chiron drag and drop functionality
38 chiron_mc.onPress = function () {
39     this.startDrag();
40 };
41 chiron_mc.onRelease = function () {
42     this.stopDrag();
43     if (this.hitTest(_root.chiron_targ_mc))
44         this._x=122;
45         this._y=78;
46     } else {
47         this._x=562;
48         this._y=342;
49     }
50 };
```

6. Test the movie to verify that it works.

The chiron_mc instance now snaps into place no matter where it's dropped. If it's dropped over the target, it snaps to the target. If it's dropped anywhere other than the target, it snaps back to its original position. Don't worry if Chiron snaps back to a position that's slightly out of line with the rest of the monsters. You'll fix this problem later in the lesson—with mathematical precision.

This snapping to position provides one form of feedback to the user, but you're not going to stop there.

7. Save your file.

Providing Dynamic Feedback

You're almost finished with the drag-and-drop functionality. However, snapping into place is hardly sufficient feedback for users. In this task, you'll add the Dynamic Text feedback that tells the user whether they dropped the monster on the correct target.

1. Select Frame 10 of the text layer in the timeline. Click in the gray area offstage to set the focus back to the Document window rather than the timeline.

You're preparing to create a new text area. You'll need to specify the frame into which you want to place the text. In order for the Property inspector to display the text settings, you must change the focus back to the Document window after you've selected the correct frame.

2. Click the Text tool in the Tools panel. In the Property inspector, set the Text Type to Dynamic Text, the Font to Verdana, Size 12, and make the Text (fill) color a dark blue (#000099). Place the cursor below the text area in the Document window, and hold down the Shift key to drag out a text field that is four lines high and about as wide as the text area above it.

The dynamic text box you create in this step will contain the text feedback for users as they drag and drop monsters in various places.

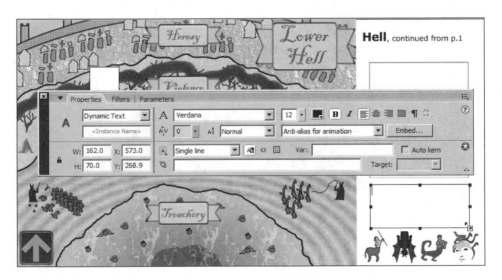

3. With the new text field still selected, use the Property inspector to give it an instance name of *drag_txt*. The Line type should be Multiline. Render Text as HTML should be toggled on, while Selectable and Show Border Around Text should be toggled off.

These settings prepare the text field so it can be used to provide feedback.

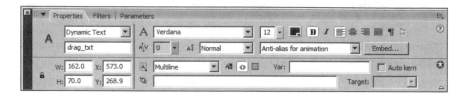

4. Select Frame 10 of the actions layer, and enter the following line of script in the Actions panel, at the end of the existing code:

```
drag_txt.htmlText="Drag a monster to its designated post.";
```

This line gives the drag_txt text field a text string to display when the movie first loads. Again, it uses the `htmlText` property, which causes the field to render HTML tags rather than plain text.

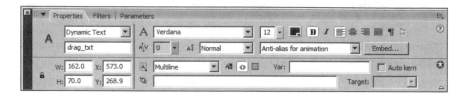

5. Test the movie to make sure the text loads.

When you test the movie, the text string should appear in the drag_txt field, in blue.

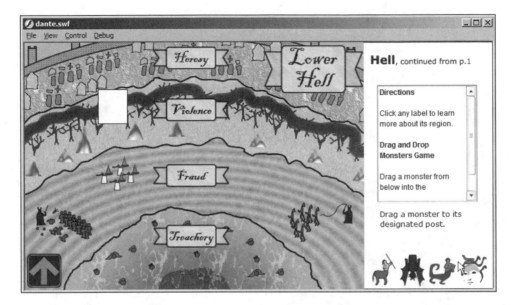

6. Return to the main movie and click Frame 10 of the actions layer in the timeline. In the Actions panel, enter the following text, below the `this._y=78;` line:

```
_root.drag_txt.htmlText="<b>Correct</b><br>Chiron the Centaur guards the
sinners immersed in the river of blood.";
```

> **Tip** *This text can be found in the script_inferno_html.txt file, beneath the Chiron heading.*

This line causes the drag_txt field to display a message confirming that the user dropped the chiron_mc instance on the correct target. Like the two lines above it, which snap the instance into place, this text is triggered to appear when the hitTest() expression evaluates to true.

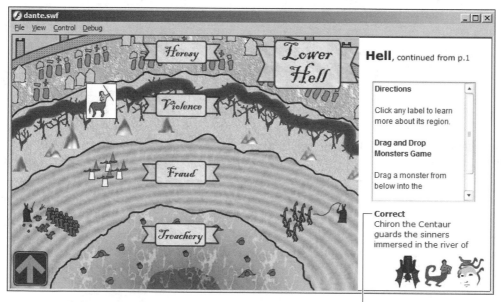

```
36  };
37  // Creates Chiron drag and drop functionality
38  chiron_mc.onPress = function() {
39      this.startDrag();
40  };
41  chiron_mc.onRelease = function() {
42      this.stopDrag();
43      if (this.hitTest(_root.chiron_targ_mc)) {
44          this._x=122;
45          this._y=78;
46          _root.drag_txt.htmlText="<b>Correct</b><br>Chiron the Centaur guards the sinners immersed
47      } else {
48          this._x=562;
49          this._y=342;
50      }
51  };
52
53  drag_txt.htmlText="Drag a monster to its designated post.";
54
```

Feedback appears when Chiron is dropped on target

7. Beneath the `this._y=342;` line, add the following line of code. Then test the movie to make sure it works.

```
_root.drag_txt.htmlText="<b>Incorrect</b><br>Please Try again!";
```

This line tells users that they placed the monster in an incorrect location.

```
36  };
37  // Creates Chiron drag and drop functionality
38  chiron_mc.onPress = function() {
39      this.startDrag();
40  };
41  chiron_mc.onRelease = function() {
42      this.stopDrag();
43      if (this.hitTest(_root.chiron_targ_mc)) {
44          this._x=122;
45          this._y=78;
46          _root.drag_txt.htmlText="<b>Correct</b><br>Chiron the Centaur guards the sinners immersed
47      } else {
48          this._x=562;
49          this._y=342;
50          _root.drag_txt.htmlText="<b>Incorrect</b><br>Please Try again!";
51      }
52  };
53
54  drag_txt.htmlText="Drag a monster to its designated post.";
55
```

Adding an Originating Target

When we first developed this project, we had the drag-and-drop scenario configured as it is at this point in the lesson. But when we did usability testing, we found that people often started to drag a monster and then changed their minds before releasing. When they changed their minds, they dragged the monster back to its starting location. Unfortunately, they were greeted with a message that said, "Incorrect. Please try again!" even though they weren't trying to drop the monster over a target. It became clear that we needed to add another target area over the originating area. This target would be neutral; it wouldn't send a correct or incorrect message to the drag_txt text field. In addition, if dropped on this target, the object would snap to its original position.

In this task, you'll add this additional functionality to the movie. Let it serve as a reminder that it's important to do usability testing early enough in the project to allow time for making significant changes.

1. Select Frame 10 of the monster targets layer. Drag out an instance of monsterTarget. Using the Free Transform tool, resize the instance to cover the entire area shared by all four monsters.

As before, you'll use hitTest() in conjunction with a new drop target. The difference this time is that instead of a separate target for each of the monsters, all four will share one target.

Normally, you wouldn't use the Free Transform tool to disproportionately resize a symbol instance, because it distorts the appearance of the instance. In this case, you can see how the black borders around the target are enlarged and blurry. But it doesn't matter here, because you're about to make the instance invisible. And invisible movie clips are just like invisible buttons in one regard: it doesn't matter what they look like.

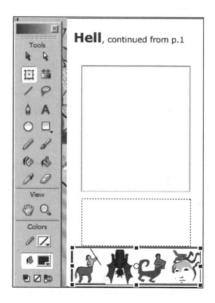

2. With the newly stretched instance still selected, give it an instance name of *start_targ_mc*.

With this instance name, you have a parameter you can test for using hitTest().

3. In the Property inspector's Color drop-down, choose Alpha, and drag the slider beside it down to 0.

This makes the movie clip instance invisible.

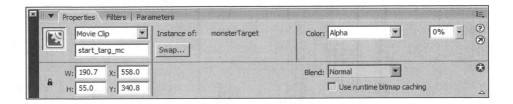

4. Select Frame 10 of the actions layer. In the Actions panel, find the code block for the chiron_mc instance, and insert the following code between the `if` and `else` blocks:

```
} else if (this.hitTest(_root.start_targ_mc)) {
  this._x=562;
  this._y=342;
  _root.drag_txt.htmlText="Drag a monster to its designated post.";
```

```
36  };
37  // Creates Chiron drag and drop functionality
38  chiron_mc.onPress = function() {
39      this.startDrag();
40  };
41  chiron_mc.onRelease = function() {
42      this.stopDrag();
43      if (this.hitTest(_root.chiron_targ_mc)) {
44          this._x=122;
45          this._y=78;
46          _root.drag_txt.htmlText="<b>Correct</b><br>Chiron the Centaur guards the sinners immersed
47      } else if (this.hitTest(_root.start_targ_mc)) {
48          this._x=562;
49          this._y=342;
50          _root.drag_txt.htmlText="Drag a monster to its designated post.";
51      } else {
52          this._x=562;
53          this._y=342;
54          _root.drag_txt.htmlText="<b>Incorrect</b><br>Please Try again!";
55      }
56  };
```

actions : 10

Line 48 of 59, Col 1

We have a variation on the if...else sequence: if...else if...else. Flash tests these code blocks in order, starting with the if block. If the if action evaluates to false, it proceeds to the else if action. If that evaluates to false, it proceeds to the next else if action (or, in this case, the final else action). You can string together as many else if actions as you need. Should any of these if or else if actions evaluate to true at any time, Flash will execute their nested statements and stop there, not checking any subsequent condition.

This particular else if line works just like the if line you created earlier: a hitTest() is performed to find out whether the chiron_mc instance was dropped over the named instance (in this case, _root.start_targ_mc). Should it evaluate to true, the chiron_mc instance is snapped back to its original position, and the drag_txt text field is reset to its initial text.

Making the Remaining Monsters Draggable

You're done working with Chiron. Its functionality is complete. You now need to apply this script to the remaining three monsters. You can copy and paste the script, because almost all of the script is the same for each of the remaining monsters, with the exception of a few particulars. In this task, you'll copy and paste the script for the remaining three monsters, and customize each script as appropriate.

1. Select Frame 10 of the monster targets layer. Drag out three new instances of monsterTarget. Using the Property inspector, place one at X 27, Y 0, and give it an instance name of *fury_targ_mc*. Place another at X 372, Y 168, and give it an instance name of *geryon_targ_mc*. Place the third at X 247, Y 345, and give it an instance name of *lucifer_targ_mc*.

Before you can do the other monsters' hit tests, you need to create and position the targets and give them all instance names.

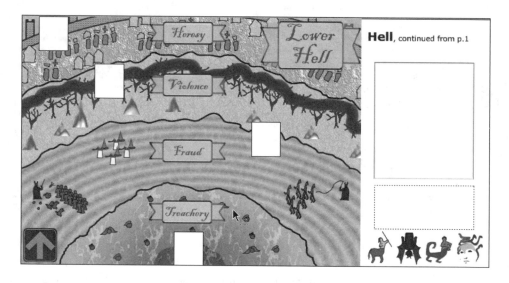

2. Select Frame 10 of the actions layer, open the Actions panel, drag to select the entire Chiron script, and copy it to the Clipboard. Position the cursor just below the end of the Chiron block and paste in the code.

```
34        lowerInfo_txt.vPosition = 0;
35        lowerInfo_txt.text = "<b>Treachery</b><br><br>The lowest of the nine circles houses the 1
36    };
37
38    // Creates Chiron drag and drop functionality
39    chiron_mc.onPress = function() {
40        this.startDrag();
41    };
42    chiron_mc.onRelease = function() {
43        this.stopDrag();
44        if (this.hitTest(_root.chiron_targ_mc)) {
45            this._x=122;
46            this._y=78;
47            _root.drag_txt.htmlText="<b>Correct</b><br>Chiron the Centaur guards the sinners imm
48        } else if (this.hitTest(_root.start_targ_mc)) {
49            this._x=562;
50            this._y=342;
51            _root.drag_txt.htmlText="Drag a monster to its designated post.";
52        } else {
53            this._x=562;
54            this._y=342;
55            _root.drag_txt.htmlText="<b>Incorrect</b><br>Please Try again!";
56        }
57    };
58
59    drag_txt.htmlText="Drag a monster to its designated post.";
60
```

`actions : 10`

`Line 38 of 60, Col 1`

Now you're ready to modify this code as needed for the lucifer_mc instance.

3. In this code block, change all instances of `chiron_mc` to `lucifer_mc`, and likewise change `chiron_targ_mc` to `lucifer_targ_mc`. Change the first set of X, Y positions to `_x=251` and `_y=347`. Change the second and third set of X, Y positions to `x=608` and `y=344`. Finally, change the text-feedback code in the line that begins `_root.dragtext.htmlText=` to the following:

```
_root.drag_txt.htmlText="<b>Correct!</b><br>Lucifer is entombed upside-down in
a frozen lake.";
```

These are all the changes necessary to customize this movie clip to the monster Lucifer. The `hitTest()` action now looks for the correct target; the positioning is adjusted so it snaps to the correct position; and the feedback text is updated to show the appropriate feedback.

```
▼ Actions - Frame

58
59 // Creates Lucifer drag and drop functionality
60 lucifer_mc.onPress = function() {
61     this.startDrag();
62 };
63 lucifer_mc.onRelease = function() {
64     this.stopDrag();
65     if (this.hitTest(_root.lucifer_targ_mc)) {
66         this._x=251;
67         this._y=347;
68         _root.drag_txt.htmlText="<b>Correct!</b><br>Lucifer is entombed upside-down in a froz
69     } else if (this.hitTest(_root.start_targ_mc)) {
70         this._x=608;
71         this._y=344;
72         _root.drag_txt.htmlText="Drag a monster to its designated post.";
73     } else {
74         this._x=608;
75         this._y=344;
76         _root.drag_txt.htmlText="<b>Incorrect</b><br>Please Try again!";
77     }
78 };
79
80 drag_txt.htmlText="Drag a monster to its designated post.";
81

                                            Script Assist
actions : 10
Line 68 of 81, Col 1
```

4. Repeat Steps 2 and 3 for the monster Geryon (the lizard-man). Change the instance name to *geryon_mc*. The first `hitTest()` should specify `geryon_targ_mc`. Change the first set of X, Y coordinates to x=375 and y=172. Change the other two sets of X, Y coordinates to x=656 and y=349. Finally, the text-feedback line should be as follows:

```
_root.drag_txt.htmlText="<b>Correct!</b><br>Geryon is the vehicle of choice
for those headed to Circle 8 and below.";
```

In this step, you're customizing the script for the monster Geryon.

```
77         }
78     };
79
80     // Creates Geryon drag and drop functionality
81     geryon_mc.onPress = function() {
82         this.startDrag();
83     };
84     geryon_mc.onRelease = function() {
85         this.stopDrag();
86         if (this.hitTest(_root.geryon_targ_mc)) {
87             this._x=375;
88             this._y=172;
89             _root.drag_txt.htmlText="<b>Correct!</b><br>Geryon is the vehicle of choice for those
90         } else if (this.hitTest(_root.start_targ_mc)) {
91             this._x=656;
92             this._y=349;
93             _root.drag_txt.htmlText="Drag a monster to its designated post.";
94         } else {
95             this._x=656;
96             this._y=349;
97             _root.drag_txt.htmlText="<b>Incorrect</b><br>Please Try again!";
98         }
99     };
```

Actions - Frame

Script Assist

actions : 10

Line 101 of 123, Col 12

5. Repeat Steps 2 and 3 for the monster Fury (the snake-haired woman). Change the instance name to fury_mc. The first `hitTest()` should specify `fury_targ_mc`. Change the first set of X, Y coordinates to x=29 and y=2. Change the other two sets of X, Y coordinates to x=706 and y=344. The text-feedback line should be as follows:

```
_root.drag_txt.htmlText="<b>Correct!</b><br>The snake-headed Furies guard the
walls of Dis.";
```

In this step, you'll customize the fourth and final monster, the Fury.

```
100
101 // Creates Fury drag and drop functionality
102 fury_mc.onPress = function() {
103     this.startDrag();
104 };
105 fury_mc.onRelease = function() {
106     this.stopDrag();
107     if (this.hitTest(_root.fury_targ_mc)) {
108         this._x=29;
109         this._y=2;
110         _root.drag_txt.htmlText="<b>Correct!</b><br>The snake-headed Furies guard the walls o
111     } else if (this.hitTest(_root.start_targ_mc)) {
112         this._x=706;
113         this._y=344;
114         _root.drag_txt.htmlText="Drag a monster to its designated post.";
115     } else {
116         this._x=706;
117         this._y=344;
118         _root.drag_txt.htmlText="<b>Incorrect</b><br>Please Try again!";
119     }
120 };
121
122 drag_txt.htmlText="Drag a monster to its designated post.";
```

6. Test the movie and try dropping each monster on its target, on an incorrect target, and on the start area. In all three cases, the monster should snap into position and the proper text feedback should appear in the drag_txt text field.

Each monster should have three unique responses, depending on where it's dropped. In addition, each should respond appropriately to its own target. If something went wrong, go back and compare your scripts with those in the directions and figures.

> **Note** *Do not skip this step! in a moment you'll switch to Dreamweaver and insert the Flash movie into its HTML document. By testing the movie, you generate a SWF from the completed version of the file. If you skip this step, you'll wind up inserting an unfinished copy of the SWF file.*

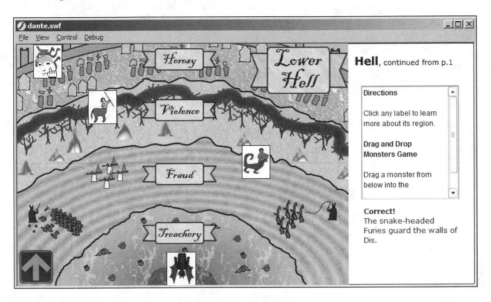

7. Save the FLA and close Flash.

Publishing the Interactive Map in the Dante Web Site

You're finished working on the interactive map of Dante's *Inferno*. But you still need to insert it into the Web site.

1. Open Dreamweaver, and verify that the Dante site is active in the Files panel. In the Files panel, double-click to open dante_map.html.

You created this page in Lesson 10, *Preparing the Dante Site*. It has only placeholder content at this point, but you're about to change that.

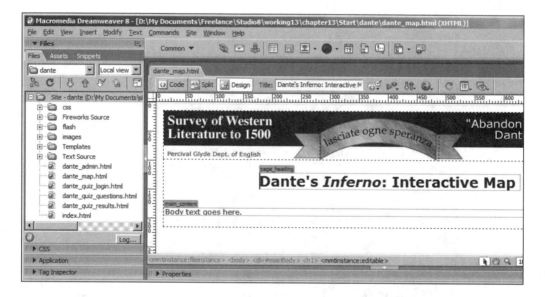

2. Drag to select the placeholder text "Body text goes here." Press Delete.

This page doesn't have any HTML text beyond the page heading. Instead, it will contain the Flash movie.

3. With the cursor blinking inside the now empty main_content editable region, in the Common category of the Insert bar, click the Media icon and select Flash from the drop-down menu.

As you probably recall from earlier Flash lessons, inserting Flash elements into HTML requires some special HTML tags. Fortunately, Dreamweaver simplifies the process of inserting Flash movies into HTML with this button.

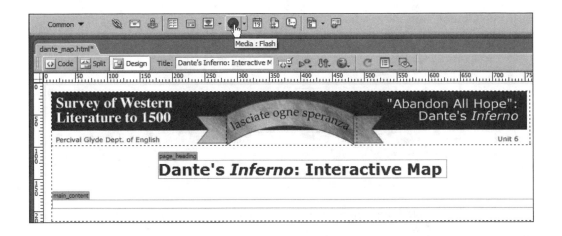

4. In the Select File dialog, navigate to the flash folder and select dante.swf. Click Choose.

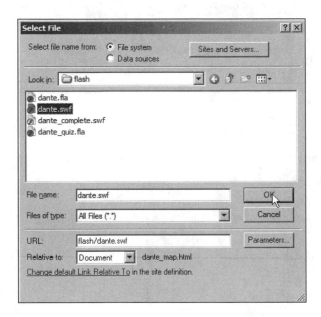

5. In the Object Tag Accessibility Attributes dialog, set Title to Dante's Inferno: Interactive Map. Click OK.

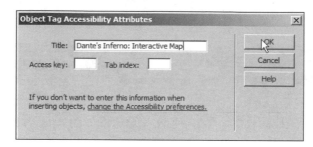

A gray box with the Flash logo appears on the page, representing the Flash movie.

Tip *You can preview the Flash movie in Dreamweaver. With the Flash movie selected, click the Play button.*

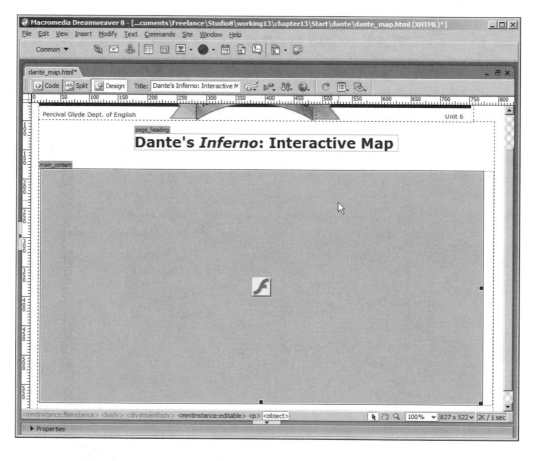

6. Click the Flash movie and press the right arrow key on the keyboard to position the insertion point just after the Flash movie. Press Enter/Return to create a new paragraph beneath the movie. Type the following, and link the word Return to index.html.

Return to the Dante site homepage.

This link enhances usability by improving navigation within the site.

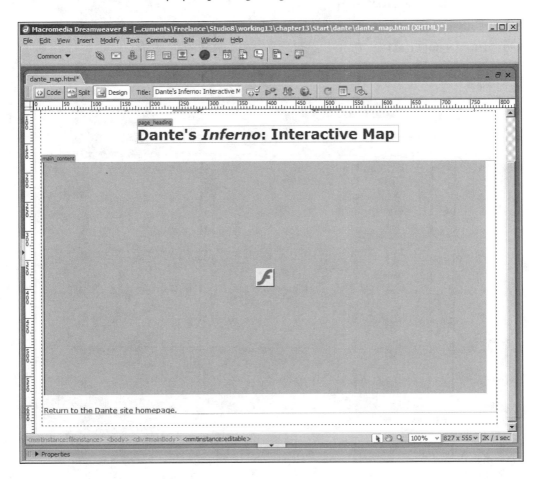

7. Save and close dante_map.html.

Also if you wish, you can test the movie inside the page by pressing F12 (Windows) or Option+F12 (Macintosh) with dante_map.html open, although nothing inside the Flash movie should have changed.

What You Have Learned

In this lesson, you have:

- Added drag-and-drop functionality to the monsters (pages 349–351)
- Created drop targets for each of the monsters (pages 351–354)
- Implemented an if…else if…else conditional script to detect where the user dropped the monsters (pages 355–366)
- Provided dynamic feedback to users, based on their actions (pages 359–363)
- Created a starting-point drop target (pages 363–366)
- Published the completed SWF in the Dante Web site in Dreamweaver (pages 372–375)

Project 2: A Class on Dante

Part 5: Dreamweaver and ColdFusion

13 Dynamic, Data-Driven Sites

The word *dynamic* means many different things in the world of Web development. You might have heard of a Web technology called Dynamic HTML (DHTML), which enables developers to control the behavior of the browser and screen content when a page is browsed. A client-side technology, DHTML runs entirely in the browser, relying on JavaScript.

Macromedia Flash developers often strive to create a "dynamic" experience, in which users have control over their experience of a Flash movie; the map of the *Inferno* you just completed is an example. Like DHTML, Flash—at least as you have used it so far—is primarily a client-side technology; all the ActionScript you wrote, all the assets

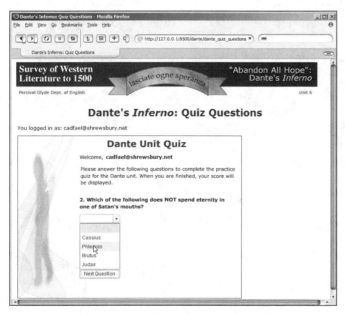

This quiz is built in Flash using components. Test data is collected in Flash and submitted to a database using ActionScript and ColdFusion.

you created, and so on are passed to the Flash player in the user's browser, and the Flash player figures out what to show the user.

From this lesson to the end of the book, "dynamic" takes on yet another, and more robust, meaning. Thanks to the power and ease of Macromedia ColdFusion, you'll create sites that act as interfaces to databases. You'll pass data between pages, enable users to view data loaded dynamically from databases, and write to databases. Later, you'll even create a quiz application in Macromedia Flash 8 that saves users' scores and identities to the database. ColdFusion is a server-side technology, which means that the code is executed on the server, and only the results are sent to the browser.

The hallmark feature of server-side dynamic sites (created with ColdFusion or an equivalent technology, such as ASP or PHP) is that page content is generated on the fly. That is, you and I might both request the exact same page (such as www.amazon.com), and yet the page we each see is entirely different. Mine greets me by name and places front and center an odd mix of computer books and mystery novels that represents my buying habits. What you see on the Amazon site is likely to be different. For starters, you won't see "Hello, Jeffrey Bardzell" at the top of your page.

You will not, in just four lessons, learn how to produce anything as sophisticated as Amazon.com's Web site. The development of Web applications is a serious topic whose mastery takes years of study and practice. The good news is that you don't need to spend years studying and practicing to create a handful of useful applications. Such Web staples as Web forms that save user input to databases take a matter of minutes (depending on their length) to set up, using Dreamweaver and ColdFusion. Developing pages that display specific database records is likewise a simple task. Using Dreamweaver and ColdFusion together, it's surprisingly easy to create environments where users have to log in to access content.

In the final four lessons of this book, you'll create a Web application that combines several of these elements. The dante_admin.cfm page displays a list of all the students in the class, and provides one-click email access to them. You'll also create a Flash-based quiz that outputs the user's test score to ColdFusion. ColdFusion then sends this data in two directions: it outputs the final test score to the browser so the user can see it, and inserts the score into the database so the instructor can see how the students are doing.

What You Will Learn

In this lesson, you will:

- Survey the completed application you will create in the next four lessons
- Learn about ColdFusion site concepts and architecture
- Define and configure the ColdFusion site in Dreamweaver
- Develop your first dynamic ColdFusion pages

Approximate Time

This lesson takes approximately 45 minutes to complete.

Lesson Files

Starting Files:

Lesson13/Start/dante/dante_admin.html
Lesson13/Start/dante/dante_map.html
Lesson13/Start/dante/dante_quiz_login.html
Lesson13/Start/dante/dante_quiz_questions.html
Lesson13/Start/dante/dante_quiz_results.html
Lesson13/Start/dante/index.html

Completed Files:

Lesson13/Complete/dante/dante_admin.cfm
Lesson13/Complete/dante/dante_map.cfm
Lesson13/Complete/dante/dante_quiz_login.cfm
Lesson13/Complete/dante/dante_quiz_questions.cfm
Lesson13/Complete/dante/dante_quiz_results.cfm
Lesson13/Complete/dante/index.cfm
Lesson13/Complete/dante/test_form.cfm
Lesson13/Complete/dante/test_output.cfm

Planning the Web Application

As always—but especially as you develop increasingly complex sites and architectures—it's essential that you have a clear vision of what you're setting out to do. Because this lesson inaugurates a whole section on ColdFusion, let's begin with the big picture.

In the real world, you'll start with a scenario—that is, your current situation and a problem that needs solving. Imagine that students are working on a unit on Dante. The unit needs to provide some content, so you created the interactive map. Also, the application would probably be more useful if students had a quick and easy way to learn who their classmates are and had hyperlinks to their email addresses—all generated from the database. Finally, students usually want some way to determine how well they're doing, so you'll create an ungraded quiz that they can use to test their knowledge.

Although you created the basic HTML pages for this application a couple of lessons ago, now it's time to get a better idea about how each of those pages fits into the overall application. The following figure shows the layout of the site, including the hyperlinks users are likely to take as they go through the site.

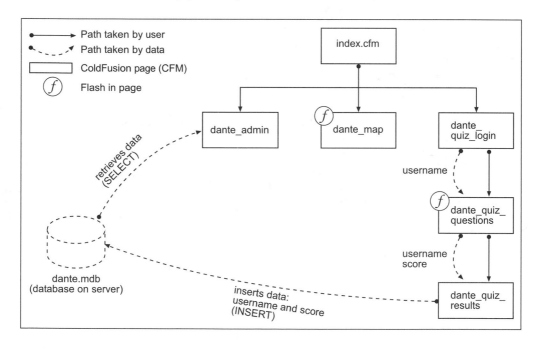

In addition to the path that users choose, this diagram also shows the paths the data takes in this application. Working with a server technology such as Macromedia ColdFusion usually involves working with data. In contrast to static Web sites, where you primarily worry about page content, layout, and graphic design, with dynamic Web sites you also send information between pages and to and from a database as each page is requested. Without this data, the Web pages don't work.

For example, dante_admin.cfm will eventually include a table of all the students in the class. The listing of students, however, is not embedded in the HTML, but rather is stored in the database. For the page to work, the page must be able to retrieve the data from the database to populate the table. If the database is unavailable, or if there's an error in the code, the data won't be returned, the table won't be populated, and the page won't be displayed. Instead, the user will see an error.

You don't need to master the specifics of this figure right now. Over the course of the remaining lessons, you'll become intimately familiar with each of the pages and learn how to send data to all the places it needs to go. The important thing for now is that you understand that a Web application is usually made up of a number of pages, which interact with each other and with one or more databases and tables to create a single user experience. That experience is made possible by collecting data from diverse sources—the user (via a Web form), the database, and so on—and using it to provide a meaningful experience.

With the big picture in place, take a few minutes to look at the final application in action.

1. Open your browser and point to http://www.allectomedia.com/dante_8/dante/.

For reasons that will be explained later, you can't open and try out the completed files in Lesson 13's Complete folder. A regular browser can't read ColdFusion pages, unless the pages have been processed by a server with ColdFusion installed. For now, go see the site on my server, where you only need a browser and the Flash player.

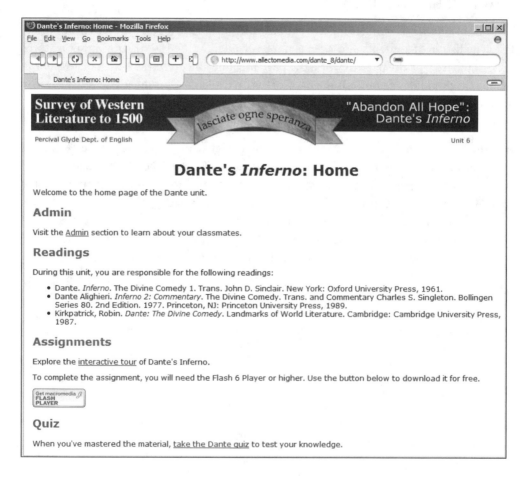

2. Click the Admin link.

This table displays all the students in the class, or'—more precisely—all the students entered in the database. Although they were added in random order, notice that they're alphabetized by last name. SQL, the language used to issue commands to databases, has built-in sorting capabilities. Notice also that on this page the user can view data, but she or he can't change it; there's no mechanism (such as a Web form) that enables the user to insert new data, update existing data, or delete data. The data on this page is strictly read-only. SQL has different commands for each of these tasks (retrieving, inserting, updating, and deleting data), and this page merely retrieves data. You'll take a closer look at SQL in subsequent lessons.

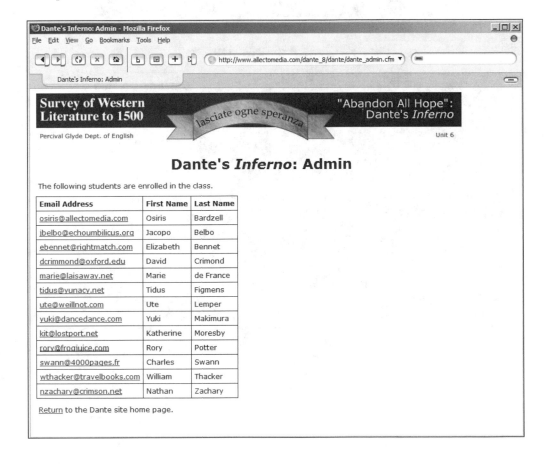

3. Return to the home page and click the interactive tour link.

This step brings up the interactive map that you designed and published in previous lessons. You're just about finished with this page; you won't be adding any database or ColdFusion functionality to it.

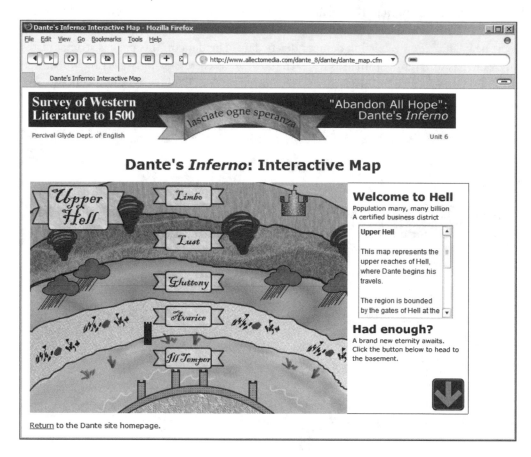

4. Return to the home page and click the "take the Dante quiz" link.

This step takes you to a log-in page. Because this log-in page is not secure, it doesn't require a password. A true log-in framework is beyond the scope of this book. Because the quiz is just for fun anyway (it isn't graded), secure log-in is not critical.

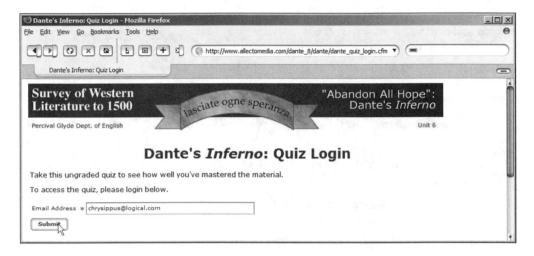

The log-in mechanism is a Web form. Later in this lesson, when the user clicks Submit on the Web form, the data she or he entered is passed to a script written to handle the data. In this case, the script that handles this data can be found in dante_quiz_questions.cfm. If you refer back to the site diagram shown earlier in this lesson, you'll notice two lines—one solid and one dashed—linking dante_quiz_login.cfm to dante_quiz_questions.cfm. The dashed line represents data; the data being passed in this case is the email address submitted with this form.

5. Enter any email address and click Submit.

The Dante quiz appears. The quiz is embedded in a Flash movie. The radio buttons and Next Question buttons are Flash components, which are prebuilt interface elements that Macromedia provides for rapid development. You'll build this quiz in Lesson 15, *A Component-Based Flash Quiz*.

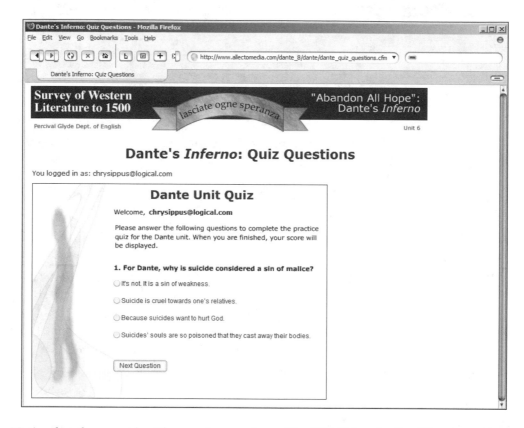

Notice that the page identifies you in two places. The HTML has the line "You logged in as: XX" where XX is the email address you provided. This information has also been passed into the Flash movie, which, as you've probably guessed, is handled by ColdFusion. The source of the data, of course, is the Web form.

Note *As an optional experiment, you can break this page. To do so, bookmark the page. Now close your browser. Reopen your browser and access the bookmark you just created. You will see an error message. Why did this error occur? Because the page depends on the data entered in the form on the preceding page (the email address). If you (or, more broadly, any users) bookmark a page in the middle of a Web application, and that page depends on certain data existing, you'll see an error because the data is not available. Good Web application design has built-in validation for all such pages: If the data is not available, the user is automatically redirected to a safe page (in this case, that would be dante_quiz_login.cfm). Again, this topic is beyond the scope of this book.*

6. **Without making any choices, click the Next Question button. When the error message appears, click OK. Answer each of the remaining questions until you finish.**

Any time you're collecting data from users, you need to ensure that they enter valid data. With a radio-button list, you only need to ensure that they make a selection. Here, the Flash quiz is programmed to display an error message when users fail to make a selection.

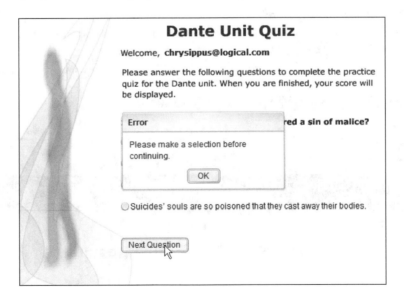

As you proceed through the quiz, notice it uses several different interface elements—not just radio buttons.

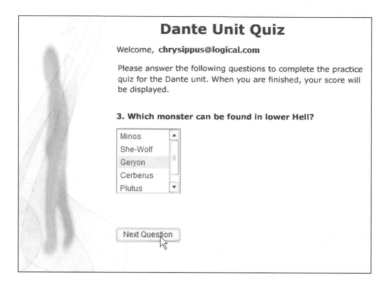

After the fifth question, your score is calculated and you are redirected to dante_quiz_results.cfm. On the Quiz Results page, your score is displayed and, behind the scenes, your score and username are saved to the database. Flash calculated the final score, but ColdFusion is used to output that score in the HTML page and save it to a database.

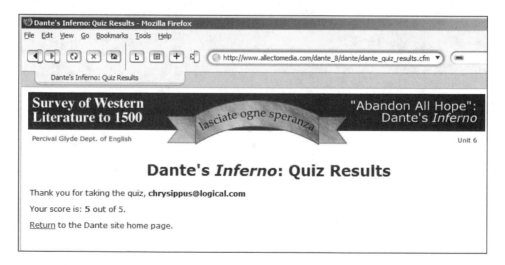

Now that you've worked through the site, return to the site diagram shown earlier in this lesson. It probably makes more sense now.

Understanding Site Definition Requirements

Defining a site for use with a server model, such as ColdFusion, ASP.NET, or PHP, is somewhat more complicated than defining a site for a static HTML site, such as the one created earlier in this book. And if you make a mistake, even a tiny one, you could have problems.

We'll walk you through the process step by step. Because people connect to servers in different ways, the process has some variations, and trying to get it right can be maddening. If you're in a networked environment, and you're connecting to a server over the network—rather than to a copy of Internet Information Services (IIS, available on Windows 2000 and XP Pro) or ColdFusion as a standalone Web server on your computer—your best resource is the network administrator, who should be able to provide you with many answers. If you're using a server on your machine (this is called a local server), the following directions should be sufficient.

Before we go into more detail, you'll need to understand a few concepts about working with server models, such as ColdFusion. (Everything we say here applies, more or less, to ASP, JSP, and PHP as well.) ColdFusion uses a custom scripting language (called ColdFusion Markup Language, or CFML) to perform a variety of tasks. These tasks include passing, manipulating, and even creating data, communicating with databases, generating email messages, and so on. None of these capabilities is native to HTML, and browsers can't perform them on their own.

Browsers read HTML, as well as a few other client-side technologies such as JavaScript, CSS, and (if you have the plug-in) Flash. But what browsers can do is limited to the client side—that is, what appears on a user's screen. Scripting languages like CFML are server-side, which means that their code resides and is processed on the server, and the user never sees the actual script—only the output HTML page.

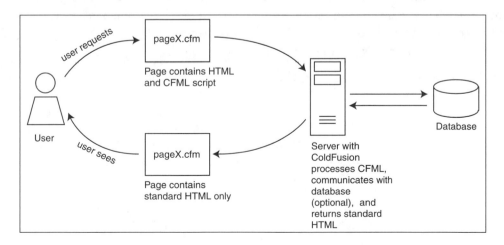

When you first start working with server technologies, you might find it confusing that two very different pages share the same name. In this figure they're called pageX.cfm. They could just as well be called index.asp, login.php, or shipconfirm.cfm. The version of the page the user requests, which happens to be the one that you, the developer, create, contains both HTML and the script, which is CFML in the case of ColdFusion. When the server processes the request, it sees the script, processes that script, and outputs a standard HTML file, with no ColdFusion script. This file appears in the user's browser as pageX.cfm. The page was generated on the fly and exists only as long as the user has it open.

ColdFusion calls the authoring version of pages that contain CFML *templates*. That is, a ColdFusion template is the page that you create and that resides on the server, but which is never seen by the user.

Now that you understand the basic process, you can see why you can't just open a completed version of the site in your browser right off the CD, as you could with the Jade Valley site. The browser would not understand the ColdFusion script inside. What's missing is the server. To view ColdFusion pages, whether they're already published on the Web or while you're developing them, they need to be processed on a server that contains ColdFusion. In other words, before you can even see the pages you create, they have to be saved on a Web server. This requirement—that pages must be saved on a server in order to be viewed—has tremendous implications for site setup in Dreamweaver. You can't simply place your local and remote file folders willy-nilly on your hard drive, as you can with static Web sites.

When you're developing dynamic sites in Dreamweaver, you typically have two versions of your site. The local version of your site sits anywhere on your hard drive; these are the files you actively work on. The remote version of your site sits on the server; these are the files you actually test in the browser. When defining a dynamic site in Dreamweaver, you'll often be defining more than one version of the site, and providing Dreamweaver with information about how to access these files in different ways (via the file system for opening and saving files; via HTTP for testing functionality).

The ColdFusion installer comes with a built-in server that will act as our local server (a server right on your computer) for this kind of testing.

> **Note** *If you prefer an alternative to ColdFusion's built-in Web server for testing, Windows 2000 and XP Pro users have access to Microsoft Internet Information Services (IIS), and Macintosh OS X users have access to Apache. Consult those servers' documentation for information on the directory in which to place your "remote" files.*

Installing ColdFusion

In order to test our ColdFusion code on your local machine, you'll download and install the ColdFusion application server.

1. Open your browser and point to http://www.macromedia.com/software/
coldfusion/trial/. You'll need to either log in if you have a Macromedia account,
or create a free account. Choose the developer edition appropriate to your
computer platform, and then download the installer.

The installer is a large file. Depending on your operating system, it could be more than 200MB. Downloading should be done over a high-speed connection.

2. Launch the ColdFusion installer and proceed with the default selections until
you reach the Install Type screen, which asks for a serial number. Check the box
for Developer Edition and click Next.

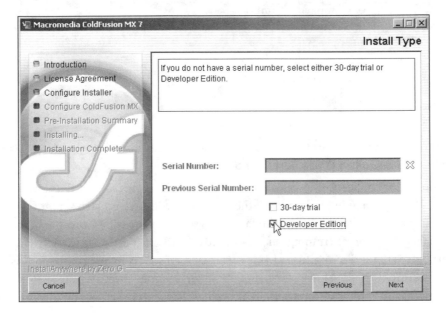

3. On the Installer Configuration screen, choose Server configuration. Click Next.

It's possible to install ColdFusion as a single server, as part of a cluster of servers (used for sites with heavy traffic), or as part of a J2EE package. For simple learning and page-testing purposes, the default single-server edition is the right choice.

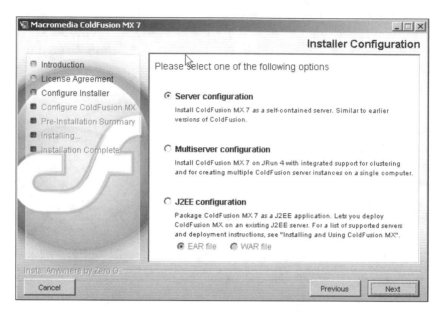

4. Continue with the default selections until you reach the Configure Web Server screen. Choose Built-in Web server and click Next.

ColdFusion is an application server; that is, its purpose is to process ColdFusion Markup Language. It's not intended to handle all the duties of a full-fledged Web server (that is, a server that interacts with Web clients such as browsers over the HTTP protocol). If you already have a Web server running, such as Microsoft IIS or Apache, you can install ColdFusion so that it ties into the existing server (in a production environment, this is the only way to install ColdFusion). If you don't have an existing server in your testing environment, you can install ColdFusion as both an application server and a Web server. Assuming that you don't have a Web server already running on your computer, you can choose this option so that you at least have a fully functional testing solution.

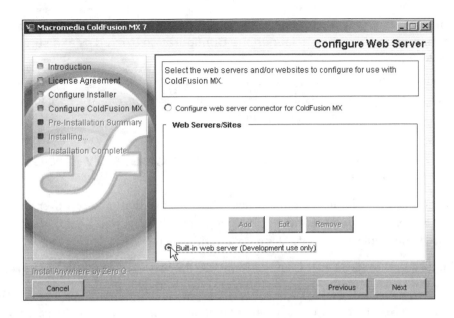

5. Enter Administrator and RDS passwords on the following two screens. Check the box enabling RDS on the RDS password screen.

Enter the same password for both the Administrator and RDS passwords. You should never use the same password on a production server, but for our purposes it doesn't matter and will make it easier to remember when we need it later.

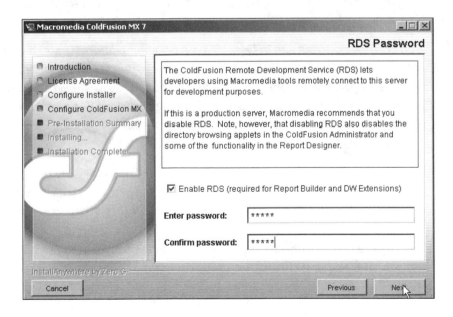

6. Continue with the rest of the defaults until the installation is complete. The last screen includes a checkbox to launch the Configuration Wizard. Make sure that it's checked before clicking Done.

The Configuration Wizard will complete the installation and launch the ColdFusion Administrator page in your default browser. You can close it for now. We'll log into the Administrator to configure other settings in Lesson 14.

Problems and Workarounds for Users Without Local Servers

If you're not running a local server, you'll have to access a ColdFusion server over a network or over the Internet to complete and test these pages. In this setup, your local files can reside on your machine, but your remote files have to reside on a server.

To gain full access to such a folder, and to configure your system to run on it, you need to contact your network administrator or Internet service provider (ISP).

A similar issue will come up in Lesson 14, *Connecting to Data Sources:* creating a DSN, or Data Source Name. A DSN is a small resource stored on the server that points to a given database and specifies what kind of database it is. When ColdFusion needs to access a database, it uses this DSN to find and communicate with the database. Because DSNs sit on the server, users who are not running local servers typically need to ask their network administrator to create a DSN for them. Creating a DSN is a one-minute process after the network administrator knows what you want to call the data source and where (and what kind) the database is.

> **Note** *You can develop your site in Dreamweaver on one platform (for example, Macintosh) and have your remote server run another platform (for example, Windows). As long as the remote server delivering the pages to the Web is running ColdFusion, the pages will be processed and delivered as HTML to the user.*

Defining the Site

In this task, you'll set up the site to use a ColdFusion environment. You already have a local version of this site, but you have not yet set up the remote version of the site, which has to be in a server folder on your hard drive (if you have a local server), a network drive, or even via FTP.

1. Open Dreamweaver 8 and choose Site > Manage Sites from the main menu. Select the dante site, and click Edit.

You'll add the remote version of the site in the coming steps.

2. If necessary, click the Advanced tab. Select the Remote Info Category. In the Access drop-down menu, choose Local/Network if your remote site is on your hard drive or on a mapped network drive; choose FTP if you have FTP access to the server.

In this step, you're telling Dreamweaver how you're accessing your remote folder to open and save files.

3. Choose the appropriate configuration settings for the option you selected in Step 2, using the specific selections below.

If you chose Local/Network as your option and you're working in a Windows environment using the built-in Web server, your remote folder must be in the following location: C:\CFusionMX7\wwwroot\dante\, as shown in the figure. Don't forget to create a dante folder in that directory.

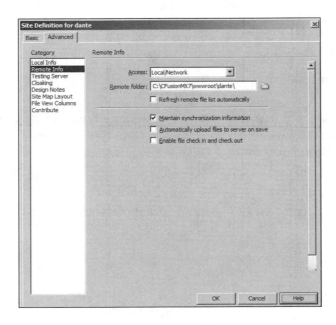

If you chose Local/Network as your option and you're working in a networked environment, whether you're a Macintosh or Windows user your remote folder should be your folder on the network appended by dante, which is the root folder for this site. Simply navigate in Windows Explorer or Macintosh Finder to the network location, and create a new folder called dante in that directory. Then select the dante directory.

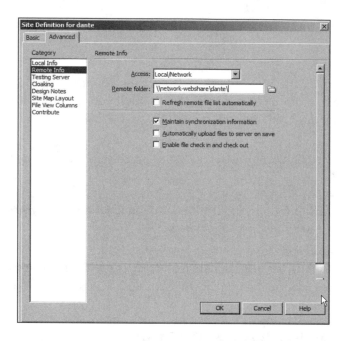

If you chose FTP, use the FTP credentials supplied by your network administrator. Because FTP information varies wildly by computer, we can't be any more specific.

All users: Leave the remaining options in this category at their defaults.

4. Select the Testing Server category. Choose ColdFusion as the Server Model. Choose the same Access option you chose in Step 3 (for example, Local/Network or FTP). Enter the same settings you did in the previous step.

In this step, you're telling Dreamweaver which server model you're using (in this case, ColdFusion) and how the server can find your files. Much of this step is a simple repeat of Steps 2 and 3, except for the all-important URL Prefix setting covered in the next step.

5. Enter the proper URL prefix, following the directions below.

The URL Prefix setting enables you to specify how the browser should access the files as the server processes them. If your pages do not preview correctly when you test them, this setting is the first place you should begin troubleshooting.

If you chose Local/Network as your option and you're working with the built-in ColdFusion Web server, your URL prefix is http://127.0.0.1:8500/dante/. The default installation of the built-in ColdFusion Web server includes a port number (8500) attached to the address of the server. If you're working in a Windows environment using IIS, your URL prefix does not, by default, include a port number, and would be http://127.0.0.1/dante/. The address 127.0.0.1, sometimes referred to as loopback, is the default address for the computer's local server. It can also be called with the more human-friendly *localhost*—for example, http://localhost:8500/dante/. Either address can be used to point to the files in your wwwroot folder.

If you chose Local/Network as your option and you are working in a networked environment, specifying the URL prefix can get a little trickier. Fortunately, your network administrator should be able to tell you what it is. Generally, the URL prefix is http:// + the server name + the path to your root folder. So, if I'm connected to a server called devserver, and my personal folder is jbardzel, then my URL prefix would be http://devserver/jbardzel/dante/. A networked server URL prefix can also contain a port number similar to the built-in server.

If you specified FTP as your method, your URL prefix is most likely a regular Internet address, possibly with a port number suffix added to the domain, as in http://www.myorganization.com:8008/jbardzel/dante/. If your site doesn't have a registered domain name (because, for example, you're testing over a home network), you can also enter the IP address of the machine with the site.

Regardless of how you connect to your remote site, your network administrator has the information you need to configure the URL prefix correctly.

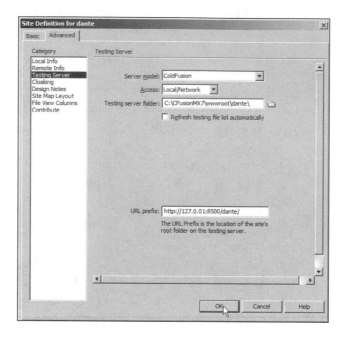

6. Accept all the default settings in the remaining categories of this dialog and click OK.

Dreamweaver scans the site and builds its cache.

7. One at a time, in the Files panel, select each HTML file and press F2. When the file name becomes editable, change the extension from .html to *.cfm*. Press Enter (Windows) or Return (Macintosh) to apply the name change. Each time the Update Files dialog appears, click Update.

In a dynamic site, the file extension is the signal the server uses to recognize that the file contains server code. If you leave the extension .html, the ColdFusion code won't get processed and the file sent back to the user will not be readable to the user's browser.

When you change a file's extension, all the links that point to it are broken. Fortunately, Dreamweaver catches this problem; the Update Files dialog presents a list of all the files that link to the original name and offers you the choice to have Dreamweaver automatically update the links in these files to the new name. In all cases you want Dreamweaver to update the files, so choose Update. Two of the files, dante_quiz_ questions and dante_quiz_results, are not yet linked to any pages in the site, so this dialog does not appear for them.

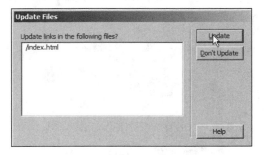

When you're finished, none of the files in the site should have the .html extension.

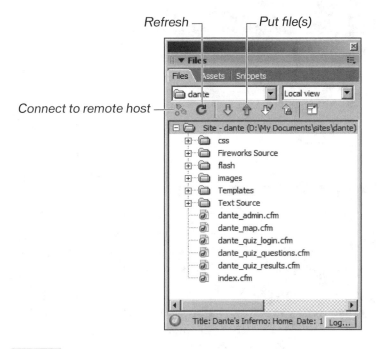

Note *At some point (but not necessarily right away), Dreamweaver rediscovers that you've made changes to the file names, and asks if you want to update the template files as well. Click OK to accept this option.*

8. In the Files panel, click the root folder, which is called Site - dante ([local root folder]). Click the Put File(s) button (the upward-pointing blue arrow button). In the dialog that asks if you want to Put the entire site, click OK.

This transfers the entire site to the remote folder. Your site is configured and you're ready to start building dynamic ColdFusion pages.

Passing Data Between Pages

You've done a lot of reading and conceptualizing in this lesson, so now is a good time to roll up your sleeves and take a stab at a simple ColdFusion technique: passing data between pages. As discussed earlier, a key aspect of creating a meaningful user experience is customizing the experience by passing relevant data between pages and/or pages and the database.

In this task, you'll create a simple Web form on one page and send that data to a second page. The second page will display the data entered on the first page. This exercise will show you how ColdFusion templates become simple HTML pages, and prove that you've configured your site correctly.

In the newly defined Dreamweaver site, choose File > New to create a new page. In the General tab of the New Document dialog, under Category, choose Dynamic Page; under Dynamic Page select ColdFusion; and then click Create. When a new untitled document appears, call it *test_output.cfm* and save it in your local dante folder. With the page still open, choose File > Save As to create a second page called *test_form.cfm*.

These two pages are throwaways that are not part of the application you'll be building. We often create throwaway pages for testing and prototyping purposes. We typically prefix the name with test_, so the test pages are grouped together alphabetically and we remember to delete them when we're finished experimenting.

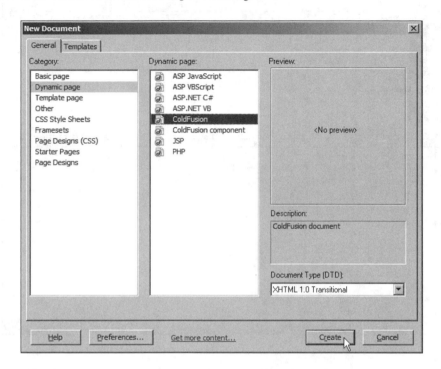

1. In the Dreamweaver toolbar, click the Show Design and Code views (Split view) button to display the document in a split window.

One way to learn how to code in a language is to look at the code generated by programs as you work. Throughout these lessons, you should try to get a feel for ColdFusion. It's an easy markup language, and there's no substitute for having some ability with the code, even when you're working in visual environments like Dreamweaver.

In fact, when you work in Dreamweaver, it's a good idea to do so in split view, especially if your monitor resolution is 1024 by 768 pixels or higher (with lower resolutions, it might get a little too crowded). If you've made it this far in the book, you should be comfortable enough to deal with the code behind the curtain.

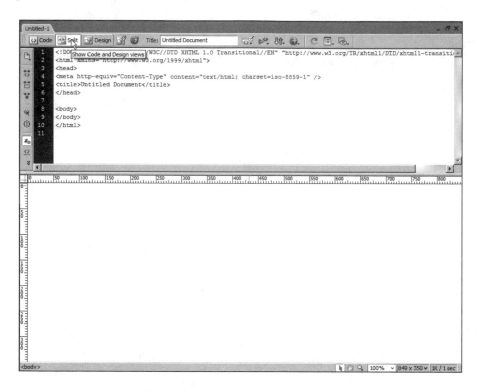

2. In the test_form.cfm page, insert the cursor after the opening **<body>** tag and press Enter/Return. Select the **CFForms** category of the Insert bar, and insert a **CF Form Field**. The cfform tag editor will open. On the General category, set the Action to *test_output.cfm*, the Method to post, and the name to *bioData*.

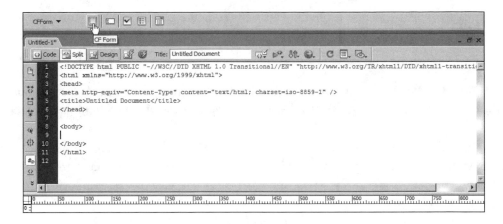

Action and method control what happens with the form data. By specifying a URL for the action, you tell the browser to send both the form data and the user to the specified URL.

The method is a little more abstract. In addition to POST, the other option in the Method category is GET. These methods are both ways of sending information from the current page to the specified destination. The difference between them is how they send that information.

The GET method appends the data to the URL itself. You've seen URLs followed by long strings of nonsense. They use the GET method. As an example, imagine your user entered Harriet as her first name. If you were to specify GET in this step, the URL that would appear after she clicked the Submit button would be http://127.0.0.1:8500/dante/test_output.cfm?firstName=Harriet. Because GET passes the data in the URL, you can see the data that gets passed, which is convenient for bookmarking. Use GET when you're querying a search engine (that is, getting data).

The POST method sends the exact same data, but it's sent encoded in the request. This method is not only more secure than GET, because it's not visible to the user, but also allows you to send more information. POST is typically used when you're sending data somewhere, such as to a database. Because it's not immediately visible in the URL, the POST method is a little more secure than GET, although the information is still sent as clear, or unencrypted, text.

In the case of the widget you're building now, either method will work. You'll use POST, which is a good default choice. Now that you've made these changes, take a look in your code and see how and where they appear.

3. Select the Miscellaneous category and set the Format to Flash. You can also choose a Skin at this time to style the look of your form. Click OK to close the tag editor.

In ColdFusion you have the option of using standard HTML forms or ColdFusion's cfforms. HTML forms are enclosed inside the <form> tags, and ColdFusion forms inside the <cfform> tags. We've chosen to use cfform to take advantage of the Flash format for a more attractive look to our form.

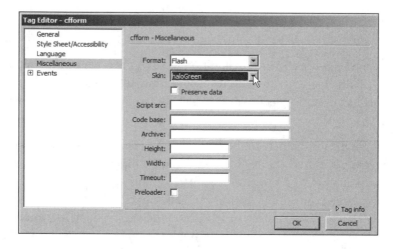

| Note | *The Flash format of <cfform> requires ColdFusion MX version 7 or higher.* |

4. Press Enter/Return to make space between your opening and closing <cfform> tags. With your cursor in the newly created space, insert a CF Text Field. The cfinput tag editor will open. In the General category, set the Type to text and the Name to *firstName*, and set Size to 20. Next, insert a new CF Text Field. Set the Type to submit and both the name and value to *Submit*.

In this form, you ask the user for her or his first name, and then send the user—as well as the data she or he entered—to the test_output.cfm page.

Each value the user enters in a form will be stored in a variable with the same name as the form element. For this reason, you should always give your form elements meaningful names. Obviously, you're not likely to get confused by a variable in a one-element form, but you should develop good habits in anticipation of working with longer forms.

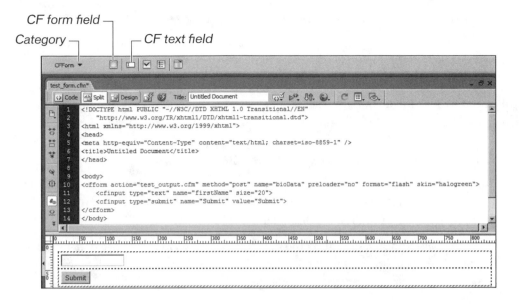

CF form field —
Category —
— CF text field

5. Right-click the cfinput text named *firstName* and choose Edit Tag <cfinput> from the list of choices. Choose the Miscellaneous category and type *Please enter your first name* in the Label field.

Functionally speaking, this step is completely unnecessary. None of these changes will affect what's sent in the POST. But the more minimalist you make your tests, the harder they'll be to understand later. It doesn't take much time to label text fields and make simple presentational changes, especially if they render the point of the page immediately obvious.

6. Save and close test_form.cfm, and open test_output.cfm.

You've completed the input page, and now it's time to build the output page, which will display the data that the input page just sent to it.

Note that while we used cfform to create our form, the same thing could have been done with straightforward HTML form tags. In addition to richer design options, cfform provides other benefits, such as form validation—but that's beyond the scope of this exercise.

7. Choose Window › Bindings to open the Bindings panel.

The Bindings panel displays variables that you can use on the page. As you will learn, there are many kinds of sources for these variables, including URLs (thanks to GET), form variables sent via POST, and data brought in from a database via a query.

Initially, a checklist appears, indicating the steps you'll need to follow to use data bindings. At this point you should have at least three of the five steps checked, which is sufficient to make use of a form variable sent via POST.

8. Click the + button near the top of the Bindings panel, and choose Form Variable from the list. In the dialog that appears, type *firstName*.

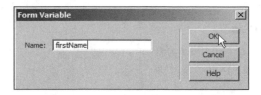

This step tells the page that it can expect to receive a variable called firstName sent from a form. You know this variable will exist, because there's a text field in the form called firstName. But Dreamweaver doesn't know this data will be available. By creating a binding, you're notifying Dreamweaver that the data will be available when the page is executed.

Note *Dreamweaver has no way to verify that the data actually will be available. You could make up fake variables and Dreamweaver would happily add them to the Bindings panel. Also note that Dreamweaver doesn't change any code in the page when you create a binding. Rather, when you use a binding—which you will in a few moments—the information you provide in the Bindings panel tells Dreamweaver how to write the code.*

When you're finished with this step, the Bindings panel changes. The checklist disappears, and in its place is a Form category. If you expand the Form category, you'll see the variable firstName with a lightning-bolt icon next to it.

9. In the main area of the document, enter the following text: *Thank you, , for providing that information*.

Again, this is static HTML. ColdFusion templates are often a combination of regular HTML and ColdFusion markup.

10. Place the cursor between the two commas, so it's snug against the second comma. In the Bindings panel, select firstName and click the Insert button.

When you're finished, the string {Form.firstName} appears in the main window, colored blue. This string is how Dreamweaver indicates a placeholder for dynamic content. You can disregard the exact formatting, because Dreamweaver's design view signifies any dynamic content this way, whether it's ColdFusion, PHP, or ASP. To learn the proper syntax, take a look in the code itself in code view.

Between the two commas, you'll see your first bit of real ColdFusion: <cfoutput>#Form.firstName#</cfoutput>. The <cfoutput> tags tell ColdFusion to write something to the page. In this case, you're telling ColdFusion to write the firstName variable that came into the page as a form variable. The pound symbols (#) tell ColdFusion that the content between the # symbols is a variable, rather than a simple text string.

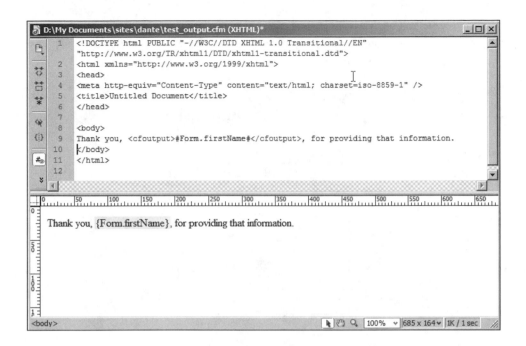

```
D:\My Documents\sites\dante\test_output.cfm (XHTML)*

 1  <!DOCTYPE html PUBLIC "-//W3C//DTD XHTML 1.0 Transitional//EN"
    "http://www.w3.org/TR/xhtml1/DTD/xhtml1-transitional.dtd">
 2  <html xmlns="http://www.w3.org/1999/xhtml">
 3  <head>
 4  <meta http-equiv="Content-Type" content="text/html; charset=iso-8859-1" />
 5  <title>Untitled Document</title>
 6  </head>
 7
 8  <body>
 9  Thank you, <cfoutput>#Form.firstName#</cfoutput>, for providing that information.
10  </body>
11  </html>
12
```

Thank you, {Form.firstName}, for providing that information.

`<body>`   100% ▾ 685 x 164 ▾ 1K / 1 sec

11. Save the page. In the Files panel, hold down the Shift key and select both the test_form.cfm and the test_output.cfm files. Click the Put File(s) button to upload the files to the server.

Note *If the Include Dependent Files dialog appears, you can choose Yes or No, because there aren't any dependent files. Dreamweaver automatically displays this dialog so you can be sure to upload any images, Flash movies, and the like when you upload the page.*

Remember, you can't test the files by just opening them in your browser. They have to be processed on the server and then sent to the browser. You accomplish that by uploading them. And now for the moment of truth!

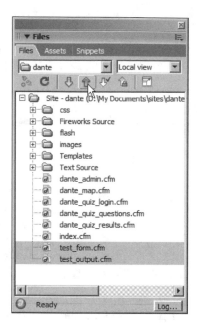

12. Select test_form.cfm in the Site panel and press F12 (Windows) or Option+F12 (Macintosh) to test the file.

Dreamweaver opens the file in your browser, using the URL prefix you specified earlier in this lesson. If you did it right, you should see the form.

13. Enter a name in the field and click Submit.

You should see the second page, with the name you entered between the commas. If you see the second page, you configured everything correctly.

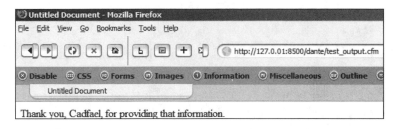

If you got an error message, then something went wrong. A number of things could have caused an error. Make sure that both the test_form.cfm and test_output.cfm files were, in fact, uploaded to the remote server. Make sure that the URL prefix is correct. Make sure that ColdFusion is actually running (Windows users running ColdFusion locally can test this by opening the ColdFusion Administrator page from the Start menu; if you can see the page, ColdFusion is running). Also, make sure that you didn't misspell test_output.cfm in the Action field of the form in test_form.cfm.

14. While still viewing the second page, choose View > Source (Internet Explorer), View > View Source (Safari), or View > Page Source (Firefox) to look at the code.

```
view-source: - Source of: http://127.0.01:8501/dante/test_output.cfm - Mozilla Firefox
File  Edit  View  Tools

<!DOCTYPE html PUBLIC "-//W3C//DTD XHTML 1.0 Transitional//EN"
        "http://www.w3.org/TR/xhtml1/DTD/xhtml1-transitional.dtd">
<html xmlns="http://www.w3.org/1999/xhtml">
<head>
<meta http-equiv="Content-Type" content="text/html; charset=iso-8859-1" />
<title>Untitled Document</title>
</head>

<body>
Thank you, Cadfael, for providing that information.
</body>
</html>
```

You'll notice right away that instead of the <cfoutput> tags, with the form variable and the pound signs (##) between the variables, all you see is the name you typed, as if the page had been hard-coded to say just that. But you know better. What you're seeing is evidence of the process depicted in the pageX.cfm figure earlier. Although two files have the same name (test_output.cfm), one has CFML code and the other contains only standard HTML. The page you're viewing was generated on the fly by ColdFusion. It exists only in your browser; as soon as you close or leave the page, it's gone forever.

What You Have Learned

In this lesson, you have:

- Learned a number of fundamental concepts about dynamic ColdFusion pages (pages 382–383)
- Explored the ColdFusion application you'll build in the remainder of the book (pages 382–390)
- Defined your site to use the ColdFusion server model and specified the local and remote folders as well as the URL prefix (pages 391–402)
- Created your first dynamic ColdFusion page, which displays information entered in a form on a different page (pages 402–413)

14 Connecting to Data Sources

In Lesson 13, *Dynamic, Data-Driven Sites*, you got your Macromedia ColdFusion site up and running. You also created a simple ColdFusion application that displayed a variable passed through a Web form from a different page. The real power of a server model such as ColdFusion is its ability to interact with data sources such as text files, XML documents, and—above all—databases. With those data sources, ColdFusion (or ASP, PHP, or JSP) can insert, edit, delete, and/or extract a particular set of data, and output that data as if it were standard HTML. This interactivity with a data source enables you to create password-protected pages, surveys, testing environments, message boards, dynamic press release applications, and so forth.

To achieve any of this functionality, you'll need to define a data source so ColdFusion knows how to find and communicate with the data. After ColdFusion knows how to access the data source—in this case, a Microsoft Access database—you'll create a page that displays data from the database live, the moment a user requests it.

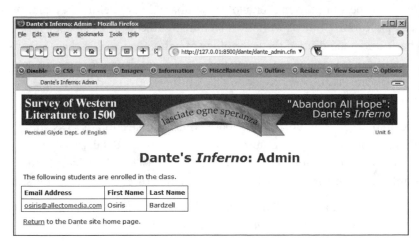

The data displayed in the second row of the table is pulled dynamically from the database.

What You Will Learn

In this lesson, you will:

- Learn foundational database concepts
- Create a ColdFusion DSN for your site
- Build a form that collects biographic information from a user
- Save the user's form data to a database
- Build a recordset from a SQL query and display live database data in the browser

Approximate Time

This lesson takes approximately 60 minutes to complete.

Lesson Files

Starting Files:

Lesson14/Start/dante.mdb (Windows)
Lesson14/Start/dante.dbn (Macintosh)
Lesson14/Start/dante/dante_admin.cfm

Completed Files:

Lesson14/Complete/dante/dante_admin.cfm

Understanding Databases

The topic of database theory is deep and entire books have been written on the subject. Serious application developers need to master a lot of database theory before they can create sophisticated applications. But, as with most technical subjects, you can get a lot done with only a basic understanding of the technology at hand. One goal in these lessons is to give you some experience working with databases, DSNs, and dynamic pages, so you can build common applications and are primed to take on more advanced books or training if you wish.

Databases are made up of a series of tables. A database table is a collection of rows and columns, and looks very much like an Excel spreadsheet. What makes database tables special is that they can link to one another. For example, imagine a small business that sells pet products online. This business's database might include three tables, as follows:

- **Customers:** This table is for a list of all the company's customers: first name, last name, street address, city, state or province, postal code, country, phone number, and so on.

- **Inventory:** This table contains a listing of all the company's products, including the name, quantity on hand, price, location, and so forth.

- **Transactions:** This table contains a listing of all the sales through the Web site. It includes the date of the transaction, total price of the transaction, name and quantity of the items sold, and the name of the customer to whom they were sold.

The magic of this setup is that the Transactions table links to the Customers and Inventory tables. Thus, for transaction number 247, rather than listing Jane Smith, 112 Cheshire Lane, Toronto, Ontario, Canada, her phone number, and all her other particulars, the table simply lists a unique ID number associated with her, and pulls up the rest of the information as needed, on the fly. Likewise, for inventory, if Jane orders six bags of catnip, the inventory amount is automatically deducted. Each piece of information needs to be maintained in only one place, and is referenced as needed by other tables.

In the remaining lessons, you will not take advantage of the relational potential of databases (we're assuming that you do not have Microsoft Access). Even so, it's important to understand what tables are, that one database can have multiple tables, and that you can establish relationships between tables.

The following figure shows the users table of the database used in this lesson. Notice that every row (technically called a record) contains an instance of every column (database columns are called fields). Although each record can—and usually does—have different information in each field, they all share the same fields; only the values in them change.

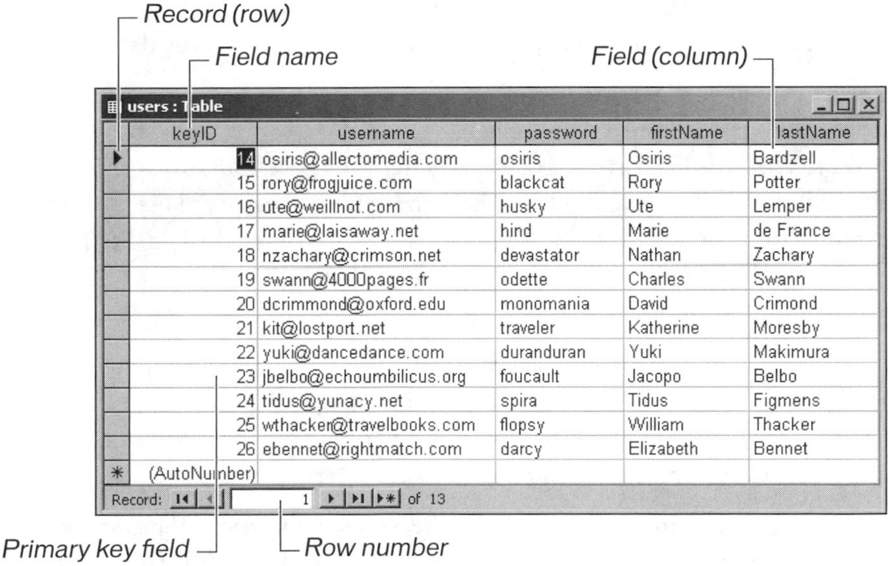

Record (row)

Field name

Field (column)

keyID	username	password	firstName	lastName
14	osiris@allectomedia.com	osiris	Osiris	Bardzell
15	rory@frogjuice.com	blackcat	Rory	Potter
16	ute@weillnot.com	husky	Ute	Lemper
17	marie@laisaway.net	hind	Marie	de France
18	nzachary@crimson.net	devastator	Nathan	Zachary
19	swann@4000pages.fr	odette	Charles	Swann
20	dcrimmond@oxford.edu	monomania	David	Crimond
21	kit@lostport.net	traveler	Katherine	Moresby
22	yuki@dancedance.com	duranduran	Yuki	Makimura
23	jbelbo@echoumbilicus.org	foucault	Jacopo	Belbo
24	tidus@yunacy.net	spira	Tidus	Figmens
25	wthacker@travelbooks.com	flopsy	William	Thacker
26	ebennet@rightmatch.com	darcy	Elizabeth	Bennet
(AutoNumber)				

users : Table

Record: 1 of 13

Primary key field

Row number

Each field has a unique name, which is how you specify the field. Records are not generally named; instead, each record has what's called a primary key: some piece of information, stored in one of the fields, that's unique and distinguishes it from every other record. In the figure you'll see a field named keyID, which is a field we created to store this unique value. You'll also notice in the last record of that field, (Autonumber) appears as the value. This means that the database table is set so that whenever a new record is created, Access automatically assigns a new number to that record, which can then be used as its primary key.

If you're working in Windows and have Microsoft Access, you should open and explore dante.mdb, which can be found in this lesson's Start folder. Don't worry if you don't have Access or if you are working on a Macintosh; the database is ready to use, and ColdFusion will be able to work with it. The Web application you create will be your interface to the data in this database.

Now that you understand what the database is, you need to understand how you configure ColdFusion to work with it. And that process requires working with Data Source Names.

Understanding Data Source Names

As mentioned earlier, a DSN is used to help a server running ColdFusion, ASP, or the like to connect to a data source. Specifically, a DSN specifies a driver (which enables ColdFusion to communicate with the specific data source you're using, such as a Microsoft Access or SQL Server database) and a path (which tells ColdFusion where to find the data source).

Individual pages can interact differently with the data source (in this project, a Microsoft Access database for Windows and a Pointbase database for Macintosh). One page might insert new records into the database. Another page might retrieve and display information from the database. Yet another might retrieve information and enable the user to edit or delete that information. Because each page potentially uses the database in a different way, specific directions for interacting with the database occur on each page.

What doesn't change from one page to the next is the relationship to the database—that is, the path pointing to the database and the driver used to communicate with it. In other words, the DSN is static across pages, even though what two given pages might do with a database can differ. (It's possible to have more than one DSN used in a site, but the information within each DSN doesn't change between pages.)

To connect to a data source from any page in the site, you simply specify the DSN (the details of doing so are covered later). When you specify the DSN, you don't have to specify the driver and the path on every page. But it also has another benefit: if the driver ever changes (for example, if you migrate your database from Access to SQL Server) or the path ever changes (say, you upload your site from your hard drive to your ISP, which uses a different setup), all you need to change are the particulars of the DSN itself. All your pages will still work without modification, because they point just to the DSN by name. The figure below illustrates the process of submitting information to a database.

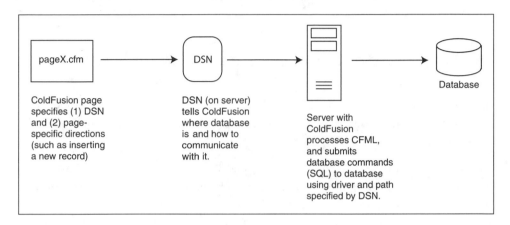

ColdFusion page specifies (1) DSN and (2) page-specific directions (such as inserting a new record)

DSN (on server) tells ColdFusion where database is and how to communicate with it.

Server with ColdFusion processes CFML, and submits database commands (SQL) to database using driver and path specified by DSN.

The separation of individual pages from DSN particulars greatly facilitates moving sites from one location to another. For example, when we uploaded the Dante testing environment application to our ISP, we sent the ISP an email telling them the name of the DSN and the name and location of the database on their server (they had specified a folder for databases when we first signed up). Within two minutes, they had written back saying that they were finished. We tested the site and everything worked. The speed of their reply is testimony to how easy it is to move database-driven sites without breaking the connectivity.

Before continuing, copy the database from the CD-ROM onto your server (you don't need to store a local copy of the database).

1. Using Windows Explorer or Macintosh Finder, browse to the Lesson14/Start folder on the CD-ROM.

The database file used from this point forward is located on the CD that comes with this book.

2. Windows users: copy dante.mdb. Macintosh users: copy dante.dbn. Access an appropriate folder on the server (see below), and paste the file into that folder.

For users developing with the built-in ColdFusion Server, the best place to store the database is in the db folder, outside the ColdFusion wwwroot folder. For Windows users with a default ColdFusion install, that is *C:\CFusionMX7\db*. For Macintosh users with a default ColdFusion install, that is */Applications/ColdFusionMX7/db*. All the documents in this folder have the appropriate permissions set.

If you're a Windows or Macintosh developer who uses a remote server, the server administrator will tell you where to put the database file. In most cases, it will be separate from the main site for security reasons.

Defining a Data Source in the ColdFusion Administrator

In this task, users running ColdFusion locally via Apache, Internet Information Server (IIS), or as a standalone Web server will define a data source from within the ColdFusion administrator.

If you're on a Macintosh or Windows machine and your remote site is on a network (or FTP) server other than your computer, the good news is that you don't have to worry about defining a data source. The bad news is that someone will have to do it for you. If you're using ColdFusion over a network on a computer other than your own, you'll need to tell that server administrator that you need a DSN created, with the name dante, that the database is called dante.mdb, and that it's a Microsoft Access database. You'll also need to tell your administrator where the database file is located. (Most server administrators store database files outside of the Web root for security, so ask your server administrator where you should put the database.) Finally, ask your administrator for the Remote Development Services (RDS) password that will enable you to access your data source while you're developing. RDS gives Dreamweaver (and HomeSite) access to the ColdFusion server, which enables you to use the Dreramweaver environment to look in your database, write server behaviors, build queries, and perform other operations that depend on information from the server. She or he will know how to take it from there.

If you're not running ColdFusion locally, skip the rest of this section and go bug your network administrator. After the administrator has you set up, skip ahead to the section of this lesson entitled "Building the Registration Form."

Note   *Regardless of your configuration, make sure you've copied the database to the Web server. You or your network administrator will need to browse to the database as part of creating the DSN, and you can do that only if the database is there.*

If you're running ColdFusion locally through IIS or as a standalone Web server, please read on. Because the specific steps vary slightly for the databases on Windows and Macintosh, we'll list the steps separately for each platform.

Defining a Data Source: Windows

1. Choose Start > Programs > Macromedia > ColdFusion MX 7 > Administrator.

This page is your interface to ColdFusion server management. Through this page you'll create DSNs, set caching and session management, and perform any number of server management tasks.

2. In the password screen, enter your password.

This is the password you chose when you installed ColdFusion.

3. In the navigation bar on the left, click the **Data Sources** link. Expand the **Data & Services** section if necessary.

The Data Sources link takes you to a screen where you can create ColdFusion DSNs.

4. In the Add New Data Source box, enter *dante* as the Data Source Name, and choose **Microsoft Access** from the Driver drop-down menu. Click the **Add** button.

Several data sources are automatically installed when you install ColdFusion, so don't be surprised if you see several listed on this screen. They're used for the tutorials that ship with ColdFusion. The tutorials are a good resource to help you improve your ColdFusion skills, and should be helpful after you finish this book (if not sooner).

Remember, a data source comprises a unique name, a driver, and a path to the database. In this step, you're taking care of two out of three of these requirements.

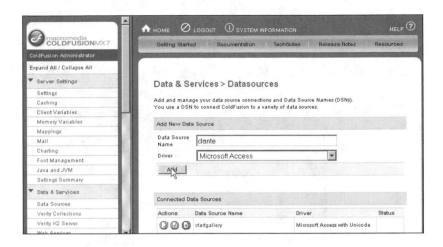

5. In the Microsoft Access screen, click the Browse Server button beside Database File. Navigate to C:\CFusionMX7\db\, select the dante.mdb file and click Apply. When you're finished, click Submit.

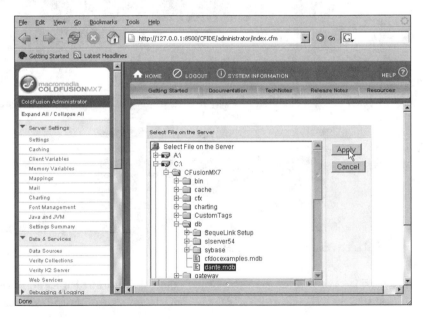

If you put dante.mdb in a different directory, navigate to it there.

In this step, you're completing the third part of the DSN: the path to the database file. When you're finished, you're returned to the Data Sources screen. The difference is that this time the dante DSN is displayed in the list of installed DSNs. The word "OK" should appear under Status, indicating that the DSN is created and ready to use.

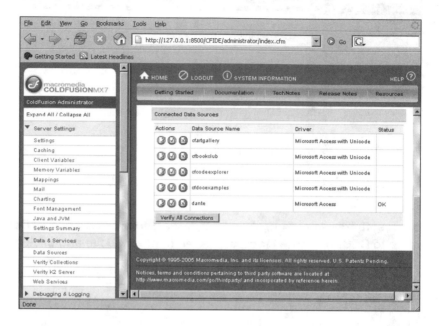

6. Click Logout to exit the ColdFusion Administrator.

You're finished creating the ColdFusion DSN, and your site is now fully ready for action.

Defining a Data Source: Macintosh

1. Launch a Web browser and open the ColdFusion Administrator login page. In the default install, the URL is *http://127.0.0.1:8500/cfide/administrator/index.cfm*

This page is your interface to ColdFusion server management. Through this page you create DSNs, set caching and session management, and perform any number of server management tasks.

2. In the password screen, enter your password.

This is the password you chose when you installed ColdFusion.

3. In the navigation bar on the left, click the Data Sources link. Expand the Data & Services section if necessary.

The Data Sources link takes you to a screen where you can create ColdFusion DSNs.

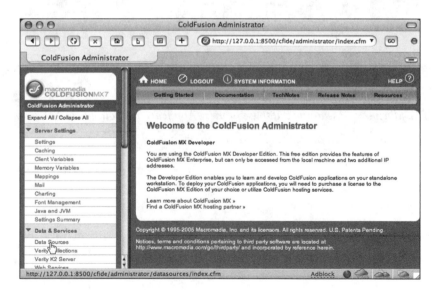

4. In the Add New Data Source box, enter *dante* as the Data Source Name, and choose Other from the Driver drop-down menu. Click the Add button.

Several data sources are automatically installed when you install ColdFusion, so don't be surprised if you see several listed on this screen. They're used for the tutorials that ship with ColdFusion. The tutorials are a good resource to help you improve your ColdFusion skills, and should be helpful after you finish this book (if not sooner).

Remember, a data source comprises a unique name, a driver, and a path to the database. In this step, you're taking care of two out of three of these requirements.

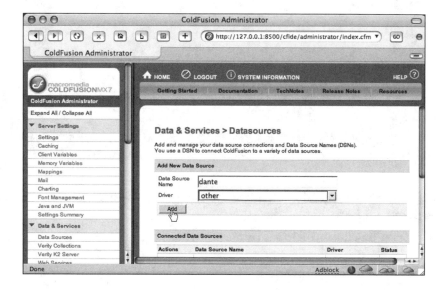

5. In the Other screen, fill in the parameters given below. When you're done, click Submit.

JDBC URL: *jdbc:pointbase:dante,database.home=/Applications/ColdFusionMX7/db*

Driver Class: *com.pointbase.jdbc.jdbcUniversalDriver*

Driver Name: *pointbase*

User Name: *PBPUBLIC*

Password: *PBPUBLIC*

At the end of the JDBC URL, enter the path to your database file. If you put dante.dbn in a different directory, put the path to it there.

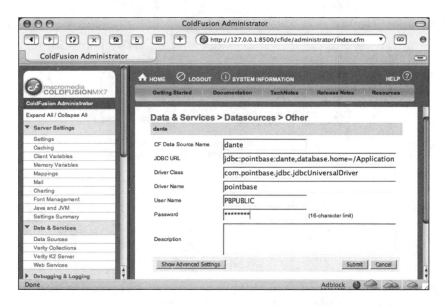

When you're finished, you're returned to the Data Sources screen. The difference is that this time the dante DSN is displayed in the list of installed DSNs. The word "OK" should appear under Status, indicating that the DSN is created and ready to use. If there's an error message, you can verify the data source by clicking the green checkmark icon in the Actions column to the left of the Data Source Name.

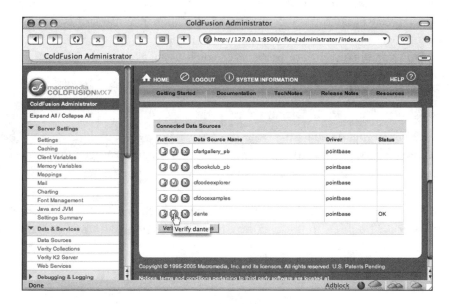

6. Click Logout to exit the ColdFusion Administrator.

You're finished creating the ColdFusion DSN, and your site is now fully ready for action.

Introducing SQL Queries

Now that you've configured your database on the server and enabled ColdFusion to see it, you're ready to start using this data in your site. In the last two tasks of this lesson, you'll retrieve data from the database and then output it into a table. To access the data from the database, the ColdFusion document needs to communicate with the database. But there's a catch: databases don't understand ColdFusion Markup Language (CFML).

The language that modern databases understand is SQL, which is pronounced "sequel" and stands for Structured Query Language. ColdFusion—like ASP, PHP, and JSP—uses SQL to obtain information from a database, just like a database programmer would. After that data is obtained, it can be manipulated and/or displayed on the page. Serious application developers need to learn quite a bit of SQL to build powerful applications. But thanks to Dreamweaver's dialog-based ways to construct SQL statements (the scripts used to access databases and the information stored in them), nonprogrammers and SQL newbies can construct SQL queries fairly easily. In this task, you'll create a bona fide SQL statement using a Dreamweaver dialog that will mask what you're doing.

1. Open dante_admin.cfm in Dreamweaver.

You'll eventually output database data into this page. Before you can do that, you'll have to configure Dreamweaver to see ColdFusion DSNs. You'll need to configure Dreamweaver only once per site, and you can have any page within the site open when you do it.

2. Choose Window > Server Behaviors. Click the fourth link in the panel, entitled Specify the RDS Login.... In the pop-up dialog that appears, enter your password.

If you're working on a machine that's running ColdFusion locally, you should enter the RDS password you entered when you installed ColdFusion.

Note *You can reset the RDS password in the Security section of the ColdFusion Administrator page.*

If you're accessing files over a network (if you had your network administrator create a DSN), you should enter the RDS password you requested from your administrator earlier in this lesson.

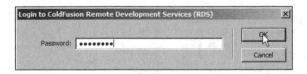

After you enter the password, you might have to wait a few moments before you return to the Application panel. When you do, go to the Database tab and choose the dante database.

3. Expand the Tables category in the database, and explore the tables. Right-click (Windows) or Control-click (Macintosh) one of the tables, and choose View Data... from the menu. After you're finished looking over the data, click OK.

Dreamweaver's Databases panel clearly provides convenient access to your data. Not only can you see the database schema (the structure of the tables and their fields), but you can even view its data right in Dreamweaver.

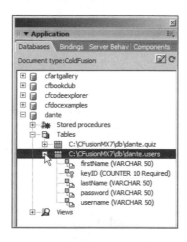

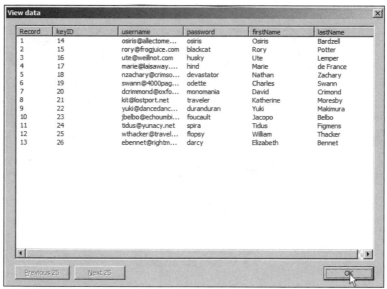

Now that Dreamweaver is seeing your data, you can start using the data. One of the most common tasks in a dynamic Web application is to retrieve a collection of data. This data might be all the data in a table, a particular subset of data from a table, or even a collection of data from more than one table. When you retrieve a collection of data from a database, it's stored in a recordset, which is a structured collection of data returned from a database and stored in the computer's memory. Once that data is in memory, you can output it into your ColdFusion pages.

Displaying data is a two-step process. In the first step, you retrieve it in the form of a recordset. In the second step, you output the data into a Web page. The first step is accomplished using Dreamweaver's Bindings panel.

4. Choose Window › Bindings to open the Bindings panel.

You use the Bindings panel as a resource for adding dynamic data to a page. In Lesson 13, you used the Bindings panel to specify a form variable (Form.firstName). This time, you're going to create a recordset.

The recordset you create will contain all the data in the users table, except each user's password and the primary key (unique ID).

5. Click the + button near the top of the Bindings panel, and choose Recordset (Query) from the menu.

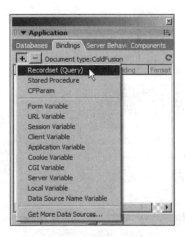

Remember, the recordset is the collection of data that is returned. The query is the SQL script that requests the information that makes up the recordset.

Because database tables can get quite large, with thousands of records (or rows), you don't want to pull all the information out of the database, especially if you intend to use only a small part of it. Overly large recordsets place an additional burden on your server and can slow overall performance. Fortunately, SQL enables you to be very specific about the data you want.

After you have made the selection, the Recordset dialog appears.

6. In the Recordset dialog, enter *rs_GetUsers* as the Name, and choose dante from the Data source drop-down menu.

The name can be anything you want. Many developers preface their recordset names with *rs_* so they're easily recognized in code.

To build a recordset, you have to specify the data. After you tell ColdFusion which DSN to use, you'll once again have access to all the tables and fields in the dante.mdb database, just as you did in the Insert Record dialog.

7. Choose users from the Table drop-down menu. When the data refreshes, click the Selected radio button in the Columns category, and Ctrl-select (Windows) or Command-select (Macintosh) the username, firstName, and lastName fields in the Column area.

In this step, you're telling ColdFusion to build the recordset from only data in the username, firstName, and lastName fields. All the data in the other fields is ignored.

8. In the first Sort drop-down menu, choose lastName, and in the second field choose Ascending.

These settings tell ColdFusion how to sort the information in the recordset. In this case, you're sorting by last name.

The final dialog should appear as in the following figure.

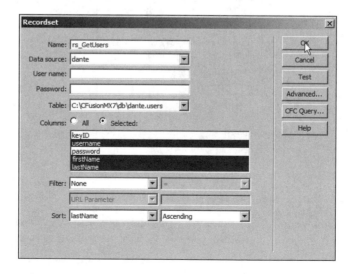

9. Before clicking OK, click the Test button.

Clicking the Test button causes Dreamweaver to show the results of the recordset you're building. This is a great way to test your SQL query without having to save the page, upload it, and test it.

You should see 13 records, listed alphabetically by last name.

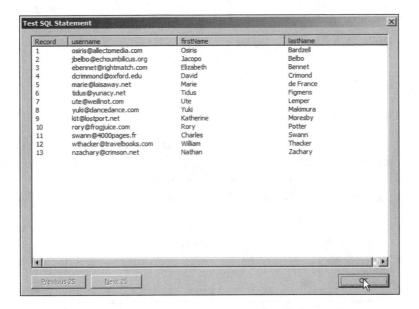

10. Click OK to exit the Test window, and OK again to exit the Recordset dialog.

The Bindings tab now lists Recordset (rs_GetUsers). If you expand the recordset, you'll see username, firstName, and lastName listed with lightning-bolt icons.

One important concept to understand about this new recordset is that just because you made it available *to* the page doesn't mean it's visible *on* the page. If you were to test the page right now, the query would run and the data would be in memory, but the resulting page would still be blank.

11. Switch to code view and look at the code at the top of the document.

You'll see the following code:

```
<cfquery name="rs_GetUsers" datasource="dante">
SELECT username, firstName, lastName
FROM users
ORDER BY lastName ASC</cfquery>
```

Sandwiched between the `<cfquery>` tags is the SQL statement you built in the Recordset dialog. The `<cfquery>` tags, as you've probably guessed, tell ColdFusion to send a query to the database. The query is the SQL statement. The recordset's name and the DSN are both passed as parameters of the `<cfquery>` statement.

As we mentioned at the beginning of this lesson, the beauty of DSNs is that you can change their particulars all you want (for example, if you migrate to a different database or server) without breaking any pages, because the pages reference only the DSN name itself.

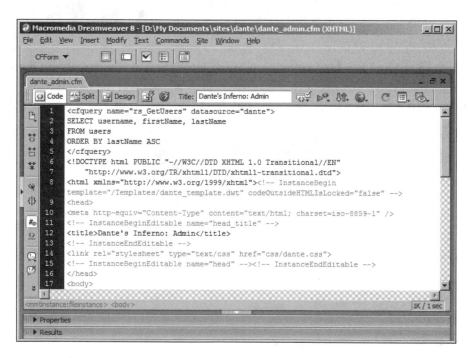

Dynamically Populating a Table

The recordset is now available to the page, and you can now output it. The recordset is eventually going to go into a table, but first you'll need to prepare the page with some static HTML.

1. Open dante_admin.cfm. Replace the placeholder "Body text goes here" with *The following students are enrolled in the class*. Press Enter or Return twice, and then type *Return to the Dante site home page*. Link the word Return to index.cfm.

You'll put the table in the blank line between the two sentences you just entered.

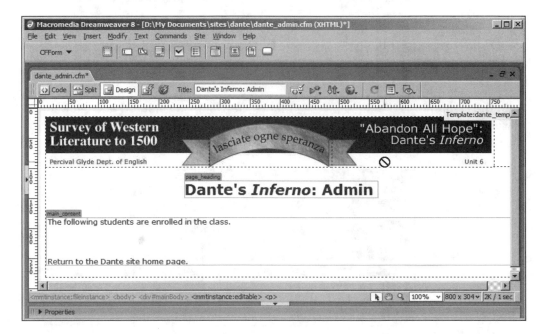

2. Position the insertion point in the blank line. From the Application category of the Insert bar, choose Dynamic Data: Dynamic Table.

The Application category of the Insert bar contains many common dynamic Web application components. The Dynamic Table is particularly convenient. You tell Dreamweaver which recordset to use, and it automatically outputs all of the records inside the table.

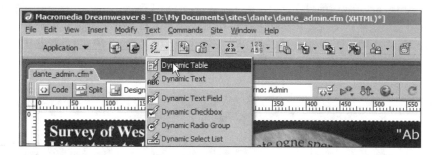

3. In the Dynamic Table dialog, verify that rs_GetUsers is selected and click the All records radio button. Leave the remaining settings at their defaults and click OK.

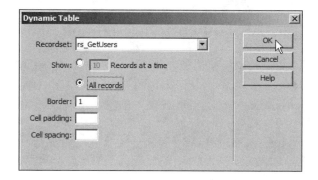

Dreamweaver generates a two-row table for you. The first row is static HTML, and it simply contains the row headings. The second row contains the dynamic data. When you test the page, however, you'll discover that ColdFusion automatically generates as many records as it needs to display all the records in the database.

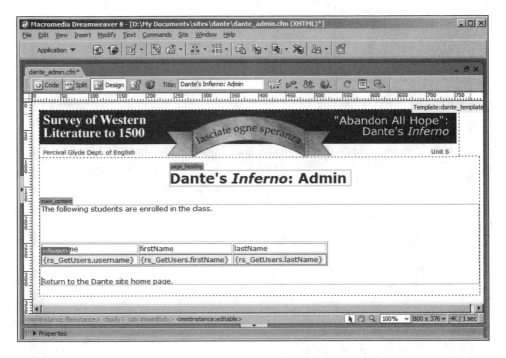

You could save and upload the page now, but before you do so there's another convenient feature you can use to test the data in your pages.

4. From the main menu, choose View > Live Data.

The table is populated with live database data. It has a yellow background, which indicates that the data can be edited. (This yellow background won't appear in the actual page; it is just a Dreamweaver visual aid.)

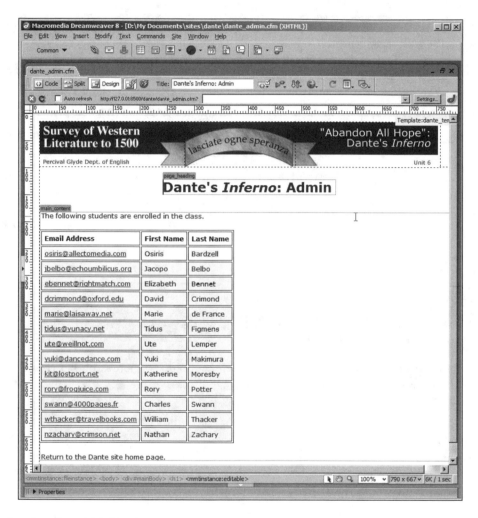

Notice that the table's headings simply repeat the column names. You can replace the headings with something more descriptive.

5. In the first row of the table, replace username with *Email Address*; firstName with *First Name*; and lastName with *Last Name*. Drag to select each new heading, and use the Property inspector to apply Bold.

This step is mainly cosmetic; no special functionality is added on the server.

main_content		
The following students are enrolled in the class.		

Email Address	**First Name**	**Last Name**
osiris@allectomedia.com	Osiris	Bardzell
jbelbo@echoumbilicus.org	Jacopo	Belbo
ebennet@rightmatch.com	Elizabeth	Bennet
dcrimmond@oxford.edu	David	Crimond
marie@laisaway.net	Marie	de France
tidus@yunacy.net	Tidus	Figmens
ute@weillnot.com	Ute	Lemper
yuki@dancedance.com	Yuki	Makimura
kit@lostport.net	Katherine	Moresby
rory@frogjuice.com	Rory	Potter
swann@4000pages.fr	Charles	Swann
wthacker@travelbooks.com	William	Thacker
nzachary@crimson.net	Nathan	Zachary

Return to the Dante site home page.

6. Save and Put the page on the remote server. Click in the Document window and press F12 (Windows) or Option+F12 (Macintosh) to test the page.

The page opens in a browser, and the data appears as expected.

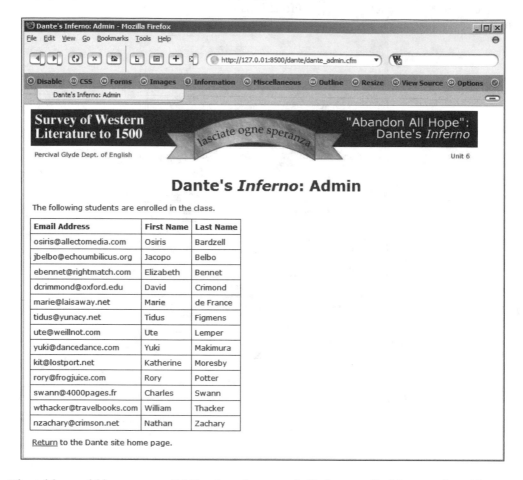

The table would be more useful if rather than merely listing email addresses, the addresses were linked. You can use ColdFusion to add this functionality, but first you should review what a regular static hyperlink looks like in HTML:

```
<a href="target_page.cfm">Clickable link text</a>
```

Creating an email link is slightly different:

```
<a href="mailto:someuser@somedomain.com">Clickable link text</a>
```

As you can see, email links are always prefaced with mailto:.

As you'll recall from Lesson 13, ColdFusion outputs dynamic data using the `<cfoutput>` tag. Return to dante_admin.cfm and toggle Live Data back off by choosing View > Live Data. If you look in the code for the table, you'll see that the email address is coded as follows:

```
<td>#rs_GetUsers.username#</td>
```

The `<td>` tags simply indicate a table cell. Remember, everything inside the pound signs (##) is a variable or expression that ColdFusion should evaluate. The code `rs_GetUsers.username` means the username variable that belongs to rs_GetUsers (the dot between GetUsers and username, which is called an access operator, indicates ownership; the item on the right belongs to the item on the left).

Now you have to put all that together. As you've probably anticipated, you'll need the following code:

```
<td><a href="mailto:#rs_GetUsers.username#">#rs_GetUsers.username#</a></td>
```

7. In code view, replace the line `<td>#rs_GetUsers.username#</td>` with the following line of code:

```
<td><a href="mailto:#rs_GetUsers.username#">#rs_GetUsers.username#</a></td>
```

ColdFusion generates an email link for each user in the database.

```
28      <table border="1">
29        <tr>
30          <td><strong>Email Address</strong></td>
31          <td><strong>First Name</strong></td>
32          <td><strong>Last Name</strong></td>
33        </tr>
34        <cfoutput query="rs_GetUsers">
35          <tr>
36            <td><a href="mailto:#rs_GetUsers.username#">#rs_GetUsers.username#</a></td>
37            <td>#rs_GetUsers.firstName#</td>
38            <td>#rs_GetUsers.lastName#</td>
39          </tr>
40        </cfoutput>
41      </table>
```

Note *If, after this step, you get an error saying you've made changes to code that is not marked as editable, click Yes and proceed to the next step. This is a known bug with Dreamweaver—all the code you're changing is marked as editable— and, at least in the context of this book, you can safely ignore it. Your edits will not be affected by future changes to the site template file.*

8. Save and upload the file. Test it by pressing F12 (Windows) or Option+F12 (Macintosh).

This time, all the email addresses should be hyperlinked. When you click one, your email editor should appear with a new message open, with the selected student already in the To line. (Don't bother sending an email message to any of these recipients, as they're all fake.)

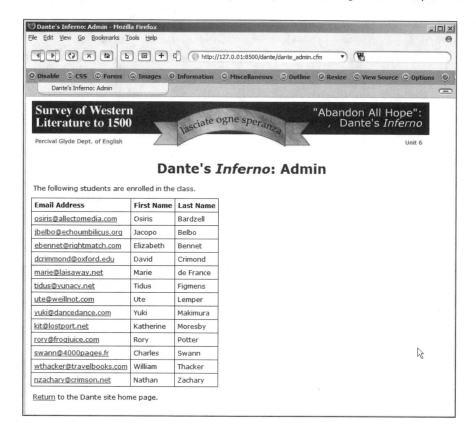

What You Have Learned

In this lesson, you have:

- Learned concepts about databases and Data Source Names (pages 416–420)
- Configured a data source in the ColdFusion Administrator (pages 420–428)
- Explored the Databases and Bindings panels (pages 428–434)
- Built a recordset using a SQL statement, and displayed its results dynamically on a page (pages 428–442)

Project 2: A Class on Dante

Part 6: Flash and ColdFusion

15 A Component-Based Flash Quiz

In this lesson, you'll complete the first part of the book's final project: a Flash-based quiz that records user's scores and identities into a database. As you look back over all you have learned, from interface layouts and static Web page design, through Macromedia Flash ActionScript and Dreamweaver and ColdFusion, you'll see that you have learned quite a bit. In this final project, you'll have a chance to pull it all together. The result combines a sleek Flash user interface, some ActionScript, a bit of ColdFusion coding, and data that gets sent in and out of Flash to a database.

Before you worry about sending data, you'll need to build the Flash interface that collects the data. Macromedia Flash Professional 8 comes with a set of components that you can use to automate interface building. You got a taste of components when you used the TextArea component in Lesson 11, *Nonlinear Flash Interactions*, and Lesson 12, *Drag-and-Drop Interactions*. In this lesson, the components you'll use are a bit more

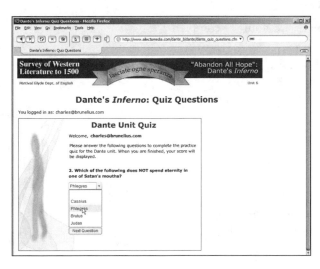

Flash Professional 8 components, such as the ComboBox component shown here, make creating Flash-based user interfaces a snap.

complicated; you'll have to set more parameters, but you'll be pleasantly surprised at how easy it is to mock up a quiz using components.

After you've built the quiz forms using components, you have to write the ActionScript to extract the data the user enters. In Lesson 16, *Flash, ColdFusion, and the Database*, you'll learn how to send that data to a database via ColdFusion, but in this lesson you'll score the results and display them in the Flash testing and debugging environment. You'll also add ActionScript that will verify that the user entered something for each question — if she or he doesn't, an error message will display.

If you want a quick refresher on how the Flash movie looks and feels, go back to http://www.allectomedia.com/dante_8/dante/ and take the test again.

What You Will Learn

In this lesson, you will:

- Build a quiz using the Flash user interface components RadioButton, ComboBox, List, and Button

- Send data into Flash from its host Web page

- Write ActionScript to collect all the data that users enter

- Deploy a custom error message movie clip symbol to display error messages

- Score the test using ActionScript, and display the user's score dynamically

Approximate Time

This lesson takes approximately two hours to complete.

Lesson Files

Starting Files:

Lesson15/Start/dante/dante_quiz_login.cfm
Lesson15/Start/dante/dante_quiz_questions.cfm
Lesson15/Start/dante/flash/flash_quiz.fla

Completed Files:

Lesson15/Complete/dante/dante_quiz_login.cfm
Lesson15/Complete/dante/dante_quiz_questions.cfm
Lesson15/Complete/dante/flash/dante_quiz.fla

Preparing the Movie

We've already created the basic shell of the movie, which is located on the CD-ROM included with this book. (We assumed you could do this yourself, but we did it for you to save you some time.) Begin by taking a few moments to look over the movie. In this lesson you'll finish setting it up so you can begin the primary development.

1. Open dante_quiz.fla.

The file is already in your site, in the dante/flash folder.

2. Review the timeline, stage, and Library.

Notice that the movie is divided into five sections. If you move the frame indicator, you'll see that the movie is divided into five screens, with one question for each screen. You'll also notice that screens 4 and 5 are completed, both in terms of the interface and the ActionScript attached to Frames 30 and 40 in the actions layer.

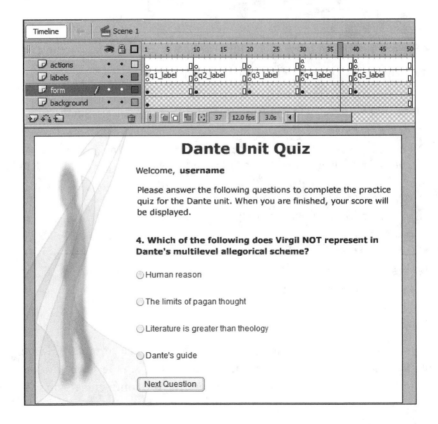

The Library already contains a number of assets, including the Button and RadioButton components. Also in the Library is a movie clip called warningDialog, which is a generic error message that you'll instantiate and program later in this lesson.

3. Click Frame 1 of the actions layer, and press F9 to open the Actions panel.

There's no script at this point, but that's about to change.

4. Type the following code in the Actions panel:

```
/********************
Enables us to access the ActionScript for components using just their names
(e.g., Button), as opposed to their full pathnames (e.g., mx.controls.Button).
It also activates code hints.
*******************/
import mx.controls.RadioButtonGroup;
import mx.controls.Button;
/******************
Initializes the movie; that is, it sets the movie's begin state.
* It stops the movie on the first frame.
*****************/
stop();
```

As you've probably guessed, everything inside the /* and */ is a comment. Flash ignores comments, but they're useful for readers, including yourself, in the event you forget how a section of code works. You can skip the step of entering the comments if you wish, but documenting your code is an important practice.

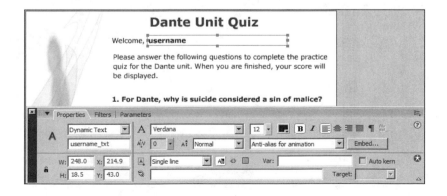

```
1  /*********************
2  Enables us to access the ActionScript for components using just
   their names (e.g., Button), as opposed to their full pathnames
   (e.g., mx.controls.Button). It also activates code hints.
3  *********************/
4  import mx.controls.RadioButtonGroup;
5  import mx.controls.Button;
6  /*********************
7  Initializes the movie; that is, it sets the movie's begin state.
8  * It stops the movie on the first frame.
9  *********************/
10 stop();
11
```

actions : 1

Line 11 of 11, Col 1

Displaying the Username Dynamically

Before accessing this quiz, the user must enter her or his name in the log-in screen. Inside the Flash movie, the username is displayed as follows: "Welcome, username." Currently, the username is hard-coded so that no matter how the user signs in, the word "username" will display in the movie. In this task, you'll set up Flash to display the name dynamically. For this step to work properly, you'll need to work in the ColdFusion file in which this Flash movie will be loaded.

1. Click the word username in Frame 1. Use the Property inspector to change its type from Static Text to Dynamic Text. Give it an instance name of *username_txt*.

By changing the word's type to dynamic and giving it an instance name, you can now change the contents of the text field on the fly using ActionScript.

2. Return to the Actions panel and click Frame 1 of the actions layer in the timeline.

You should see the script you typed up in the previous task. You'll now add to that.

3. At the bottom of the current script, add the following code:

```
var username:String;
username_txt.text = username;
```

In the first line you declare a new variable, called `username`, and tell Flash that it's a `string` (that is, text as opposed to a number or an array of data, for example). ActionScript 2.0, introduced in Macromedia Flash MX 2004, enables developers to specify the variable type of all their variables, which helps with debugging. Notice that you're not assigning a value to this variable—more on that in a moment.

In the second line, you're populating the content of username_txt with the value of username. This might surprise you, since you still haven't assigned a value to the `username` variable. The reason you don't need to assign a value to this variable is that one will have already been assigned; it will be passed into the Flash movie from ColdFusion. In other words, as soon as the movie loads it will have a username variable with a value (an email address) already available. Thus, in this code all you're doing is officially declaring the variable and making its value appear onscreen via the username_txt text field instance.

4. Update the comment just above the script you added in Step 3 with the following information:

```
* Populates username_txt with the value of the username variable
```

Make sure you put this line inside the comment block!

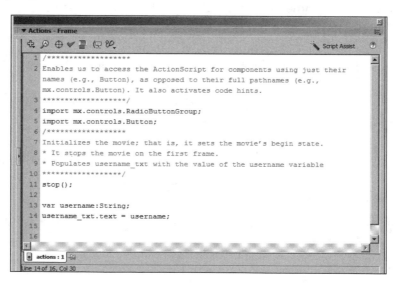

Next, you'll build the HTML/ColdFusion required to make this work.

5. Choose Control › Test Movie, and close the movie after it starts playing.

Selecting Text Movie is the quickest way to generate a SWF based on the current state of the FLA. You aren't really testing the movie, so you can close it as soon as it opens.

Obviously, the movie is far from complete, but it's sufficient to put in a ColdFusion document.

Preparing the ColdFusion Pages

In this task, you'll prepare the dante_quiz_login.cfm page and the dante_quiz_questions.cfm page. You'll complete the third page—dante_quiz_results.cfm—in Lesson 16.

1. Open dante_quiz_login.cfm in Dreamweaver. Add three paragraphs of text, as follows, to the main body of the document. After the second line, press Enter/Return twice before adding the last line. Link the word Return to index.cfm.

```
Take this ungraded quiz to see how well you've mastered the material.
To access the quiz, please login below.
Return to the Dante site home page.
```

The third line is supposed to be blank; that's where you'll add the form in a moment.

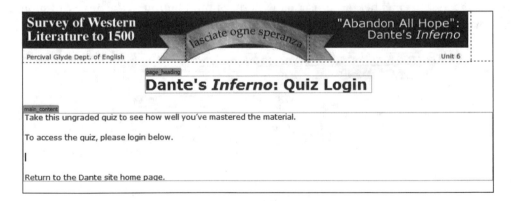

2. Switch to either code view or split view for the following steps. Select the code   between the opening and closing <p></p> tags which form the blank line you created in the previous step.

The code   represents a non-breaking space, and was inserted by Dreamweaver to give content to the paragraph you created for the blank line. As you'll recall, it's considered bad HTML form to have tags that lack content, such as opening and immediately closing <p></p> tags. The non-breaking space is invisible, so it doesn't mess up your page—but it's technically content, so the HTML is still well formed.

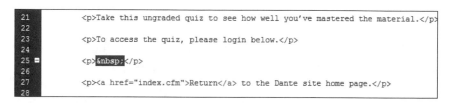

3. Use the CFForm category of the Insert bar to insert a CF Form. The cfform tag editor will open. In the General category, set the Action to dante_quiz_questions.cfm, the Method to post, and the name to *frm_login*. Select the Miscellaneous category and set the Format to Flash. You can choose a Skin at this time to give your form a particular look. Click OK to close the tag editor.

This step creates the basic functionality of the form. Now all the form needs is a field to enable the user to enter her or his username, and a Submit button so she or he can submit the form.

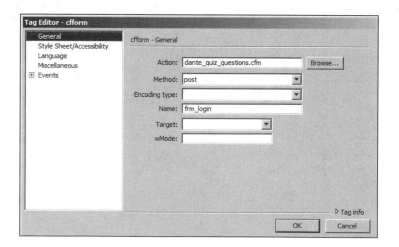

4. With the insertion point inside the `<cfform>` tags, insert a CF Text field from the insert bar. The cfinput tag editor will open. On the General category, set the Type to text, the Name to *username*, and the Size to *30*. In the Validation category, check the Required checkbox, set Validate to email, and set Validate at to onSubmit. In the Miscellaneous category, type *Email Address* for the Label. Click OK to close the tag editor. Dreamweaver will insert the code to create the cfinput element.

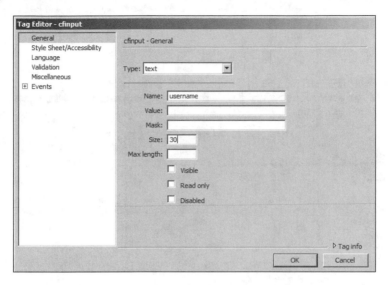

ColdFusion's Flash forms not only provide elegantly simple design and layout tools, but they also give you other useful capabilities. When you check Required, ColdFusion will mark the field with a red asterisk to indicate that the field is required. When you set Validate to email, the form will know that it must contain a properly formed email address. The Validate at value tells ColdFusion when to check both the existence and format of a value in this required field. By setting the value to onSubmit, you've chosen to have the browser check when the form is submitted.

```
<p>
    <cfform action="dante_quiz_questions.cfm" method="post" name="frm_login" preloader="no" format="flash" skin="halogreen">
        <cfinput type="text" name="username" label="Email Address" validateat="onSubmit" validate="email" required="yes" size="30">
    </cfform>
</p>
```

5. To complete the form, you must insert a Submit button. With the cursor at the end of the first `<cfinput>` tag, press Enter/Return to make room for another form input. Insert another CF Text field from the insert bar. The cfinput tag editor opens. Set the Type to submit, and both the name and value to *Submit*. Click OK to close the tag editor.

The form is now ready for use.

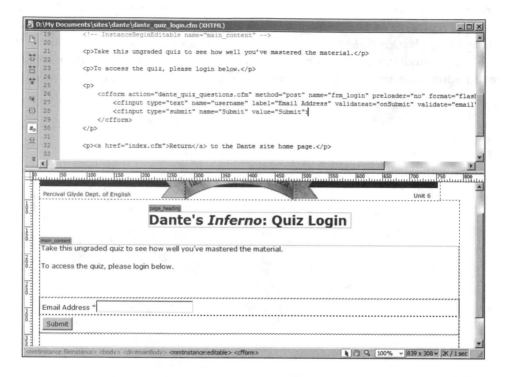

6. Save, Put, and Close dante_quiz_login.cfm.

It's easy to forget to Put files when you're finished working on them, so get in the habit of putting files just before you close them.

7. Open dante_quiz_questions.cfm. In the Bindings panel, select New Binding (+) › Form Variable. In the Form Variable dialog, name it *username*.

As before, creating the binding tells Dreamweaver how to find data that you expect to be available to the page.

8. Replace the placeholder body text with *You logged in as:* and press Enter/Return once to create a new paragraph beneath it.

You'll dynamically output the username after the colon in the first line, and you'll insert the Flash movie in the second line.

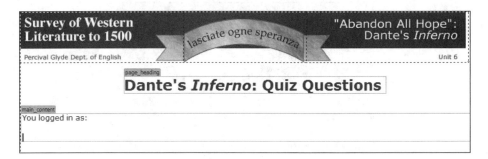

9. From the Bindings panel, press and drag the username variable onto the page, to the right of the colon in the first line.

As before, Dreamweaver writes a `<cfoutput>` tag into the code. At runtime, ColdFusion will replace `<cfoutput>#form.username#</cfoutput>` with the email address entered into the form on dante_quiz_login.cfm.

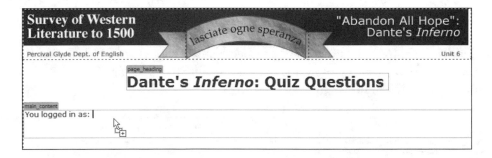

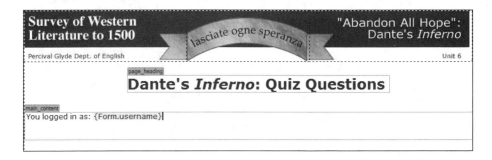

10. Position the insertion point in the blank line just below the first line, and choose Insert > Media > Flash. Navigate to and select flash/dante_quiz.swf. The Object Tag Accessibility Attributes dialog box appears. Set the Title to *Dante's Inferno: Quiz Questions* and click OK.

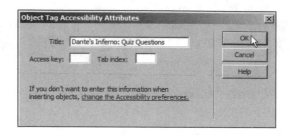

This step inserts the Flash movie into the page, but it doesn't yet insert the username variable Flash movie.

Flash has numerous options for sending data in and out. One of the simplest is to pass the variable in as a part of the request for the movie. When you insert a Flash movie into HTML, you provide the URL specifying where the movie is located.

11. Click to select the Flash movie, and switch to code view.

If you look at the code, you'll see the Flash movie's URL referenced twice. Inserting Flash movies into HTML pages requires a bit of redundancy, because Internet Explorer deals with media players like the Flash player differently than Netscape and other browsers. Specifically, the HTML includes both the <object> and <embed> tags, which are used to insert special media files into browsers. Both tags require that you specify the URL pointing to the plug-in file (in this case, a Flash SWF).

```
21    <p>You logged in as: <cfoutput>#Form.username#</cfoutput></p>
22    <p>
23      <object classid="clsid:D27CDB6E-AE6D-11cf-96B8-444553540000" codebase="http://download.macromedia.com/pub/shock
24        <param name="movie" value="flash/dante_quiz.swf" />
25        <param name="quality" value="high" />
26        <embed src="flash/dante_quiz.swf" quality="high" pluginspage="http://www.macromedia.com/go/getflashplayer" ty
27      </object>
28    </p>
```

You can append name–value pairs to these URLs. When you do, those variables are available in the main timeline of the Flash movie. Thus, if you wanted to pass the variable pairing username=yuki@sheepman.com into your Flash movie, the URL for the <object> and <embed> tags that insert the Flash movie would look like this:

```
flash/dante_quiz.swf?username=yuki@sheepman.com
```

The question mark separates the file from the variable(s). In this case, only one name–value pairing follows. The only catch is that you don't know the value in advance; you'll need to capture the username entered into the form. This problem can also be resolved with the ever-useful <cfoutput> tag.

12. In code view, append ?username=<cfoutput>#form.username#</cfoutput> to each of the two URLs. Each URL should read as follows:

```
"flash/dante_quiz.swf?username=<cfoutput>#form.username#</cfoutput>"
```

The <cfoutput> block will be resolved before the page is sent back to the browser, so by the time the Flash movie is requested, the correct data will already exist and be inserted into the Flash movie.

```
21    <p>You logged in as: <cfoutput>#Form.username#</cfoutput></p>
22    <p>
23      <object classid="clsid:D27CDB6E-AE6D-11cf-96B8-444553540000" codebase="http://download.macromedia.com/pub/shock
24        <param name="movie" value="flash/dante_quiz.swf?username=<cfoutput>#form.username#</cfoutput>" />
25        <param name="quality" value="high" />
26        <embed src="flash/dante_quiz.swf?username=<cfoutput>#form.username#</cfoutput>" quality="high" pluginspage="h
27      </object>
28    </p>
```

13. Save and Put dante_quiz_questions.cfm. Also, be sure to Put flash/dante_quiz.swf.

You're ready to test this portion of the pages/movie.

14. Select dante_quiz_login.cfm in the Files panel, and press F12 (Windows) or Option+F12 (Macintosh). Enter an email address in the form and click Submit.

The second page, dante_quiz_questions.cfm, should load, and the Flash movie with it. The username variable should be resolved in both the regular page and the Flash movie.

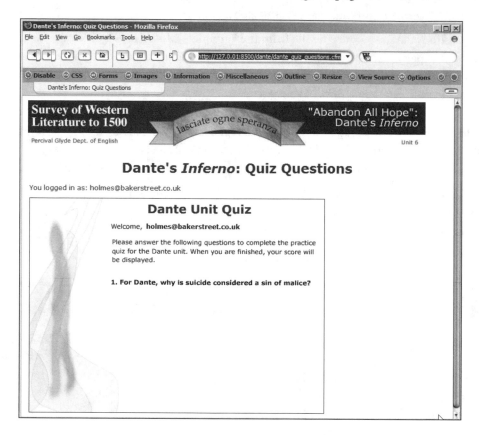

If you got an error, make sure that you uploaded all three files, and that you tested starting from dante_quiz_login.cfm. If you try to test dante_quiz_questions.cfm, you'll get an error, because that page depends on a form variable called username to have been submitted, and that variable exists only if you access dante_quiz_questions.cfm from dante_quiz_login.cfm.

Building the Quiz Interface with Components

In this task, you'll return to Flash and build the quiz interface using Flash components. When you're finished, the first screen of the quiz will look complete. It won't work yet (that will require a little ActionScript), but at least it will look right.

1. Return to Flash and open dante_quiz.fla, if necessary.

You can close Dreamweaver now. You won't need it for this lesson.

2. Click Frame 1 of the form layer. Open the Library panel (Window > Library). Press and drag an instance of the radio button onto the stage, and position it below the question.

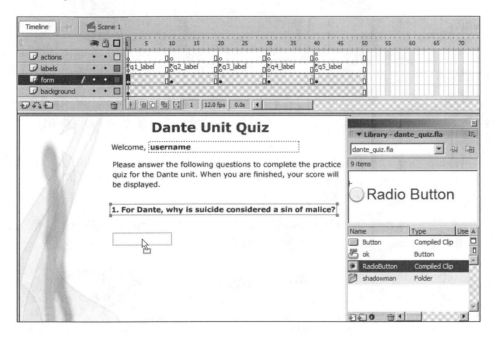

Using components is usually a simple matter of drag and drop. If you have trouble aligning the radio button on the first try, just let it go, and then reselect and drag again.

Flash's new auto-alignment feature (represented by the dashed line that sometimes appears when you drag an object around) should help you get it right.

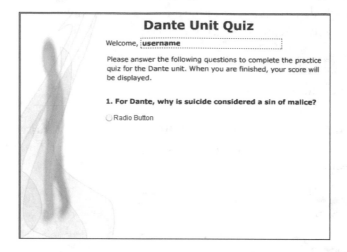

3. With the radio button still selected, in the Parameters tab of the Property inspector (which should be activated automatically), click in the Label field and type *It's not. It is a sin of weakness*.

Press Enter/Return to apply the value. This text string now appears beside the radio button, where it previously said "radio button." When you label each radio button, your user knows what she or he is selecting.

Notice that part of the label is truncated. The label area beside the button is wide enough to accommodate the words "radio button," but does not accommodate the full text string.

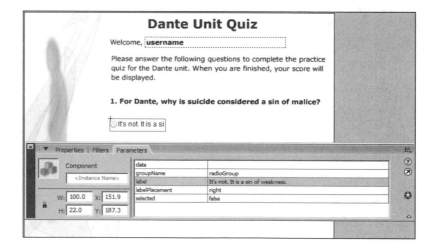

4. Select the RadioButton component instance and, using the Free Transform tool, drag the box to the right to make the entire label visible.

Customization does not affect the functionality of the component. It just makes the full label readable for the user.

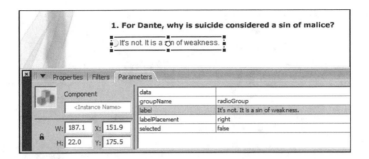

5. With the radio button still selected, set the Data to *a* and the Group Name to *q1_radio* in the Parameters tab of the Property inspector.

The Group Name setting is critical; this is the name of the radio group, and the name under which the actual data will be stored. The Data setting is also vital; the value you enter is the value that will be stored if the user selects this particular button. Therefore, if the user selects this radio button, Flash will know that the value of q1_radio is a. If the user selects a different radio button (although you haven't created it yet), Flash will know that the value of q1_radio is b, c, or whatever the Data setting is for that button.

This radio button is now good to go. Of course, by itself it doesn't make much of a group.

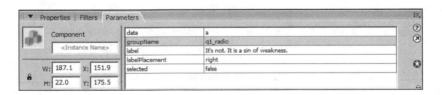

6. Copy the radio button and paste three copies of it, one below the other. Change the labels and data values as follows. All should have the Group Name set to q1_radio. When you're finished, adjust the length of the label areas to accommodate the long labels.

Label: *Suicide is cruel towards one's relatives. Data: b.*

Label: *Because suicides want to hurt God. Data: c.*

Label: *Suicides' souls are so poisoned that they cast away their bodies. Data: d.*

In this step you individualized each of the buttons, both for the user (by changing the labels) and for the computer (by changing the Data values). In spite of this individuation, the buttons all still belong to the same radio button group, q1_radio.

Remember not to change the Group Name; all four should be q1_radio.

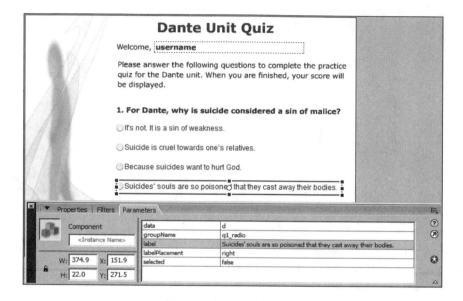

7. Drag an instance of the Button component onto the stage.

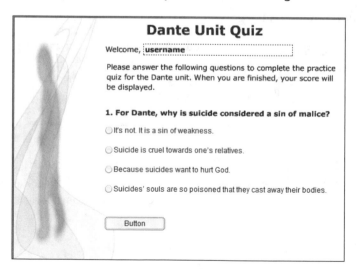

The Button component is going to be the Submit button, so you have to configure it to fulfill that role. To do so, you should first understand how Flash handles a form made of components.

While Flash component forms might resemble HTML forms in many ways, they're not identical. There is no overarching `<form>` element in Flash, as there is in HTML. And remember that the HTML `<form>` element has an `action` attribute that lets you specify what the Submit button should do (such as `POST` the information to another page).

Because Flash doesn't see these elements as a part of a larger form, there's no way to tell it unilaterally what to do with all of this data. Telling Flash to do something with the data requires ActionScript, which you'll write later. Clicking this Submit button will serve as the event that triggers a custom function, much like the ones you've written throughout this book, all of which used the following syntax:

```
myButton_btn.onRelease = function() {
  // some code here;
};
```

8. With the button still selected, enter *Next Question* as its label. Give it an instance name of *q1_button*.

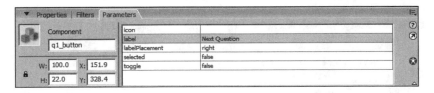

The instance name, as you probably remember from earlier lessons, is this object's unique ID. Thanks to this ID, this object can now be seen and/or manipulated by ActionScript. Again, the Label value is for the user. It has no effect as far as Flash is concerned.

Note *You might remember that for all the buttons we've used up to this point, we've added the _btn suffix to the instance name to indicate that it's a button. So you might be surprised to see that the instance name on this button is _button. The reason for the change is that the Button component is distinct from the standard Button symbol in Flash, however confusing that might seem.*

You're now finished with this screen.

Scripting the First Question

Now that the interface is laid out, we can write the script that accesses the data in the radio group. All four radio buttons belong to the same group, so only one of them can be selected at a time. To find out which one the user selected, we simply need to access the data of the selected item in the radio group. ActionScript makes this easy, as you will soon see.

1. Click Frame 1 of the actions layer, and press F9 to open the Actions panel.

The script you wrote earlier is still there.

2. Below the existing code, add the following code:

```
/****************
When the Next Question button is clicked:
* Goes to the next screen
****************/
q1_button.onRelease = function() {
  gotoAndStop("q2_label");
};
```

You've already seen several scripts just like this, so it should be familiar to you by now. Of course, it doesn't actually access any of the data.

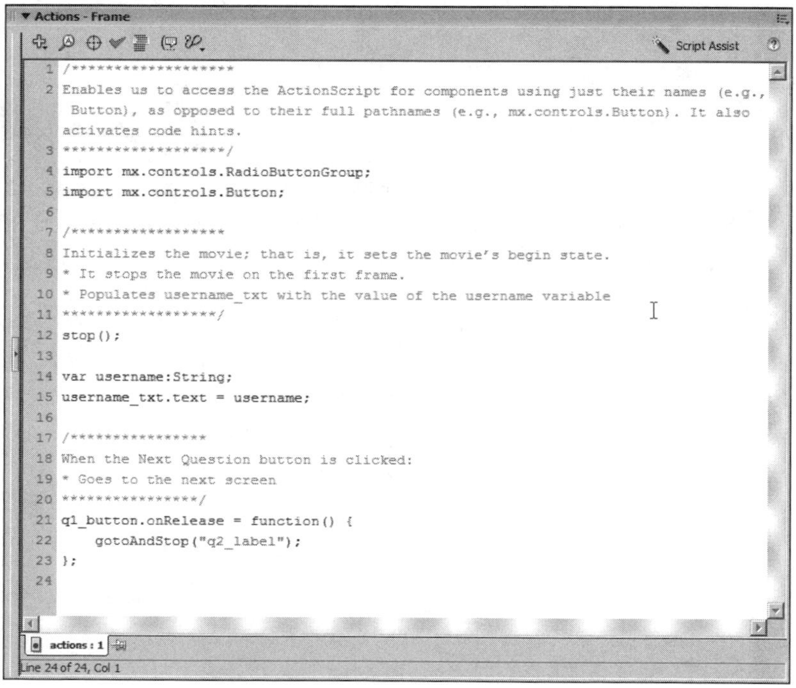

3. Add the following code just above the `gotoAndStop()` line. Test the movie, make a selection, and click **Next Question**.

```
trace(q1_radio.selection.data);
```

```
▼ Actions - Frame
⊕ 𝒫 ⊕ ✔ ⎯ 🖵 ℗                                    Script Assist  ⑦
 1  /********************
 2  Enables us to access the ActionScript for components using just their names (e.g.,
    Button), as opposed to their full pathnames (e.g., mx.controls.Button). It also
    activates code hints.
 3  *********************/
 4  import mx.controls.RadioButtonGroup;
 5  import mx.controls.Button;
 6
 7  /******************
 8  Initializes the movie; that is, it sets the movie's begin state.
 9  * It stops the movie on the first frame.
10  * Populates username_txt with the value of the username variable
11  *******************/
12  stop();
13
14  var username:String;
15  username_txt.text = username;
16
17  /*****************
18  When the Next Question button is clicked:
19  * Goes to the next screen
20  *****************/
21  q1_button.onRelease = function() {
22      trace(q1_radio.selection.data);
23      gotoAndStop("q2_label");
24  };
25
────────────────────────────────────────────
 actions : 1
Line 22 of 25, Col 33
```

Both pieces of this line are probably unfamiliar: the `trace()` method and the parameter you're passing to it, `q1_radio.selection.data`. The `trace()` method is used for debugging. When called, it writes into the Output window (see the figure) whatever parameter is passed to it. In this case, you're passing `q1_radio.selection.data`. Flash evaluates this parameter and returns a value: a, b, c, or d. Let's break the code into its parts, remembering that everything on the right side of a dot belongs to whatever is to the left of the dot: `q1_radio` refers to the Radio Group (remember how all four radio buttons listed `q1_radio` as the Group Name?). The next part, `selection`, refers to whichever individual radio button the user selected within that group. Finally, `data` refers to the data value you specified in the Property inspector for each radio button.

If you close the movie and test it a few times, you'll see that each time you make a selection, a, b, c, or d displays in the Output window. If you don't choose any of the options and press the Next Question button, Flash displays undefined in the Output window.

You've figured out how to get your data, but you aren't doing anything useful with it yet. You'll use this data for two purposes: to verify that the user selected one of the options (you don't want users to continue unless they've made a choice), and to determine whether the user chose the correct answer, so you can score the quiz.

Validating Component Data

In this task, you'll ensure that users actually make a selection before they click the Next Question button. If they don't make a selection, they'll see an error alert message and won't be able to continue.

The error message is an instance of the Alert component. The Alert component can be configured with a message, title, and a selection of built-in buttons (OK, Cancel, Yes, and No). We'll use the OK button. If a user does not choose an option, we'll show the Alert component with our message, asking the user to make a selection.

In order to use the Alert component, you need to have it in your project's Library. You can add it to the Library by creating an instance of the component one time. You don't need to keep the instance you create.

1. Open the Components panel (Window > Components). Expand the User Interface group, if necessary. Double-click the Alert component to place an instance of the Alert component on the stage. If it's not already selected, click the instance and press Backspace or Delete to remove it.

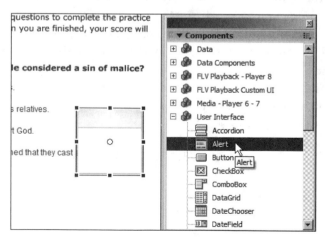

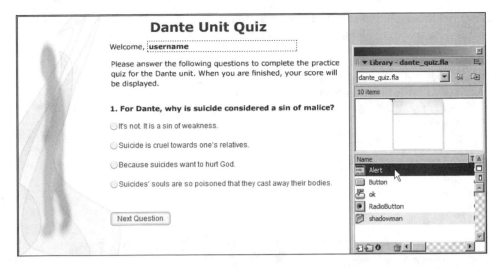

You can now call up the Alert whenever you need it.

2. Click Frame 1 of the actions layer, and press **F9** to open the Actions panel. Just below the `import mx.controls.Button;` command near the top, add the following code:

```
import mx.controls.Alert;
```

As with the RadioButtonGroup and Button components, this code allows you to access the Alert component throughout your project using just its name, rather than its full path. It also allows you to use code hints for the component in the Actions editor window.

In the next step, you'll amend the script to call the Alert component and set its parameters. The trick is to figure out how it will work. As you'll recall from earlier experiments with the `trace()` method, when you take the first screen of the quiz, one of five results is returned: a, b, c, d, or undefined. The latter occurs when nothing is selected, which is what you want to test. Thus, implementing this feature will consist of an `if` block that checks for the presence of undefined, and either calls your error alert message or proceeds to the next screen.

3. Amend the **q1_button** script to read as follows. After you've entered the code, test the movie and click Next Question without making a selection. Update the comment to describe the new functionality.

```
q1_button.onRelease = function() {
  if (q1_radio.selection.data == undefined) {
    Alert.show("Please make a selection before continuing.", "Error",
Alert.OK);
  } else {
    trace(q1_radio.selection.data);
    gotoAndStop("q2_label");
  }
};
```

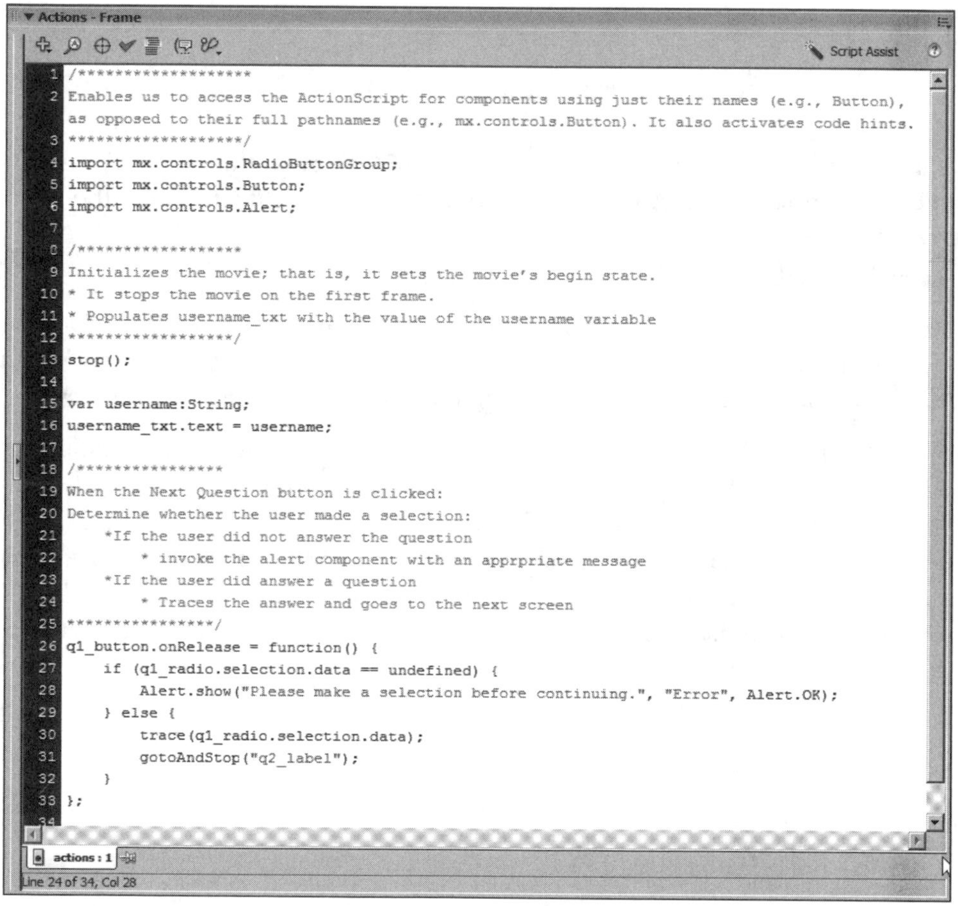

```
▼ Actions - Frame                                                                    ⬚
  ⬚ 🔍 ⊕ ✔ ☰ 🖵 ⅋                                              ✎ Script Assist  ⓘ
   1  /********************
   2  Enables us to access the ActionScript for components using just their names (e.g., Button),
      as opposed to their full pathnames (e.g., mx.controls.Button). It also activates code hints.
   3  ********************/
   4  import mx.controls.RadioButtonGroup;
   5  import mx.controls.Button;
   6  import mx.controls.Alert;
   7
   8  /******************
   9  Initializes the movie; that is, it sets the movie's begin state.
  10  * It stops the movie on the first frame.
  11  * Populates username_txt with the value of the username variable
  12  ******************/
  13  stop();
  14
  15  var username:String;
  16  username_txt.text = username;
  17
  18  /****************
  19  When the Next Question button is clicked:
  20  Determine whether the user made a selection:
  21      *If the user did not answer the question
  22          * invoke the alert component with an apprpriate message
  23      *If the user did answer a question
  24          * Traces the answer and goes to the next screen
  25  ****************/
  26  q1_button.onRelease = function() {
  27      if (q1_radio.selection.data == undefined) {
  28          Alert.show("Please make a selection before continuing.", "Error", Alert.OK);
  29      } else {
  30          trace(q1_radio.selection.data);
  31          gotoAndStop("q2_label");
  32      }
  33  };
  34
   ◀                                                                                   ▶
  🗎 actions : 1 🖼
  Line 24 of 34, Col 28
```

When you test the movie, you should see the error message if you click the Next Question button without making a selection.

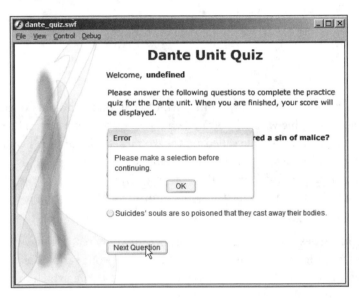

This script deals with two possible scenarios and responds to each differently. If the user doesn't make a selection, q1_radio.selection.data will be undefined, and the error alert message will pop up. If the user does make a selection, the movie will advance to the next screen.

One problem remains: we're not scoring the quiz for correctness. You'll take care of that problem now.

Scoring the Quiz

Scoring the quiz is a critical part of this application. Fortunately, it's easy to implement. You'll create a new variable called score and initialize it to 0. Then you'll test each response against the correct answer, and if there's a match you'll increment the score by 1.

1. With Frame 1 of the actions layer selected, open the Actions panel. Just under the stop() action near the top, add the following script:

```
var inited:Boolean = false;
if (!inited) {
  var score:Number = 0;
  inited = true;
}
```

This is an initialization script. You want the script to run once, and only once. To ensure this, you'll create a variable with a Boolean data type, which means it can be true or false; in this case, you'll create a variable called inited. You'll set this variable's value to false initially. Then you'll have a script inside an if statement. As you'll recall, if statements run only if the condition specified in parentheses is true. The if statement checks to see whether the inited variable is false (the ! operator means "not"), and if inited is false, the code inside the curly braces is executed.

Two lines of code are executed inside the if block. The first creates a new variable with the Number data type, and initializes it to 0. No other part of your script does anything with this variable yet. The second line sets the value of inited to true, which means that the if block won't execute again.

You should also update the comment above this block to summarize this new block of code.

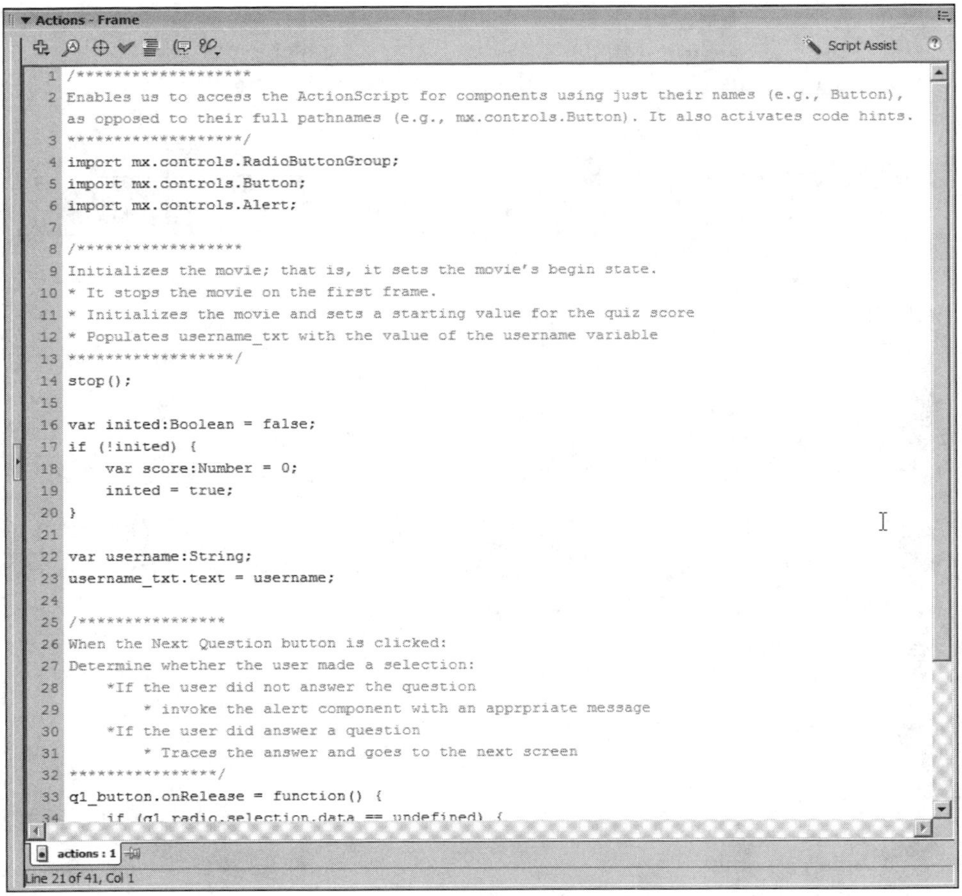

```
1  /*****************
2  Enables us to access the ActionScript for components using just their names (e.g., Button),
   as opposed to their full pathnames (e.g., mx.controls.Button). It also activates code hints.
3  *****************/
4  import mx.controls.RadioButtonGroup;
5  import mx.controls.Button;
6  import mx.controls.Alert;
7
8  /*****************
9  Initializes the movie; that is, it sets the movie's begin state.
10 * It stops the movie on the first frame.
11 * Initializes the movie and sets a starting value for the quiz score
12 * Populates username_txt with the value of the username variable
13 *****************/
14 stop();
15
16 var inited:Boolean = false;
17 if (!inited) {
18     var score:Number = 0;
19     inited = true;
20 }
21
22 var username:String;
23 username_txt.text = username;
24
25 /*****************
26 When the Next Question button is clicked:
27 Determine whether the user made a selection:
28     *If the user did not answer the question
29         * invoke the alert component with an apprpriate message
30     *If the user did answer a question
31         * Traces the answer and goes to the next screen
32 *****************/
33 q1_button.onRelease = function() {
34     if (q1_radio.selection.data == undefined) {
```

In the next step, you'll add to the q1_button code block so that the score will be incremented if the user answers the question correctly.

2. In the **q1_button** code block, just before **trace(q1_radio.selection.data);**, add the following code block. Update the comment above accordingly.

```
if (q1_radio.selection.data == "d") {
  score++;
}
```

This code block tests to see whether the data in the radio button the user selected matches "d," which is the correct answer to the question. If there is a match, the user answered correctly, and 1 point is added to score. Note that score++; is a shortcut. In longhand, it means score = score + 1;.

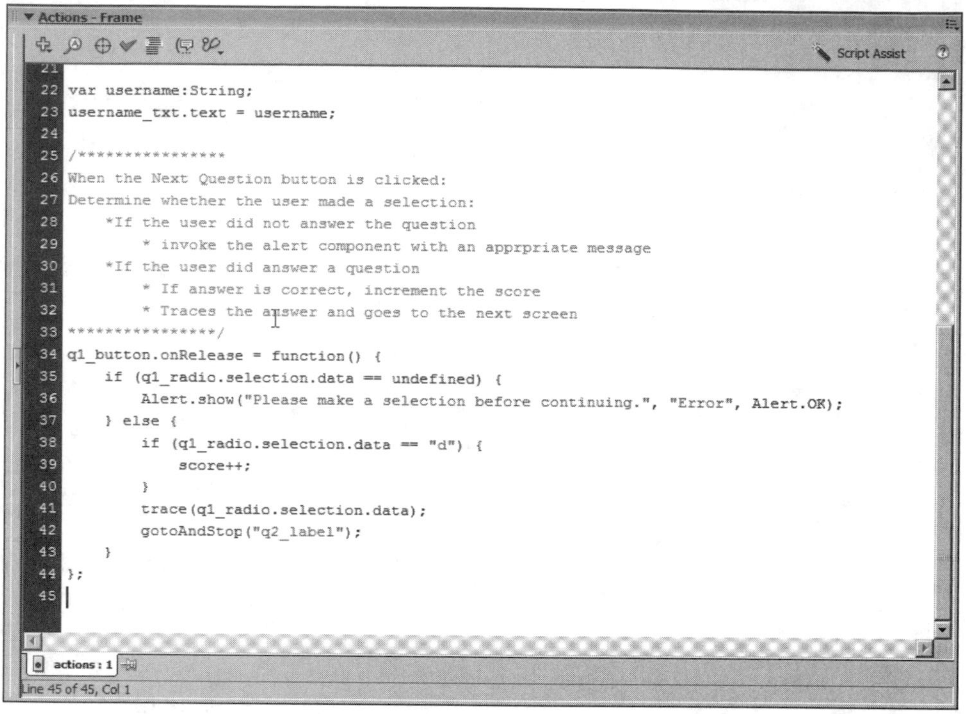

```
21
22  var username:String;
23  username_txt.text = username;
24
25  /****************
26  When the Next Question button is clicked:
27  Determine whether the user made a selection:
28      *If the user did not answer the question
29          * invoke the alert component with an apprpriate message
30      *If the user did answer a question
31          * If answer is correct, increment the score
32          * Traces the answer and goes to the next screen
33  ****************/
34  q1_button.onRelease = function() {
35      if (q1_radio.selection.data == undefined) {
36          Alert.show("Please make a selection before continuing.", "Error", Alert.OK);
37      } else {
38          if (q1_radio.selection.data == "d") {
39              score++;
40          }
41          trace(q1_radio.selection.data);
42          gotoAndStop("q2_label");
43      }
44  };
45
```

3. Add a new line of code just above or below the existing **trace()** line in this block, as follows. Then test the file, choosing the fourth radio button once, and choosing any other radio button once.

```
trace("The current score is " + score);
```

```
 21
 22 var username:String;
 23 username_txt.text = username;
 24
 25 /****************
 26 When the Next Question button is clicked:
 27 Determine whether the user made a selection:
 28     *If the user did not answer the question
 29         * invoke the alert component with an apprpriate message
 30     *If the user did answer a question
 31         * If answer is correct, increment the score
 32         * Traces the answer and current score and then goes to the next screen
 33 ****************/
 34 q1_button.onRelease = function() {
 35     if (q1_radio.selection.data == undefined) {
 36         Alert.show("Please make a selection before continuing.", "Error", Alert.OK);
 37     } else {
 38         if (q1_radio.selection.data == "d") {
 39             score++;
 40         }
 41         trace(q1_radio.selection.data);
 42         trace("The current score is " + score);
 43         gotoAndStop("q2_label");
 44     }
 45 };
 46
```

actions : 1

Line 45 of 46, Col 3

You're outputting the current score value in the Output window, which will enable you to verify that the code is actually working. Because you're now tracing two values to the Output window, you might find it hard to figure out which is which. To prevent this problem, you add the string "The current score is" to the parameter, which will make the output easier to read.

When you test the file, the output block displays the selected option and the score. The score updates to 1 if you select the fourth option, and remains at 0 if you do anything else.

Adding and Scripting a ComboBox Component

The first question is complete; now you just have to worry about the next four. Actually, it's not as bad as it appears, because two have been done already (questions 4 and 5), and the other two are remarkably similar to the question you just did.

1. Click Frame 10 of the forms layer. From the Components panel, drag in an instance of the ComboBox component. Use the Property inspector to give it an instance name of *q2_combo*.

The ComboBox component is superficially quite different from the RadioButton component, but under the surface its functionality is quite similar.

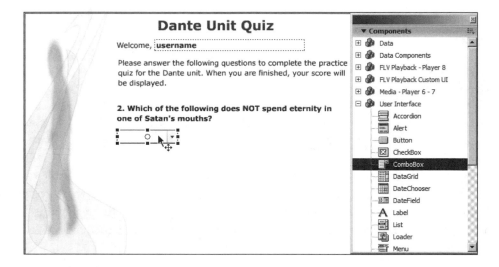

2. In the Parameters tab of the Property inspector, double-click the Data field. In the Values dialog, click the + button and replace the default text with *999*. Repeat this process four more times to create the values a, b, c, and d. Click OK.

You're creating the data values that will be submitted when the user clicks the Next Question button for this screen.

3. Double-click the Labels field and add five labels. The first value is three spaces, the next four are *Cassius*, *Phlegyas*, *Brutus*, and *Judas*. Click OK.

You're populating the items that will appear in the ComboBox. Notice that the five labels are correlated to five data values.

Four of these label/data combinations are straightforward, but one might seem odd. The one with three spaces for a label and a data value of 999 will be the default option, and you'll write the validation script so that if the data entered by the user is 999, you know the user didn't make a selection. You can't test for undefined, like you did with the radio buttons, because a ComboBox always returns a value, even if the user didn't specify one. The value that's returned is the first item by default, so by making the first item a dummy item with a dummy value you can still verify that the user made a selection.

4. With Frame 10 of the forms layer still selected, drag an instance of the Button component to the stage. Give it an instance name of *q2_button*. Change its label to *Next Question*.

Put the instance near the bottom of the stage. Remember that the ComboBox is a pop-up menu, and will expand in size when the user clicks it. By placing this button near the bottom, you leave room for the ComboBox to operate normally.

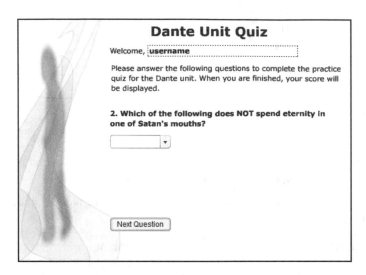

Now it's time to write the script. Fortunately, it's almost identical to the script you created on the first frame.

5. In Frame 10 of the actions layer, in the Actions panel, enter the following script (optionally, you can copy the relevant portion of the script from Frame 1 and customize it). Place it at the end after the existing code.

```
q2_button.onRelease = function() {
  if (q2_combo.selectedItem.data == 999) {
    Alert.show("Please make a selection before continuing.", "Error",
Alert.OK);
  } else {
    if (q2_combo.selectedItem.data == "b") {
      score++;
    }
    trace(q2_combo.selectedItem.data);
    trace("The current score is " + score);
    gotoAndStop("q3_label");
  }
};
```

This script should look quite familiar. You're merely replacing a couple instance names (instead of q1_button, you now use q2_button; likewise, you replace q1_radio with q2_combo). In addition, the correct answer is now "b," rather than "d." The only other difference is that instead of accessing the data with `selection.data`, you use `selectedItem.data`. Macromedia used slightly different method names for equivalent functionalities in the two types of components (RadioButtons and ComboBoxes).

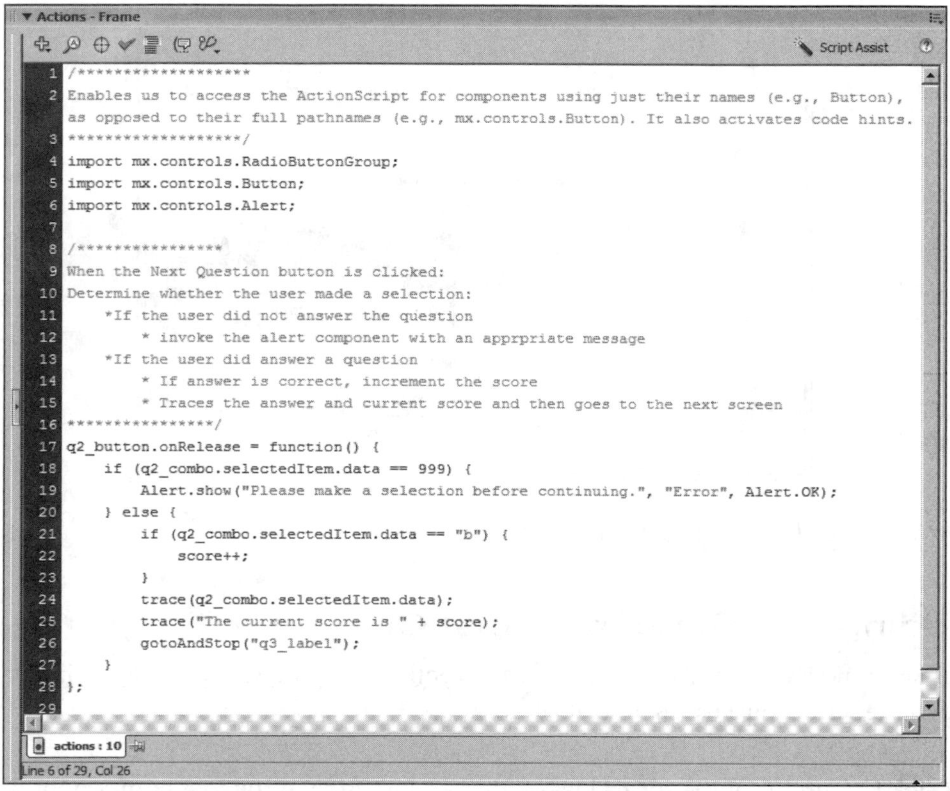

```
1  /*******************
2  Enables us to access the ActionScript for components using just their names (e.g., Button),
   as opposed to their full pathnames (e.g., mx.controls.Button). It also activates code hints.
3  *******************/
4  import mx.controls.RadioButtonGroup;
5  import mx.controls.Button;
6  import mx.controls.Alert;
7
8  /*****************
9  When the Next Question button is clicked:
10 Determine whether the user made a selection:
11     *If the user did not answer the question
12        * invoke the alert component with an apprpriate message
13     *If the user did answer a question
14        * If answer is correct, increment the score
15        * Traces the answer and current score and then goes to the next screen
16 *****************/
17 q2_button.onRelease = function() {
18     if (q2_combo.selectedItem.data == 999) {
19        Alert.show("Please make a selection before continuing.", "Error", Alert.OK);
20     } else {
21        if (q2_combo.selectedItem.data == "b") {
22            score++;
23        }
24        trace(q2_combo.selectedItem.data);
25        trace("The current score is " + score);
26        gotoAndStop("q3_label");
27     }
28 };
29
```

6. Test the movie.

It's always a good idea to make sure things work before moving to the next task. If you choose the fourth radio button and the second item ("Phlegyas") in the ComboBox, you should end up with a score of 2.

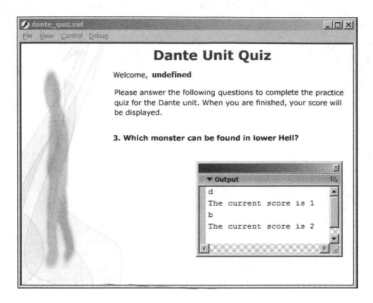

Now you're ready to put together the third quiz question.

Adding and Scripting a List Component

This task is nearly identical to the previous task, both in the process of creating the interface and in the script you'll use to make it all work.

1. Click Frame 20 of the forms layer. Drag an instance of the List component onto the stage, and give it an instance name of *q3_list*. Drag an instance of the Button component onto the stage below the List component, give it an instance name of *q3_button*, and change its label to *Next Question*.

The interface of the third question is almost finished, but you still need to populate the List with labels and data.

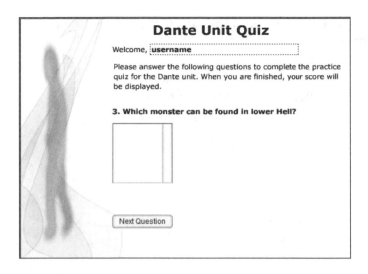

2. Select the List instance. In the Parameters tab of the Property inspector, populate the Data with *a*, *b*, *c*, *d*, and *e*. Populate the Labels with *Minos*, *She-Wolf*, *Geryon*, *Cerberus*, and *Plutus*.

As with the ComboBox, the Labels are the text users will see onscreen, and the Data is what will be passed with the form when the Next Question button is clicked.

Note *You don't need an empty choice with a data value of 999 for the List. If no item is selected, the data value will come back as undefined, as it did with the radio buttons.*

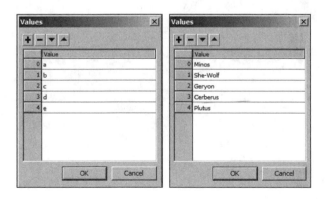

Now the interface is complete, and you need only the ActionScript to make it work.

3. Click Frame 20 of the actions layer, and in the Actions panel, enter the following script after the existing code.

```
q3_button.onRelease = function() {
  if (q3_list.selectedItem.data == undefined) {
    Alert.show("Please make a selection before continuing.", "Error",
Alert.OK);
  } else {
    if (q3_list.selectedItem.data == "c") {
      score++;
    }
    trace(q3_list.selectedItem.data);
    trace("The current score is " + score);
    gotoAndStop("q4_label");
  }
};
```

Again, you can copy and paste the script from Frame 10 into Frame 20 and customize it by changing all instances of q2_button to q3_button and all instances of q2_combo to q3_list, as well as changing 999 to undefined, "b" to "c", and q3_label to q4_label.

You're almost ready to test the movie, since the last two questions and their scripts have been written. Before you test it, though, you'll make one further change so you can see the final score and verify that the scoring is working correctly.

4. Click Frame 40 of the actions layer, and in the Actions panel, find the following comment: // Insert code here to send data to ColdFusion script. Just before this comment, insert a new line, as follows:

```
trace("The final score is " + score + " out of 5");
```

You'll send the code to ColdFusion in Lesson 16. By adding this trace() line, you'll get visual feedback when you press the Next button, so you'll know the scripts are all working.

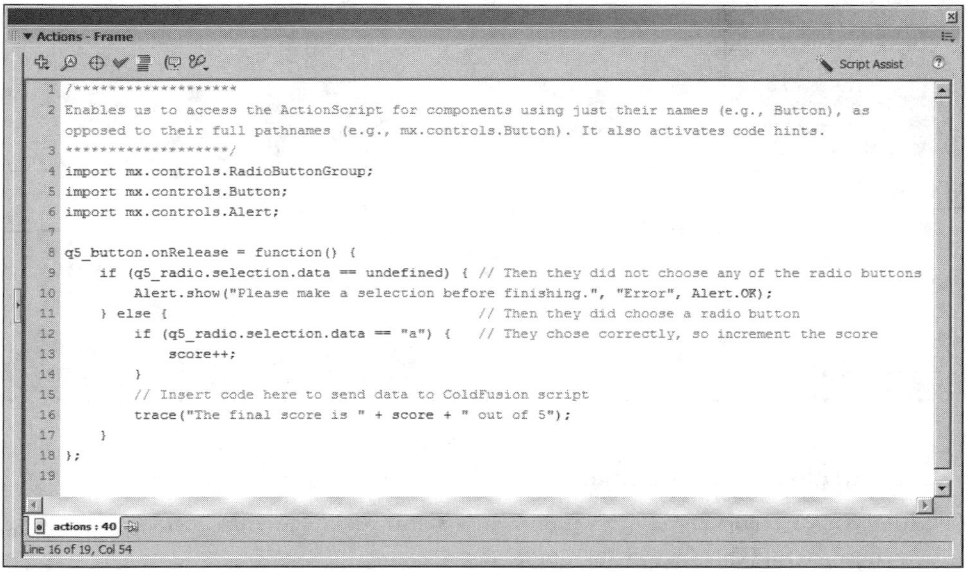

5. Test the movie and take the quiz.

The correct answers are as follows:

1: Suicides' souls are so poisoned that they cast away their bodies.

2: Phlegyas

3: Geryon

4: Literature is greater than theology.

5: A pit

Now that you know the correct answers, go through the quiz and answer all the questions correctly to ensure that your final score is 5. When you click Finish, nothing will happen, except that the Output window will display the final score. Next, go through the test again, deliberately missing a couple questions, and make sure the score is still correct. Finally, go back through the quiz and try to click the Next Question/Finish button on each screen without making a selection. On all five screens, you should be blocked by the error message.

6. **Save and close dante_quiz.fla.**

If you like, you can test the movie as it currently stands inside the browser, so you can see your username while you answer the questions.

Note   *When you're testing Flash movies in a browser, the Output window doesn't display. The Output displays only inside the Flash-authoring environment.*

What You Have Learned

In this lesson, you have:

- Prepared the movie for development (pages 447–448)

- Implemented a text field that displays the username (pages 449–451)

- Prepared a ColdFusion page that passes the username as a variable into Flash (pages 451–458)

- Laid out a radio-button interface for the first question (pages 459–463)

- Written the ActionScript needed to handle the radio group (pages 464–466)

- Used trace() to output data in the debugger (pages 464–466)

- Implemented an error-catching mechanism, including a movie clip and the ActionScript needed to show and hide it as necessary (pages 466–469)

- Scored the quiz as users take it (pages 470–473)

- Laid out a ComboBox form element and prepared the ActionScript needed to get the data and score it (pages 474–478)

- Laid out a List form element and prepared the ActionScript needed to get the data and score the quiz (pages 478–482)

16 Flash, ColdFusion, and the Database

In this lesson, you'll complete the Dante quiz project. From the title of this lesson you might think that this is the hardest lesson in the book; in fact, the hard part is already behind you. In this lesson, you'll connect all the pieces—Flash, the HTML pages, and the database—and do little else. Working with ColdFusion is like hooking up a VCR to your cable and your TV: the complicated parts are in the TV and VCR, but all you need to worry about is connecting a few wires from one component to the other.

You'll save two pieces of data in Macromedia Flash—the username and score variables—into a database. You'll then send this data to ColdFusion, and then ColdFusion will insert it into a database.

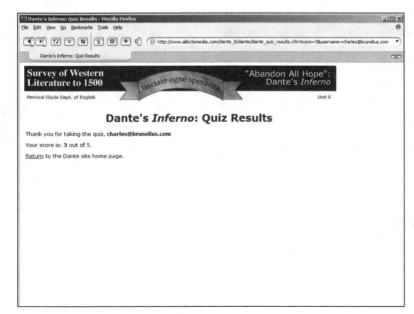

This page is accessed via Flash, which sends data via the URL (notice the variables in the URL) when it calls the page. ColdFusion outputs the URL data in the page and also inserts the data into a database.

Flash offers several means of sending data in and out of a ColdFusion (or ASP, PHP, or JSP) script. Some of these options are robust, such as Flash Remoting and Web Services, while other options are comparatively simple. One useful technique is to use Flash's `LoadVars` object, which makes it easy to send and load name-value pairs from a text file or ColdFusion template. An even more primitive — but effective — approach is to pass data via the URL. As you'll recall from Lesson 15, *A Component-Based Flash Quiz*, when you inserted the Flash movie using HTML's `<object>` and `<embed>` tags, you appended a variable: `flash/dante_quiz.swf?username=<cfoutput>#form.username#</cfoutput>`. This variable was sufficient to get the `username` variable into Flash. One or more variables appended to the end of a URL in this way is called a querystring, and is a common approach to sending data between pages. In this lesson, rather than bringing data into Flash using a querystring, you'll send data out of Flash, using a querystring.

What You Will learn

In this lesson, you will:

- Finish the Flash quiz, sending data to ColdFusion
- Use ColdFusion to output the data in the HTML page
- Use ColdFusion to insert the data into a database
- Improve security by moving the data out of the URL

Approximate Time

This lesson takes approximately 45 minutes to complete.

Lesson Files

Starting Files:

Lesson16/Start/dante/dante_quiz_questions.cfm
Lesson16/Start/dante/dante_quiz_results.cfm
Lesson16/Start/dante/flash/dante_quiz.fla

Completed Files:

Lesson16/Complete/dante/dante_quiz_questions.cfm
Lesson16/Complete/dante/dante_quiz_results.cfm
Lesson16/Complete/dante/flash/dante_quiz.fla

Sending Data from Flash to ColdFusion

The Flash movie is nearly complete. The only remaining task is to have the Finish button load the ColdFusion page and send the data to it.

1. Open dante_quiz.fla in Flash. Click Frame 40 of the actions layer and open the Actions panel.

You'll see the final script in the movie. In each of the four preceding scripts, after incrementing the score (if appropriate), the script used `gotoAndStop()` to advance to the next screen. Question 5, however, is the last screen. Rather than advancing to a new screen, you want to load dante_quiz_results.cfm.

2. Replace the comment "`// Insert code here to send data to ColdFusion script`" with the following code.

```
getURL("dante_quiz_results.cfm");
```

The `getURL()` behaves much like the <a> tag in HTML: it opens a new page in the browser.

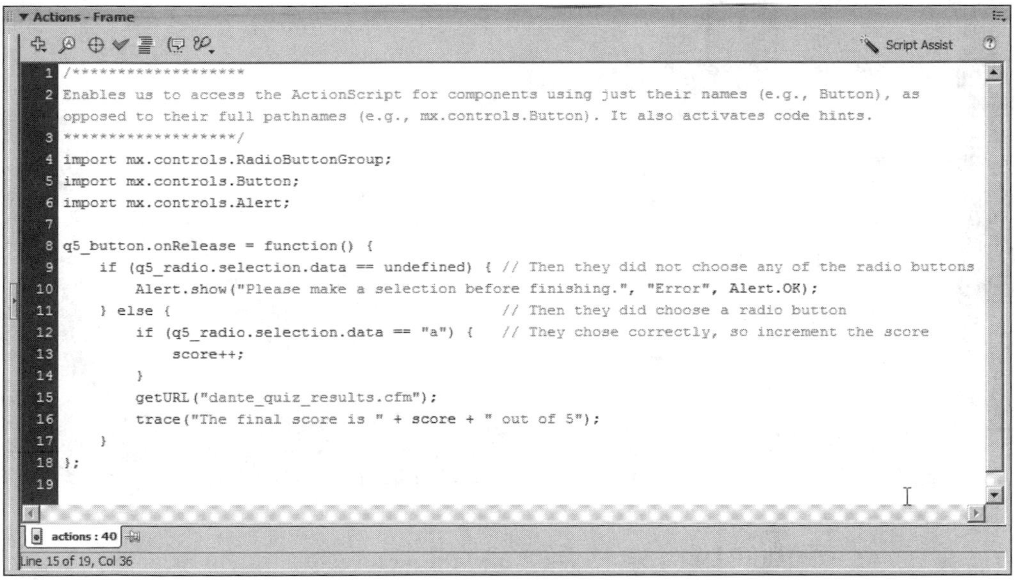

At this point, though, no data is being sent. You need something like this:

```
getURL("dante_quiz_results.cfm?score=5&username=osiris@allectomedia.com");
```

The problem is that you can't hard-code the values of the score variable ("5") and the username variable ("osiris@allectomedia.com"). You'll need to have Flash insert those values on the fly. Earlier, faced with the same challenge in a ColdFusion page, you used `<cfoutput>` to solve the problem. Obviously, `<cfoutput>` is not available in Flash. But an equivalent is.

3. Revise the `getURL()` line as follows:

```
getURL("dante_quiz_results.cfm?score=" + score + "&username=" + username);
```

Text inside quotation marks is ignored by Flash, which simply passes that text as is. However, the text outside the quotation marks is evaluated by Flash. The + symbol between the text strings in quotes and the variable names outside the quotes are used to glue the pieces together; the programming term for this is concatenation. Thus, if the current value of score is 3, and the current value of username is rory@frogjuice.com, this line will be converted to the following, and will be sent as a request to the server.

```
getURL(dante_quiz_results.cfm?score=3&username=rory@frogjuice.com)
```

```
/*******************
Enables us to access the ActionScript for components using just their names (e.g., Button), as
opposed to their full pathnames (e.g., mx.controls.Button). It also activates code hints.
*******************/
import mx.controls.RadioButtonGroup;
import mx.controls.Button;
import mx.controls.Alert;

q5_button.onRelease = function() {
    if (q5_radio.selection.data == undefined) { // Then they did not choose any of the radio buttons
        Alert.show("Please make a selection before finishing.", "Error", Alert.OK);
    } else {                                    // Then they did choose a radio button
        if (q5_radio.selection.data == "a") {  // They chose correctly, so increment the score
            score++;
        }
        getURL("dante_quiz_results.cfm?score=" + score + "&username=" + username);
        trace("The final score is " + score + " out of 5");
    }
};
```

4. Create a SWF (Control > Test Movie), and then close the movie after it appears. In Dreamweaver, find the dante_quiz.swf in the flash folder (within the Files panel) and upload it to the remote server. Click dante_quiz_login.cfm and press F12 (Windows) or Option+F12 (Macintosh). Complete the quiz, and then click the Finish button.

When you choose Control > Test Movie, you create a new version of the SWF file, complete with the new code. But you can't really test the movie in the Flash environment, so close it right away and go to Dreamweaver.

When you're finished taking the quiz, you should see dante_quiz_results.cfm. This page has nothing on it yet, beyond the placeholder text. But that doesn't matter; you'll fix that soon enough. Most importantly, notice in the address bar of the browser that the username and score variables have been passed into the URL. Because ColdFusion can see querystrings like this, you'll be able to grab that data and make use of it.

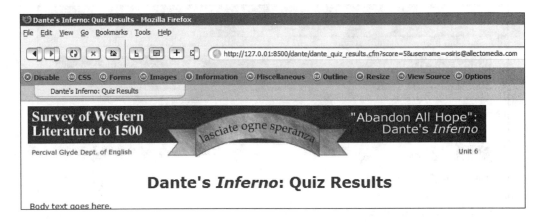

5. Save and close dante_quiz.fla.

Now it's time to return to Dreamweaver.

Outputting the Data in the HTML Page

When it loads, dante_quiz_results.cfm now has two variables available in its URL (that is, as a querystring). In this task, you'll output those two variables into the HTML page.

1. In Dreamweaver, open dante_quiz_results.cfm.

The other pages of the site are finished, so this is the last page you'll need to work on. It needs to accomplish two things: provide feedback, in the form of a quiz score, to the user; and insert a new record into the database.

2. Replace the placeholder text with the following. Link the word "Return" to index.cfm. Make both sets of "XXX"s bold.

Thank you for taking the quiz, XXX

Your score is: XXX out of 5.

Return to the Dante site home page.

As you probably guessed, XXX is just placeholder text, which you'll soon replace with dynamic data.

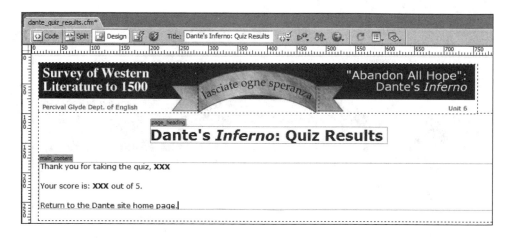

3. In the Bindings panel, click the New Binding (+) button to create two new URL variables: *username* and *score*.

Creating bindings notifies Dreamweaver that this data will be available to the page, but creating bindings does not actually change any code in the page. Creating bindings makes it easy to insert dynamic data in a page so you can output it.

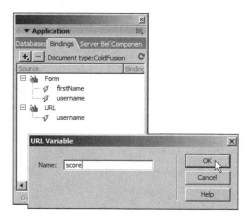

4. Select the first set of "XXX"s in the Document window. In the URL category of the Bindings panel, click to select username. Click the Insert button at the bottom of the panel.

Dreamweaver writes the code necessary to enable ColdFusion to output the value of the URL variable username in HTML code. As you probably guessed, Dreamweaver inserted a `<cfoutput>` tag.

5. Repeat Step 4 to insert the URL.score variable in the second set of "XXX"s. Save and upload dante_quiz_results.cfm.

The page is now set to output both variables from Flash. You're ready to test the page.

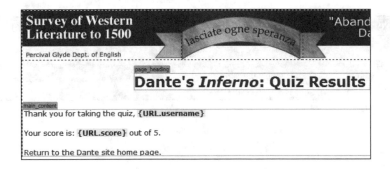

6. In the Files panel, select dante_quiz_login.cfm and press F12 (Windows) or Option+F12 (Macintosh). Enter an email address and take the quiz.

When you're finished taking the quiz, the email address you entered in the form two pages ago, as well as your score, are output.

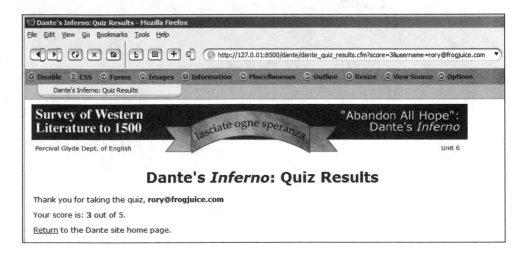

Inserting the Data into a Database

In this task, you'll insert the username and score into the database. To do so, you'll have to hand-code a SQL query.

1. Still in dante_quiz_results.cfm, switch to code view and scroll to the top of the page. Add several blank lines above the opening <!DOCTYPE> tag.

The query is not a part of the HTML output, so it makes sense to put it outside the HTML document. By putting the query above the beginning of the HTML document, you ensure that if for some reason the query doesn't work, the rest of the page will not process either, but will instead display an error message.

2. Begin the query by typing the following code:

```
<cfquery name="insertQuizScores" datasource="dante">
</cfquery>
```

Leave a blank line between these two lines.

The <cfquery> tag is used to query databases, whether you're merely selecting data or actually modifying it, by inserting new records or updating existing records. The name attribute is an arbitrary name you give your query. If you were returning records, you would need the value of name to output them using <cfoutput>. This query won't return any records (it only inserts them), so the value of name doesn't matter too much. The datasource attribute enables you to specify the ColdFusion DSN, which, as you'll recall, tells ColdFusion where the data is located and in what format (Microsoft Access, etc.).

You'll place the query between the opening and closing <cfquery> tags. It's this query that gets sent to the database. In this case, you'll write a query that inserts data. An insert query in SQL has the following basic syntax:

```
INSERT INTO someTable
  (
  fieldName1,
  fieldName2,
  fieldName3
  )
VALUES
  (
  'Value1',
  'Value2',
  'Value3'
  )
```

The first set of items lists the names of the fields in the database table into which you want to insert data. The second set of items lists the data that you want inserted. The two sets are correlated; in this example, 'Value1' will be inserted into fieldName1 of the someTable table; 'Value2' will be inserted into fieldName2, and so on.

To insert the quiz data from the Flash quiz into the database, you'll need something like this:

```
INSERT INTO quiz
  (
  username,
  score
  )
VALUES
  (
  '[the username supplied in the URL variable]',
  '[the score supplied in the URL variable]'
  )
```

The tricky part is the part in the square brackets; you'll need to figure out how to get ColdFusion to supply that data for you.

3. Between the opening and closing <cfquery> tags, insert the following code:

```
INSERT INTO quiz
  (
  username,
  score
  )
VALUES
  (
  '#url.username#',
  '#url.score#'
  )
```

Just as it does with the <cfoutput> blocks you've seen before, ColdFusion evaluates the variables inside the pound signs (##) before it sends the results to the database. Thus, when this command is sent to the database, the variables have already been replaced with their actual values.

```
<cfquery name="insertQuizScores" datasource="dante">
    INSERT INTO quiz
    (
    username,
    score
    )
    VALUES
    (
    '#url.username#',
    '#url.score#'
    )
</cfquery>

<!DOCTYPE html PUBLIC "-//W3C//DTD XHTML 1.0 Transitional//EN"
    "http://www.w3.org/TR/xhtml1/DTD/xhtml1-transitional.dtd">
<html xmlns="http://www.w3.org/1999/xhtml"><!-- InstanceBegin template="/Templates/dante_template.dwt"
<head>
```

4. Save and upload dante_quiz_results.cfm. Test dante_quiz_login.cfm and take the quiz again. After you're finished, leave the browser open.

It works! How do you know? If you don't see an error, it must have worked. If ColdFusion had any trouble, it would have generated an error message. But an even more reliable way to verify that your data has been successfully inserted is just to go in and look at the table.

Survey of Western Literature to 1500

lasciate ogne speranza

"Abandon All Hope": Dante's *Inferno*

Percival Glyde Dept. of English

Unit 6

Dante's *Inferno*: Quiz Results

Thank you for taking the quiz, **silk@drasnia.net**

Your score is: **5** out of 5.

Return to the Dante site home page.

5. With any page in your site open, switch to the Databases panel. Expand, if necessary, the dante database. Expand the Tables category. Right-click (Windows) or Control-click (Macintosh) the quiz table, and choose View Data.

In the View Data window, you'll see all the records in the quiz database. The email address and the score you just created are listed. Success!

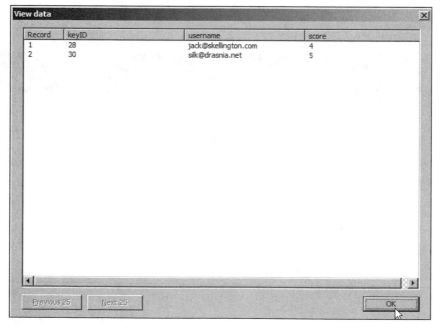

Improving the Security of the Application

The application is fully functional. Still, a rather obvious security problem exists as the application currently stands. The ColdFusion scripts on dante_quiz_results.cfm that insert the data into the database and output the scores on the page both depend on the URL variables. However, the address in the URL is fully editable!

1. **In the browser's address bar, change the score to *0*, and revise the username to the email address of someone you don't like. Press Enter or Return.**

The page reloads with the new data, and sure enough, your victim has been added to the database with a score of 0.

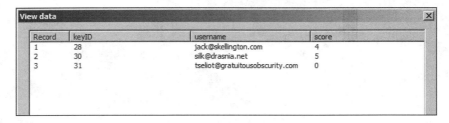

You need to find some way to get this data out of the URL.

Do you remember the earlier discussion about GET versus POST in the information about forms? With GET, data is submitted as a querystring via the URL; with POST, data is submitted in a way that it's invisible—and not editable—to the user. Ideally, we could submit the data from Flash using POST, rather than as a querystring. We can.

2. In Dreamweaver, open dante_quiz_questions.cfm. In Design view, click to select the gray rectangle representing the Flash movie. In the Property inspector, click the Edit button.

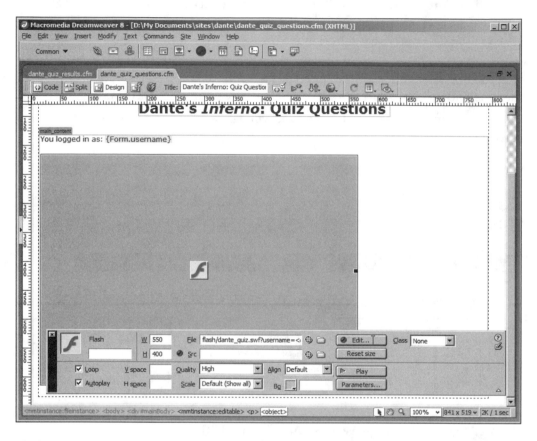

Flash opens, with the FLA file already active. If you're prompted to choose a file, choose dante_quiz.fla. This is a convenient shortcut. After Flash opens, you'll see a Done button in the top-left corner. When you're finished making changes to the file, click this button. Flash will regenerate a new SWF file and also save the FLA.

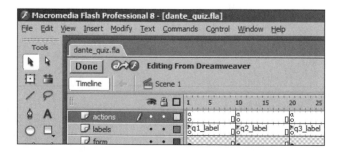

3. Click Frame 40 of the actions layer, and open the Actions panel. Revise the getURL() line to remove the variables, as follows:

```
getURL("dante_quiz_results.cfm");
```

Now, no variables will be sent, which is not what you want. But you don't want the variables passed through the URL, so you'll have to remove them from the URL.

The getURL() method, like many Flash methods, has optional parameters in addition to its required parameter (the URL itself). The two optional parameters are target and variables. The target parameter enables you to specify which browser window you want to open the requested URL. The default is the same window that called the file, or _self. If you don't specify a parameter, Flash assumes you mean _self as the target. The other parameter, variables, causes Flash to send all the variables on the timeline to the requested URL as part of the request. The variables parameter has only two options: GET and POST. You should recall the discussion about GET and POST earlier in a book, but as a quick review, GET sends the variables in the URL, while POST sends the variables as form data. So to retrieve data sent via GET in ColdFusion, you use #url.myVariable#, and to retrieve data sent via POST, you use #form.myVariable#. POST is the option you want.

The only catch is that in order to specify this variables parameter, you also have to specify the target parameter, even though the default (_self) is fine.

```
▼ Actions - Frame                                                    Script Assist

    1  /*******************
    2  Enables us to access the ActionScript for components using just their names (e.g.,
       Button), as opposed to their full pathnames (e.g., mx.controls.Button). It also activates
       code hints.
    3  *******************/
    4  import mx.controls.RadioButtonGroup;
    5  import mx.controls.Button;
    6  import mx.controls.Alert;
    7
    8  q5_button.onRelease = function() {
    9      if (q5_radio.selection.data == undefined) { // Then they did not choose any of the
       radio buttons
   10          Alert.show("Please make a selection before finishing.", "Error", Alert.OK);
   11      } else {                                    // Then they did choose a radio button
   12          if (q5_radio.selection.data == "a") {   // They chose correctly, so increment the
       score
   13              score++;
   14          }
   15          getURL("dante_quiz_results.cfm");
   16          trace("The final score is " + score + " out of 5");
   17      }
   18  };

    actions : 40
Line 15 of 18, Col 34
```

4. Revise the `getURL()` line one last time, as follows:

```
getURL("dante_quiz_results.cfm", "_self", "POST");
```

Don't misspell anything or leave out any commas or quotes.

Again, this line will send all the variables on the main timeline to dante_quiz_results.cfm, using POST.

5. Click Done to return to Dreamweaver. Use the Files panel to upload (or put) dante_quiz.swf on the remote server.

The SWF file is re-exported and the FLA is saved. Unfortunately, the SWF is not uploaded to the server, so you'll have to upload the SEF manually.

One more change is necessary. The file dante_quiz_results.cfm is expecting two URL variables: username and score. You even created bindings for them. But they won't be available any more. Instead, they'll be available as form variables. You'll need to update dante_quiz_results.cfm, or you'll get errors.

6. Open dante_quiz_results.cfm. Create bindings for two form variables: username and score (username might already exist; if so, don't redefine it).

Dreamweaver now knows the data will be there, but the page is still looking for the wrong data.

7. In the Document window in design view, click to select {URL.username}. In the Bindings panel, click the username variable in the Form category, and click Insert. Repeat the process to replace {URL.score} with {Form.score}.

You've taken care of the `<cfoutput>` blocks. But don't test the file yet; remember there are two more places inside the `<cfquery>` block where the URL variable is used.

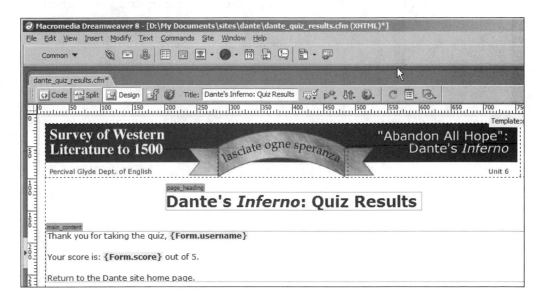

8. Switch to code view, scroll to the top. Change `#url.username#` to `#form.username#`. Likewise, change `#url.score#` to `#form.score#`.

Now the query will use available data as well.

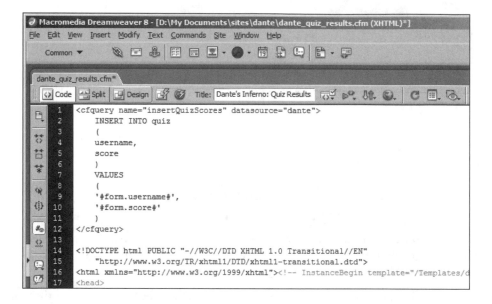

9. Save and upload dante_quiz_results.cfm. Take the whole quiz again, starting from dante_quiz_login.cfm.

This time, when you get to the last page of the quiz, the username and score are both displayed and inserted into the database, but you can't edit them via the URL.

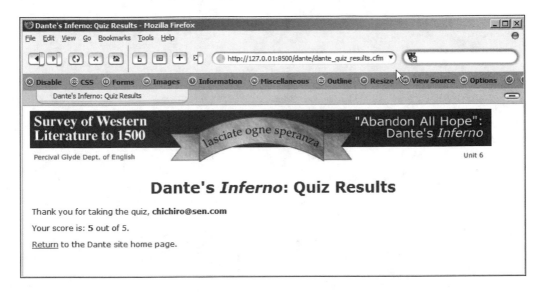

The project is finished, and now you have a good idea of the basic structure of dynamic sites with Flash interfaces. As you get more serious about Flash front-ends for database-driven sites, be sure to check out some of the data-passing techniques not discussed in this beginner's introduction, especially the loadVars object in Flash and—if you want to go all the way—Flash Remoting, which enables you to work with ColdFusion and other middleware business logic much more robustly.

For the final part of the book, you'll learn to set up your site for Contribute users to maintain, so you don't have to do everything by yourself!

What You Have Learned

In this lesson, you have:

- Sent data from Flash to ColdFusion by passing it in a URL (pages 487–489)
- Output URL variables to HTML, using ColdFusion (pages 489–491)
- Used <cfquery> in conjunction with SQL's INSERT statement to insert data into a database (pages 492–496)
- Used the getURL() method's optional variables parameter to pass data more securely from Flash to ColdFusion (pages 497–503)
- Updated the ColdFusion template so that it could see the variables in their new location (pages 497–503)

17 Decentralizing with Contribute

As a Studio 8 developer, your favorite feature of Contribute 3 probably won't be its interface, one of its features, or some nifty command. More likely, your favorite feature will be some tedious content update task you *won't* do—because someone else can! Contribute 3 frees designers and programmers from Web-content maintenance tasks and lets content experts take ownership of their own content, without having to go through the IT staff every time they need to make a small change on the site. This accessibility is made possible by Contribute's unique browse-edit-publish paradigm, sophisticated administration options, secure reviews prior to publishing, and integration with Microsoft Office products. Given that Contribute also provides cross-platform and multi-browser support, Web maintenance has never been easier and more efficient.

Contribute's Browse-to-Edit paradigm makes web maintenance a breeze.

In this lesson, you'll be working in both the Dreamweaver and Contribute environments to become familiar with key Contribute features such as connections, browse and edit modes, and page update using CSS. You'll also learn to create an efficient workflow by integrating Dreamweaver and Contribute.

What You Will Learn

In this lesson, you will:

- Configure a Web site in Dreamweaver for Contribute users
- Create and export a connection key for users
- Use the connection key to create the site connection in Contribute
- Edit a page in Contribute
- Publish the edited page

Approximate Time

This lesson takes approximately 60 minutes to complete.

Lesson Files

Starting Files:

Lesson17/Start/dante/index.cfm

Completed Files:

Lesson17/Complete/dante/index.cfm

Configuring a Site in Dreamweaver for a Contribute Site Administrator

Thanks to the seamless integration between Contribute and Dreamweaver, you can configure your site for Contribute users without leaving the Dreamweaver environment. To do so, you use Dreamweaver's Manage Sites dialog.

1. Open Dreamweaver. Choose Site > Manage Sites... from the main menu, and with the dante site selected, press the Edit button. The Site Definition for dante window opens.

Because the Contribute configuration is accessible from within the Site Definition window in Dreamweaver, you'll need to edit the Dante site definition to prepare it for Contribute-based editing and maintenance.

2. With the Advanced tab selected, choose Contribute from the Category column on the left. Select the Enable Contribute compatibility checkbox to activate a Dreamweaver pop-up window. Click OK to enable the local use of Design Notes, the upload of Design Notes, and the Check In/Out feature.

This step allows you to configure Contribute for site-maintenance tasks. Enabling Design Notes and Check In/Check Out in Dreamweaver allows you to use Contribute's compatibility features with the Dante site.

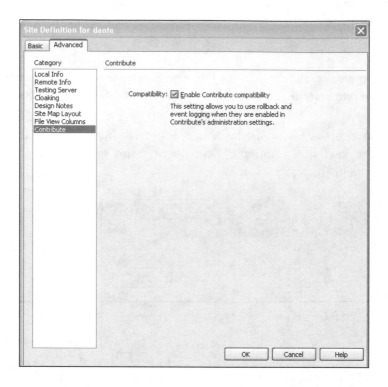

3. In the Contribute Site Settings window, type the name of a designated Contribute user and his email address in the text boxes. Click OK to return to the Site Definition for dante window.

When you provide the user information, Contribute is able to assign the user appropriate permissions. You'll first create an account for the Dante site's administrator, so that he can use all Contribute's updating features with no limitations.

Contribute has three default roles: administrator, publisher, and writer. The administrator, who has the most powerful of the three roles, can create new roles and modify existing ones, add users to the site, and send connection keys to new users so that they can access the site. A site can have only one administrator. Publishers are users who can create, edit, and publish pages. Writers can only create and edit pages; they can't publish pages. Writers need to send their pages to either an administrator or a publisher for review prior to publication.

4. In the Site Definition for dante window, enter the Site root URL. Click the Test button to test the connection.

The Site root URL must be the same as the URL Prefix (specified in the Testing Server tab, and set in a previous lesson) in order for Dreamweaver to create a successful connection to Contribute.

Note *If you're running ColdFusion as a standalone Web server, the site URL will be http://localhost:8500/dante. If you're using a different ColdFusion server, enter its URL.*

After you click the Test button, Dreamweaver displays a pop-up window that tells you the connection was successful.

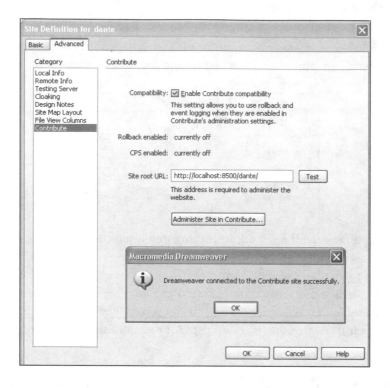

5. Click OK to dismiss the connection-successful pop-up and return to the Site Definition window. Click the Administer Site in Contribute button. In the Contribute dialog that appears, select Dreamweaver-style editing as the editing experience and click Yes.

Because you're creating an account for the site administrator, you need to choose Yes to make sure that Contribute recognizes and configures the role of this person.

As the Contribute site administrator, you'll need to make decisions regarding the types of code-editing experience you'll provide for the people who perform maintenance tasks. Two options are available in Contribute: one-line line breaks, as in standard word processors (where pressing Enter/Return moves the cursor down a single line); and two-line line breaks, as in Web-page editors (where pressing Enter/Return moves the cursor down two lines, creating an extra line of space between the two paragraphs). To ensure better code, choose the Dreamweaver-style editing option. With the Dreamweaver-style editing option selected, the code will be clean and will include <p> tags. If you choose the Word-processing option, the resulting code will have large quantities of inline styles.

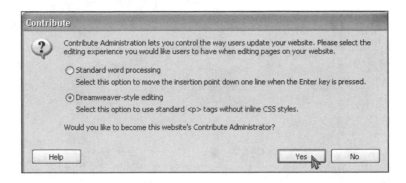

Now that the connection for the site is successfully established, you can administer Contribute use within Dreamweaver.

6. In the Administer Website dialog that appears, click Edit Role Settings to explore what types of page editing a Contribute Site Administrator is allowed to do. Do not change any default settings. Click Cancel to return to the Administer Website window.

As mentioned earlier, the site administrator has the most page-editing privileges. The site administrator is allowed to publish files to the Web server, edit any files in any folder, create a new page, and insert images.

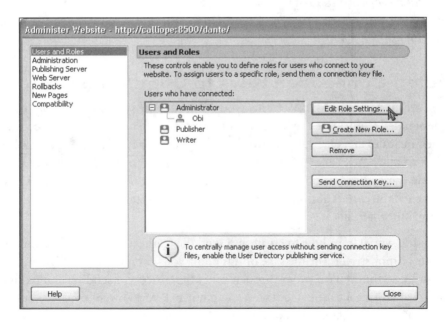

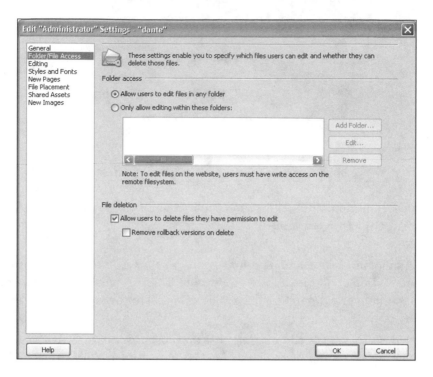

Tip *Whenever you create a new user who can update your Web site using Contribute, you can use the Edit Role Settings window to customize the editing settings for that user.*

Sending Connection Keys to Contribute Users

After you set up connections to Web sites, you can distribute site connection information to the designated Contribute users. Contribute embeds such information in a connection key, which includes and encrypts password, network, and/or File Transfer Protocol (FTP) log-in information. You can email the connection key (with the file extension .stc) to the appropriate users, or save it onto the network for users to download. All the user has to do is double-click the connection key file, and Contribute will start up and import the connection automatically.

In this section, you'll learn how to create and send the connection key to the dante site's Contribute administrator. For the sake of this book, you will role-play both administrator and end-user, so that you can work through the entire process of sending and receiving keys as well as editing a page in Contribute. In a normal workflow, of course, you may decide to opt out of either or both of these roles, depending on your team's needs.

1. With the Administer Web site window open, click the **Send Connection Key** button.

This button opens the Send Connection Key Wizard (Windows) or Export Connection Key Assistant (Macintosh).

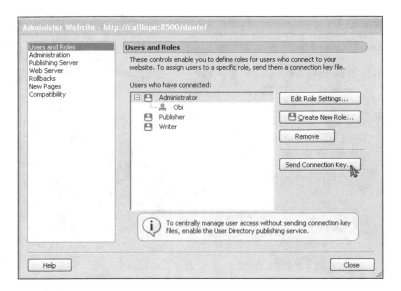

2. Accept the default setting to send the current connection settings to the user, and click **Next**.

The step confirms that the connection key is issued and sent to the user.

3. In the Role Information window of the Connection Key Wizard, select Administrator as the user role. Click Next.

This confirms the designated user as a Contribute site administrator.

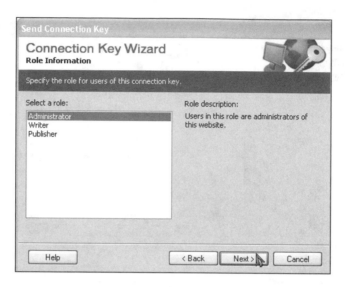

4. In the Connection Key Information window of the Connection Key Wizard, select Send in email to export the connection key file. In addition, enter a password for Contribute to use to encrypt the connection key. Click Next to advance to the Summary window.

Because Contribute will prompt your users for the password before they import the connection key, you'll need to write down the password you enter in this screen and give it to your users.

Note *Do not include the password in the email message, because that would defeat the purpose of password-protecting the connection key! Anyone with this key and its password becomes a full administrator of your Web site. Send the connection key using a different medium, such as a hand-written note or a phone call.*

Before you click the Done button, carefully verify the settings in the Summary page. Contribute now creates a new connection key for the user, assigning him the role of administrator.

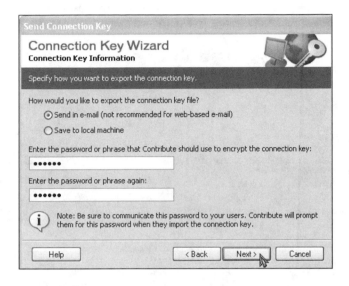

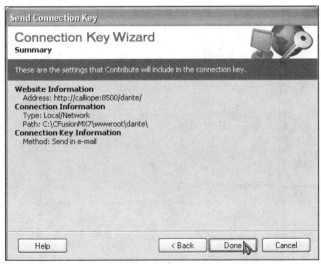

5. After you complete the wizard or assistant, Contribute creates an email message with the connection key attachment. Enter the designated user's (in this case, your) email address in the To box, and send the email message.

Your e-mail client sends the message with the connection key attachment to the user (that is, you; check your email to make sure it arrived).

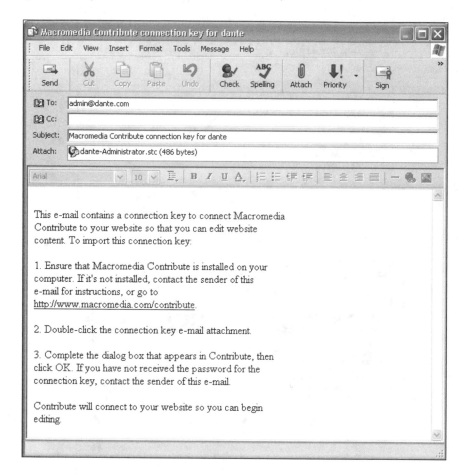

6. Close the Administer Web site window. Contribute prompts you to enter a password for the administrator. Enter a password, which should be different from the one the user will receive.

This completes the process of creating and sending the connection key to the Contribute user.

Creating a Connection in Contribute

After you send the email message to the designated Contribute user, he will need to open the message and its attachment to initiate the Contribute Web site connection process. In this section, you'll play the role of the end user to learn how to set up the connection within Contribute with the aid of the connection key.

1. Open the email message and download the dante-Administrator.stc connection key to your Desktop.

After the connection key is downloaded to the user's (in this case, your) Desktop, all he has to do is double-click the connection key file to initiate Contribute's connection to the Web site. The user can then begin editing the content.

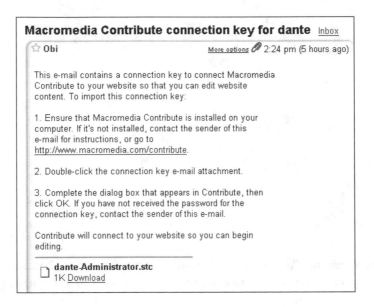

2. Double-click the connection key on the Desktop, which opens the Import Connection Key Wizard. Enter the name, email address, and connection key password.

Because you (in the role of administrator) created this connection key for the Contribute site administrator, you need to enter the name and email address of this individual. This is the same information you provided within the Dreamweaver environment in the previous section (again, this was presumably your own information).

The password should be identical to the one you created earlier for the connection key.

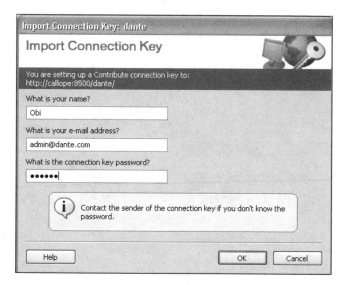

3. Click OK to initiate the connection-creation process within Contribute. After the connection is successfully created, you'll see the Dante site within the Contribute environment.

The home page of the Dante site appears in Contribute, indicating that Contribute has successfully created a connection to the Dante site.

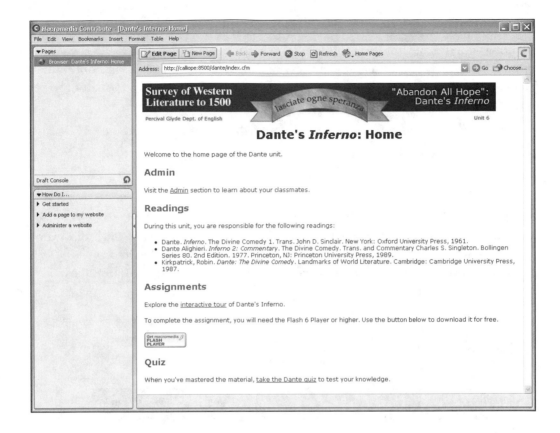

4. Take a few moments to explore the Contribute interface.

Contribute operates in two modes: browser and HTML editor. When you first open Contribute to access a site, you're viewing the site within its browser; pages are rendered as they would be in a regular browser, hyperlinks work, and so on. To navigate the site within Contribute, you can use the navigation bar or links on the site, or use the browser's Back and Forward buttons.

When you're ready to edit a page, you'll click Edit Page in the main menu. After a few seconds, Contribute will download the page and all its assets (such as images) to a local folder, and switch to HTML editor mode. Within this mode, the user can (depending on the permissions assigned to the connection) edit text, insert and remove images, create tables, format text, create new pages, insert hyperlinks, and so on.

Performing Simple Editing Tasks in Contribute

Working with text and images in Contribute is similar to working with them in a word processor. You can make formatting choices using the toolbars and menus in Contribute, and in return, Contribute will convert your decisions into proper HTML formatting to be rendered on the Web.

In this section, you'll learn how to perform simple editing tasks in Contribute.

Before learning how to edit a page in Contribute, you must return to the home page of the Dante site.

1. Click the Edit Page button in the main menu to access Edit mode in Contribute.

You'll notice that the main menu now contains a different set of options, which allow you to edit and format text and other common HTML objects. Because the site was constructed using a Dreamweaver template, Contribute recognizes and respects the blue borders surrounding the page's body text and heading.

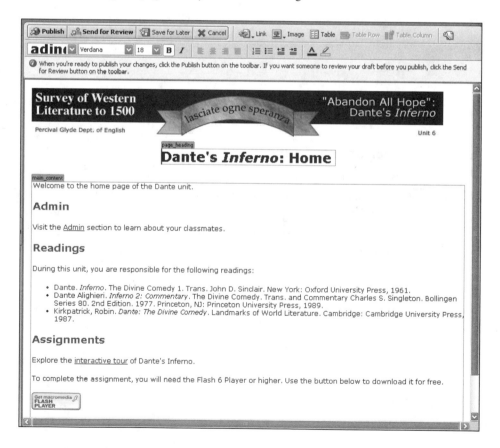

2. Under Assignments, change Flash 6 Player to Flash 8 Player.

As in a word processor, when you want to change text in Contribute, you must first select the word or phrase you want to change, and then type the new text in its place.

Assignments

Explore the _interactive tour_ of Dante's Inferno.

To complete the assignment, you will need the Flash 8 Player or higher. Use the button below to download it for free.

3. Under Assignments, make the text Flash 8 Player or higher bold by highlighting the text block and clicking the Bold button in the text formatting toolbar.

You can also right-click (Windows) or Control-click (Macintosh) and select Bold from the contextual menu.

Note _The right-click option for making text bold is not available if you're working in a table._

4. Position your cursor at the end of the sentence under the Quiz section, right after the word knowledge, and press Enter/Return. Type the word _Questions_, press Enter/Return, and then type _Contact your instructor if you have any questions about the unit_.

The text is not yet formatted particularly well, but you'll fix that in a moment.

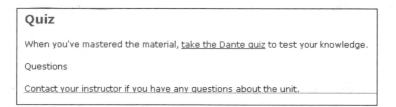

Quiz

When you've mastered the material, _take the Dante quiz_ to test your knowledge.

Questions

Contact your instructor if you have any questions about the unit.

5. Select the word Questions, and choose Heading 2 from the Style pop-up menu in the text formatting toolbar.

When you made the connection to the Web site in Contribute, the CSS styles you defined in earlier chapters are made accessible to Contribute users, allowing them to modify the text using the same styles to maintain a consistent look. If the Style menu is not enabled, your Contribute administrator has restricted the site so that you can't apply these styles.

Tip   *Alternatively, you can select Format > Style, and then select an appropriate style (Heading 2 in this case) from the pop-up menu to apply the style to the text block.*

Publishing the Draft and Reviewing the Page

Contribute saves what you've done so far as a draft of the Dante site's home page, stored on your hard drive. No one can see the new changes yet. You'll need to publish the updated page.

Before publishing the draft, Contribute allows you to preview it in a browser or obtain approval or feedback from others. If you wish, you can choose to publish it at a later time or cancel the draft.

In this section, you'll learn how to publish the updates you just made and make the page live.

1. Click the Publish button in the main menu to publish the draft. Contribute displays a pop-up window, indicating that the page has been successfully published to the Web site.

Contribute replaces the existing page with the updated version.

2. Click OK to complete the publishing process. Contribute switches back to browse mode.

In the browser mode, review the changes you've made.

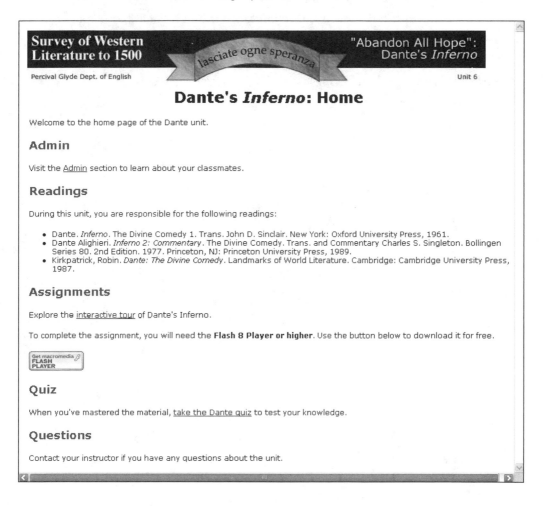

As a site-maintenance tool, Contribute provides smart features such as rollbacks, source editing, integrated image editing, drag-and-drop linking, shared assets, and more. Explore these features and learn to keep the content of your Website up to date easily and efficiently.

What You Have Learned

In this lesson, you have:

- Learned how to configure a Web site for Contribute users from within Dreamweaver (pages 507–512)
- Understood the process of creating a connection key (pages 512-516)
- Become familiar with the Send Connection Key Wizard (Windows) or Export Connection Key Assistant (Macintosh) (pages 512–516)
- Created a connection in Contribute (pages 517–519)
- Performed simple page-updating tasks in Contribute (pages 520–522)
- Published a page to the Web server (pages 522–524)

Index

dragging in Flash 8, 232

hiding gray line behind, 55

opening in Flash 8 Symbol Editing mode, 261–262

C

canvas

displaying in Fireworks, 9

repositioning graphics in, 11

Canvas Color box in Fireworks, using, 25

canvas size, determining for buttons, 38–39

CD Form Field, inserting in test_form.cfm page, 404

cell padding, specifying for tables, 178, 179

cell spacing, specifying for tables, 178, 179

cells in tables, moving content to, 180

CF Forms, inserting, 452. *See also* forms

CF text field icon, identifying, 407

CF Text fields, inserting, 453

cfform tag editor, opening, 404, 452

<cfform> tag, Flash format of, 406

cfinput tag editor, opening, 406, 453

.cfm extension, changing .html extension to, 400

CFML (ColdFusion Markup Language), description of, 391

<cfoutput> tags, using, 410, 441, 455, 457

<cfquery> tags

explanation of, 434

using, 493

characters

making draggable, 354

selecting with Pointer tool in Fireworks, 31, 32

Check In/Check Out, enabling in Dreamweaver, 508

checkerboard pattern, creating in Fireworks, 25

circles

dragging with Pointer tool in Fireworks, 12

formatting size and location of, 41

modifying in Fireworks, 11

selecting in Fireworks, 14, 43

classes, instantiation of, 314

Clipboard, copying text to, 171

code, examining, 413

code hints, enabling in ActionScript, 323

Code View button, effect of, 110

code view, displaying Flash movies in, 456

codec, configuring, 280

ColdFusion

evaluation of variables inside pound signs (##) by, 494

example of, 410

features of, 394

forms available in, 406

installing, 393–396

scripting language used by, 391

sending Flash data to, 487–489

ColdFusion Administrator, defining data sources in, 420–428

ColdFusion environment, setting up site for use of, 396–402

ColdFusion Flash forms, features of, 453

ColdFusion pages

preparing for Flash-based quiz, 451–458

reading, 384

viewing, 392

ColdFusion templates, description of, 392, 410. *See also* templates

color palettes, choosing, 78

color swatches, displaying in Fireworks, 23

colors. *See also* Fill Color

applying to logos, 14–18

customizing slice colors, 64

representing in Fireworks, 78

columns

creating in tables, 178

in database tables, 417

ComboBox component, adding and scripting in Flash-based quiz, 474–478

Command+C (Macintosh), copying shapes with, 12

Command+Enter (Mac), testing movies with, 284

Command+F8 (Mac), creating button symbols with, 39

Command+N (Mac), opening Fireworks documents with, 38

Command+Return (Mac), testing Flash movies with, 318, 354, 357

Command-Select (Windows), selecting fields in Column area with, 432

comment lines (<!-- and -->), deleting, 110

comments (//), adding to code, 328

comments (/* */), examples of, 448

comments, simplifying, 334

Common category of Insert bar
    Image option in, 182
    Table button in, 178
components. *See* Flash components
Components panel, opening, 466
compression, determining for video, 281
connection keys, sending to Contribute users,
    512–516
connections, creating in Contribute, 517–519
contact information, reorganizing with tables,
    178–181
content_main editable region, creating, 162–163
content_special, entering in New Editable Region
    dialog, 164
Contribute
    applying styles in, 522
    browser and HTML editor modes of, 519
    changing text in, 521
    configuring for site maintenance tasks, 508
    creating connections in, 517–519
    default roles in, 509
    displaying Site Settings window, 509
    editing pages in, 519
    line-break options in, 510
    performing editing tasks in, 520–522
    publishing drafts and reviewing pages in,
        522–524
    sending connection keys to, 512–516
    using Design Notes with, 507
Contribute dialog, selecting Dreamweaver-style
    editing option in, 510
Contribute site administrators, configuring
    Dreamweaver sites for, 507–512
Convert to Blank Keyframes option in Flash 8,
    choosing, 217–218, 224
Convert to Keyframes option in Flash 8, choosing,
    246, 262
Convert to Symbol option in Flash 8, choosing,
    234, 245, 251
Copy Up Graphic button in Fireworks, effect
    of, 48
.copyright custom class, creating, 143
Create Motion Tween option in Flash 8, choosing,
    247, 250
Crop tool, using, 63, 90
CSS (cascading style sheet)
    aligning objects with, 185

applying as inline style, 148
overview of, 135–136
selecting CSS blocks, 152
using <div> tags with, 148
using css folder, 105
CSS classes, creating, 136, 142–144
CSS layers
    creating in Dreamweaver, 115–119
    exporting Fireworks slices as, 84–89
CSS panel, editing #main_content in, 154
CSS reference, displaying, 136
CSS Rule Definition dialog, displaying, 140–141,
    143, 154, 155
CSS styles
    advantage of, 136
    applying, 144–148
CSS Styles panel
    creating custom classes with, 142
    opening, 137
Ctrl+C (Windows), copying shapes with, 12
Ctrl+Enter (Windows), testing Flash movies
    with, 318
Ctrl+Enter (Windows), testing movies with, 284,
    354, 357
Ctrl+F8 (Windows), creating button symbols
    with, 39
Ctrl+N (Windows), opening Fireworks
    documents with, 38
Ctrl-Select (Windows), selecting fields in Column
    area with, 432
curly braces ({}) in Flash 8 scripts, explanation
    of, 258
Customers table, description of, 416

D

Dante project. *See also* Web sites
    adding hotspots to, 334
    adding originating targets to, 363–366
    applying unordered list to, 305
    breaking pages in, 389
    creating drag-and-drop targets in, 355–358
    creating placeholder pages for, 296–299
    defining, 293–295
    drag-and-drop interactivity in, 351–354
    editing, 396–402
    formatting home page for, 299–308
    providing dynamic feedback in, 359–363

dynamic data, adding to pages, 431
dynamic feedback, providing, 359–363
dynamic sites, developing in Dreamweaver, 392
Dynamic Table dialog, displaying, 436
dynamic text fields in Flash
    overview of, 319
    preparing, 324–326
Dynamic Text, selecting, 359

E

Edge
    changing from Anti-Alias to Feather in
        Fireworks, 15–16
    changing to Feathered in Fireworks, 24
Edit mode, accessing in Contribute, 520
Edit Role Settings option, selecting in Administer
    Website dialog, 511
editable regions
    designating, 161–164
    impact of, 182
Editable setting in Parameters tab, changing to
    False, 338
Ellipse tool
    selecting in Fireworks, 10
    using with button over states, 46
    using with button symbols, 40
<em> tag, adding italics with, 306
Email Link dialog, displaying, 176
email links, creating in database tables, 440–441
email messages, sending for Contribute
    connection keys, 516
<embed> tags, using with Flash movies, 456, 457
embedded style, applying CSS as, 148
empty tag. See <img> tags
Encoding screen for video, Show Advanced
    Settings button on, 279
error messages, as instances of Alert
    component, 466
events
    relationship to interactive Flash movies, 254
    relationship to objects, 313
events.htm file
    dragging Point to File icon to, 175
    linking outreach page to, 175
    using with Flash video, 285
events.htm file, selecting, 173

Export Connection Key Assistant, opening on
    Macintoshes, 513
Export dialog box, accessing, 86, 91
Export HTML File option, selecting from Source
    drop-down menu, 91
Export Movie option in Flash 8, choosing, 265
Extension Manager, 119–124

F

F6 key
    Convert to Keyframes in Flash 8, 263
    inserting keyframes with, 212
F8 key, converting bitmap graphics to symbols
    with, 352
F9 key, opening Actions panel with, 316, 327, 353,
    464, 467
F11 key, opening Fireworks Library with, 321
F12 key (Windows)
    previewing pages in browsers with, 114, 181,
        184, 187, 192, 194, 268, 269, 286, 288
    testing files with, 412, 442
    testing Fireworks documents with, 50
    testing Flash movies in Web pages with, 375
    testing forms with, 458
    testing Web pages with, 440
Feather Edge in Fireworks, changing to, 15–16, 24
field names, identifying in database tables, 417
fields
    selecting in Column area, 432
    specifying in database tables, 418
files
    previewing in browsers, 181
    saving in Fireworks, 10, 30
    testing, 442
    uploading to servers, 411
Files panel
    description of, 108
    location of, 108
fill, explanation of, 5
Fill Color. See also colors
    changing in Flash 8, 262, 263
    setting for rectangles, 59
    setting in Fireworks, 14, 22
filters, using in Fireworks, 31–32
Firefox, examining code in, 413
Fireworks documents, testing, 50

J

Jade Valley project. *See also* Web sites
  choosing template from Files panel, 137
  creating navigation bar for, 51–55
  developing page-slicing scheme for, 62–65
  developing site banner for, 55–57
  finalizing design for, 57–61
  linking to home.htm, 195
  optimizing and exporting interface design
    for, 84–87
  saving as template, 159
JDBC URL, entering for Macintosh data
    sources, 426
JPEG (Joint Photographic Expert Group) format,
    guidelines for use of, 72
JPEG - Better Quality option, selecting, 76, 77, 82

K

key frame placement, configuring for codec, 280
keyboard shortcuts
  for Actions panel, 464
  for Convert to Keyframes in Flash 8, 263
  for converting bitmap graphics to symbols, 352
  for copying shapes, 12
  for creating button symbols, 39
  for Dodge tool in Fireworks, 26
  for inserting keyframes in Flash 8, 212
  for opening Actions panel in Flash 8, 316, 327,
    353, 467
  for opening documents in Fireworks, 38
  for opening Fireworks Library, 321
  for pasting shapes, 12
  for previewing pages in browsers, 114, 181, 184,
    187, 192, 194, 268, 269, 286, 288
  for selecting fields in Column area, 432
  for testing files, 412, 442
  for testing Flash movies, 318
  for testing forms, 458
  for testing movies, 284, 354, 357, 375
  for testing Web pages, 440
keyframes in Flash 8
  creating, 246
  creating temporal structure with, 211–213
  example of, 206
  explanation of, 205

inserting, 212
inserting blank keyframes, 217–218, 224
opening in Over button state, 262
representation of, 211

L

L (left) coordinates, specifying for layer position,
    117, 118
labels
  adding to Flash-based quiz, 475
  creating temporal structure with, 211–213
labels layer in Flash 8, selecting frames in, 212
Latin text, inserting, 124
layer positioning, specifying in Property
    Inspector, 117
layer styles, defining in external style sheets, 149
layers
  creating with CSS and `<div>` tags, 148
  naming, 116
  naming in Flash 8, 208
layers in Flash 8
  adding, 274
  adding content across, 213–216
  creating, 207
  naming, 274
  selecting frames in, 210
Layout category
  choosing from Insert bar, 115
  choosing from Insert menu, 146
leading, setting in Fireworks, 28
`<li>` (list item) tags, using, 188, 189
`<li>` tags, using with Dante site, 305
library, 221–222
Library in Flash 8. *See* Flash 8 Library
Library panel. *See also* Fireworks Library; Flash 8
    Library
  commands in, 53
  opening, 459
line breaks, creating, 181, 190
Line tool in Fireworks
  selecting, 58
  using with button instances, 55
  using with site banners, 56
Line tool in Flash 8, selecting, 223
Line Type, setting to Multiline, 325

Pointer tool in Fireworks
  changing font Color with, 59
  dragging circles with, 12
  optimizing navigation bar with, 83
  selecting characters with, 32
  selecting objects with, 14
  switching to, 76, 80
  using, 82
  using with button over states, 47
  using with buttons, 43
POST versus GET, 405, 497, 499
pound sign (#)
  identifying named anchors with, 157
  using with ColdFusion and database tables, 441
  using with ColdFusion tags, 410
Preview tab in Fireworks
  options on, 74
  using with button over states, 50
primary key fields, identifying in database tables, 417
Products label image, inserting banana.jpg below, 129
products.htm page
  creating, 173
  modifying, 185
Progressive download option, using with video, 277–278
properties, relationship to objects, 314
Property Inspector in Dreamweaver, 107
  Align Center button in, 185
  Alt field in, 112
  Bold option in, 191
  Format drop-down of, 301
  Link field in, 193
  Link field of, 307
  Ordered List button in, 189
  specifying layer positioning in, 117
Property Inspector in Fireworks
  context-sensitivity of, 41
  naming button instances with, 54
  setting fonts with, 61
  setting Stroke and Fill with, 46
  setting Stroke with, 57
  using Stroke Options in, 42
Property Inspector in Flash 8
  applying Alpha color with, 252–253

  changing font size with, 230
  checking size of stage in, 204
  description of, 202
  Frame Label field in, 212
Publish button in Contribute, accessing, 522
publisher role in Contribute, description of, 509
Put Files icon, identifying, 401
Put Images in Subfolder option, description of, 87
px, specifying after number values for layer positions, 118

Q

q1_button code block, adding, 471–472
q1_button instance, naming, 463
q1_radio radio button group, creating, 462
q2_button instance, naming, 475
q2_combo instance, naming, 474
q3_list instance, naming, 478
q1_button script, amending, 468
question mark (?), using with URLs and name-value pairs, 457
QuickTime, convert to FLA, 275–284
quickTip architecture, planning, 320
quickTip instance, opening in Symbol-editing mode, 324
quickTip interactions. *See also* Tooltips
  preparing for, 318–320
  scripting, 327–336
quickTip movie, preparing, 324–326
quickTip_mc instance, naming, 326
quickTip_txt dynamic text field, location of, 326, 331

R

R keyboard shortcut, using with Dodge tool in Fireworks, 26
radio buttons
  adding text strings next to, 460
  using Data setting with, 461
  using Group Name setting with, 461
RadioButton instance in Flash, selecting, 461
raster graphics, explanation of, 5
RDS passwords. *See also* passwords
  entering in ColdFusion, 395
  resetting, 429
recipes.htm page
  creating, 173

finishing, 190–192

opening, 188

Recordset (Query) option, choosing from Bindings panel, 431

recordsets, building, 431

Rectangle tool, selecting in Fireworks, 22–23, 57, 59

rectangles, drawing in Document window, 58

red asterisk (*) In ColdFusion, meaning of, 453

Reference panel, CSS reference in, 136

Refresh button in Site folder, effect of, 173

Refresh icon, identifying, 401

Registration, setting for symbols, 352–353

relative URL, definition of, 176

remote host icon, identifying, 401

Remote Info category

accessing in Category list, 102

selecting, 397

remote servers, uploading dante_quiz.swf on, 500

Render Text as HTML option, selecting, 325–326

Required option, using with ColdFusion Flash forms, 453

Role Information window of Connection Key wizard, selecting user role in, 514

rollover effects, adding to buttons in Flash 8, 260–265

root folder

defining, 103

importance of, 102

row numbers, identifying in database tables, 417

rows

creating in tables, 178

in database tables, 417

rs_GetUsers recordset

listing, 433

verifying, 436

rs_GetUsers.username code, explanation of, 441

S

Safari, examining code in, 413

sans-serif fonts, using with screen-based content, 139

Save As Template dialog, displaying, 160

Save Style Sheet File As dialog, opening, 138–139

screen graphics, standard size for, 9

scripted animation in Flash 8, explanation of, 244

scripts, adding to Actions panel, 259

Scripts pane in Flash 8, typing scripts into, 255

scrolling, managing, 186

scrolling text areas, creating with components, 337–340. *See also* text

Search Exchanges option, using with placeholder text, 120

Section 508 Guidelines for accessibility Web site, 66

security, improving for Flash-based quiz, 497–503

Select File dialog, displaying, 373

Select Image Source dialog, displaying, 128, 183

Selected radio button in Columns category, accessing, 432

Selection tool in Flash 8

dragging buttons with, 232

dragging graphic symbols with, 246

using, 225

using with button graphics, 228

using with text, 220, 230, 245

selectors in CSS, explanation of, 135

_self as target in Flash, significance of, 499

Send Connection Key button, clicking, 513

Send Connection Key Wizard, opening in Windows, 513

Server Behaviors, choosing, 428

server technologies, diagram of, 391–392

servers

installing ColdFusion on, 394

uploading files to, 411

workarounds for users without local servers, 396

shape tools, toggling through in Fireworks, 10

shapes

copying, 12

drawing for logos, 5–13

using vector graphics with, 6

Shift-constraint technique, using with ellipses, 10

site accessibility, enhancing, 65–67

site banners, developing, 55–57

Site Definition dialog, accessing Local Info category of, 101

Site Definition for dante window

entering Site root URL in, 509

opening, 507

sites. *See* Web sites

in Flash 8 library, 221

naming, 352

previewing in Library, 52

types of, 318

T

T (top) coordinates, specifying for layer position, 117, 118

Table dialog, displaying, 178, 179

table width, measurement of, 179

tables. *See also* database tables; HTML tables

exporting slices as, 89–94

inserting, 178

Tag Selector

description of, 108

location of, 108

selecting <div#logo> in, 149

selecting <div#special_content> from, 163

tags, nesting, 136

target parameter of getURL(), description of, 499

<td> tags

using, 177

using with table cells, 441

template.htm file

exporting and reviewing, 86

naming, 86

templates. *See also* ColdFusion templates

advantages of, 159

converting Web pages to, 159–161

modifying, 192–195

purpose of, 162

using Assets panel with, 173

Templates folder, managing, 160

temporal structure, creating with keyframes and labels, 211–213

Test button in Recordset dialog, clicking, 432–433

Test Movie option in Flash 8

choosing, 243, 253, 256, 259, 264, 329

creating new version of SWF files with, 489

using with Flash-based quiz, 451

using with Upper Hell, 341

test_form.cfm page

creating, 402

inserting CF Form Field in, 404

saving and closing, 408

testing, 412

test_output.cfm

creating, 402

opening, 408

Testing Server category, selecting, 398

text. *See also* scrolling text areas; type

adding hyperlinks to, 127

changing in Contribute, 521

copying to Clipboard, 171

inserting placeholder text, 119–124

resizing in Fireworks, 29

wrapping around images, 186

text areas

dynamic population of, 340

preparing for creation of, 359

text blocks

repositioning in Fireworks, 21

resizing in Fireworks, 28

selecting in Fireworks, 20

text boxes

assigning instance names to, 325

converting to graphic symbols in Flash 8, 245

selecting in Flash 8, 245

text placement, correcting in Flash 8, 225

Text Source folder, contents of, 295

Text tool in Fireworks

using with buttons, 44

using with logos, 18, 27, 29, 61

Text tool in Flash 8

changing button text with, 233

using, 214, 224

using with button graphics, 228

text_files folder, opening from Files panel, 170

.text_nav class, applying to paragraph, 147

.text_nav custom class, creating, 143

TextArea component

adding default text to, 339

enlarging, 338

textures, applying to logos, 14–18

<th> tags, using, 177

TIFF format, advisory about use of, 71

timeline in Flash 8

components of, 206, 207

Insert Layer button in, 274

making extra room in, 210

manipulating space used for rendering of, 208

scrubbing, 250

titles, modifying for Web pages, 109, 297, 374
Tools panel in Fireworks, tools available in, 10
Tooltips, displaying in Flash 8, 201–202. *See also* quickTip interactions
`#top` hyperlink, creating, 157–158
`trace()` action
   debugging with, 357
   replacing, 358
   using with Flash-based quiz, 465, 481
Transactions table, description of, 417
transform handles in Fireworks, identifying, 12
triangles
   deleting, 236
   designing for button graphics in Flash 8, 227–228
   selecting in Flash 8, 233
tween animation in Flash 8, explanation of, 244
type. *See also* text
   adding to logos, 18–21
   applying to logos, 27–30
type effects, applying with Fireworks, 30–33
Type tool in Fireworks
   using, 59
   using with button over states, 50

U

`<ul>` (unordered list) tags, using, 188, 305
undefined, checking for presence of, 467
Ungroup option in Flash 8, using, 234
unordered list, 305
Up button state in Fireworks
   copying, 48
   description of, 37, 81
   previewing, 50
Up button state in Flash 8, description of, 261
Update Links dialog, displaying, 159
Update Pages dialog, displaying, 194
Update Template Files dialog, displaying, 193
upperInfo_txt instance, naming, 338
URL Prefix, setting for ColdFusion access, 399
URL variables, creating from Bindings panel, 490, 500–501
URLs (uniform resource locators)
   appending name-value pairs to, 457
   for ColdFusion Administrator login page for Macs, 424

entering in Link field of Property inspector, 177, 307
   making uneditable, 497–503
   specifying for actions, 405
   using relative and absolute URLs, 176
URL.score variable, inserting in "XXX"s, 491
{URL.username}, selecting in design view, 501
U.S Section 508 Guidelines for accessibility Web site, 66
User Name, entering for Macintosh data sources, 426
username URL variable
   creating, 490
   selecting, 491
username variable, declaring, 450
username_txt instance, naming, 449
Users table, structure of, 417

V

Validate option, using with ColdFusion Flash forms, 453
variables
   declaring, 450
   displaying with Bindings panel, 408
   evaluating inside pound signs (##), 494
`variables` parameter of `getURL()`, description of, 499
vector graphics
   drawing for button symbols, 41
   explanation of, 5
   using textures with, 17
   using with simple shapes, 6
vector masks, creating in Fireworks, 24
video. *See also* Flash videos
   avoiding embedding of, 278
   compression options for, 279–282
   converting to FLV format, 275–284
   deploying in Flash 8, 277
   hosting options for, 276
video layer, selecting frames in, 276
video streaming servers, example of, 276
View Data window, displaying records for quiz database in, 496
View Source option, using, 89
`_visible` property, using with movie clips, 328
`vPosition` property in `TextArea` object, explanation of, 344